W9-BRD-226

Praise for *Mailer: His Life and Times*

"Try dipping into Mr. Manso's interviews without at once becoming addicted. Try just skimming the text without getting hooked in the stage-by-stage unfolding of Norman Mailer's career. You can't."

—Christopher Lehmann-Haupt, *The New York Times*

"A sort of sprawling, late-into-the night party. *Mailer* gives you an enjoyable time."

— *The New Yorker*

"Mostly the book is grand gossip, a sort of portable Hamptons, Everyman's own private literary soiree."

—*Time*

"A rare and unprecedented document. . . . Bigger even than Mailer."

—*Mark Harris, Los Angeles Times*

"May well be the year's best read."

—Niven Busch, *San Francisco Review of Books*

"An irresistible, exciting experience."

—*Publishers Weekly,* boxed review

Praise for *Brando, The Biography*

"Monumental. . . . The book's organizing narrative is a morality of waste, such as American tragedies are always supposed to offer . . . pursued with the diligence and the desire for completeness that we associate with loving labors."

—Michael Wood, *The New York Review of Books*

"Stunning."

—*Vanity Fair*

"Staggering."

—*Mirabella*

"A page-turner."

—*Kirkus Reviews*

"Marlon Brando emerges in Pater Manso's massive biography as a more complex, but also more sympathetic, figure than the one revealed in [Brando's] own memoir."

—Jay Carr, *Boston Globe*

"An exhaustive, incisive biography."

—Jack Kroll, *Newsweek*

Praise for *Ptown: Art, Sex, and Money on the Outer Cape*

"An eloquently written, in-your-face cri de coeur about the so-called 'gay takeover' and resultant 'great philistine shift' that has transformed the sleepy little hamlet into what one local activist derides as a 'gayted theme park.'"

—Alex Beam, *Boston Globe*

"Kicks up the sand."

—*Vanity Fair*

"Unsparing, to say the least."

— *The New York Times*

"A blistering critique . . . Manso's point is a good and important one."
—Andrews Sullivan, *The Daily Dish*

"The story of gentrification unfortunately is all too familiar. . . . At the risk of wrongfully being called homophobic, Manso examines the exclusionary policies used by affluent gays to make Provincetown wholly their own."

—Jonathon Keats, *San Francisco Examiner*

"Manso's storytelling skills are evident as he guides readers through the Cape Cod settlement's evolution. And he delivers with gusto on the promise of the book's 'art, sex and money' subtitle."

—*Time Out New York*

"This is nonfiction, and the tales are all true, no matter how bizarre."
—*Sunday Advocate*

REASONABLE
DOUBT

ALSO BY PETER MANSO

Ptown: Art, Sex, and Money on the Outer Cape

Brando: The Biography

Mailer: His Life and Times

The Shadow of the Moth: A Novel of Espionage with Virginia Woolfe
(with Ellen Hawkes)

Faster! A Racer's Diary

Running against the Machine: The Mailer-Breslin Campaign

REASONABLE DOUBT

THE FASHION WRITER, CAPE COD, AND THE TRIAL OF CHRIS McCOWEN

PETER MANSO

ATRIA BOOKS

NEW YORK   LONDON   TORONTO   SYDNEY

ATRIA BOOKS

A Division of Simon & Schuster, Inc.
1230 Avenue of the Americas
New York, NY 10020

Copyright © 2011 by Peter Manso

All rights reserved, including the right to reproduce this book or
portions thereof in any form whatsoever. For information, address
Atria Books Subsidiary Rights Department,
1230 Avenue of the Americas, New York, NY 10020.

First Atria Books hardcover edition July 2011

ATRIA BOOKS and colophon are trademarks of Simon & Schuster, Inc.

For information about special discounts for bulk purchases,
please contact Simon & Schuster Special Sales at
1-866-506-1949 or business@simonandschuster.com.

The Simon & Schuster Speakers Bureau can bring authors
to your live event. For more information or to book an event,
contact the Simon & Schuster Speakers Bureau at
1-866-248-3049 or visit our website at www.simonspeakers.com.

Designed by Jill Putorti

Manufactured in the United States of America

10   9   8   7   6   5   4   3   2   1

Library of Congress Cataloging-in-Publication Data

Manso, Peter.
Reasonable doubt : the fashion writer, Cape Cod, and the trial of Chris
McCowen / Peter Manso.—1st Atria Books harbk. ed.
    p. cm.
Includes bibliographical references.
1. Worthington, Christa, 1955– 2. McCowen, Chris. 3. Crimes of passion—
Massachusetts—Truro (Town)—Case studies. 4. Murder—Massachusetts—Cape
Cod—Case studies. 5. Trials (Murder)—Massachusetts—Cape Cod—Case
studies. I. Title.
HV6534.T78M36 2011
364.152'3092—dc22

                                                          2011009329

ISBN 978–0–7432–9666–3
ISBN 978–1–4391–8744–9 (ebook)

To the brothers Baldwin—Jimmy and David—
who came back every now and then
to help get me through this

Read this: The unexamined life isn't worth living, but the examined life will make you want to die.

—CHRISTA WORTHINGTON

The more we look at her, the uglier she gets.

—CAPE AND ISLANDS DISTRICT ATTORNEY MICHAEL O'KEEFE

Race is somewhat ambiguous in its concept.

—BARNSTABLE SUPERIOR COURT JUDGE GARY NICKERSON

I would still be asking you to convict if the defendant were white and facing the same evidence.

—PROSECUTING ATTORNEY ROBERT WELSH III

I thought McCowen, a black man, was unjustly accused, and, boy, was I right.

—DEFENSE ATTORNEY ROBERT GEORGE

Your Honor, all I can say is that I'm an innocent man in this case . . . and that's how I'm going to go out.

—DEFENDANT CHRISTOPHER MCCOWEN

In my old age I have about come to believe that the whole of written history is miscreated and flawed by these discrepancies in the two ideals systems: the one of how we would all like to believe humanity might be, but only the privileged can afford to believe it; and the one of how we all really know humanity in fact is, but none of us wants to believe it.

—JAMES JONES

CONTENTS

INTRODUCTION

The American murder trial as a metaphor for the nation as a whole has become, in recent years, almost a cliché. Our best writers have seized upon it as a vehicle of self-expression. Academics argue over its myths and realities. The producers of TV series capitalize on its imagery, earning the networks heady profits second only to those raked in by Oprah. At some point or another, almost every American, rich or poor, white or black, has confronted the American justice system and its complexities—with pride, skepticism, awe, revulsion, or a combination of all these.

I began this project with the assumption that the Christa Worthington murder would be the basis for my "trial book" (every journalist wants to do a trial book), that it would take only eighteen months to complete, and that my involvement as the author would be no different from my involvement in the half-dozen other books I've written, even though I'd known Christa Worthington, my neighbor in the town of Truro on the tip of Cape Cod, Massachusetts, for more than a dozen years.

Like so many assumptions, these proved false, largely because of what I found while digging into the crime, its investigation by the Massachusetts State Police, and the trial I'd planned to cover in the style of the late Dominick Dunne, notebook in hand, memorializing courtroom events in a so-called objective manner. Instead, I wound up lending assistance to the defense team and soon found myself in a great deal of trouble—specifically (not to say surreally), hauled into court, where I was indicted on a series of felonies after voicing my belief, both in print and as a guest commentator on Court TV, that the Cape and Islands district attorney in charge of the case (and also the case against me) was an ambitious, racially insensitive politico who'd cut corners in the courtroom and during the three and a half years he'd supervised the police investigation. My run-in with the lawman, however, is a story for another time.

I began the project in spring 2005, shortly after the arrest of Christopher McCowen, thirty-four, a black trashman with a borderline IQ. A layman, I lacked any close familiarity with the law or the courts. It did not take long to learn that the typical criminal trial is a deeply flawed process; narrative and storytelling, not evidence, determine many a trial's outcome. The art of jury selection—voir dire, as it is called—is also critical, more so than most people would imagine. Experienced practitioners know that jurors, ordinary Americans of ordinary intelligence, have a way, as Harper Lee put it, of "carrying their resentments right into the jury box."

The best trial lawyers also know that judges, the vast majority of whom are white, must be educated as much as possible, within the limits of protocol, when the defendant is black; the court should never be allowed to sidestep the issue of race, although most judges will try.

None of this should come as a surprise. The principal figures in every jury trial are ego-driven mortals, each with his own agenda: DAs want to win in order to get reelected (and perhaps slake a native bloodlust); expert defense lawyers work out authority issues while running high-profile, publicity-generating cases; and, again, jurors are not self-sacrificing citizens driven by common sense as most will vote in a way that reinforces who they are, what they believe in, what they value the most. The jury room is a stage, a pulpit, as the Oscar-nominated film *12 Angry Men* illustrated more than fifty years ago.

Even judges with tenured appointments are part of this food chain. Bound by precedent, they rule on evidentiary questions with the record ever in mind, and those who aspire to an appellate bench or to political office have every reason to interpret the facts of the case narrowly, to preserve the status quo. Even when their choices are blatant and obvious, trial judges are the most protected element in our court system, rarely questioned.

There are, of course, dedicated lawyers and truly disinterested jurists, just as there are prosecutors who can see their way to dropping a case against a defendant wrongly charged. But recent history has forced such folks to work overtime. The Vietnam War, the Wall Street financial scandals originating in the early '80s, the callow adventurism of the Bushes, Sr. and Jr., at home and abroad (made worse by the mainstream press's failure to expose them), all have had a lasting effect. Lying, bending the rules, and a growing readiness to abandon constitutional safeguards have invaded the popular culture and courts alike, sanctioned by the events of September 11, 2001, and their progeny.

This is no small matter, obviously. The normally staid *New York Times* has pointed out that the Federal Bureau of Investigation, the Office of Homeland Security, and other federal agencies have improperly obtained more than 8,500 telephone accounts from 2003 to 2006 without following legal procedures. Next to the financial sector, local representatives of the law-enforcement community have most taken this new value system to heart. "Testilying," for example, has become common, police officers bending the truth while on the witness stand. Another form of police misconduct is the withholding of exculpatory evidence; the ACLU, the Innocence Project in New York City, the Center on Wrongful Convictions at Northwestern University, and a rash of appellate court rulings across the country have shown that hundreds of criminal defendants have been set up by less-than-honest cops. Equally alarming, the local courts have been loath to blow the whistle during this time of orange alerts and nationwide anxiety. Better we overlook the bad apples than risk besmirching the much-needed good guys.

Of course, there is another view. Conservatives such as Sean Hannity will argue that there is nothing new here so much as what's happening is just a Hobbist reassertion of the human condition, and, yes, we should feel all the more blessed for it. But before jumping into this little book of mine, I'd scarcely realized how bad, *how dark,* things had gotten on Cape Cod, my childhood summer home of art openings and clam bakes, until I had read through the Massachusetts State Police file, case number 02-102-0900-0007, *Comm. v. McCowen*; consisting of forensics, criminalistics, and surveillance reports, DNA screenings, polygraph results, police interviews, and internal memos. The file was a journalistic gold mine, as were the minutes of the grand-jury proceedings since what both showed was a miasma of law-enforcement shortcuts running through the case like mold on a particularly smelly blue cheese. The local legal community had become so ingrown, so incestuous, that the courts looked upon the cops as family, and given the pressure on police to find Christa's killer, it seemed nobody and nothing was safe, least of all the Constitution.

It took no genius to see this as much of what the DA and the cops did was right out in the open. The file showed, for example, that my own phone records had been grabbed without a subpoena or court order the day after Christa's body was found; my wife, who is not a professional journalist protected as I am by the First Amendment, had her records pried out of Verizon and during the investigation the records of at least forty-five others were obtained via demand letters to a compliant Verizon, as well. My DNA was snatched, along with the DNA of a half-dozen other locals, swabbed from discarded cigarette butts and cast-off water bottles. We were not suspects but, rather, "persons of interest," meaning that police felt no compunction about violating our privacy even as they couldn't determine that any one of us was materially relevant to their probe, either.

If pressed, these investigators would probably defend their actions on the grounds of thoroughness. But that argument is limited. Time and again, while conducting my interviews, I heard locals speak of being confronted by plainclothes detectives banging on their doors, unannounced, at 9:30 P.M., which on off-season Cape Cod is the equivalent of midnight. One suspect, Christa's onetime boyfriend Tim Arnold, was grilled for several hours while confined at a Cape-area psychiatric facility, in open defiance of his lawyer's insistence that interviews be cleared in advance. Arnold was sedated at the time but that made no difference to detectives, who apparently failed to consider that the Effexor and amnesia-inducing lorazepam Arnold was taking might render their truth-gathering efforts less than reliable, at best.

Then, too, on the third anniversary of Christa Worthington's death, the frustrated investigators, after going to the FBI for pointers, conducted a DNA sweep of our sleepy little town of Truro wherein they intimidated reluctant donors by threatening to record license-plate numbers on a "special list." The ACLU and the *Boston Globe* called the sweep something just short of a fascist outrage; the story made *USA Today* and the *New York Times*, but what the public never learned was that the majority of the 150-odd swabs collected were never even turned in for analysis. Rather, the samples languished in DA Michael O'Keefe's office until Christopher McCowen was arrested in April 2005, four months after the sweep, more than *a year* after McCowen's DNA was collected. It, too, had sat on the shelf in O'Keefe's corner office while Truro trembled.

In addition, the director of the Massachusetts State Police (MSP) crime lab was discharged after more than twenty-five DNA samples were misfiled, while five of the thirteen fingerprints lifted from the Truro murder scene turned out to belong to local police and EMTs. Inexplicably, key evidence, including fibers and even vaginal combings, were never tested.

But disorganization, incompetence, and a corrupted crime scene were business as usual. An MSP report dated December 10, 2002, "Blood Sample of Anthony R. Smith for Comparison in Worthington," documented the nadir of police misconduct. Here, lead detective Christopher Mason reported that he'd requisitioned two vials of Smith's blood from the coroner's office and delivered it to the crime lab for analysis without, it appears, a court order or family permission. Anthony Smith was the son of a stubborn defense witness who would insist to the end that he'd seen a truck or van speeding out of Christa's driveway the day before her body was found; the driver was white, not black like Christopher McCowen. Mason was covering all bases, as he usually did, since he is a very thorough man. But he ran roughshod over the Fourth Amendment in the process, displaying utter insensitivity to a parent's grief. Smith, who lived with his father, the stubborn witness, had recently taken his own life.

The rationale for this official act of quasi-vampirism was nothing more than unverified telephone hotline tip that Smith "lived in the area," according to Mason's report of May 16, 2003.

Nothing tied the young man to the murder, not even remotely.

But beyond the blindness of such efforts, the file revealed a world of drug-dealer snitches protected by police, and a particularly self-invested DA. The new off-season Cape Cod was made up of single welfare mothers, wild-eyed alcoholic wife abusers, "wash-ashore" laborers living on food stamps while waiting for the tourist restaurants to reopen in May, and an ever-growing horde of teenagers dragged into court up and down the Cape, their OxyContin-fueled lifestyles combining with post-9/11 jitters to empower the cops like nothing anyone had ever seen before.

It was after plowing through the file that I began interviewing people on both sides of the law. Almost all interviews were face-to-face, not on the telephone, and often the drama that accompanied these encounters was as illuminating as the words themselves, for once again I found myself on a Cape Cod I'd only heard about. The former director of the Cape NAACP, for example, insisted on coming to my house for our meeting, then excused himself when it was only late afternoon, apologizing that it wasn't wise for a lone black man to drive the Truro-Orleans stretch of Route 6, the "gauntlet," as he put it, after dark. Not long afterward, a white drug dealer, a Truro-Wellfleet townie with deep local connections, told me that at night he always drove with his interior lights *on*. Why? So the "*federales*," he explained, would know who was behind the wheel, not pull him over. As one local journalist reminded me, the Cape is only an hour and a half's drive from Charlestown, home of Boston's infamous busing crisis, and the situation wasn't helped any by the fact that African-Americans make up only 1.6 percent of the Cape's population, a minuscule fraction of the 13.5 percent national average.

My interviews continued right through the trial, which was a David-and-Goliath proposition from the start. The DA threw his full staff onto the case the way Rommel used his tanks to overrun North Africa. Day after day, a dozen or more of his lawyers, researchers, interns, and secretaries filled the lawyers' dock on the left side of the courtroom, just as the commonwealth had the resources of the State Police and state crime lab. Attorney Robert George, by contrast, was flying solo. George fought the good fight, but in the end, he lost. Most reporters covering the trial felt his client deserved a hung jury, at least; according to nearly 40 percent of those responding to a *Cape Cod Times* poll conducted after the verdict, the defendant's color made the difference.

It is an open question whether any defense lawyer—even Clarence Darrow or Perry Mason, for that matter—could have won the case in that courtroom, with that judge, that jury.

I openly sided with the defense—supplying research, feedback, and editorial contributions to briefs and motions—out of the belief that the trial's racist subtext was substantive and real. As I told the *Boston Globe*, it would take moral impotence to miss prosecutor Robert Welsh's strategy: playing to jurors' biases while simultaneously insisting that race had nothing to do with the proceedings. A black garbageman charged with the rape and murder of a white Vassar grad? On traditionally conservative Cape Cod where even JFK had not gotten the local vote in what was then the closest presidential election to date? Whom did Welsh think he was fooling?

Republican governor Mitt Romney's announcement of prosecutor Welsh's appointment to a district court judgeship at the start of deliberations was another outrage. Few people on Cape Cod, white or black, did not know that during the past century, local judgeships had been held by the prosecutor's great-grandfather, grandfather, and father. Still another Welsh ran the court clerk's office in the Cape's outermost district court. The nepotism was offensive, but Romney's timing was worse. Welsh, with his Plain Jane suits and humorless, rubbery face, was a Babbitt ready-made for skewering, a smug Tea Party Republican who thought he could get away with anything. I do not exaggerate. Halfway through trial, our prosecutor cum newly appointed judge had the audacity to claim he did not to have the probation file on one of his major witnesses. He did have that file; he had to. Yet he got away with his lie, as has been documented in the defense's brief to the Supreme Judicial Court, the state's highest tribunal.

Given the importance of injecting some balance into all of this, I made it a point to share all research with the court and the prosecution. This was de rigueur. One of George's motions, charging the prosecution with withholding exculpatory evidence, announced my contributions in its opening pages so as to send the message that nothing underhanded was going on. Even so, a Harvard journalism professor queried by the *Boston Globe* alleged that my "loss of objectivity" called into question anything I might write about the trial, which, then as now, I answer by taying that the prof didn't recognize alternative reportorial strategies. Aside from the access it got me, my alignment with the defense became so widely known that even a year after the verdict I was sought out by one juror's relative, a black woman in her seventies, who claimed that her nephew had been an unabashed racist since the age of fifteen and lied during the jury-selection process meant to sift out bias. On this, I notified the court, and the woman was called as a witness at a postverdict hearing.

The disparity between the prosecution and defense arsenals was a constant, and if my participation would help level the playing field, so be it. Black people too often get screwed in America, and on that issue I have never been, nor will I ever be, prepared to brook debate even when it's coming from Harvard.

Did all of this affect my ability to report the trial fairly? Unlikely. My involvement provided a unique vantage point, not to say access to the aforementioned materials that I would not otherwise have had. Robert George and I talked daily during the trial process and then throughout three years of postverdict motions and appeals.

Did I talk to the other side? After speaking with Michael O'Keefe before trial, I approached the DA, Welsh, and lead detectives on multiple occasions and was rebuffed, orally and in writing, as were all other reporters I know of who requested one-on-ones with the prosecutor. This is the DA who storms out of press conferences, snapping, "You must be kidding" or "Grow up," when he doesn't like reporters' questions.

Some will fault George's defense as understaffed, sometimes underresearched, and underfunded, and perhaps worse yet for my involvement. I say that without Robert George's energy and commitment, the sheer loudness of his pugnaciousness, Chris McCowen would have disappeared like so many other uneducated, marginally functioning defendants in courts across the country. McCowen would have been swept through the process with no one the wiser, another casualty of our lopsided justice system. Innocent or guilty, the vast majority of indigent defendants *do* suffer that fate. The corridors of local courthouses across the country are filled with attorneys looking for cases, ready to be court-appointed and step in at a moment's notice. Their prep work is nil. They cop plea bargains. They neither test the system nor challenge prosecutors nor protect the rights of the individuals they claim to defend.

McCowen's trial was expected to take two weeks, not five. Day to day, George stuck, a high-priced criminal defense lawyer stepping into William Kunstler or Charlie Garry country. He didn't have the politics (perhaps a plus), but he had something out of the ordinary, something genuine, even if he overly enjoyed being surrounded by reporters. Maybe he realized that this was the case of his career, that rare shot that lawyers, like athletes, get but once or twice in a lifetime. Or maybe it was nothing more than the sentiment he expressed after the verdict, while wrestling with whether he could afford to take on the appeal. "Now my kids won't think I just represent bad guys," he said. "Maybe they'll understand that defense lawyers can do something that's useful and important."

His work *was* useful. The system I'd observed over the previous months was too ready to do what it shouldn't. George challenged that, stamped his foot. His resolve had as much to do with prosecutorial irregularities and bad calls from the bench as with McCowen's innocence or guilt, as well it should have. That's what we have defense lawyers for.

Readers will draw their own conclusions. My account of the trial relies on the official transcript of 3,878 pages. I've condensed that record, using ellipses and paraphrasing, ever mindful of remaining faithful to the content of all testimony, sidebar exchanges, and rulings from the bench. Readability was a major consideration, but I consciously erred on the side of inclusiveness and accuracy.

Much of the information in this book is based on my interviews, many done "on background" for reasons already acknowledged. Granted, this is not the best arrangement. But such confidentiality was necessary to secure the subjects' cooperation, in some instances because of the menacing air surrounding the case. In verifying key matters, especially criminal activities or persons and events impinging directly on the murder, I insisted on at least two, preferably three, sources, as well as confirming documents. Material gleaned from MSP interviews and incident reports was always checked.

Some potential sources repeatedly refused to talk even after a year or two of my nagging, worried that the murderer was still "out there." But many also feared local police in Truro, Wellfleet, and Eastham, who wield the power to inflict a drunk-driving bust or do a pot search at two A.M. So real was the fear factor that several sources called me after interviews, wanting to retract their comments. Not once in my career have I had to fall back on anonymous sourcing as I have for this narrative.

On the other hand not all was so grim. A number of individuals stepped forward unsolicited, among them a former assistant district attorney, now in private practice, who introduced himself on the checkout line at a local supermarket; his information proved invaluable to my understanding of the personalities and social world of the Cape's court system and law-enforcement agencies. Another ex-prosecutor explained District Attorney Michael O'Keefe's foibles—his heavy drinking, priapic tendencies, blind ambition, and racial insensitivity. Not so surprising was the help I received from McCowen's girlfriend, Catherine Cisneros, and from his father and stepmother, who provided the defendant's childhood medical records and other documents, in addition to explaining what life was like for a black child growing up in rural southwestern Oklahoma.

Other sources were people whose trust stemmed from my book *Ptown: Art, Sex, and Money on the Outer Cape,* which does not shy away from discussing the ongoing class war between locals and wealthy summer visitors. Happily, a number of these individuals worked in local town offices and in district and superior courts; they guided me to records buried in dusty files and offered sub-rosa tips about local officials. One Truro selectman, for example, was quietly shouldering two OUI convictions; a third would land him in jail, my tipster pointed out, explaining that this was "why the bastard keeps backing the police."

By the time I finished writing, the core documentation for this project filled sixteen three-ring binders and seven file boxes, not counting interview transcript and the trial record. Unlike the Massachusetts State Police and FBI, I used a cassette recorder to memorialize my 200 or so interviews. I also filled nine of my beloved French Rhodia notepads inside the courtroom.

In the end, I called several out-of-town friends, well-known lawyers, and also one of the most celebrated PIs in the country, a man who'd worked with the defense for the Oklahoma bomber and also on the case of John Walker Lindh, the California youth who joined the Taliban. I did this for a reality check. Was I exaggerating about the cops, who were, after all, trying to nab a killer? Was the misconduct of the prosecution really as egregious as I was saying? The collective reply was, "It's very bad. These guys were out of control. Had your man been tried in Boston, even Dayton, Ohio, it probably would have turned out differently."

Again, readers will draw their own conclusions. New developments in the McCowen case will unfold within the year. The account that follows is based on the best information and documentation available now.

THE MURDER

Like any other bleak winter day, Sunday, January 6, 2002, was gray and windy, the metallic smell of rain heavy in the air. Cape Cod knows only three colors in winter: gray, darker gray, and the muted green of omnipresent scrub pines, somber hues that only add to the depression that engulfs many locals during this phase of the year. As Henry David Thoreau once observed, "It is a wild place, and there is no flattery in it."

Just outside the kitchen of the bungalow at 50 Depot Road, Christa Worthington's green Ford Escort was parked, as usual, at the top of her long driveway. A plastic Little Tikes car belonging to her daughter, Ava, was not far away, waiting to be used once more come spring. The telltales were barely noticeable at first glance: on the flagstone walkway curving back to the house lay a barrette, also a pair of eyeglasses near the Escort's driver's door. Under the front tire was a wool sock, its mate several feet away in a flower bed. Farther away still, south toward the woods, a set of keys lay on the ground on the Escort's passenger side, as if someone had flung them from the house.

Inside, the home seemed too small for its contents. What was always known as the "back door" led into the kitchen, which was Cape Cod tiny, a mere 120 square feet, not accounting for the appliances, the free-standing cabinet just behind the door, and the counters. The table was covered with newspapers, old mail, flyers, and notes. Toys scattered across the floor made the room even smaller.

Dirty dishes overflowed in the sink. Food-encrusted pans covered the burners of the galley-style stove opposite the doorway. At the right rear corner, the room opened into a narrow hallway that led to the living room. Along the right side of the hallway, on the easterly side of the house, were two doors: one led to Christa's study, the other to the bathroom. In the study, a lone desk lamp illuminated a room nearly as cramped as the kitchen and just as messy, with a floor-to-ceiling stack of cardboard file boxes, plastic bins, a desk and chair, piles of magazines, and more loose paperwork. A Dell laptop computer, its screen still glowing, reported that the last user had logged off the Internet.

In the northwest corner of the house, the living room offered a "million-dollar" view of the salt marsh leading down to Pamet Harbor, then the bay and Provincetown, with the Pilgrim Monument in the distance. Paintings by Christa's mother, Gloria Worthington, covered the walls. Two couches, a coffee table, a Christmas tree, and Christa's childhood piano made this space cramped, too. The couches were littered with coats and books. On the far side of the living room, the north end, the so-called front door was locked. It had not been used in years, the kitchen entry being closer to the driveway turn-around where occupants always parked. The door to the bedroom, kitty-corner to the locked front entry, was shut, too. More toys strewn across the floor made the living room hard to navigate.

The little girl who owned the toys, barely two and a half, managed the transit with no problem. She had turned on the television to play her favorite video but hadn't been able to figure out how to get the VCR tape into the machine. She'd put it in end first, then tried it sideways, then upside down. She soon stopped, wondering when her mother was going to wake up.

Despite the mess, the house appeared to be in its natural state, unaffected by the force of a struggle. The only aberration lay on the floor in the hallway: a woman's body, naked from the chest down. Her head leaned toward her right shoulder, and blood had pooled on the floor below her swollen mouth. On her bare stomach were tiny red handprints.

The little girl made her way back toward the kitchen, stopping to tug at her mother again. She was hungry and equally starved for attention. She had never gone this long without talking to an adult. Most of all, she missed her mother's smile, her cooing sounds. Earlier, she had tried to clean her mother as her mother had so often cleaned her, using a hand mitt to wipe up the blood.

In the kitchen, she poured herself a bowl of Cheerios, a skill she'd recently acquired. She added milk to the bowl, barely noticing the bloodstains she left on the glass bottle of organic milk her mother always bought. Her hands were covered with blood. It was under her fingernails and in her hair. She ate a little but did not finish. Her attention wandered again.

The late-afternoon sun began to set. The day had almost passed, and her mother still had not gotten up. She grabbed a bottle of apple juice from the refrigerator and put it down next to her mother, then curled up beside her on the floor. Her mother had said she would have to stop nursing soon, but for the moment, she gave up on the juice for the familiarity of her mother's nipple.

Most eyes in Massachusetts that Sunday were on the New England Patriots, winners of five straight games and closing out a Cinderella season. The Patriots needed a victory to clinch the AFC East division title and a loss by the Oakland Raiders to seal an improbable bye in the first round of the playoffs. The victory was almost a certainty, their opponents being the Carolina Panthers, a team in the midst of a fourteen-game losing streak. Still, New England was leading just 10–3 at halftime when Robert Arnold, in his late seventies, went to pick up his son, Tim, age forty-four, in Wellfleet.

Since his brain surgery seven months earlier, Tim suffered double vision and balance and coordination problems, and he couldn't drive. He normally lived with his parents, but since mid-November, he'd been house-sitting for friends in Wellfleet. His father was picking him up so Tim could do his laundry at home.

By the third quarter of the game, the clothes were in the dryer and the Patriots had jumped ahead 24–6. Tim decided to call Christa Worthington, an ex-lover who remained a friend, to see if she still wanted to go out for Sunday night dinner. He had suggested Saturday, but she had said no. Tim had gotten the impression she was going off-Cape to see her dad. When she didn't answer, he thought she might still be away. He left a message on her answering machine and went back to the game.

A half hour later, with New England up 38-6 and running out the clock, Robert Arnold was ready to drive the six miles back to Wellfleet. Noticing a flashlight Tim had borrowed from Christa, he suggested they return it on the way. Robert grabbed the flashlight, Tim picked up the laundry basket, and they got into Robert's seven-year-old Ford Windstar.

As Robert drove around Old County Road and then cut back up Depot, Tim wondered whether he should return the flashlight unannounced. Christa had chastised him before for showing up without calling, and although he'd left her a message, she hadn't given him the OK to come by. Seeing her always stirred emotions. Just two months earlier, he had written in his journal: "There is such an ache where she and Ava used to be. The first Father's Day gift she gave me was a picture of Ava in my arms. Ouch. That hurts badly. Especially now that I can look back and see how little she was involved."

Often, he'd tried to convince himself that he had the upper hand, writing in his diary that she could be "impatient, angry, hostile, unpleasant," and that he had "left her several times because she was so difficult, so cutting, so caustic, on the attack." But he couldn't give up the idea of the two of them together.

He decided it would be best just to leave the flashlight on her back porch.

As they slowed to take the left into Christa's driveway, it was Robert who first saw two copies of the *New York Times* in familiar blue plastic wrappers. Tim got out and grabbed the papers. They drove up the 175-foot drive, a narrow dirt road topped with weeds and crushed clamshells. As it curved to the left near the house, Tim was surprised to see Christa's car. He also noticed the light on in her study. It was dusk.

He got out, flashlight and newspapers in hand, crossed the flagstone walkway, and went up the three steps to the kitchen landing. The rickety wooden storm door was closed. The inside door stood open more than halfway. Looking inside, as he later recalled, he immediately saw Christa on the floor with Ava. The child appeared to be breast-feeding. He thought it an odd place to nurse, then remembered that Christa would often stop whatever she was doing to give Ava her breast, no matter where.

When he called out, Ava's head popped up. The little girl ran to him as he stepped into the kitchen, putting the newspapers down. Ava was a talkative child, but at this moment, she said nothing, only clung to him. He took the three or four steps across the kitchen with her in his arms and looked down at Christa. She was naked from the chest down, a bathrobe and black fleece shirt around her shoulders. Her legs were splayed. Her right knee was bent, pointing at the ceiling. Her left leg was bent at the knee, too, but entirely flat on the ground.

Tim blinked, having trouble with what he was seeing. Her lips were horribly swollen, as if she had been hit, and much blood had run down the side of her face onto the floor. Some of it was still wet, glistening. Her eyes were wide open, staring at the ceiling, unfocused. He looked into her eyes, and all he saw was white. In a daze, he reached down and touched her cheek. It was cold. Panic rushed through him. He looked for the phone, a cordless model that should have been on its cradle on the wall but wasn't.

With Ava still in his arms, he stepped over the body and into the living room. The television was on, a children's show. The flashlight was still in his hand, and he put it down on a windowsill to turn the TV off, then stepped back over the body and reached down to check Christa's pulse. Nothing. The open bathroom door was just beyond her head. Inside, he saw blood on the rim of the sink and a red-stained wash mitt on the floor underneath. Ava's little step stool was there, too. The child, he realized, had tried to clean her bloodied mother. He forced himself to whisper comforting words to Ava as she clutched him.

He looked around the kitchen once more, remembering that the inside door had been open. Christa must have just gotten home. What could have happened so quickly?

He carried Ava out to the Windstar. His father had already turned the van around, so that it pointed downhill, back toward the road.

As Tim climbed inside, he said, spelling for the sake of the child, "Christa is D-E-A-D," his voice shaky. They sat in stunned silence, the only sound the whirr of the vehicle's heater. Then Tim said, "I can't find a phone anywhere."

Robert left the Windstar to go inside. As he later testified in court, first he could bear only a quick glance at the body as he looked around the kitchen, putting his hand against the wall to steady himself. He had never been in Christa's house before and wasn't sure where to look. The place was cluttered. He looked at Christa again. He was a retired veterinarian; he'd seen death before but not like this. The right side of the young woman's face had been beaten, contusions covering her upper lip, nose, and forehead, and smeared streaks of blood laced her chest and abdomen. Her lips were swollen but pulled back, exposing her teeth, gleaming reddish from the blood she'd aspirated.

He stepped over the body to check the living room. No phone. Quickly, he returned to the Windstar.

They sat in the van in silence again, both rattled, having trouble deciding what to do. After a moment, Tim passed Ava to his father and went back inside. Again, he checked the kitchen, the living room; he opened the bedroom door and took a quick look, remembering other times when Christa's phone was difficult to find, a cordless in a cluttered house. He turned around for the second time, deciding that the only recourse was to go back up the path to his father's house to call from there. He left the house without noticing Christa's cell phone on the kitchen table. It was on, the illuminated screen revealing a lone 9.

As in 911.

He ran up the 100-yard path to his father's house, then dialed the police emergency number. It was just before 4:30 P.M. In a surprisingly coherent voice, he told the dispatcher he thought Christa Worthington had fallen down her stairs. The Truro police switchboard logs report him saying, "I think she is dead."

Robert continued to wait in the minivan, holding Ava, who rested her head against his neck. Although he never talked about it later, he had to have smelled both Christa's blood and Ava's dirty diaper.

Meanwhile, Christa's cousin Jan Worthington, a member of Truro's rescue squad, was reading the newspaper at her North Pamet Road home two miles away when her pager went off. The dispatcher announced: "You have a rescue call—50 Depot Road, the Worthington residence—for an unconscious, unresponsive female."

Jan thought of her mother, Cindy, who had a pacemaker. The address was wrong, but errors like that were made all the time. She drove as fast as she could, slowing only when she pulled abreast of her parents' house on the opposite side of Depot from Christa's, several hundred yards west. No cars, no activity.

She turned back to Christa's driveway. At the top of the hill, she saw Tim Arnold standing next to his father's minivan.

"It's Christa. I think she's dead."

She ran up the steps and stopped at the landing. Through the kitchen door, Jan saw Christa on her back, wearing what appeared to be a green bathrobe bunched up around her shoulders. Her legs were in a weird position, "akimbo," as Jan later described them. She turned back to Tim, screaming for an explanation. He repeated that maybe Christa had hit her head and fallen. But he didn't know.

She again yelled at Tim, telling him to call the police. He said he couldn't find the phone, forgetting that he had already called 911. Jan panicked and ran down the driveway, screaming, "Call the police! Somebody—call the police!" Halfway down the drive, she met the ambulance that had just returned from Hyannis and was minutes away when the emergency call for 50 Depot Road came in. Paramedic Jeff Francis, responding from his nearby home, followed in his car. All of them later recalled Jan's shrieks.

Francis was the first official responder to step inside. The ambulance crew followed, one carrying the "first-in bag," three others bringing the defibrillator and oxygen. They flipped the light switch near the kitchen table, and Francis noticed a pool of blood about eight inches by fourteen inches around Christa's head. He bent to feel the pulse on her neck.

"Code ninety-nine!"

The patient was not breathing. He instructed the crew to clear an area so they could move the body. They slammed the open portable dishwasher shut, slid it back to create space, and began moving toys away from Christa's feet. The body had stiffened in its awkward position. "Code thirteen," Francis reported on his radio, meaning that rigor had set in. They gave up on moving her.

Two members of the ambulance crew later recalled seeing the sea-green bathrobe around Christa's shoulders and two bloody handprints on the flat of her stomach. Fecal matter was under her and between her legs, blood behind her ear. They used a brown blanket from the couch to cover her body. A plastic yellow disposable blanket from the ambulance was also put on top of the body.

The deputy fire chief and two emergency medical technicians had arrived. The kitchen was getting crowded. Outside, a second ambulance pulled up, then a Truro police lieutenant and the Truro fire captain. Cars and trucks were parked end-to-end along the narrow driveway, and Jan was still screaming. She stopped only with the arrival of her father, on foot, from across the road. The ambulance crew searched the house, looking for the baby, whose toys and handprints were everywhere.

Outside, Tim Arnold explained that Ava was safe in the Windstar with his father. Someone brought out a supply of diapers, and EMT George Malloy carried the little girl down the driveway to Jan's parents' home. Malloy would state that the child, whom he held in his arms for the next hour, "never once stopped shaking."

He added, "Anybody who says she didn't see what happened up there is totally crazy."

Later that evening, the long probe into Christa Worthington's murder began.

THE INVESTIGATION

Cape Cod was carved by the advance and retreat of the Laurentide ice sheet during the Pleistocene geological era. But within only thousands of years, scientists say, it will be completely submerged, swallowed by the hungry Atlantic Ocean. Technically a peninsula, the Cape is unofficially recognized as one of the largest barrier islands in the world, shielding much of the Massachusetts coastline from ravaging North Atlantic storms. And it pays the price, especially during the winter months. Jutting into the open ocean, the narrow sand spit is subject to massive erosion, with winds and tides routinely washing out beaches and destroying barrier islands. Outer Cape towns know these phenomena best, Provincetown at the tip of the arm-shaped landmass, tiny Truro just to its south.

Truro is not a town accustomed to attention. Provincetown draws its share, in large part because of its geographical status as the tip of sublime Cape Cod, its long-standing history as an arts colony, and its uncontested international reputation as *the* gay vacation mecca. Wellfleet to the south also has a large tourist draw. But Truro is pastoral, the most rural of the Cape's fifteen towns. Residents embrace its tranquillity. But Christa Worthington's murder rendered quietude a thing of the past.

For the media, the case had it all: sex, money, violence, and the pathos of a little girl found next to her mother's dead body. Coverage was intense—TV satellite trucks swept into the sleepy little town like a school of hungry sharks, jockeying for parking space along narrow Depot Road even before daybreak on Monday, January 7, the morning after the body was discovered. As suspects slipped in and out of the news, people chose favorites, as if those named were competing on *American Idol*, not possible perpetrators of a ghastly, cold-blooded murder.

People who knew Christa Worthington described her as obdurate, short-tempered, high-strung, and bright; she was also confused, in the last months of her life unable to decide whether to leave Truro or stay. The media would portray the victim's short life in an altogether different light, suggesting that this privileged Vassar graduate had everything go her way until her murder. In one account after another, Christa spent her early twenties in Manhattan, dancing the '70s away at Studio 54. In Paris, she enjoyed the perks of working for Fairchild Publications, publishers of the fashion trade journal *Women's Wear Daily* and its gossipy sister *W*. She hobnobbed with aristocrats, millionaires, fashion moguls, and celebrities, then moved on to a freelancer's life in London. After a string of affairs with various Brits and Americans, she moved back to New York, reclaiming the co-op she owned in a turn-of-the-century building overlooking Gramercy Park, writing freelance for the *New York Times, Elle*, and other national glossies. Eventually, she returned to her house in quiet Truro to live off the occasional published piece and her private income. At forty-two, she discovered she was pregnant. The baby, fathered by a rough-and-ready, philandering ex-fisherman, was born out of wedlock. For Christa, the child's arrival was a miracle.

These reports were a fairy tale. The glitzy celebrity life and the cherished child were real, as were other aspects of the story, but the trajectory of Christa Worthington's life was far, far more complicated. Despite her advantages—wealth, education, and moderate good looks—she was not happy. Nor had she found lasting peace with the birth of her wonder child. Christa struggled with decisions, second-guessed herself; she solicited advice from friends and relatives, only to reject it. She was intelligent but addicted to self-help books and given to self-pity. Despite an inheritance of a half-million dollars cash and two Truro homes, she obsessed over money and was often miserly. She knew right from wrong but used people. She was by nature secretive and rarely "shared," least of all with family members, who branded her a neurotic, then tried to cash in on her death with lawsuits, media interview fees, and screenplay deals. Worthington family testimony would paint a Christa who bore little resemblance to the woman others knew. And it wasn't just townsfolk who said so.

Close friend Leila Levinson had seen a masochistic side when the two were at Vassar: "She didn't have the capability to have a normal, functional, committed relationship with a man . . . and there was a real attraction to the illicit." Levinson visited Truro several times, the two staying at Christa's grandparents' house. "Her grandmother, Tiny, was a major figure for Christa," said Levinson. Tiny's independence and disregard of other people's rules appealed to her favorite granddaughter. And Tiny's affairs were not always discreet. Once locals learned that Tony Jackett had fathered Christa's child, they recalled Tiny choosing local Portuguese fishermen as lovers, class differences notwithstanding. One of Tiny's most high-profile *amours* was the great bass and film star Paul Robeson, who was performing at Provincetown's West End Theatre at the time. An avowed Communist, Robeson was eventually hounded by McCarthyism and forced into exile in the Soviet Union. He was a black man. Tiny had always been Christa's role model.

Knowing Christa and her history, Levinson had no problem believing she'd have a secret affair with her African-American garbageman. Ben Brantley, nowadays the *New York Times* drama critic, who was Christa's supervisor at *W*, told police Christa had been "attracted to difficult men. There was always something dramatic going on with Christa."

While in Europe, she had a long-term affair with an Englishman, a heavy drinker, who tried to pitch her out a window at one point in their tempestuous relationship. He was but one of several lovers. She also spent considerable time with gay friends, serving in one high-profile case as a well-acknowledged "beard."

Levinson said Christa had a "total lack of interest in the reliable good boy. What was her driving dynamic? What was she seeking? That was the mystery about her. There was a very high-strung side to her, a side . . . that she couldn't handle."

After living in Paris and England, she returned to the United States, working at *Elle* for two years before leaving to freelance. It was about then that she began her relationship with Gloria Vanderbilt's son, Stan Stokowski, brother of now–CNN newscaster Anderson Cooper. When Stokowski broke it off and started seeing another woman, Christa began stalking him.

The next man in her life was the Amazing Tarquin, a.k.a. Thomas Churchwell, who, when not performing at strip clubs, did magic tricks at the bar across the street from Christa's Gramercy Park co-op. Visiting the bar with a friend one night, Christa found herself courted by the strange, tuxedoed magician, whose tricks, she later recalled, "made you think he could read your mind."

By the end of that first evening, the magician had rolled a cocktail napkin into a perfectly shaped rose on a stem and asked her for her telephone number. Two weeks later, she helped him move out of his cubicle at a Bowery flophouse and into her apartment. It was a mistake. When Tarquin unpacked, she discovered he "smelled." He insisted he was the "artistic heir" to Houdini, whose name was tattooed across his wrist. He forced his sketchbooks on her, hyperrealistic drawings of naked virgins and strippers with plucked eyebrows and shaved pubic hair. He called it his "art." To Christa, confiding to her diary, it was sick porn.

For a woman drawn to difficult men, Tarquin was a prize. Even Christa's doorman, who'd watched the magician tumble out of the neighborhood bar, tried to warn her. She didn't listen. Nutty as the arrangement was, she tried to treat it as a joke, striking a superior pose that only revealed her vulnerability.

"I always wanted to keep a man in a cage, a well-cared-for pet," she wrote in her diary, sublimating her complexities into the opening scene of a would-be novel. "This arrangement seemed fair to me. An improvement for him, and company for me. The cage I built was made of money, of which I had very little. But I had more than he did. . . . I'd let [him] out. [He] would roam and run free but [he'd] come back for food and water and petting. That was the plan."

Her sick little scenario didn't work. Tarquin was an insomniac and wouldn't let her sleep. He'd watch daytime TV, hour after hour, "inane shows," as Christa saw it, and he smoked up the apartment, his ashes spilling out of the ashtrays onto her carpet and furniture.

If she said anything, he'd fly into a rage, screeching, "You won't let me be *me!*"

Later on, back in Truro, Christa would write a short story, "The Magician," subtitled "How I Got Taken by a B.U.M." One particularly telling passage read, "I was making life undignified for him. I was humiliating him. I was being a bitch. . . . I liked being with a B.U.M."

Her closest friends subsequently told police, as did Arnold, that Christa always needed "to have the last word." Even during Tarquin's rants, she wouldn't back down. If she felt she was starting to lose the argument, she'd pick up a book or a vase and throw it at him. Tarquin later said she once pulled a knife—an event that Christopher Mason would incorporate into his interrogation of McCowen.

By spring 1996, Christa told Tarquin she wanted him out. Petrified, she changed her locks. Lonely as never before, she had a fling with a TV producer, a quickie that only made her lonelier.

The relationship's end seemed to harden her resolve to have a baby, as if the disastrous seven-month affair had wasted too much precious time. Her biological clock was ticking. She went to a fertility center to research artificial insemination, then wrote a surprisingly frank piece for *Harper's Bazaar* on single motherhood. She attended meetings of Single Mothers by Choice and represented the group on the Leeza Gibbons TV show. Predictably, she set herself up for another crushing setback.

She went to a gynecologist, then sought a second opinion. Both physicians said she was premenopausal and might not be able to have a child. She wept for most of a week, then left the city to be with her mother, recently diagnosed with cancer. She spent that winter in Hingham, then moved to Truro for the summer, settling into Tiny's beach shack, "The Hut," which was one of two properties willed to Christa's father when his parents died; the other was 50 Depot Road. Constructed of driftwood and old timbers, the one-room shack sat on the sand not a hundred feet above the high-water mark at Pamet Beach, adjacent to the town landing and the harbormaster's office. It was the kind of place where people spend much of the time on the porch, bare feet propped up on the railing, drinks in hand, surveying the boats and minding other people's business.

Christa had barely unpacked when she began drifting over to chat with harbormaster Warren Roderick. She usually had a complaint: the proposed town pier or a kayaker who'd beached in front of the Hut on "her" property.

An easygoing middle-aged man who loves to gab, Roderick indulged her. He also introduced her to his assistant, Tony Jackett, who'd recently lost his fishing boat and was working part-time at the landing to make ends meet. Jackett was forty-seven, dark-skinned, with jet-black hair. John Dos Passos had contrasted the "dark and marvelously good-looking" Provincetown Portuguese with the local Yankees and their "hard-looking hatchet faces."

Married for twenty-seven years and the father of six, Tony was nonetheless known as a ladies' man. His relationship with Christa was long, intense, and invisible. Another old Vassar friend of Christa's thinks it wasn't the first time Christa operated undercover. This woman remembers the day they graduated. She and Christa were walking through the lobby, when a married professor "pulls her to him and he kissed her on the mouth. I'm going, like, what the hell? . . . Both have this secret smile, and I was wondering if she slept with him."

If so, the tryst didn't allay what her friend saw as Christa's basic unhappiness. "She seemed like the loneliest person in the world. . . . I think of her as muddy water."

Christa's affair with Jackett continued for more than two years. Until she got pregnant her relatives knew nothing about it—these same relatives who would take the witness stand to assert that if Christa had been having an affair at the time of her death, they would surely have known.

District Attorney Michael O'Keefe would later announce that the investigation into Christa Worthington's murder would begin with those closest to the victim—her family—and proceed outward in concentric circles. What O'Keefe and his detectives did not realize was that the Worthington family was a Truro dynasty, living in a world the police would never fully comprehend.

Christa was raised in Hingham, a commuter town south of Boston, but Truro was the family seat. The Worthingtons, like other staunch Yankee families, had made themselves a legend on Cape Cod, and since the early eighteenth century, Truro itself had kept a guarded distance from its neighbors, bawdy Provincetown and Catholic North Truro. The town was arguably the most proper on the Outer Cape, and the Worthingtons, starting with Christa's great-grandparents, Robert Briggs and Velnette Cheney Worthington, were proper people. They'd arrived in 1905, not artists or writers like so many other big names associated with Cape Cod, but landowners and business-people, the epitome of white WASP-itude, some said, going all the way back to the *Mayflower*.

The eldest of Robert and Velnette's four sons was Christa's grand-father. John Worthington summered at the family home for years, often rising at four A.M. to go out on commercial fishing vessels, many manned by locals of Portuguese descent. In 1926, he married Ada "Tiny" Warden, and at the height of the Great Depression, they set-tled in Truro full-time, buying a ramshackle house on Depot Road overlooking the Pamet River, not far from the town's only harbor, where the Pilgrims came ashore three hundred years earlier. John purchased the fish-processing plant at the end of Pond Road, a mile from Depot, installed modern equipment, and was soon shipping a dozen tons of fish daily to New York City and points west. More than half the town's menfolk worked for him.

It proved synergistic: the cold-storage plant being the area's larg-est employer translated into John Worthington serving three terms as town selectman, as well as doing stints on the planning board and the zoning board of appeals, positions that put him in touch with the local bank. With the plant's success, he started to buy up property, then more property. By the start of World War II, he and Tiny had amassed upward of twenty acres along Depot Road and in the Pond Road area near the fish plant. He kept his purchases as contiguous as possible, amassing large blocks of land. He lent money to folks struggling with property taxes; when they defaulted, the deeds went to Worthington.

Today, a three-quarter-acre lot on Depot Road sells for close to

$1 million. John Worthington, who died in 1988 at age ninety-one, was the buccaneer who saw it coming.

Locals still talk of John *and* Tiny, who was as charismatic and vibrant as her ex-pilot, entrepreneurial husband. Nearly six feet tall, she drove an ambulance during World War I, where she earned her nickname wearing men's combat boots, size ten. This woman was the first and last person to swim in the Pamet every season; she was a devout reader of Christian Science and the Bible; she was outspoken, was well versed in barnyard epithets, and had a repertoire of ribald songs to embarrass her friends and children.

Born in Buenos Aires, she grew up in London and trained as a nurse, then studied acting in New York. Children and the move to Truro ended her dramatic career. Instead, she founded a company that made clothing and fashion accessories from fishnets. Fishnet Industries was so successful that she opened shops in Manhattan and Miami, employing as many as fifty local women to provide for clients such as the Duchess of Kent, who owned eight of Tiny's fishnet turbans.

Big John and Tiny stood as heroic figures to the Worthingtons who followed, and it was not just the money. Ex-Marine John flew a Stinson monoplane across the country when he was a salesman, competed in air races, and once took his plane under Manhattan's George Washington Bridge on a dare. He donated land for public beach access during his tenure as selectman and was a leading advocate for the Cape Cod National Seashore, established by JFK in 1961, which now engulfs, and safeguards, almost three-quarters of Truro's landmass. In Truro, the Worthingtons mattered.

The oldest of Tiny and John's offspring lived almost opposite Christa on Depot Road. John Worthington Jr. and his wife, Lucinda, called Cindy, had five daughters, three of whom lived on the Cape year-round. Jan, the oldest at fifty-four at the time of Christa's murder, was a Truro police and fire station dispatcher, a selectperson, and a member of the town rescue squad. After Christa's murder, she became the family spokesperson, a role she combined with her experience as a TV writer to snag contracts with HBO and Lifetime TV to write a docudrama about her cousin's murder. Christa was not particularly close to her relatives; she told a childhood friend her cousins made her "feel like a misfit." After prodding by police on the night the body was found, Jan admitted she'd had little contact with Christa over the past few years. The information she did have came from her connection to the Truro rescue squad and—rumor had it—various men she served with.

Next in line was Pam, who was closer to Christa than the others. Pam and her husband, Teddy, also lived on Depot Road, although financial problems ultimately forced the sale of their home just as they lost their second, more modest place to foreclosure in spring 2007. Patricia, the youngest, turned her inherited Cape home into a small farm, where she offered horseback-riding lessons. She once made the newspaper for keeping a 198-pound goat next door to the summer digs of ex-Clinton labor secretary Robert Reich. From all reports, Reich had the sense not to complain. An outsider grousing about a local might suddenly find himself without a plumber, or other workmen, in a time of need. Patricia had little to do with Christa or with the investigation, but her marriage would dissolve in the wake of the murder, as would Pam's.

Although more than two dozen investigators and forensics experts were involved in the search for Christa's murderer, it was MSP Trooper Christopher Mason and MSP Sergeant William Burke who quickly emerged as the lead figures assigned to CPAC, the elite Crime Prevention and Control unit run by Cape and Islands District Attorney Michael O'Keefe. Earlier in his career, Burke had worked as a Dennis cop; the younger, fair-haired Mason had been a Cape-area game warden. A number of people were to wonder if the length of the investigation, and its many twists and turns, made them desperate to make an arrest.

At first, their primary target was Tony Jackett, the self-ingratiating ex-fisherman and married father of six. Jackett was Provincetown's shellfish warden, Truro's assistant harbormaster, and the father of Christa's child. He had carried on his secret, long-term affair, then walked away when Worthington told him she was pregnant and planned to keep the baby. Christa kept hoping Tony would come back.

He didn't. Instead, he managed to hide the child from his wife for more than two years, no mean feat in a place as small and gossipy as Ptown-Truro. Police knew Jackett had engaged in other affairs before and during the time he was with Worthington, just as they knew he'd bungled a big Colombia-Ptown dope run back in the 1980s. The guy could operate under the radar. He had talked to investigators about his smuggling the night the body was found, even though the record of the episode had been sealed in exchange for his cooperation before the grand jury, when he'd "ratted" on friends. On the record, Jackett's only crimes were a goodly number of fishing violations and a speeding ticket.

Early on, the detectives asked Jackett to come to the Truro police station to expand on the statement he had given to locals Sunday night. He didn't expect wires to be hooked up to his arm to gauge his pulse, respiration, and blood pressure; although caught off guard, he managed to keep his cool through the preliminary chat with the polygraph examiner, then deal with the big questions: "Did you stab Christa?" "Did you stab Christa in the house?" "Do you know the location of the weapon used in Christa's death?" The examiner's four-page report concluded, "No significant physiological responses were observed when the relevant questions were asked."

Tony's wife, Susan, underwent the same procedure eleven days later, on January 22. Still in the early stages of the investigation, police had not ruled out the possibility that a woman could have killed Christa, despite the ferocity of the single stab wound to her chest. Susan had eventually learned of Ava's existence and decided to keep her marriage intact by trying to bring the child into the Jackett family circle. Christa accepted the idea at first but had second thoughts, recognizing the financial and educational abyss between them. She wrote in her diary, "Read this: The unexamined life isn't worth living but the examined life will make you want to die. How does someone just go and get married and make babies when young, like T's family? They are an endangered species, a working class protected by a gentle environment and tight-knit community."

Police knew Susan served as her husband's alibi, claiming she was with him most of the weekend of the murder. But she, too, "passed" the polygraph, which allayed suspicion.

What police did not realize was that Susan Jackett's attempts to play Happy Family were not altogether successful. Relations between Christa and Tony were quite strained, as Christa (and her lawyer) pressed him for support and health insurance for their daughter. Some said the Jacketts' family plan and their custody battle for Ava after the murder were nothing more than an attempt to gain control of Christa's estate, valued at almost $1.5 million, counting the real estate. Jackett's annual earnings were south of $40,000, and before the dust settled on the McCowen trial, he would be moonlighting as a newspaper delivery boy.

Police didn't dismiss Jackett, but by the end of January, other candidates drew their attention, chief among them Tim Arnold.

A once-handsome man with a fondness for modernist authors such as Giovanni Verga and Gabriel García Márquez, at the time of the murder, Arnold had put on considerable weight following brain surgery. With a beard and long, scraggly hair, he looked unkempt. Sometimes he wore an eye patch; without it, he squinted to correct double vision, making him look stranger still. At High Toss Pizza, where he frequently breakfasted, employees called him Tappy Tim. Some locals doubted that he could have physically committed the act; at times, he struggled just to pour a cup of coffee. Still, after grilling him on January 6, 9, and 13, and again a year later, on January 18, 2003, police could not dismiss the idea that he was capable of the murder.

Their reasoning was simple: Tim had picked up Ava and carried her through the house to his father's van outside, then run the 100-yard, potholed path through the brambles back to his father's house to call 911. A man in a state of strong emotion, charged with adrenaline, could also have delivered the deadly knife thrust and used the missing Panasonic cordless handset to beat his victim bloody.

In their profile of Arnold, police noted that he had been diagnosed with attention deficit disorder as an adult and had been seeing Yarmouth therapist Carole Seibert regularly. He took 15 milligrams of Effexor each day and 75 milligrams of Remeron, another antidepressant, at night.

He had been married for twelve years, and his ex-wife lived off-Cape in Southboro, Massachusetts, with their two children, ages ten and twelve. Before his divorce, Arnold taught at a Manhattan private school, done illustrations for Hallmark greeting cards, and wrote five children's books. In recent years, he'd struggled unsuccessfully to find work, one of the reasons his marriage ended.

Tall and blond, he resembled actor Jeff Bridges and had grown up in Worthington, Ohio, a fact that amused Christa the sophisticate. The two began dating in the fall of 1999, when Ava was five months old, each needing more than just a bedmate for the cold months ahead. Tim took Christa's single-motherhood in stride, along with her frumpy appearance. He understood, as only a parent can, the demands of a baby.

Tim offered Christa intellectual substance she had not found in the uneducated Tony. They took walks through the marshes and dark green moors along the Pamet, discussing books, ideas, and politics, and by midwinter, she invited him to move in. Although they were intimate, Christa chose to sleep in the downstairs bedroom with Ava. As Tim would later recall, "She was tense. There wasn't enough psychological room in the same bed. She never got enough sleep. So I went upstairs. But then she'd complain if she heard me walking around up there."

Tim soon became Ava's father figure, the necessary male presence. But as much as Christa cherished this and found Tim easy to talk to, they were soon fighting.

"We drove each other crazy," he later recalled, explaining that polite disagreements often escalated into loud yelling. Sometimes they argued over money, sometimes about Christa not wanting to have sex as often as Tim did. She could get vindictive if things didn't go her way. Tim's response was to leave the house to cool off. On one occasion, he returned to finish the fight after Christa had slammed the kitchen door and locked the dead bolt. He'd tried to push the door open; Christa told others he had tried to break it down. To police, the description bore an eerie similarity to the crime scene.

In July 2000, the relationship grew too contentious, and Tim returned to his parents' place. But the two continued to see each other into the fall. He was unable to work because of his cerebral circulatory problem, in addition to depression, and he was having dizzy spells. Money was another problem. Even before she told him to move out, Christa had complained to Vassar classmate Sharon Ferrito that Arnold was broke. The "financials," she'd explained, were central to any relationship. He also had unresolved anger issues, she said, and she was troubled by his "weird" behavior.

Police determined that this was a man who couldn't give up the idea that Christa might have been in love with him despite their problems. They saw it as a fatal attraction.

But in order to point the finger at Tim Arnold, they had to show how he got from Wellfleet, where he was house-sitting, to Christa's house in Truro six miles away. He could have hitched a ride or taken a taxi. But after four weeks of investigating, police found no one who had given Tim a lift.

What they did find was that on Friday morning, January 4, Tim walked his dog, had his coffee at High Toss Pizza in Wellfleet, then returned to the house to paint until ten A.M. He'd gone to the library for a couple of hours before getting a sandwich at Box Lunch, then spent the rest of the day writing and painting back at the house. After dinner, he went to bed at ten P.M.

On Saturday, his routine was similar, except that he stayed home all day after breakfast at High Toss.

On Sunday, he woke at six A.M., walked his dog, and returned to bed. At 10:30, he again had breakfast back at High Toss, returned to the house, gathered his laundry, and was there until his father picked him up in the afternoon. From Christa's caller ID box, police knew he had called her at 1:53 P.M., then again at 4:01 P.M., from his father's house.

Contacts at both Cape Cab and Mercedes Cab in Provincetown led nowhere. But despite the dearth of evidence to place him at the scene, police wouldn't dismiss their suspect.

In June, Detective Mason interviewed Arnold again, telling him police thought he had hounded Christa, that he had not been able to "take no for an answer." Because she rarely bothered to delete messages on her answering machine, they knew how often he'd called her; one day, after Thanksgiving, he left seven consecutive, increasingly whiny messages. In the last, he'd become petulant—"I think you made it clear where you stand on the issue of friendship. . . . So at this point, don't expect me to be around." A few days later, he called and repeated himself, saying, "I don't think we should see each other."

Mason recalled in his report, "I asked Arnold what, if anything, he and Christa planned to do if she met 'Mr. Right.' Arnold stated that he and Christa had agreed to 'phase out' when that time came. I asked Arnold if that agreement to be phased out of Christa and Ava's life was acceptable to him, and he stated that he had agreed because he thought it would be best for Ava."

Trooper John Mawn was in the room during this interview, and Mawn's more aggressive questioning made Arnold tense, which made the investigators get more suspicious. Tim agreed to turn over his Compaq laptop and his journals, but the next day, he hired a criminal defense attorney, Russell Redgate. Redgate contacted the DA's office, making it clear that all future police contact was to go through him.

Even so, a few days later, on June 15 or 16, Arnold telephoned Detective Bill Burke to say he had forgotten something that could be important. He was worried that his handprint would be found on the outside of Christa's bedroom window. Eight to ten months earlier, he had stopped by her house after jogging. When she didn't answer the door, he went around to the side and looked in the window to see if she was home. Christa was in bed, and he admitted she was startled.

Later, when author Maria Flook, researching a book on Worthington's death, suggested to DA Michael O'Keefe that the killer might have been a third person, someone who watched Christa come home with another man, then kicked the door down, the DA had responded, "Now, who do you think that is?" Arnold's alleged attempt to push the door in after an argument made it easy to envision that possibility, especially now that he had admitted to "spying" on his ex through the bedroom window.

Tim's journal rendered an even clearer picture of his infatuation. But the journal entries also reflected frustration that the killer had not yet been caught: "I do want this to be solved. It has to be. I've got to know what happened. . . . It is so intensely appalling to know that she felt this pain, the horror that she did, and I want justice, justice to be served."

Police remained suspicious for the next six months, even though no further evidence materialized. On January 17, 2003, after the first anniversary of the crime, the Worthington family announced a $25,000 reward, and Arnold learned that he was still the chief suspect. Later that day, his therapist came to believe he was suicidal and referred him to Cape Cod Hospital's psychiatric unit. That evening, Tim was transferred to a Department of Mental Health unit in Hyannis.

Police seized the opportunity, and the next day, Mason and Burke appeared at Arnold's bedside. Ignoring lawyer Redgate's letter to the DA, the detectives conducted their interrogation for three hours. Mason told Arnold what they already "had" on him, and Arnold admitted that he and Christa argued almost daily but reminded them that he had been physically disabled and could not have committed the crime or kicked in the door. The detectives wondered how he knew the door had been kicked in, since there was no footprint on it. Arnold said he thought he saw one, then said someone at the scene, perhaps an EMT, had told him so.

Mason explained that police had never believed that Arnold's physical state at the time of the murder eliminated him and pointed to how he'd been able to carry Ava through the house and run through the woods. Arnold's statements and actions, Mason said, were "consistent" with someone involved in the murder.

Arnold resisted.

Mason repeated: Tim had been fit enough to run through the woods, uphill, to dial 911.

At that point, Arnold reasserted his right to counsel.

After the detectives left, he was so shaken that he had to be transferred to a more secure facility in Pembroke. Russell Redgate was but a hair's breadth from filing a civil-rights suit.

By now, the prime suspects—Tony Jackett and Tim Arnold—had both passed the polygraph. But Christa's father, Christopher "Toppy" Worthington, as well as Toppy's girlfriend Beth Porter and Porter's boyfriend Ed Hall, would all fail the same exam.

The senior Worthington had married outside his narrow WASP world. His wife, Gloria, who died a few days before Christa's little girl was born, was Italian-American by birth, grew up in a working-class neighborhood, had no college degree, and incurred the disapproval of the family by being pregnant at the time of the marriage, which, it turned out, was not a good one. A part-time still-life painter, Gloria had mostly artistic friends, drove an unfashionable (by South Shore standards) VW Bug, and took in feral cats. Toppy had a succession of girlfriends and at times drank heavily. Later in life, Christa attended meetings for children of alcoholics.

While in his early sixties, Toppy, a graduate of the exclusive Kent School, Harvard, and Harvard Law, had abandoned his successful legal career as an assistant state attorney general and then private practitioner to become a bicycle courier for a Boston-based delivery service. If this struck investigators as odd, odder things were to come. Shortly before her murder, Christa told friends in New York and Truro that she was afraid her father was frittering away Ava's inheritance. Records from the Boston-based money-management firm handling both Christa's and her father's accounts showed he was making monthly withdrawals of $2,000 to $3,000, the funds wire-transferred directly to his young girlfriend, Elizabeth Porter, a heroin addict he'd met through an escort service. In addition, Toppy was making daily cash withdrawals of $100, $200, sometimes $250, from ATMs. He had bought Porter a computer, paid medical bills for treatment of her ulcers and other ills, and covered her rent for more than a year. For 2001 alone, Toppy's withdrawals totaled $139,666, a sum separate and apart from his funding of the modest $162,500 Weymouth home he bought months after wife Gloria's death and the sale of Christa's childhood home in Hingham.

According to a number of her friends, as well as her accountant, Christa could not stop talking about ways to stanch the money flow, even though she knew nothing about Porter's past. Police learned that Porter's boyfriend, Edward Hall, also an addict, was living with her, albeit on the sly so Toppy wouldn't find out. Together, the two consumed upward of twenty-five bags of heroin daily, paid for with Worthington money. Hall actually met Toppy a few times, once to pick up cash when Porter was too sick to do it. Beth had introduced him as her "gay" black friend who was studying to be a nurse.

Suspicions about Toppy Worthington—if not of the crime, then at least of complicity—were fueled by his behavior once told of his daughter's murder. His brother John had called him with the news from the Cape, and instead of immediately driving to Truro, he'd escorted Porter back to her apartment in Quincy, then returned to his house in Weymouth to feed his cats. It was after nine P.M. before he appeared in John and Cindy's kitchen at 53 Depot Road, which had become ground zero for police and family members shortly after Arnold discovered the body.

But that evening, when Detective Burke began to describe what had happened, Toppy's behavior grew stranger. He interrupted to ask if Christa was found lying on her back? And did she have bruises on the right side of her face? Burke, a twenty-year veteran who'd run more than fifty murder investigations, was taken aback. He hadn't seen the body, but he'd seen Polaroids, and that was exactly how the victim was found. This information had not yet been released to the family. Asked if someone had told him, Toppy replied no, he simply was trying to determine whether the assailant was right- or left-handed. He then remained silent for the rest of Burke's briefing.

Toppy said he had last seen Christa on Christmas Day, when she appeared concerned about something "because her door was locked." No one had told him about her injuries, he reiterated. As for his daughter's life in general, he said, Christa was involved in a child-support battle with Jackett, who "gave no assistance to Ava other than health insurance"; Tim Arnold was magnificent, very gentle with Ava; and Christa had a trust fund worth more than $500,000, not counting the value of her house. What Toppy failed to mention was that his daughter had recently hired a private investigator to look into an aunt's sale of property in Florida, suspecting the proceeds weren't being divided as her mother's will dictated.

Beth Porter failed her polygraph on January 14, piquing investigators' interest further. The examiner, Trooper Christopher Dolan, concluded that Porter had "significant physiological responses" to the questions "Did you stab Christa in that house?" and "Did you plan with anyone to harm Christa?"

"It is the opinion of this examiner," Dolan wrote, "that Ms. Porter practiced deception during this examination."

Mason felt it was time to apply pressure. Porter gave them the leverage they needed the next morning, when police found her and Hall on a stairway in Boston's South End with a packet of heroin and a syringe. Hall, who had done time for drugs, was held in lieu of $500 cash bail that he could not raise. Porter faced an additional charge for violating probation from a 1999 heroin conviction. With a prison sentence looming, the waiflike twenty-nine-year-old provided Mason with a more accurate version of her relationship with the victim's father: she and Hall discussed the money flow ending "all the time," she said. Toppy had been telling her for years that he'd be cutting back but so far had never carried through with the threat, so she'd never really been worried.

Prodded about her whereabouts the weekend of January 4–6, she said she usually got up early and woke Worthington with a phone call around seven A.M. Mason asked if these were independent recollections or if she had discussed her whereabouts over the weekend with Hall or Worthington. What did she remember about Friday evening? What was her relationship with Christa? What was Hall's real feeling about Worthington cutting off the money supply?

He also asked when she was last on Cape Cod. She said that "several years ago," she and Hall had taken the ferry to Provincetown and stayed at the Sandcastle condos, where her father, a cop, had a time-share. Hall, she said, did not have a driver's license, and they had no access to a car.

The detective asked if Worthington had ever proposed to her, and she said he had, two or three times. When Mason asked why she hadn't married him, he got no response.

He came back to Christa. Why had Porter never met her? Beth's response was that she felt "awkward," even though Toppy had offered to introduce her "many times." She didn't want to meet Christa, she said. When Mason asked if Porter was in Worthington's will, Porter said no.

By nature cautious, Mason wasn't satisfied. When he told Porter she'd flunked the lie-detector test, she became agitated and claimed she'd been "dope sick." He reminded her that the information she'd given in their first interview had been riddled with lies, at which point she demanded to be taken home. As she rose to walk out of the interview room, the detective stopped her with an upraised hand: police wanted to search her apartment and analyze her Compaq computer. She had no choice but to consent.

Porter was not in great health. On January 18, a week after Christa's standing-room-only burial service, Toppy took Porter to Boston Medical Center's emergency room; she was suffering from pneumonia. The *Boston Herald* had a cameraman in place, as if Elizabeth Taylor were being wheeled into Cedars-Sinai in Beverly Hills. Porter was now hot news, in the papers almost daily, "a high-risk drug offender" with thirteen prior warrants, five probation violations, four convictions for heroin possession, and an arrest for passing a bad check at a local supermarket back in 1993.

None of this, of course, displeased Mason and Mawn. It upped the pressure. On January 24, with Eddie Hall's release from the Nashua Street jail, the investigators turned their attention to him, hoping to make inroads there. The interview took place in Boston, inside Mason's cruiser, just before seven P.M. Hall admitted almost immediately that he'd once heard Porter say she wished "that bitch" was dead, referring to Christa. But he denied any involvement in the murder. On Friday, January 4, he said, he took a Quincy cab into Boston, specifically to the Cherry Street and Grove Hall area of Mattapan, to score some heroin. When he returned to Porter's apartment, she was upset because she'd wanted cocaine, and he had to go back into Boston, this time using the train. The two spent the rest of the day at home, getting stoned. By nightfall, he was "too high" to work and called in sick. He often went to work high on heroin, he told Mason, but he wasn't used to being "coked out," and his eyes were "pinned."

On Saturday, he slept in while Porter got up early to go shopping with Toppy. She was gone only an hour and returned with a bag of things Toppy had bought for her. Hall's memory was that they stayed at the apartment the rest of the day except when he went out to score more heroin.

On Sunday, Hall hung out "elsewhere" in Quincy. When he returned in the early evening, he found Porter upset about the death of Toppy's daughter, as if everything had become too much for her.

Asked about Christa's resentment of her father's spending money on Porter, Hall acknowledged that Worthington had told his daughter that some of the funds he gave to Porter were for medical bills and that Christa had wanted him to get his girlfriend on MassHealth. Hall wasn't worried about the money "drying up," because he'd always known the "free ride" was going to end. He denied any efforts to approach or kill Christa, denied ever having been to Truro. Asked why Porter had been reluctant to turn over her caller ID box, Hall admitted she hadn't wanted the phone numbers of her drug connections falling into the hands of police. The cell phone he and Porter used was the only one they had, a prepaid TracFone that Worthington bought. Hall said he had encouraged Porter to stay with Worthington rather than risk exposure to multiple partners. Porter, he said, refused to have intercourse with Worthington "because she wasn't attracted to him." Their morning meetings involved the exchange of oral sex for money and lasted no longer than ten minutes.

For the most part, Hall's story coincided with Porter's. Most important, she was home all weekend except for two meetings with Toppy, the first early Saturday morning to purchase a twenty-dollar fake Oriental rug, then on Sunday when he picked her up during the Patriots game. The only part of the account that differed from Porter's was that Hall was with her that day; she was not alone.

Police might not have believed their alibis, but one fact was clear: neither Hall nor Porter owned a car. Unless police could explain how the two got to the Cape, they were at a dead end.

The media of course had been riding the connection between the seventy-two-year-old Harvard-educated Worthington and Porter the hooker, who initially identified herself as Christa's "stepsister." Both the *Globe* and the *Herald* soon revealed another sordid link: Porter was tied to the high-profile prosecution of Dirk Greineder, a Wellesley doctor convicted the previous summer of murdering his wife. She had testified before a grand jury that she met Greineder in 1998 while working for her usual escort service and that the successful allergist had wooed her in a hotel suite with champagne and chocolate-covered strawberries. The *Herald* reported that Worthington, "a widower and retired prosecutor for the civil bureau of the

Office of the Attorney General," was paying Porter's rent and had recently renewed the yearlong lease on her Quincy apartment.

Mason and Burke might have been cheered by this, but they were getting nowhere with Hall, and Toppy's gray 2001 Toyota Echo came up clean except for some medium-length brown hair found near the passenger seat, its significance unclear. The big news was that Toppy had blown his polygraph on January 15, the same day the Porter-Greineder story broke. Once more, examiner Dolan found that the subject "practiced deception." Worthington "exhibited significant responses" to ten questions, among them "Since Dec. 25, 2001, did you go to Christa's house with anyone?" and "Did you plan with anyone to harm Christa?"

A do-over was discussed, but detectives decided to "lean on" him instead. In a previous interview with Trooper James Massari and Sergeant Robert Knott, Toppy admitted that he and Christa hadn't spoken much during the past year because of his relationship with Porter. Their exchanges were "strained," "tense," "difficult," all the more so because Christa made her resentments known not just to him but to her "many" friends and relatives. As for the weekend of January 4–6, Toppy was uncertain about what he did Friday but knew he didn't go out at night. On Saturday, he got up early, stopped at an ATM on the way to Porter's, then took her to a Kmart, where he exchanged a vacuum cleaner and bought a coat and a pair of pants. The two then went to Building 19, a cut-rate outlet, where he bought Porter her rug before driving back to her apartment. He returned home at one P.M. Later, he went back to Building 19 to buy more clothes. Between three and four, he got a haircut, leaving a three-dollar tip, then bought a cup of coffee and drank it "at the harbor" before returning home for the night at 4:30 P.M.

Sunday was not as active. Around noon, he left his house to go to Dunks in Hanover for coffee and a doughnut, then drove through Cohasset. When he got home, he watched the Patriots game until he picked up Porter, who returned with him to his house.

Mason wasn't satisfied, but a subsequent search of Porter's living quarters turned up a receipt dated January 5; it was from Wal-Mart, not Kmart, but it verified that Worthington had been in Weymouth that morning.

Porter continued to make headlines as the month drew to a close. On January 29, she defaulted on her court appearance, then turned herself in two days later, saying she'd been "sick." The next day, paramedics and police responded to a 911 call from Worthington's address, where they found Porter semiconscious, having trouble breathing. Weymouth police officer Francis Beatrice interviewed Toppy and found him as arrogant and uncooperative as Burke had earlier.

Beatrice reported: "He showed me three hypodermic needles in the utensil drawer in the kitchen. He stated he found these in the bedroom next to the victim. He stated these are what she used to OD. I secured these and asked if there was [*sic*] any more. He stated he would look when he got time [*sic*] but was not willing to look at this time with me present. I asked if these were her drugs. He stated they were. . . . I asked if he knew where she got them. He stated he didn't know but she had been doing this for five years. At first he stated he was her sponsor as in drug rehab. Further into the conversation I managed to ascertain that Ms. Porter was in fact his girlfriend. He stated she was an addict going through treatment and he was trying to help her. . . . He also stated that this could possibly violate her probation and to go easy on her."

Then the lonely seventy-two-year-old WASP added, implausibly, one more detail: "She will be moving in with me this May."

Back on the Cape, Keith Amato was the next to attract attention. Married to Tony Jackett's daughter, Braunwyn, Amato had been seen at Christa's house the summer before the murder, using her outdoor shower. The Amato marriage was rocky, and Keith resented Tony, which might have led to the rumors that Keith had been having an affair with his father-in-law's ex-lover.

For some, either scenario made sense: Tony, the sly risk taker, wanting Christa off his back; or Keith, in too deep after he and Christa, both angry with Tony, decided to pay him back by taking pleasurable revenge.

The idea was buttressed by the kindly Diana Worthington, Toppy's younger sister, of all people. She told investigators that her niece once intimated that she was seeing "a son" of Tony Jackett. If Christa had actually switched from father to son, Diana hadn't wanted to hear about it, and the subject was dropped. Still, locals speculated that Christa might have been referring not to one of Tony's three sons but to Keith, his son-in-law. Police shared that suspicion.

Amato also seemed a likely candidate because of his age, thirty-seven. And the more detectives dug into it, the more they realized that Amato's marriage was not just on the rocks but terminal, something Keith hadn't been straight about.

Amato was cut of different material from his wife and father-in-law. A broad-shouldered five-foot-eleven, he'd grown up in affluent Huntington, Long Island, and was busted for felony cocaine possession in the late 1980s; his parents' money kept him out of jail. Although he never completed college, he was bright, with a hip, articulate New York style that was as much a part of his persona as his Dean Martinish good looks. His marrying Jackett's daughter could only be explained by Braunwyn Jackett's own good looks; blond with high "cat cheekbones," she carried herself with a saucy aloofness many young men found alluring. The two were not intellectual equals.

The weekend of Christa's murder, Keith had been juggling two jobs, working as an assistant carpenter in Wellfleet from 8:00 A.M. to 2:30 P.M. both Friday and Saturday; then as a cook at night at High Toss Pizza, Tim Arnold's favorite breakfast spot. Through three interviews with police, he claimed to have interacted with Christa only four times: when she initially met the Jackett family in June as part of "the big reconciliation"; when he bumped into her with Ava and Arnold later that month at Pamet Harbor, which was the one time he used her outdoor shower; and later that summer, in August, when he ran into Christa and Ava at a concert on the Truro green. He did not see her again, he said, until the Friday before Christmas, when she came into the pizza parlor.

Amato expected police to press him. Word was out that investigators were growing frustrated, and he'd read that a witness had reported seeing a black van-type vehicle leaving Christa's driveway. Amato's Ford Bronco was black and had a license tag ending with the same numbers the witness claimed he'd seen, 17 or 18. On June 13, police brought him to the second-floor conference room at the Truro police station for his third interview. Mason and Burke produced Amato's home telephone records, asking him to identify each and every call. Amato explained that several other people lived at his address; not all of the calls were his. The officers told him to try anyway. Soon they became more confrontational, claiming they had a source who was positive he'd seen Keith kiss Christa in public, a subject that had come up before. Now they said they didn't believe his claim that it was only a friendly hello-type peck. They pushed him to elaborate on his relationship with Braunwyn, to admit that he and his wife were splitting.

For Amato, this was a sensitive area. His eight-year marriage was, indeed, at its end, and he didn't know what to do about it. During the winter, Braunwyn had taken off for Colorado, partly to escape the pressure-cooker atmosphere of the Jackett household brought on by Tony's infidelity but also to get away from Keith. In Colorado, she had become pregnant after a fling with an ex-boyfriend. Keith's life was in shambles. Under pressure, he admitted it. Halfway through the interview, when the officers revealed that they knew about his suicide attempt the previous summer, he unraveled. Only three people knew about the attempt: his therapist, his wife, and his father-in-law, Tony. Amato believed that Tony was pointing the finger at him, perhaps to shield himself or his wife, Susan. As he tried to process, the third detective in the room got louder. According to Amato, Detective Mawn slammed his hand on the table and bellowed, "This is a murder investigation, and if we so choose, we will turn your life inside out!" Massachusetts was planning to bring back the death penalty, Mawn added, without lowering his eyes.

Imperturbable Mason, sitting on the opposite side of the conference table, piped up to say he knew Amato was lying. It was now more than three hours into the interview; Amato would later testify that the room was "spinning." He shoved his seat back from the table, got to his feet, and halted the interrogation. "I know how you guys can frame people!" he yelled. "I'm not one of these dumb locals. My parents have money; they'll get me a lawyer if I need one, goddammit!"

Mason and Mawn left the room; Burke reentered. Amato claims Burke threatened him, saying that the difference between "telling the truth" and continuing to lie could be a sentence of twenty-five years as opposed to life. The time had come, Burke counseled, for Amato to "make the right decision."

Amato left the station. Outside, he vomited in the bushes.

For the time being, the cops were to leave him alone. Instead, they interviewed hundreds of others, on the Cape and off, from the Boston area westward to Menomonie, Wisconsin.

Closer to home, broader, more amorphous issues were at work. Whether or not investigators were ready to acknowledge it or were even aware of it, these factors pointed to the most likely suspect to date.

Late in 2001, the Cape Cod Drug Task Force, made up of local, state, and federal agents, had begun a push to recruit small-time dealers as informants, hoping to nail the big-time players. The local drug underground was not ignorant of this campaign; it was everywhere. More and more charges against two-bit pushers were being dropped. Rumors circulated about the reasons; the Cape's tight-knit communities tightened further.

On the Cape, as elsewhere, drugs of choice can be seasonal, in one year, out another. At the time of the Worthington murder, the prescription painkiller OxyContin had come into its own, hotter even than Percocet. Also available that winter were Ecstasy, psychedelic mushrooms, cocaine, brown heroin, and never-ending supplies of pot, grown in local basements, in remote areas of the National Seashore Park in Truro and Wellfleet, and brought across the bridge from off-Cape. According to the U.S. Department of Health, in 2002, Massachusetts ranked fourth in the nation for drug use, pharmaceutical and non-. Statewide, among rural areas, Cape Cod topped the list.

With the Cape's long winters, exacerbated by wet springs and the seesaw seasonal economy—unemployment in Provincetown, for example, pushes 50 percent during the off-season—too much empty time equals drugs and alcohol, as well as their attendant problems.

In Wellfleet, the onetime whaling port bordering Truro to the south, when those winters finally subside, springs bring an influx of psychoanalysts and academics such as linguist Noam Chomsky and historians Doris Kearns Goodwin and the late Howard Zinn, as well as dozens of lesser-known professors from Harvard, Tufts, MIT, and other Boston institutions of higher learning. Spring also brings out the Wu-Tang

Clan, not the best-selling New York City rap group but, rather, a "crew" of local bad boys formed at nearby Nauset High in the '90s, whose members commonly lollygagged up and down Wellfleet's quaint Main Street, three or four abreast, hats on sideways, in a stylized, threatening shuffle. Anyone coming the other way would have little choice but to step off the sidewalk, precisely the group's objective: they *owned* the street, just as they owned the benches in front of Town Hall.

Any half-intelligent, half-cosmopolitan adult would find the wannabe rapper chants of these white kids laughable. But to leader Jeremy Frazier, nicknamed "Wu," he and his pot-smoking boys were "gangstas," the toughest, roughest, meanest hombres to come down the pike.

The Frazier family went back four generations in Wellfleet, but it was Jeremy's father, Michael, a.k.a. "Froggy," whom people talked about. Covered in tattoos, his hair long and often rubber-banded in a ponytail, Froggy had a well-earned reputation as a Harley-riding, boozing, gnarly bar fighter who would pop open a beer at eight A.M., although most say he stopped drinking when Jeremy, a.k.a. "Tadpole," was born. In his youth, even fellow bikers avoided Froggy, because he was usually too drunk to ride with. When they made their annual pilgrimage to Laconia, New Hampshire, for the big motorcycle rally, they were forced to leave him behind; he'd been banned from too many places along the way. "Whenever he went into a bar," recalled one, "it was like you'd turn around, he'd be pissing on the floor, some punk-ass thing like that that might have amused him but in the whole scope of things didn't do anything but make us have to move on."

Some Wellfleet locals say even the police were cautious around Froggy, because when he was drinking, "he scared the crap out of them." One recalled that he was "a bully, and mean . . . I mean *really* mean." And, conveniently, his youngest brother, "Bubba," served on the Truro police force until a personal-injury settlement allowed him to set up a business leasing dumpsters and portable toilets up and down the Cape.

Fourth-generation Jeremy emerged as a class bully even before high school. When his name came up in connection with the Worthington murder, one Wellfleet woman recalled that she had never wanted to be left alone in a room with him: "Even as a kid, he freaked me out. He's creepy."

This was not an isolated view. Parents of Jeremy's contemporaries did not want the junior Frazier inside their homes because he stole. He carried a knife in his back pocket that he'd learned to flick open using one hand, and according to a classmate at Nauset High, he "used to pull it out all the time and play with it while talking to you."

At the time of the murder, twenty-one-year-old Jeremy Frazier was a known dealer. "Everyone knew where to get your drugs," said one Wellfleet-Eastham local. "And everyone knew about the Wu-Tang Clan," added the man's wife. A mother who'd watched Frazier grow up remembered another parent telling her about Jeremy's gang "putting drugs" into other kids' drinks at parties, adding "I wonder why he is still wandering around loose." Said another, "Jeremy was selling blow, too, everybody knew that. Like, Friday night, Jeremy would be out at a party" with "a pocket full of fucking bags, you know?"

"I watched as they became more and more violent. I watched it go from marijuana to cocaine," said Wellfleet detective Michael Mazzone.

Dave Amerault, a close friend of Chris McCowen, the black man police would arrest for the murder in 2005, remembers that Frazier came to McCowen's place at least several times a week. For Frazier, with his affected hip-hop persona, McCowen was the real thing: black, with a prison record and a seemingly endless array of willing women. On the Cape, with few blacks and prejudice pervasive, McCowen found a welcome with Frazier and his gang.

"They'd always do their deal," recalled Amerault, a local plumber. Jeremy would "stay for about a half-hour, twenty minutes, smoke a joint, then leave."

While the self-titled "Wu" might have been a major supplier to the local high school and blue-collar crowds, he was not the area's biggest dealer but a middleman, at best. This did not matter. He kept a high profile and flaunted the lifestyle, gold chains, zircon-encrusted watch, and all. People wondered why he never got caught.

Frazier allegedly had close ties to the off-Cape drug world, but he mostly hung out at a house in nearby Provincetown that served as a social center for the drug crowd. Among the group were ten to fifteen inner-city types, some from New York, several black. The older, tougher, more experienced city dealers found his constant posturing annoying. When he was coked up, said one, he simply couldn't control himself. Tripping on Ecstasy made him think he was "fucking in Hollywood all the time."

Yet when the grand jury eventually indicted Christopher Mc-Cowen, it did so on the basis of testimony from just three people: Chris Mason, the Massachusetts State Police detective who led the investigation; MSP crime-scene services expert Sergeant Monte Gilardi; and the drug-dealing, knife-wielding Jeremy Frazier, who, it turned out, had for years been an undercover informant for the cops.

But if Frazier was a druggie and snitch, so, too, was McCowen. The difference between the two was that McCowen was black, without local moorings, an easy target.

Christopher McCowen had arrived on the Cape in June 1995, a six-foot, muscular man four months past his twenty-third birthday and recently released from a Florida state prison after serving two years for grand theft auto. He'd previously done time for petty theft and receiving stolen property but had no history of violent crime. At the Hyannis bus station, he was met by Pam Maguire, his white girlfriend and mother of his two-year-old daughter. They'd met in Key West. Maguire had grown up in Eastham, next to Wellfleet, and the move to Massachusetts was to be a new start for this man. Six and a half years later he would be indicted for Christa Worthington's murder.

Cape Cod is a strange place for an African-American. Cape Verdeans live there, shanghaied by whaling captains starting in the early nineteenth century, then put to work in the cranberry bogs. But black men, Southern blacks whose origins go back to slavery, have always been rare. McCowen was thus something of a novelty, an attractive man with hazelnut skin, brilliant white teeth, and an ease with women. Racial prejudice on Cape Cod is no different from anywhere else in America, but women liked Chris, always had, because of his easy manner and his ability, as he put it, "to bullshit 'em." By the time of his arrest, McCowen had gone through several major relationships, all with white women. He'd fathered three children with three different girlfriends. And he'd gathered a circle of friends and employers who insisted, whatever his flaws, that Chris was incapable of murder.

Those who knew him well reported that marijuana was as important to him as women; he smoked daily, and to keep himself supplied, he did what many heavy marijuana users do: he dealt. Chris went with the flow, often following the path of least resistance. His job as a garbageman took him into the homes—and, according to those who knew, the beds—of a number of women along his zigzagging route that stretched from Ptown 35 miles up-Cape to Dennis.

From time to time, he got rejected. But in light of later events, it's important to note that rejection didn't seem to bother him. If a potential conquest said No, he simply moved on down the bar. One woman who rebuffed him laughed as she remembered how calmly he backed off: "He'd just, like, move on to the next chick." His propensity for womanizing led to friction with whatever woman he was living with, not surprising considering the extent of his infidelities. But the phrases people most often used to describe him were "easygoing," "eager to please," "a get-along guy," "never really disagreed with anybody."

Few on the Outer Cape were aware that when he was a toddler growing up in hardscrabble Oklahoma, the man they called Black Chris had been diagnosed as mildly retarded. At four months, he'd been rushed to the hospital with a head injury, diagnosed as epileptic, and placed in the custody of his paternal grandmother. His unmarried seventeen-year-old mother was either unable or unwilling to administer to his special needs, and he saw her only intermittently; after he was sent to Florida at age fifteen to live with his father, he never saw her again. His grandmother was nurturing, the most important figure in his life, and when she died in 2005, he was unable to attend her funeral. He was already in jail.

Chris held down a job, but tests showed that his ability to express himself, or to understand what others said, was below normal. His IQ registered at 76, placing him just above "retarded" on the Wechsler scale. Going along with things you don't understand can be easier than trying to figure them out. To his friends, it made perfect sense that McCowen so willingly talked to the police the night of his arrest;

it wasn't in him to say he didn't want to talk, just as he also believed he could "bullshit" people when he had to. As defense lawyer Robert George would argue, he thought the police were on his side; he'd been reporting to them for two and a half years, "turned" after getting caught with a parole-violating hash pipe in the late '90s.

One of the more major ironies was that McCowen had met with police on Tuesday, January 8, 2002, less than forty-eight hours after the discovery of Worthington's body. Mason's investigation was just gearing up, with interviews of the Jacketts, the Worthingtons, Tim Arnold and his father, the EMTs, and Truro Fire Department personnel, as well as Ava's nanny, yet there was Chris, chatting away with the cops inside an unmarked police car in the Orleans Stop & Shop parking lot. Present were two members of the Wellfleet PD and Sergeant John Santangelo, representing the Cape Cod Drug Task Force. According to Santangelo's report, McCowen said Jeremy Frazier received a couple of pounds of cannabis every few weeks and was also dealing cocaine. He mentioned two other dealers: "Sly," who lived off Exit 7 of Route 6, and Sean "Muddy" Murphy, the DJ at Rick's Outer Bar in Eastham, where Chris had worked as a bouncer. McCowen offered to make a "buy" for the cops, saying he could easily do so along his garbage route.

To many observers, neither McCowen nor Frazier had the fortitude to become a serious drug dealer, as both were "functioning drug addicts." McCowen never seemed to have any money, and Frazier, a man of little discipline, couldn't handle having an ounce of coke "in his face" without using it up.

Drugs cemented their relationship, and Frazier's undisclosed police connections would play an important part in the investigation. Later, some people said it was incomprehensible that police summoned Frazier before the grand jury without running his arrest record or that Michael O'Keefe, the tough, hands-on DA, was unaware of the man's street rep. But those people were mistaken. The cops had known for years; they just looked the other way.

Now, though, by June 2003, investigators were desperate. Truro townsfolk feared the murder would never be solved. The Worthington family, in addition to posting their $25,000 reward, had petitioned the state attorney general to take O'Keefe off the case—not only because he "lacked perspective" but because the DA had blabbed to writer Maria Flook, calling Christa a sexually promiscuous slob. The press had grown critical, too. One headline, "More Theories Than Answers," summed up most people's feelings. The story read, "For months now O'Keefe and his investigators have been on a frantic and frustrating search that was going nowhere."

Mason, Burke, and their team had, indeed, been working overtime. They interviewed "persons of interest" in a half-dozen states, throughout Massachusetts, and in New York City. They quizzed Worthington's former publishing colleagues and ex-lovers. They checked employee records at the Stop & Shop where the victim had last been seen alive on Friday, January 4. They spoke with her psychiatrist, her accountant, her optometrist, her writing instructor, even her Weight Watchers coordinator and a female "organizer" she had hired to straighten out her life. They obtained UPS records tracking delivery of her new Dell computer. They pulled her stock records and even reviewed her 1040s. They searched Tim Arnold's Compaq hard drive for the words "Christi," "Christa," "Base64," "Death," "Murder," "Knife," "Stab," and "Ava." In a separate operation, the MSP Computer Forensics Unit extracted Arnold's Internet history.

They had to deal with crank stuff, too, the volume nearly overwhelming. It's not uncommon for nuts to come out of the woodwork with high-profile murder cases, but these were off the charts: one hotline tipster directed police to an individual in the mid-Cape area who "was acting as a con man" posing as a Scottish nanny. A self-admitted car thief in Vermont, a recovering alcoholic, had been in a bar and run into an individual called "Bubble U," who could not stop talking about Truro and the Worthington investigation. A psychic talked about "auras" and "emanations" from the caller's deceased daughter that, if properly "related to," would lead police directly to the killer.

Pity the cops. Every lead had to be followed.

By January 2005, after two conferences with FBI behavioral assessment experts in Quantico, Virginia, police conducted their controversial DNA sweep of all age-eligible men in Truro, which the *New*

York Times called "an unusual last-ditch move." The ACLU jumped in, faulting the DA's office for deliberately ignoring constitutional guarantees of privacy. The worst part was the intimidation: Mason himself had stood in front of Truro's post office in the January cold, buttonholing prospective donors, saying that anyone who refused to be swabbed would have his plate numbers added to a "special list."

By now, Mason and Burke had also interviewed McCowen, initially on April 3, 2002, then again two years later, when Chris volunteered his DNA. On April 14, 2005, three months after the Truro sweep, they interviewed him once more, after his arrest. It was only then that Jeremy Frazier was questioned and swabbed. He was given a lie-detector test the next morning. Unlike Christa's father, he passed.

On May 5, almost three weeks later, Frazier was interviewed a second time. Police ran a check on his T-Mobile cell phone. They tested a leather jacket, a sweater, pants, and boots obtained from his home; all proved negative for blood.

Frazier was asked to review the statement he'd given on April 14, when he denied knowing Chris McCowen. He enumerated the events of January 4, 2002, saying he got a ride home that evening from either Eli Auch or Shawn Mulvey, another drug dealer. He acknowledged that he'd sat with McCowen at the kitchen table at the party they'd all gone to in Eastham, then admitted he'd met McCowen, a.k.a. Black Chris, back "in either 1999 or 2000." According to Mason's report, Frazier stated he "did not know Christa Worthington" but had moved her belongings from storage into her home after her death while working for Magnum Movers. He was not asked to respond to McCowen's allegation that it was he, Frazier, who had stabbed Worthington; Mason's questioning was designed to secure confirmation that McCowen, the suspect now arrested, had gone to Truro that evening alone.

The omission was glaring. Also absent were any questions related to Frazier's criminal history, as if it didn't matter. But they would have done well to ask Frazier about his activities as a thief, undeniably part of McCowen's explanation for what took place at Worthington's the night of the murder. Eric Kinton, another local street tough, would later testify that Frazier approached him about robbing a woman's home "in Truro" for jewelry, coins, and money. The woman was "a rich bitch."

Kinton's description of Frazier as a thief wasn't isolated. "Jeremy, he stole *anything.* Fucking break in your house, steal your stereo, your booze," said another local, insisting on anonymity while recalling that it was common for area youths to break into vacant vacation homes during winter months. Some said one of Frazier's later jobs, driving a truck solo up and down the Cape, provided a ready sales platform for his hot goods. But despite his reputation as a man who stole, dealt drugs, carried a knife, and threatened people, Frazier was never seriously investigated. Instead, police swallowed his alibi for the evening of Christa's murder, even though the person he claimed he'd been with said he was not.

When McCowen was told the night of his arrest that his DNA matched sperm found on Christa Worthington's body, he said the two had sex the Thursday before her murder, when he stopped at her house on his regular garbage run. Police found this scenario impossible to believe; rich white women do not climb into bed with black trashmen. Those who knew Chris's winning ways and Christa's sexual history were not so sure. The commonwealth's medical examiner was to acknowledge in the courtroom that there were no signs of rape.

And so police settled on Chris McCowen and his borderline IQ. Detectives questioned him for more than six and a half hours. The interview was never taped. Police claimed that McCowen "confessed." Their written statement placed him at the scene but didn't put the murder weapon in his hand. After a three-and-a-half-year investigation that many saw as sloppy in the extreme—it had taken twenty-four months to swab Christa's doorknob, for example—police announced that they'd solved the case. It was time for trial.

THE TRIAL

Day 1, Monday, October 16, 2006

Christa Worthington's murder had been in the news for a long, long time and the trial of the man accused of the heinous crime began in mid-autumn, when the sky was no longer hazy with summer heat and the wind had started to swing around to the north. The foliage on the bowerlike maples along Route 6A leading to the Barnstable County Superior Courthouse was a rich yellow, on the brink of turning cranberry, then brown before the leaves would be swept away by the salty winds and the Cape would turn the corner into winter. The day was as beautiful as it gets, the stuff of every New England postcard.

Although the first day of trial would be devoted to jury selection, the courthouse parking lot was chockablock with network TV trucks, their dish antennas straining skyward. Inside the large granite building, once regarded as the purest expression of the New England neoclassical revival, several dozen reporters were crammed into the carpeted, wood-paneled balcony of the main courtroom, among them three representatives of Court TV assigned to cover the proceedings live, start to finish. In the gallery below, curious citizens vied for spectator seats despite the unspeakable discomfort of the straight-backed, hardwood "Puritan" benches arranged in two aisles. Above, suspended from the ceiling, hung two-hundred-year-old chandeliers and the court's famous hand-hammered bronze codfish, six or more feet in length, homage to the industry that once supported Cape Cod.

The crowd must have been disappointed. The day's drama was to play out at sidebar, the small arena next to the judge's bench, out of earshot for spectators and media, alike.

As the masses continued to pour into the building, defense attorney Robert George was trying to get out. He moved for a change of venue, supporting his motion with a box of press clippings with headlines like "Black Trash Hauler Ruins Beautiful White Family" and "Black Murderer Apprehended in Fashion Writer Slaying." The experienced defense lawyer didn't expect Judge Gary Nickerson to relinquish the high-profile case, but he wanted the press coverage solidly on the record. The murder had gone unsolved for thirty-nine months; during that time, the public had been inundated with hundreds of stories in the Boston and Cape media whose underlying message was "white beauty ravaged by black beast." George argued that it would be impossible for McCowen to secure a fair trial in this atmosphere.

Short of stature, Robert George was himself a study in contradictions. A Lebanese-Syrian "tough guy" who'd taken on the McCowen case as a court-appointed lawyer, he'd grown up in Boston, where his Antiochian Orthodox priest father led the largest Middle Eastern parish in New England. Originally, Bob wanted to become a cop. He majored in criminal justice at Northeastern University, later graduating from Suffolk Law School, the alma mater of many Boston-area pols and power brokers. The three years he served in the Norfolk County District Attorney's Office introduced him to homicide cases and led him to decide he'd rather defend than prosecute: "I don't want to fall back on the old clichés like we're gunslingers—you know, *High Noon*, Gary Cooper, that whole thing—but trial lawyers are a different breed of cat. You've got to be able to cross-examine a witness and, as the words are coming out of the guy's mouth, figure out how to turn them to your advantage. Improvisation is key, in addition to connecting with jurors who may not be your cup of tea, nor you theirs."

No smooth-talking Ivy Leaguer, he was like a cross between John Belushi and Humphrey Bogart, and for the next twenty-five years at the bar, he represented alleged major mob figures such as Darin Bufalino, Jimmy Martorano, and Francis "Cadillac Frank" Salemme, onetime head of the Boston Mafia. A number of his colleagues in the close-knit world of Boston's criminal-defense bar were a touch surprised, some also envious, when he took on McCowen, the indigent black garbageman, although, truth be told, previously he had successfully defended another black man falsely accused of murder. Some saw it as a publicity stunt. Yet for all his macho bluster, he claimed he didn't take the case for publicity alone: "I took it because I thought McCowen, a black man, was unjustly accused, and, boy, was I right."

Sincere or not, George's explanation evoked another fact of his biography: while the attorney-to-be was still in law school, his priest father deserted the family for the West Coast, leaving George, his brother, and their mother behind. Robert George had not come up the easy way. A solo practitioner, he worked out of a small Newbury Street office, assisted by a savvy middle-aged woman who'd been answering his phone for ten years. He was "street." He'd worked since the age of fifteen, parking cars, tending bar, and whatnot; his cultivated "ders" and "dems" belied the fact he was an up-to-date, out-of-the-ordinary attorney with little tolerance for pretense.

Nickerson shortly denied the change-of-venue motion, as expected, but George was positioned to raise the race issue throughout the trial, laying the groundwork for appeal, if necessary. Moving forward, he introduced into evidence the large poster of Worthington's face that for the last two years of the investigation had been plastered all over Cape Cod and eastern Massachusetts, offering the $25,000 reward put up by the Worthington family. This particular copy was stamped with large red block letters, reading, "SOLVED." It had been posted on the district attorney's website since McCowen's arrest and widely reproduced in the press. Holding the poster aloft, George argued that it was the function of the trial to prove his client guilty or not, but the district attorney had here taken it upon himself to proclaim that the defendant, without benefit of any process whatsoever, was the killer. The poster had likely been seen by everyone in the jury pool.

Nickerson, a tall, white-maned stereotypical New Englander if ever there was one, allowed that if it proved impossible to select a "fair and impartial jury" locally, he would reconsider change of venue. George believed it was impossible. Blacks, he explained, totaled less than 2 percent of the Cape's population, more than 4 percent below the state average and almost 11 percent below the national one. Potential jurors' names are pulled from voter registration lists, then chosen randomly by town clerks; on the Cape, the poor and people of color are not socially integrated but, rather, seasonal, transient workers who are far less likely to register to vote.

But George knew there was a bigger problem. Legal scholars and jury specialists agree that it is nearly impossible to detect prejudice in a jury pool; most people hide their biases. In the majority of states, attorneys are given the right to question prospective jurors during the selection process, known as voir dire. In Massachusetts, it is the judges who inquire, not the lawyers, and the questions are thus a compromise between those requested by the defense and those posed by the prosecution. Some analysts call the judge-dominated voir dire backward; others say it's "tradition." Nickerson and the two lawyers had little disagreement over the standard queries: "Does the potential juror have any personal connection to those involved in the trial?" "To police or to lawyers?" "Does the candidate have a friend or relative who was attacked or raped or murdered?"

But the race questions caused arguments. Given that the Massachusetts rules of procedure also don't allow follow-up questions from the lawyers, it would be up to the judge to dig deeper, to ask a follow-up that might reveal buried bias. Nickerson wanted to ask if the allegation that a black man raped and killed a white woman would "make it impossible for the juror to make a fair judgment." For George, that didn't cut it; the query was too obvious. Nickerson came back with an alternative: "Would the juror more readily believe the testimony of a white person over that of a black, or vice versa?"

George shook his head. He preferred a blunt approach: "Do you believe that blacks are more likely to commit crimes than whites?"

Prosecutor Robert Welsh, a plain-looking man, objected. George cited studies proving that the direct question is the most effective. Nickerson finally agreed to adopt George's language.

Another argument kept the three at sidebar. George wanted jurors to be asked whether they believed someone might confess *falsely*. The heart of his defense was that the police interview with McCowen on the night of the arrest had been mishandled, that information stemming from it was inherently unreliable. Again, Welsh objected. George argued, and Nickerson finally adopted the wording, "Do you have any preconceived opinion as to whether a person can falsely confess to a crime?"

This question would draw the longest pauses over the next two days, with many prospective jurors saying they didn't understand it or that the idea of false confessions was something they'd never thought about.

It was almost noon when bailiffs finally led the juror pool into the courtroom. Up in the balcony, reporters leaned forward, looking for faces they might recognize and counting the number of blacks in the group. Of sixty-seven bodies present, only one seemed African-American, a middle-aged man in the front row, wearing a worn red-and-black-checked shirt and several days' worth of stubble.

Nickerson disputed the number. "Race is somewhat ambiguous in its concept," he offered, sonorously. "There are at least two other individuals in the jury who have facial characteristics that may be derived of African-American heritage. So there is [sic] three, perhaps." Since George had not backed up his objections to the racially lopsided pool with case law, jury selection began.

Now, with great formality, the court clerk announced the three indictments against Christopher McCowen: Murder. Aggravated rape. Aggravated or armed burglary.

Nickerson cautioned the press against approaching members of the jury pool, and then selection began.

"Is anyone related to, or have any other relationship with, any individuals involved? If so, raise your juror's card," the judge asked, reading a list of nearly one hundred witnesses. Seventeen of the sixty-seven raised their cards. For reporters who'd been covering the Worthington case from the beginning, the most incendiary name on the list was that of Jeremy Frazier.

That Nickerson recognized Frazier's name was doubtful, and he moved on. None of the candidates acknowledged a personal interest in the case. But sixteen admitted to forming an opinion, six to harboring prejudice toward the case, and thirty-one went on record as having a medical condition or children at home that would hinder their ability to serve.

When individual questioning began, the race factor emerged quickly, along with a panoply of human foibles too bizarre to fabricate, not to mention the incestuousness of ocean-bound Cape Cod where everyone seemed to know everyone.

The second potential juror said he believed blacks were more likely to commit crimes than whites, a conviction he derived from "my father's teaching of prejudice." The middle-aged man, sporting a greasy, graying ponytail, said he had tried to quash such racist ideas, but certain experiences "triggered" them. He was dismissed.

What seemed to surprise no one was the matter-of-factness with which this information was delivered, as if there were such people in the world (at least the world of Cape Cod) whose point of view here, like their choice of an auto, say, or their preference for bluefish over mackerel, had to be accepted. Was this the exception? Yes and no. The vast majority denied racial bias, but some said they couldn't set aside what they already knew about the case, or they admitted that they believed McCowen was guilty. One woman had lived on the same street as the defendant and felt intimidated by him; another worked with the Department of Social Services and had dealt with his children. One man acknowledged that his wife's rape at age fifteen might affect his judgment; another knew a member of the investigating team; another was a social worker at the Plymouth County Correctional Facility and in the Barnstable and Falmouth juvenile courts.

It was a Nathanael West procession of oddballs and ordinaries that demonstrated just how tiny a place the Cape really is. The pool came overwhelmingly from the mid-Cape, not the more liberal communities that begin beyond Orleans and extend to Provincetown. One woman with frizzy hair proved how difficult it might be to choose a juror from the Outer Cape; although she had once worked for the Truro police chief's wife, she was dismissed because she thought serving was too great a responsibility, and she felt unable to set aside all she'd heard about the murder: "I think if we could somehow wipe everything out that we've read about—you know, about O'Keefe, all of the things that have gone on. But, you know, who hasn't read about it? Maybe somebody that lives in the woods and doesn't buy a newspaper."

By the end of the day, George had used eight of his fourteen challenges. Three jurors had been dismissed by the court, one because
she was related to the victim of a sex crime, another who said he
tended to believe police and thought McCowen guilty, and another
who was the mother of a Boston cop and who, when asked whether
she had formed an opinion about the case, replied defensively, "if a
person is guilty, they should be punished."

So far, three women and three men filled six of the sixteen seats
designated for twelve jurors and four alternates. It was going to be a
long haul.

By now Nickerson was starting to come into focus. With his nasalized
basso profundo, the Judge carried a definite aura, supported by his
reputation as learned, even bookish, and able to recite an impressive
range of case law from the bench, mid-motion. He was intolerant
of unprepared lawyers and was known to censure those who hadn't
done their homework. But beneath his traditional magistrate's robe,
the judge wore chinos and boat shoes. Standing six-foot-two, he drove
a nondescript VW Passat that lurched sideways every time he climbed
into the driver's seat. Before assuming his seat on the bench, he'd
been a well-respected criminal-defense lawyer who set precedent with
a case that went to the SJC, the highest court in Massachusetts, limiting police officers' authority in search-and-seizure situations. He'd
served in the DA's office, so he knew that side of the law, too, and
acted briefly as a special prosecutor for the U.S. Attorney's Office in
Boston.

George had never tried a case in Nickerson's court before but
knew that his wealth of experience made him a special judge on the
Cape. But Nickerson was not originally assigned to preside over the
McCowen trial; the court calendar had dictated his colleague, Judge
Richard F. Connon. But on September 27, 2006, weeks before trial
began, Connon, in what was the first of many bizarre episodes in a
bizarre case, was forced to forfeit his plum assignment: he had managed to break his leg by running himself over with his own golf cart.

Nickerson now called those chosen and the remainder of the pool back into the courtroom. At his Phineas T. Bluster best, he instructed, "Those of you who live with somebody, you know what's going to happen. You're going to go home. And that special someone is going to look at you . . . very excited . . . and you're going to look them square in the eye and say, 'I can't talk about it.' And they're going to say, 'Aw, honey, you can tell me.' *Don't take the bait!*"

In the weeks to come, the admonition would emerge as one of his many set pieces. He would goad and joust with Robert George, largely but not exclusively in the privacy of sidebar conferences, two entirely different temperaments butting heads as Welsh, the starchy career prosecutor, looked on, tonelessly.

The battle was just beginning.

Day 2, Tuesday, October 17

Court TV, *48 Hours, Dateline,* NPR and numerous Boston stations, along with reporters from a dozen newspapers, including the *New York Times* and AP, were summoned to meet with Nickerson downstairs in the courthouse conference room before the start of the next day's proceedings, ostensibly to go over the judge's "media order." Nickerson had definite ideas about who would be where. The public had a right to know, and the court was cognizant of reporters' problems, but first and foremost, there had to be guidelines. Court TV, the judge announced, would run the only live feed. Its principal camera would be set up to the right of the main entry; its request to run a football-sized robotic camera up-front was granted, with the understanding that it would be positioned next to the judge's bench opposite the jury box, would have no audio, and would be shut off during sidebars and whenever McCowen conferred with his attorney. The microphones on the clerk's desk, the witness stand, and outside the jury box would be shut off at those times as well.

The same rule applied to still photographers. One at a time in the balcony, all photos pooled.

The defense had not yet filed its response to the judge's denial of the change-of-venue motion; back upstairs in the courtroom, George apologized for the delay, acknowledging that the jurors were ready to go at nine A.M. Nickerson took note.

So did the prosecution. The half-dozen off-duty local lawyers taking in the show weren't surprised, for while George might have had more murder trials under his belt, the forty-one-year-old Welsh was known to be a workhorse. He was thorough, not imaginative or daring, but he knew how to press an advantage. It was in his DNA. His father was the affable 2nd District Court Judge Robert Welsh Jr.; his grandfather, Robert Welsh Sr., sat on the Cape Cod bench for close to forty years, while even his great-grandfather had been a jurist. Assistant District Attorney Robert Welsh III was part of a legal dynasty, not to mention also a paratrooper which belied the flabbiness of his premature double chin.

Welsh had gotten the plum Worthington assignment by default, much like Nickerson. His boss, Michael O'Keefe, who had become the Cape and Islands district attorney eleven months after Christa's murder, often boasted that he'd seen the body of every Cape murder victim since 1974. According to one oft-repeated story, he kept his scanner on day and night when he was a cop in order to be among the first to arrive at murder scenes, earning the nickname "Hammer Head." Those who knew him realized that when he arrived at the grisly Worthington scene, he was already calculating the case's political potential. But somewhere along the way, as the Irish say, he lost the run of himself. His most embarrassing moment, still talked about, was when *Invisible Eden: A Story of Love and Murder on Cape Cod* hit bookstores in spring 2003. O'Keefe had shared confidential police information and crime-scene photos with author Maria Flook, who faithfully reported it all. She quoted the DA calling Christa Worthington "an equal opportunity employer" who would "[expletive] the husbands of her female friends, the butcher or the baker." He called her a "slob," adding, "The more we look at her the uglier she gets."

According to both Boston dailies, the DA met the long-haired author in bars at odd hours for interviews. In one off-the-wall episode, he showed her a police photograph of Worthington's bikini underpants spread across the victim's bed, commenting, "These are all Victoria's Secret." But the zinger was when he greeted Flook at his home "wearing only a white towel snugged around his hips" after showering, a scene rendered in near-cinematic detail in Flook's "kiss-and-tell" book. Both the author, a married mother of two, and the DA denied any impropriety. Nobody bought it. Declared the *Boston Herald*, "It's a toss-up whose reputation suffers more than O'Keefe's: the author's or the dead woman." The *Globe* viewed the revelations in Flook's "sex-omatic" tell-all as toxic to the DA's "professional reputation." *Time* chimed in, quoting a Boston University professor of legal ethics, "For a prosecutor to make comments like that about the victim is absolutely reprehensible."

Even before the book hit the *New York Times* best-seller list, the Worthington family lodged a complaint with the State Attorney General's Office, demanding that the priapic DA be yanked off the case. Amyra Chase, guardian of the victim's daughter, seconded, flailing O'Keefe for releasing intimate details of the investigation.

Visibly shaken, O'Keefe announced that he had telephoned the Worthingtons to express regret for his language—"that was certainly not meant for publication." In a subsequent interview with *People*, he repudiated Flook's book as "a blend of fact with fiction," then claimed he'd been misquoted.

One weepy neighbor came to the DA's defense, explaining that his divorce in the late '90s had left him "devastated." This only aggravated the situation. Courthouse regulars, reporters, and local pols all knew that his bar-hopping started long before his wife walked out, and they weren't reluctant to talk about it. One assistant DA insisted that while O'Keefe was second-in-command to DA Phil Rollins, he'd chased after the assistant's wife, who worked in a nearby courthouse. Another spoke of his openly enjoying a less than innocent dance with a stranger at a mid-Cape bar while his then-wife looked on. "He was boozed," said the witness. "He couldn't help himself." In another account, O'Keefe was spotted at the Hyannis Mall, not far from the Barnstable courthouse complex, ogling a teenage sales clerk. The newsman who reported the story said it was "about the millionth one of those I'd heard about."

Jokes about the DA circulated like ragweed pollen during a bad hay-fever season. With the Flook flare-up, the big question had been, would he keep his job? Sharing crime-scene photos and details of an ongoing murder invest with a flirtatious female author? O'Keefe had always been known as extra-secretive with investigative information; now he was perceived as a wacko, the DA who couldn't keep his zipper shut.

There was more, though.

An ex-Barnstable County Sheriff's Department detective reported another episode, more alarming than the rest. Called to a Brewster murder scene on a Saturday night, the detective found one of the DA's CPAC-ers in the victim's master bedroom, searching the bureau; when he balked at this obvious breach of crime-scene protocol, the trooper told him to mind his own business. Weeks later, the two lawmen met by chance, and the trooper laughingly volunteered that he'd found the object of his search, a videotape that had nothing to do with the murder. Rather, it showed Michael O'Keefe and one of the Cape's most respected defense lawyers frolicking with several bimbos in a hot tub. With them was the murder victim, a high-profile drug dealer, who had been an O'Keefe snitch. The detective asked about the fate of the video and got the answer he expected: "Ha! Long gone, I assure you."

Said Seth Rolbein, editor-publisher of the *Cape Cod Voice* and one of few locals unafraid to speak about O'Keefe on record, "He's a skirt chaser. He just can't help it . . . the little head talks to the big head, and that's his deal."

And the big head didn't seem to control the busy mouth, either. Several months before the start of the trial, he and I had been talking in his office for nearly an hour, the only time the DA granted me an audience. When I stood to examine the notorious "Wanted" poster, its bright red, three-inch-diagonal banner reading "Solved!", suddenly, the man rose. He'd been scoping me out and now stepped between the door and his visitor to declare, "The worst thing to happen to American justice was the O.J. case! This verdict is going to turn that around!"

"The O.J. case"? What did O.J. Simpson and Christopher Mc-Cowen have in common except black skin?

O'Keefe's ego and ambition, it seemed, blinded him to reality, but he was also handicapped by his appearance. With his small, lipless mouth and receding chin, he resembled nothing so much as a nib-bling chipmunk. He wore expensive "Hollywood" business suits, glen plaids and faint pinstripes, the trousers with a knife-edge crease to them, set off with heavy gold cuff links and rep ties. He peered over the tops of rimless granny glasses, and his drugstore hair dye was so dark and monotone it looked like shoe black. One courthouse em-ployee said the DA's "toupee" gave him "a Sid Vicious look."

He seemed sad, and a bit desperate, when he'd enter the court-room to instruct an assistant or monitor the proceedings, his strut rem-iniscent of Charlie Chaplin's goose step. But the inappropriateness of his behavior with Flook notwithstanding, it was he who was controlling the case. Thanks to his mentor, Rollins, he knew how. He'd needed a replacement with a low profile. In Rob Welsh, he had one.

A man who shunned the limelight, Welsh was married with two sons, was a graduate of Georgetown University and Suffolk Law School, and had successfully prosecuted six first-degree murder cases. He did have areas of amazing ignorance, however—or maybe Welsh just took certain things for granted. During the first round of jury selec-tion, when George cited African-American population figures for the Cape, he'd responded, "I don't have any independent knowledge of these statistics nationally or statewide or countrywide," as if he nei-ther saw nor cared what bearing the 1.7 percent statistic might have on selecting a jury. Not good news for a black man about to be tried for the murder of a white woman. Nor the stuff any media-savvy pros-ecutor would want the *New York Times*, the *Boston Globe*, or Court TV to sink their teeth into.

Still, Welsh was Goliath; George was David. Preparing for the Cape's most high-profile trial in forty years, the DA's office tapped all of its many resources; George hadn't even managed to fax his appeal. He told Nickerson that his associate was on vacation at California's Legoland, his secretary wasn't due from Boston until later in the af-ternoon, and he needed fifteen minutes.

"Why do you need fifteen minutes to push a button?" Nickerson asked, irked by the defense lawyer's tardiness.

"Well, no, give me five minutes. But the fact is I am also asking you to stay the proceedings . . . until we hear if the SJC is going to have a hearing on this matter."

Nickerson had gone through the three dailies available on-Cape— the *Cape Cod Times*, the *Boston Globe*, and the *Boston Herald*—and he'd seen nothing in print that wouldn't come out during the trial, he explained. He was about to go on but was interrupted by George fumbling with paperwork.

He stopped and told the clerk to pass the defense lawyer a staple remover. "The last we need is for you to sever the top of your finger, Mr. George," he said, adding, "not that I'd suggest you'd get a stay in whatever fashion you could, but I'd rather you use the puller-out thing there."

George's smirk said *asshole*, nothing less. Rustling the papers, he later admitted, was intentional.

For all his bluster, Nickerson persevered, and at 9:20 A.M., the jurors finally filed in, a new pool having been added to those left over from the day before. George called for another sidebar and challenged the panel, seeing just one black person in the group. Nickerson saw three. He denied the motion.

By the two P.M. lunch break, George had the SJC decision: appeal denied. The judge who ruled, Roderick Ireland, was the first black jurist ever to sit on the SJC. In 2010 he would become Chief Justice.

Race remained at center stage. One juror, asked whether he would be likely to believe a white person over an African-American, said he wasn't biased but that "a lot of crime is committed by blacks" as a result of "poverty and social economic situations," then qualified, "I don't think that they're predisposed to be any more violent than anyone else."

Nickerson ruled the juror indifferent. The "they're" struck him as meaningless.

George protested.

Nickerson paused, reviewed the transcript, then reversed himself.

Another prospective juror was dismissed after saying that the blacks-and-crime question depended on "what part of the country you're talking about," then added that he'd be likely to believe police officers or doctors over lay people. Another candidate said he could be biased about race because blacks were largely poor. Nickerson excused him, too.

Not all of those who were vague on the race question were dismissed. George was forced to use another precious challenge on one who said, "Statistically, it's true that blacks commit more crimes than whites," then added, disingenuously, "Whether I believe that or not, I haven't formed an opinion."

Hardship and media coverage were factors in most of Nickerson's dismissals. But finding a prospect who did not know one of the witnesses was particularly difficult. Those excused for cause included one man who'd worked with the Wellfleet police for eleven years, another who was the shellfish warden in Brewster and knew Tony Jackett. One had done legal work for Christa. Another lived 400 yards from the murder site and boasted of golfing with one of the Worthingtons.

By day's end, seven jurors had been added to the six previously selected; two were black, a man and a woman, both middle-aged. The defense attorney had used all of his peremptory challenges. Welsh had used only four.

Day 3, Wednesday, October 18

By 11:15 Wednesday morning, jury selection was complete. Juror questionnaires identified the panel.

Vernon J. "Norm" Audet, age sixty-three, was a college graduate and co-manager with his wife of a self-storage unit in Mashpee at the very foot of the Cape. He had two daughters, one a lawyer, the other a Florida deputy sheriff. Audet's wife, Kathy, had also been in the juror pool; Nickerson asked them to decide which one would serve, so the other could run the business.

Roshena Bohanna was a black nursing-home administrator originally from Monroe, Louisiana, in her early thirties. She and her husband brought their three children to Cape Cod looking for a life "less complicated." Her vision of an idyllic existence by the seashore was soon to be shattered.

Carol Cahill, forty-four, with a master's in education, was a special-needs teacher with three children ages twelve, fourteen, and sixteen. Her husband was a pharmaceutical sales rep.

Marlo George, thirty-seven, was a Barnstable High School teacher with two children ages seven and four. Her husband wholesaled organic foods.

Eric Gomes, thirty-five-ish, managed a bar in Mashpee, where he was born. A high school graduate, Gomes was a dark-skinned Cape Verdean, one of the two blacks on the panel.

Rachel Huffman, twenty-two, was an administrative assistant at Falmouth Town Hall; unmarried, she had a two-year-old daughter with her black live-in boyfriend, as police and other jurors would soon learn.

Charles E. Ivers, fifty-nine, was a gray-haired social worker employed by the Department of Youth Services in Plymouth, with three grown children and a wife who worked in health care.

Jack Kanis, fifty-four, was previously an "institutional security officer" in Paterson, New Jersey, and now worked for the Department of Youth Services. He had one grown child and a wife who was a special-ed teacher. Kanis dressed all in black and wore medically mandated dark glasses; already the press had dubbed him "Mick Jagger" and "the rock star."

Alice Tuttle, sixty-eight, was a real estate agent from Mashpee. She and her husband, a sand and gravel company employee, had no children.

Robert Lyon, forty, was an antiques and jewelry dealer with three children ages eleven, thirteen, and fifteen. His wife was a personal trainer at a local gym. He wore a sports jacket and trademark bowtie.

Matthew Maltby, forty-seven, had an associate's degree in culinary arts and a job with Sysco Foods. He was the father of two teenagers, his wife was a hairdresser, and his mother was a probation officer.

Taryn O'Connell, thirty-three, held a BS in criminal justice from Roger Williams University in Rhode Island, although her paralegal work for a local attorney mainly involved real estate closings. She had two children with her electrician husband, who worked off-Cape, frequently in Boston.

Mary O'Prey, sixty-three, a former summer resident of Mashpee, had recently moved to the Cape full-time after working as a grant writer for a Bronx nonprofit. Her husband was a teacher, and they had no children. O'Prey's bone-white hair and matronly outfits reminded a number of courtroom observers of the late Oscar-winning actress Maureen Stapleton.

Eventually appointed jury foreman, Daniel Patenaude, fifty, chiseled and six-foot-two, was a guidance counselor at Mashpee High School. He held two master's degrees and had a grown son and a wife described as a "self-employed retreat worker."

Sally Ann Powers, sixty-seven, was retired but previously held the baffling title of "career center operator" at Braintree High School. She and her high school teacher husband had four children.

Laura Stacy, forty-seven, was an insurance claims analyst. Her husband worked at Massachusetts Maritime Academy, and they had two teenagers.

With two blacks on the sixteen-member panel, George figured it was as good as he could get on Cape Cod. Was he happy? No, not so much as resigned to playing out the hand he'd been given. As with artists and poets, with defense attorneys hope springs eternal.

Before opening statements, Welsh informed Nickerson that he'd received a four-page letter McCowen had written to his friend, Dave Nichols, a white man living in South Wellfleet, saying he had consensual sex with Worthington on Thursday, January 3, the day before the murder.

The letter had followed a circuitous route, Welsh explained, coming to him through attorneys handling a civil lawsuit the Worthingtons had initiated against McCowen's employer, Cape Cod Disposal. It echoed a statement McCowen made to defense psychologist Eric Brown, but since the statement was made—and the letter written—*after* McCowen's arrest, the claim had to be questioned. Discovery rules obligated Welsh to disclose the letter, but he asked Nickerson to exclude it as "hearsay." It should be admitted into evidence only if McCowen took the stand to face cross-examination.

Nickerson agreed. Evidence offered to exculpate the accused was not admissible unless a corroborating circumstance or first-person testimony established its trustworthiness. I.e., McCowen had to testify.

At 11:24, court officers led the jurors back into the courtroom. Welsh delivered his opening statement in a style true to his reputation, flat and plodding. But it didn't take a gifted orator to do what he had to, the tableau of Christa and Ava more than did the job: the mother, beaten and stabbed, with the blood-covered two-year-old trying to nurse from her half-naked, rigor-mortised body.

Welsh explained that the commonwealth's case would revolve around McCowen's DNA, found on Worthington's breast and in her vagina, and on the defendant's ability to describe the crime the night he was arrested, supplying details only the killer would know. McCowen had accused another man, but Welsh promised to call a witness who would provide an alibi for that individual. Shaking his head as though he, too, was nearly overcome by the crime's brutality, Welsh cautioned the jury against viewing the evidence through the prism of race.

"This case has to do with a horrendous crime," he said, "with an individual matching the DNA. The color of his skin has nothing to do with it."

He finished in twenty-nine minutes.

Studies show that almost 70 percent of murder trial jurors make up their minds immediately after opening statements; the night before, Robert George had spent hours preparing. As he rose, he hoped to identify those who were with him and those who were not and learn whom, in particular, to address.

He began by assuring the jurors that he would not fill the morning with idle chatter: McCowen was on trial solely because of his race and economic status. The evidence said so.

The arrest was based on "a false assumption that a Vassar-educated, 46-year-old, world-traveling, wealthy heiress could not possibly have had consensual sex with a black, uneducated, troubled garbageman."

For thirty-nine months, police said they were searching for Christa's last lover, but when they arrested McCowen, that lover became a sexual predator. Police hadn't looked for a rapist before, he repeated, "because you will hear from the doctors there was no evidence of rape." McCowen had never been a suspect, and during his two interviews with police he "did the only smart thing he has done in this whole case, he told them he didn't know her. And he was right— because when he did admit he knew her, he got indicted for murder."

Look closely, he urged. The commonwealth's case is nonexistent: no fingerprints, no forensic evidence of any kind, no witness to tie the defendant to the crime.

He closed after twenty minutes, and it was impossible to tell which of the two had made the greater impression, Welsh or George who'd paced constantly and, unlike the prosecutor, spoken without notes. But jurors appeared riveted when the prosecution's first witness now took the stand. Tim Arnold, age forty-eight, wore a preppie blue blazer, rep tie, and gray flannel trousers, his graying hair paradoxi- cally in a ponytail. His walk skewed the image further. He moved un- steadily, advancing sideways in a series of crablike movements. Jurors knew he'd been Christa's lover and was found her body; they didn't know about his brain surgery.

Welsh asked him to describe his actions when he entered Chris- ta's house the afternoon of January 6, 2002. He began haltingly. "I came into the house and called her name. I saw Ava's head pop up." Arnold stopped, squinted, closing his left eye to correct double vi- sion, then resumed his account. After feeling Worthington's cheek, he roamed the house with Ava in his arms, searching for the phone. After depositing the child with his father outside in the van, he'd run up the path between Christa's house and his father's to call police.

He had lived with Worthington and her daughter for about ten months, moving out a year before the murder, he explained. Not long after the breakup, he had corrective surgery for a neurological condi- tion. The surgery had not been entirely successful, leaving him with his vision problem and a lack of sensation on one side of his body.

He gripped the rail of the witness box for support, and a tendril of hair from his ponytail flopped over his temple. He seemed sad, beaten, as he went on about living with Christa.

They argued frequently when they cohabited from May 2000 to February or March 2001. But they'd remained friends after the breakup, even though Christa had thrown him out, because of his relationship with Ava, whom he "loved like a daughter." Since then, he'd mostly lived at his parents' house. Money problems contributed to their breakup, but so did his sex drive. More and more toward the end, Christa rebuffed his overtures.

But she had helped him through his medical crises. Their relationship, he reiterated, remained "Okay" and "Cordial."

Knowing that Arnold was vulnerable because of his difficulty accepting his ouster from Christa's house—on her voice mail, he'd ranted, then desperately begged that she see him again—Welsh had the witness explain that he'd seen Worthington at Thanksgiving and Christmas.

Arnold testified that Christa usually kept her cell phone in her Escort wagon's glove compartment and that she used reading glasses, both significant pieces of evidence: the glasses and the car keys were found on the ground outside, the phone on the kitchen table. He then added that Christa "would sometimes meet people she wasn't really familiar with outside of her house." If she saw someone coming up the drive, he explained, "she would go outside, not let them in." To hammer home the importance of this last statement, Welsh produced a photo of the rear of Christa's cottage. Arnold indicated that his ex-housemate would stop visiting strangers at the kitchen steps.

Arnold's testimony about discovering the body was to be his primary contribution to the prosecution's case.

He had last seen Christa on January 2, when they had tea at her house. By the time he left, it was dark outside, and he'd borrowed a flashlight. He talked to her on the phone two days later, a Friday, when they made tentative plans for Sunday dinner. On Sunday, he called to confirm but got no answer.

Asked if he had phoned Christa again from his parents' house, Arnold was unsure. "I think I may have called to see . . . I think I probably did, yes."

With the Patriots game almost over, his father suggested they return the flashlight on their way back to Wellfleet. As they approached Christa's drive, they saw two *New York Times* papers in familiar blue plastic wrappers and stopped to pick them up; one paper was dated Saturday, January 5, the other Sunday. At the top of what Arnold called the "long, looping driveway that comes straight in for a while and then bends up around the house," he was surprised to see Christa's car. "When I didn't get her on the telephone I thought that maybe she was in—away visiting her father."

He had admitted to police that Christa had told him never to drop by unannounced. Nonetheless, he decided it would be "kind of rude" to leave the flashlight on the back porch, so he knocked, then noticed the door was ajar. "And I looked in, and I saw her lying there with Ava. And my first thought was that that was a really strange place to nurse."

She was on the floor, half in the kitchen, half in the hallway that led to the bathroom and the front of the house, he explained. When he called her name, Ava's head popped up, but "her mother did not answer. . . . I went over to see what was the matter . . . and as I got closer, I could see that there was . . . blood around her head."

Christa was wearing a bathrobe. It was open, the lower part of her body exposed. Her "right leg was up. Her knee was up in the air. The foot was flat on the ground," and her legs were "somewhat spread apart."

When he touched her cheek, "she was cold." He realized she was "probably dead."

He said he didn't know she'd been stabbed. He believed she might have fallen down the stairs, which were just around the corner from her body.

He paused. Even from the far rear of the courtroom, observers saw him sway. As he reached out for the rail once more, Welsh displayed a photo that gave gruesome credence to his description: Christa, nude from the waist down, a black top pushed up to expose most of one breast, her legs splayed, her face a horribly swollen mask of pain, teeth stained red from blood she'd aspirated. An image worthy of Hieronymus Bosch, the photo was meant to remind jurors of their obligation to exact revenge.

George called for a sidebar, objecting that "the inflammatory effect of the photograph far outweighed its probative value." Welsh countered, saying he planned to offer ten such exhibits but would settle for three. Nickerson said he would rule on each photo's probative value as the trial progressed.

Arnold resumed. Carrying Ava in his arms, he looked around the house for the phone, then went outside to his father's van. His father went inside but couldn't find the telephone, either. Tim went in to look again, then ran, "as best I could," up the path to his family's home to call 911.

Welsh played the police tape. Arnold's voice blanketed the hushed courtroom. "It's Christa Worthington," he said, his breathing labored. "I think she fell down or something, I think she's dead."

Official EMT reports indicate that Jan Worthington, Christa's cousin, arrived "a short time later," just before the first wave of ambulances came up the hill at 4:34, six minutes after Arnold's call. Jan was screaming, yelling, Arnold said.

"She wanted to know what happened." He told her he didn't know.

Police and EMTs were "kind of all coming at the same time," he said. "So I went back outside." Paramedics were to recall Arnold sitting on the ground, zombielike, staring into space.

Arnold now testified that Jan's father, John Worthington, took Ava from his father's vehicle. But he was wrong. George Malloy, a local CPA who'd served as an EMT on the Truro rescue squad for nearly fifteen years, took the child and carried her down to John and Cindy Worthington's home several hundred feet west on Depot Road. A father of two, Malloy would later claim that Ava "couldn't catch her breath, she just kept sobbing."

The description of the murder scene complete, Welsh returned to the witness's knowledge of the house, using a photo of the kitchen that included the butcher block and knives. Again, George objected. The knives in the photo weren't linked to the crime, since "no forensic testing was done on them." The prosecution didn't have a murder weapon; it shouldn't pretend otherwise.

Welsh said the butcher-block photo tied in with the upcoming testimony of Detectives Mason and Burke, who would allege that the murder weapon had likely been taken from it. The photo showed the butcher block near the hallway, where the body was found. Nickerson told him to proceed.

"Did you kill Christa Worthington, sir?" Welsh asked Arnold directly.

Arnold still gripped the witness box, now with both hands. "No," he answered in a soft, distant voice. In the past, investigators had repeatedly called him the killer.

At 3:02, following the afternoon recess, court resumed.

Before George began cross-examination, Welsh challenged a CD the defense planned to introduce into evidence. It contained phone messages Arnold had left on Christa's voice mail, but it had been edited. The tape had recorded over itself, so the calls were not sequential. Welsh wanted the jurors so informed.

George knew that Arnold's affection for Ava and his physical difficulties would make him a sympathetic figure. He'd need to walk a fine line: too tough, he'd sway jurors' sympathy toward the witness; too lenient, he'd lose an advantage that might free his client.

He took Arnold back to the moment when police spoke to him outside the house, after the arrival of the paramedics, when he told them he believed Christa had fallen. Familiar as he was with the house, he must have known that this was impossible; the stairs were around the corner from the hallway where the body was found. Arnold shook his head, denying that he'd said she might have fallen. Jan Worthington said it, not him.

Long-smitten Arnold acknowledged that the next day, Monday, police asked for his computer and journals, both mirroring his thoughts about Christa and their rocky relationship. The computer contained a letter he'd written to Christa but never sent. "I think it had to do with the father of her child," he testified, referring to Jackett. He admitted that he loved Ava, that she was like his own child in "some ways," that the letter was "angry," and that he "was upset" when he wrote it.

He also acknowledged he'd told police that he and Christa had stopped being intimate in January 2001, twelve months before her death. He recalled trying to kiss her while they were watching television once, when "she turned away." In happier times, when they were intimate, their lovemaking usually took place "outside of the bedroom. Either in the room where I was sleeping, or in the living room where the sofas were."

George asked about his employment history, another source of friction between Christa and the impoverished writer. His last part-time job was with Truro's Council on Aging. Before moving to Truro, he had been a teacher at Manhattan Country School, and he held a master's degree in early childhood and elementary education. In 1988, *Winter Mittens* was published, his book about a little girl who rubs her hands together and causes a horrendous blizzard; her town loses power, and she's stranded in the dark. George wanted to use the book to suggest that Arnold was not as calm as he appeared.

"It is a nightmare, or is it a kid's story?"

A "kid's story," Arnold said.

George moved to enter the book into evidence. Welsh objected.

"Is there any relevance to the thing?" Nickerson demanded.

George said it was relevant to Arnold's "long history of deterioration before he moved into Christa Worthington's house. "And then, when she put him out, the inference could be that he didn't take it well."

But what did *Winter Mittens* have to do with any of that? Nickerson repeated.

"Well, it's a pretty horrible story, Your Honor."

"If you can link it in some fashion, I'll certainly allow it in," Nickerson said.

George agreed; they should mark the book for identification and argue about its admissibility later. He returned to Arnold's history. The witness explained that he had worked for his wife of twelve years, doing color plates for textiles. After their divorce in 1996, he moved into his father's house and started therapy at South Bay Medical Center in Yarmouth. His counseling was ongoing when he moved in with Christa, and it continued through the year preceding her death. It had nothing to do with their breakup, he said.

Arnold admitted he'd told the police that he and Christa used to fight all the time, that she could be cruel and abusive. He also admitted that his third interview with detectives had become confrontational. Before that, even, he'd hired an attorney.

George switched to the computer and journals he'd turned over to police, holding up a photocopied journal page, which he asked Arnold to read aloud.

Arnold began slowly. "*Why if I do not believe in spirits do I feel you come near and hold onto me?*" He struggled, again covering his left eye. "*Do I wish you had held me more often . . . and shown me more love . . .*" George prompted, "Really?" Arnold, reluctant, answered, "Perhaps."

"*I know you were meant no harm,*" George continued, pushing the witness. Tired-looking, Arnold faltered again.

"OK, then I'll read it for you," George said. After each passage, Arnold nodded and admitted that the words were his.

"*You died and your last thoughts were of horror at your death*"?

"*I so much wanted to tell you how much your life meant*"?

"*I feel you all around me*"?

"*Ava, you cleaned your mother's bleeding chest. You didn't know what end to which she came. Maybe you thought, as I did, she had fallen down*"?

"*I saw the single wound that killed her; that made her drown in her blood*"?

George continued, "You also wrote, '*What will I do? How will I do well for Ava and my own children? What is right? What is good? What is merely foolish?*' Did you write that as well?"

"Uh-huh, yes," answered Arnold, deflated.

Trooper Mawn had used two pages from Arnold's notebooks when questioning him. George produced them and again asked the witness to read.

He complied: "*Why was I taking care of someone else's child? Because I loved her with every part of myself, of course. Christa, I have not felt you here, not the way I did. You come to me with a gift, a part of yourself that I might use if I can only hang onto it. I am confused about what it means that we will always be . . . always love each other. That I was so . . . lucky to know you. . . . Yes, both of these things. But maybe you were lucky to know ME.*"

George paused, then asked Arnold if he'd told the troopers how he felt about Christa Worthington using him as a babysitter.

"I mentioned that, yes," Arnold admitted, adding that "at times" he felt Christa was using him.

During the interview, Trooper Mawn asked most of the questions while Mason watched. Arnold hired attorney Russel Redgate because he believed police exhibited more than a passing interest in him.

Asked if detectives believed he killed Christa, he replied dolefully, "As it turns out, I think that's what they thought. Yes."

George had set down the diary pages and picked up a long rubber-tipped pointer, the kind lecturers use in front of large audiences, which he'd begun waving around erratically. Nickerson interrupted. "Mr. George, put that stick down, please."

George thanked him, not too convincingly.

"And I'm sure the jurors in the front row thank us also," the judge boomed, eliciting laughter from jurors and spectators.

George nodded once more and returned to the floor plan of 50 Depot Road, asking Arnold to point out his movements inside the house. Arnold said he'd gone as far as the bedroom door. He'd stepped over the body once to get there and then again, coming back. He'd touched Christa's cheek only once. When he entered the house the second time, he basically retraced his steps, circling the living room. The house was messy, he said, but the house was always messy. Pressed, he admitted that he didn't see the rugs amiss or any lamps turned over and had not noticed the broken door lock until one of the police officers pointed it out.

He remembered the study light being on but was not sure about other lights inside the house.

Visibly exhausted, he repeated himself, unprompted: he'd stepped over Christa's body in a frantic search for the phone, concerned only with finding a way to call for help.

It was four o'clock. Gary Nickerson said, "The court will adjourn and reconvene at nine A.M. tomorrow. And jurors . . ."

George turned back to the defense table, not wanting to hear the rest. The end of Arnold's testimony had been a rehash, dramatically flat. But it left the door open for the next day's reentry.

Day 4, Thursday, October 19

Robert George spent the night alone at his family's beach cottage in East Dennis, not ten miles from the courthouse on Route 6A. He got little sleep. He'd moved his operation down from Boston to spare himself the daily commute, and most days, after court, he headed straight to the cottage to catch up with the business of his busy criminal practice. After a nap, he'd return to McCowen's case, preparing for the next day. Now, with Arnold's testimony, he changed his routine. He skipped the nap, and went straight to work.

Arnold, with both means and motive, was logically the killer. Having followed that track, George decided to use the witness to damage the police and elicit testimony about how detectives treated him, in contrast to how they treated McCowen. The idea was that this evidence might have real impact; for years, Cape Codders had called many of their cops cowboys. And worse.

Back in the courtroom, George wanted to set up ELMO, a projector that allows juries to see exhibits without "publishing"—physically passing the objects or paperwork from juror to juror. Nickerson was skeptical. The machine was large; it interfered with the public's view of the witness box and, possibly, Nickerson himself. The judge suggested putting it on a lower platform. He ordered it turned off when not in use; its light, he claimed, was distracting.

Nickerson was cranky for another reason. He had scheduled a conference to discuss Court TV's coverage, and George had arrived late, again. Without referring to the defense attorney by name, he announced to the court that in "future instances of tardiness," he would bring in the jurors who would "see who is holding them up as they're in the back patiently waiting to be put to work."

This wasn't the end of the judge's performance. He went back to grousing about ELMO. "If you haven't got this piece of equipment already set up . . . and ready to go, then let's wheel it out of here." He might have added "dammit." George met his stare with a pseudo-apologetic head bob. It was becoming a game, this ritual wrestling between the two. In a studentlike, deferential voice, George asked if he could proceed. Nickerson had no choice; he nodded.

George resumed his cross, showing Arnold eight photos of the Worthington house interior sans the dead body. He asked if the witness had entered the study while searching for the phone. Arnold said no. George asked him to look at the photo of the study more closely.

"Does this appear to be a telephone answering machine on the desk?" he asked, pointing.

The day before, Arnold had testified that the phone in the study was the only landline in the house; Christa got the cordless wall phone after he moved out. Asked why he hadn't looked for the phone in the study, he said he assumed it was not working or maybe "wasn't there anymore." None of it made sense. When George pressed, the witness admitted that he had left messages on that very machine.

Like a cartographer, George now walked him through the rest of the crime scene, using the floor plan still on the easel. He asked Arnold to diagram his progress with large red-dot stickers, an exercise he would repeat with every witness who was at the house on January 6. The adhesive one-inch dots were visible from the rear of the gallery. In time, the sheer number would all but completely obfuscate the floor plan, dramatically illustrating how thoroughly the crime scene had been corrupted, literally "stepped on."

Outside, it was "snow-ish, sort of," Arnold continued. The front door was ajar; he didn't know whether he pushed the door panel or used the handle to enter. He insisted he did not turn on any lights but did turn off the VCR and the TV.

Already, the floor plan had three dots.

When George raised the subject of past boyfriends, Welsh objected on relevancy grounds. Nickerson gave defense counsel leeway since it was cross-examination.

Arnold answered the question by saying he knew of one of Christa's past beaus, Gloria Vanderbilt's son. Christa took the breakup so badly she moved to Truro. Why, George asked, were police interested in Christa's past lovers? Arnold replied, "Because it would say something about her character, I guess. I think that's what they were going for."

"Were her romantic affairs only involved with men of status?"

"Obviously not."

He almost sneered. The allusion was, plainly, to Tony Jackett, portrayed in the media as a gigolo who'd lost both his fishing boat and his house, whose wife worked multiple jobs to help support the family. Jackett was not in the courtroom, but he didn't have to be. Most Provincetown-Truro locals knew what the tabloidy producers of *48 Hours* and *Dateline* did not: that Jackett had run out on Christa and Ava, refusing to have anything to do with, or for, his child for the first two years of her life.

With that question, Arnold seemed to gain some equilibrium, as if his comment fulfilled something inside him. George alluded to the notion that Christa might have had an encounter with her gar-

bageman, and then he attacked: When Arnold was the primary suspect, hadn't police treated him harshly? During his second interview,
hadn't Detective Mason asked if Christa felt he was "a pest," insisting
that he call ahead whenever he wanted to visit? The shift in the cops'
attitude made Arnold hire a lawyer, no?

Welsh rose to ask for a sidebar, where he requested a limiting
instruction, telling the jury that "no negative inference" was to be
drawn from Arnold's availing himself of counsel.

Since George's goal was to expose the detectives' harsh interrogation techniques, he could live with this. "Whatever you want to do,
Judge," he said. He knew Arnold's testimony had been prepped and
primed by the prosecution for weeks now, although the staties had
once been disposed to arrest him for murder.

Nickerson raised an issue of his own. "I know there was a moment
of pique, Mr. George, over the ELMO. But let me be clear. You had a
lot of notice and a lot of time to set that equipment up. Even though
it wasn't set up the way I suggested, I still don't mind it being there.
But when you turn the thing on and the color is so far off compared
to what the actual photograph is, it's not representative of—"

"I want the record to be clear that I agree with you," George interrupted, "that that is a crappy ELMO. But I'll try to fix it during lunch."

He nodded furiously, doing his penitent shuffle even though he'd
actually used the word, "crappy." Nickerson wanted to go on about
the ELMO but couldn't, and George knew it.

Quickly, the defense lawyer resumed cross, establishing that attorney Russell Redgate had sent a letter to the DA's office making
it clear that the lawyer was to be present if Arnold was interviewed
again. The letter stressed that all interrogations were to be taped and
that investigators were to stay off the Arnold property unless they had
a valid warrant.

Arnold testified that Redgate was not present when police subsequently came to him in January 2003. But before that fourth interview, he had contacted police on his own, Tim explained, to tell them
about fingerprints he might have left on Christa's bedroom window.
He told Sergeant Burke that he'd gone for a run and that "it was my
custom to stop at her house and say hi in the morning after the run.

But on this occasion, she was in bed or . . . I think she had gone in for a nap with Ava."

The incident couldn't have occurred later than May 2001, he conceded, because he had brain surgery on May 29 of that year.

"So . . . I came to her house. I knocked on the door. She didn't answer . . . and then I got a little concerned, you know, because she wasn't responding. So I went around to look in the window to see, to make sure she was OK and sleeping with her child."

George pressed for the less benign version of the story. Arnold admitted that Christa had looked up from her nap and seen him. He couldn't remember whether she was dressed or not but recalled that she "was annoyed."

The former boyfriend grew visibly sullen, reluctant. George's subsequent questions were met with "I don't remember," "Probably," or "Not really." Asked if he had last been intimate with Christa in January 2001, as he'd told police, he hedged. "That was my estimation."

Arnold's fourth and last interview was preceded by an official police press conference during which, he said, "I became aware that they thought I was the killer." He was on antidepressants and in counseling at the time, partly because of anger-management issues tied to Christa. On three separate occasions, he'd admitted that the relationship was troubled, that they "argued all the time," and now he reluctantly acknowledged that he'd often have to leave the house to cool off following their arguments.

"Now, why would you do that?" George pressed. "Why would you have to cool off before you would go back? Were you afraid you would do some harm?"

"No, I was not."

"You ended up in a hospital, didn't you? A mental-health facility in Dennis, Massachusetts?"

"Yes."

This last line of questioning was a little lame, although it served to establish that Arnold's Dennis therapist considered him a suicide risk and had him check into Cape Cod Hospital's Department of Mental Health Unit. It was there that police questioned him on January 18 while he was medicated and in bed.

Arnold explained that they'd asked whether he wanted to call Redgate and that he might have said no. Pressed, he acknowledged that he was in no condition to make that decision. Police didn't video-tape him, despite Redgate's demand that all interviews be recorded. Nor did they offer him another opportunity to make a phone call.

Mason and Burke pumped him for "about three hours," he said. And although some questions focused on his mental state, the detectives didn't inquire about his medications. Mason did most of the questioning.

"He asked you immediately after he saw the condition you were in about your romantic relationship with Christa Worthington and how it ended up, didn't he?" George asked.

"I think he—yeah."

Mason said he'd heard that the two argued about the frequency of sex, then went on to say investigators had learned that Arnold wanted more sex, Christa less, and that Christa could be cruel during these arguments, sometimes driving Tim from the house.

George handed him Mason's January 18, 2003, report about the incident when he allegedly tried to break down the kitchen door.

Arnold looked at it, then recalled Mason's questioning. He recounted the incident in detail: "I remember I was doing dishes, and we had an argument in the kitchen. And I . . . I left. . . . She locked the door. I think I still had a key and came back and opened the door and continued doing the dishes. And she didn't realize I had come back into the house, and she was startled when I did."

"And did she then put you out again?" George asked.

"I think she did."

"Did you tell the police that she had bolted the door and that you attempted to push it in but you didn't break it?"

"He remembered that incident; I didn't."

"Did Trooper Mason tell you that you were pushing in the door? Did he tell you that?"

"Yes."

Presented with a photo of the door, broken after the murder, he admitted it was the same dead bolt. He'd reminded police that he was physically disabled at the time of the murder, but they said his run through the woods to call 911 was evidence of his ability to commit the crime.

Arnold's knowledge of Christa being stabbed was also incriminating, Mason said. Tim explained that he'd gotten this information secondhand, from an EMT, or from Truro police Sergeant David Costa. It didn't matter. Mason accused him of killing Christa. Burke made the same accusation, he testified, the two "going back and forth."

"And when you told them, sir, that you did not kill Christa Worthington, what was said to you?"

"That oh, yes, I had."

"Well, you just told them you hadn't. They said that you had. Did they arrest you?"

"No."

"And when they said that you had, what did you say?"

"I repeatedly said I hadn't. . . . They kept repeating that I had. And then they finally ended the interview."

The hospital incident provided plenty of drama, but George had saved his biggest jab for last. Just the week before, while coaching him for his upcoming testimony, Welsh had told Arnold that his DNA matched semen found on a blanket at the murder scene, a defense lawyer's gift from on high. George now casually dropped it into the mix, earning a small collective gasp from the courtroom.

"So, in your case, sir," he asked, "at least your semen being found at the scene wasn't enough to cause your arrest, was it?"

Welsh jumped to his feet, objecting on relevancy grounds. Nickerson sustained. It didn't matter. George turned his back on the witness, striding away like a matador who had just finished off his bull with a triumphant *veronica*. He'd gotten it in. The jury had heard.

At morning recess, Nickerson called another sidebar, concerned about the overcrowded courtroom but also unable to let go of George's tardiness. "Gentle persuasion has not worked with you, Mr. George," he chastised, eliciting another exaggerated mea culpa from the lawyer.

Nickerson announced that the courtroom had reached its saturation point. Every seat was filled but people were still streaming in, jurors were becoming distracted. He didn't want spectators standing in the back. The solution was to post a court officer at the door to control admissions.

But the judge failed to address a corollary issue: the Worthington family and friends numbered ten, at most, leaving empty one of two full rows reserved for them. They'd been assigned a chaperone from the DA's office to escort them in and out as if they were royalty, just as they'd been given access to the judge's elevator. In addition, their seats were cheek-on-jowl with the jury box, too strategically located for comfort; Toppy, Cindy, any of them, could literally reach out and shake hands with jurors, or maybe even pat one of them on the shoulder. Meanwhile, McCowen's father and stepmother, who'd driven up from Virginia, had been thrown in with the general audience, with no guaranteed seating at all. The arrangement left elements of the press wondering what was, and wasn't, special about Cape Cod.

When the jury returned from break, Welsh tried to restore their faith in police. Trooper Mawn was confrontational at the June 13, 2002, interview, not Mason, Arnold agreed. At the hospital on January 18, 2003, he told Mason and Burke that he was willing to speak, distinguishing them from abrasive, threatening Mawn.

Welsh also got Arnold to clarify the door-pushing episode, stressing that he had supplied "the facts and details" to Mason, not vice versa.

"Did you ever have a chance to review Mason's report relative to that?" Welsh asked.

"Yes."

"And it's fair to say that Mason wrote up that statement as some inadvertent pushing on the door, correct?"

"That's right."

No sooner had Welsh posed the question than he knew it was a mistake. He wrapped up by asking if Arnold had felt coerced. "Was your will overborne so that you confessed to a crime you didn't commit?"

"No."

As Welsh headed back to the commonwealth's table, George leaped to his feet. "Is it your testimony that you were allowed to review the police report in this case?" he demanded, indignant.

"I did see them, yes."

"So, you were allowed to check whether the police wrote you an accurate interview?"

"Well, I was asked to say whether I felt this reflected what happened or not."

"Do you know if they offered anyone else the right to proofread and correct their interviews?"

Welsh objected. Nickerson sustained.

Arnold said he'd been allowed to review the reports of all of his interviews, including the confrontational Mawn interrogation of January 6.

"Well, what won you that right over anyone else?" George demanded, pointing out that the defendant hadn't been granted review.

Welsh objected. Nickerson sustained.

George moved on, unruffled. He asked about Mason's delving into Arnold's sex life with Christa, how he knew about the stab wound, how he was physically able to kill her.

Mason's demeanor remained low-key, even as he asked accusatory questions, Arnold replied.

"That low-key demeanor" doesn't make the interrogation "any less dangerous, does it, sir?"

Again, Welsh objected. Nickerson sustained.

The content of Mason's questions was anything but low-key, Arnold agreed.

George asked if he believed Mason really thought he was the killer. Welsh objected. Nickerson sustained once more, forcing George to rephrase: "Did you believe at that time that if you falsely admitted to committing the murder of Christa Worthington, that Trooper Mason would believe you were telling the truth?"

Welsh objected. Nickerson sustained.

"No further questions," George said, turning away.

Robert Arnold, Tim's father, was next. The retired eighty-one-year-old veterinarian accepted a seat in the witness box, then carefully put his cane between his knees. It was a good touch. He and his wife usually wintered in Columbus, Ohio, he said, but in 2002, they'd stayed in Truro, primarily to be close to Tim, still recovering from surgery.

On January 6, 2002, as emergency personnel worked inside the cottage, Robert Arnold sat in his minivan, holding Ava. Her head rested on his neck, but he knew she wasn't asleep. "I smelled the smell of blood," he said.

Some of his testimony—where he parked, whether the ground was moist from snow, whether Tim reentered the house—conflicted slightly with his son's. But it was obvious that he had been well coached. His answers, delivered almost methodically to Welsh's questions, dovetailed with Tim's. He had picked Tim up at halftime so he could use the Arnolds' dryer; at Christa's, they found newspapers in the driveway; Tim had been in the house only a few minutes before coming out with Ava, mouthing, "Christa is D-E-A-D."

It was his idea, not Tim's, to return the flashlight. Jan Worthington was first on the scene, followed by other medics. "In fact, it looked like half of Truro arrived," he said. Inside the house, he'd had to steady himself by keeping his hands against the wall. "I'm a veterinarian, and I've seen death before," he added, "but not in humans."

On cross-examination, George was more concerned with where Robert Arnold had parked. As with Tim, he asked Robert to place a red dot on the crime-scene diagram.

When he waited in the car with Ava, the elder Arnold said, he did not pay much attention to Jan or to the comings and goings of rescue personnel. He did recall that they could not maneuver around Jan's pickup or the other vehicles. "There was a line of them down the driveway."

The next day, he confronted Tim. "I think that's the first question anyone would ask of their son or daughter. 'Let's get it from the start. Did you kill Christa Worthington?' I told him, 'I have to ask you,' and he said, 'No.'"

George thought the testimony odd. "It wasn't the normal reaction of a parent," he later said, although he wasn't about to pursue it.

Next up was Jan, who identified herself as "Janet Warden Worthington." The formality was surprising. Locally, Christa's older cousin was known as the town's chatty police dispatcher, a selectman, a member of the rescue squad, and a social gadfly who had played a role in

one of Truro's more amusing incidents. Local police and fire departments received radio calls one afternoon from Sergeant David Costa,
requesting assistance. Costa and Jan, who were busy in the backseat
of his cruiser, had locked themselves in. The rumor began: Jan and
the married Costa were prisoners of love.

Jan's carefully selected dark outfit couldn't hide her fifty-plus chub-
biness; her neck scarf didn't help much, either. Her best feature was
her golden blond hair, but there was too much of it, as if she feared,
perhaps, that a proper coif would leave her armorless. She described
herself as a "writer," as well as a part-time dispatcher, volunteer EMT,
and firefighter. She grew up in Needham, while Christa lived in Hingham, both Boston suburbs. Their families spent holidays together. For
most of their adult lives, she and Christa had maintained a strong relationship. They'd lived in the same Manhattan building for a year, dated
jointly, and later, when Christa worked in Europe, she'd once visited
Jan in California. The relationship was eventually to change, however.

The Worthingtons owned multiple homes in Truro, including
four on Depot Road, Jan explained. Christa lived at number 50, Jan's
parents at number 53, her sister Pam at number 49, and an aunt and
uncle had an address in the high 60s. Another uncle lived nearby on
North Pamet Road, not far from the residence Jan was renting at the
time of Christa's death. Her other sister Patricia lived on Pond Road,
a mile or so from the family compound on Depot, where Jan would
later build a home behind her parents' house.

On January 6, when she received the emergency call with a Depot
Road address, she knew immediately that it was a family member.

"I thought perhaps it could be my mother because she has a pacemaker." She thought maybe the 911 dispatcher had gotten the house
number wrong.

Welsh asked her to detail her first actions.

"I jumped out of my truck and ran over to Tim and said, 'Is there
someone in the van that needs help?' . . . He said, 'No, it's Christa. I
think she's dead.'"

Once inside the house, Worthington said, "I saw my cousin lying
on the floor between the kitchen and the hallway. She was naked
from the waist down, and her legs had been pulled apart."

"Objection to 'pulled apart,' Your Honor," George boomed.

"Her legs were apart," Jan repeated, after getting instructions from Nickerson not to speculate about "the mechanical means" by which they arrived at that position. "Her right leg was bent, and her—the heel of her right foot was jammed in the lower part of the bookcase in the hallway. Her left leg was open to the left. She's lying on her back."

Most of the lights were on, including the Christmas tree lights. It was dusk, she added.

Welsh once again displayed Exhibit 4, the photo of bloody Christa, dead in the hallway. After removing glasses from her purse, Jan looked, then looked away, saying that was how she remembered the body, except that one of Christa's feet was on top of some books in the bookcase. Her voice trembled.

Jan said she "took enough steps over to her to see if she were breathing." She was not. "I put my hand on her left carotid artery. She had no pulse. I knew she was dead."

Asked what she did next, the witness answered, "I was frightened because I didn't know what had happened; but I thought that she had been murdered."

"What did you do, is the question," the judge admonished her, now for the second time. "Not what you thought."

She "went to look for a phone." She knew the rescue squad was en route, she explained, but she wanted the police to arrive first. "Because I thought it was a crime scene, and there was nothing to do to bring her back. She was dead."

Unlike the Arnolds, Jan did not step over the body to look for a phone. Instead, she went outside, where she told a just-arrived rescue worker to use the radio.

She then started to cry and asked Tim how this could have happened. He said "something about maybe she could have fallen down the stairs."

Patrolman Meredith Allen was the first officer to arrive, four or five minutes later. In the interim, four or five rescue workers had already driven up, entered the house, and called in a Condition 13, confirming that Christa was dead. Allen ordered everyone to leave the house.

Jan said she then walked down the driveway, where she encountered her father, John, coming up, and she told him Christa was dead, "that something terrible had happened." A few minutes later, EMT George Malloy was seen coming down the drive, cradling Ava in his arms, and Jan took them to her parents' place across the road. Once there, the three went into the living room. "I sat with George while he comforted Ava; and after a few minutes, we undressed her to make sure she had no wounds on her."

Ava's clothes were streaked with blood, Jan said, mostly on her pajama bottoms from sitting on the floor beside her mother's body. She also had a full diaper and diaper rash. "We got a new diaper and clean clothes for her."

During the next two hours, others gathered at the senior Worthingtons' home, including Christa's father, Toppy, Tony and Susan Jackett, neighbor Francine Watson Randolph, and, of course, Truro and state police. One by one, detectives questioned individuals in the dining room.

Welsh moved on to the rape, eliciting repeat testimony that Christa's legs were "apart and at an odd angle" several times more before ceding the floor to the defense.

George began seven minutes before one P.M., when court was scheduled to break. Quickly, he revisited Jan's writing background, knowing that it was far less than she intimated; Jan just might make a fool of herself.

"What kind of a writer are you?" he asked gruffly. "I mean, what do you write *about*?"

"I was a television writer for about fifteen years," she said.

"Are you a screenwriter?"

"Yes."

She went on to list her credits: "Heartbeat," a Danielle Steel adaptation for NBC; "Perfect Strangers," another Danielle Steel adaptation; "Romance on the Orient Express" for NBC. "I had *Three Wives* episodes. I have written a lot of movies . . ."

"Any murder mysteries?" George asked, seemingly lamely.

"I wrote a *Movie of the Week* based on my cousin's murder."

For the moment, he let this pass. "Any others? Wasn't there one, 'Police Centerfold'?"

"*Police Woman Centerfold,*" she corrected him tartly, "about a woman who had been a police officer in Ohio who posed for *Playboy.*"

Jan had pinned her hopes on screenwriting, George had found out. She'd organized a gala premiere for the 1983 *Police Woman Centerfold* film, even sent gilded invitations, only to suffer the humiliation of the C-grade film going nowhere. Eventually, Jan was forced to leave LA, return home to Truro, file for bankruptcy, and take her present job manning the local police switchboard.

After the lunch break, George resumed. More recently, Worthington received $60,000 from Grossbart/Barnett, a career-reviving movie deal about her cousin's murder, the "*Movie of the Week*" she'd mentioned earlier. But her movie had not yet been made.

Asked when she had sold the rights, she replied, "As soon as I could."

George, faking shock, urged her to explain.

Worthington testified that she wrote the screenplay about Christa's murder and sold it early on, "so no one else would sell the story."

"So, you sold it early on so no one else would *get any money* from it?"

"No, so no one else would exploit it."

"And you received sixty thousand dollars for exploiting it yourself?"

"That's not how I see it."

He asked if she'd put that money in the reward fund the family had established in December 2002 in an effort to apprehend Christa's killer.

Welsh objected. Nickerson sustained.

George persisted. "Did you contribute any money whatsoever from that sixty thousand dollars to the reward fund?"

Again, Welsh objected; again, Nickerson sustained.

"Did you contribute any of the money to a trust fund for Ava when you took the sixty thousand dollars?"

Welsh objected again. This time, Nickerson called for a sidebar. "How is the disposition of the money relevant?" he asked George. "I mean, I can understand how the taking of money is relevant."

Jan had opened the door to the exploitation issue, George answered him. If Jan were not exploiting Christa's death, then, of course, the money wouldn't be used for anything but the benefit of the family. The defense was entitled to explore how she profited from her "Who Killed Christa?" project. Given the witness's high-toned stance, they wanted to explore her motive: altruism or greed?

The assistant DA saw it differently. As he tried to make his case, Jan, alone on the stand, looked plaintively at her family sitting twenty feet away, as if hoping someone would rescue her.

"I didn't object when Mr. George asked, 'Did you make any money off of it?'" Welsh argued. "But in terms of where the money went after that, I think, is beyond the bounds of relevance."

The judge wasn't so sure. "She volunteered the 'exploitation.' It wasn't something that, shall we say, Mr. George crafted a . . . trap for her to walk into."

He held up his hand, took a minute to think, then shook his head. He would give the defense a modicum of wiggle room. "I'll let you have one or two questions on it, Mr. George, then move on."

George continued to push, none too gently now. When Jan repeated that she'd sold the rights because she wanted "control" over the project, he pounced, moving in on her hard.

"So no one else would get the money?" he snapped.

"So no one else would exploit it," she said, trying to remain firm.

George asked what she'd done with the $60,000. Welsh objected. "No, I'm going to allow it," Nickerson interrupted him.

Jan admitted that she had not put aside any of the money toward the reward or toward Ava's future, an admission that "sucked the air out of the courtroom," according to Rose Connors of the *Cape Cod Voice*. Instead, she'd used the money to support herself. She would establish a scholarship at Truro Central School in Christa's name, she said, if the movie was ever produced and turned a profit.

Her testimony struck her Truro neighbors, many watching on Court TV, as less than truthful. A new VW and a sporty Audi convertible sat in Jan's driveway. The past two summers, Jan had often been seen driving the white Audi, top down, her untamed golden hair streaming in the wind.

George wasn't through. "You have cut business deals with other media outlets as a result of telling your story, haven't you?"

"No."

She was lying, and he knew it. The lawyer took a long, theatrical pause.

"Well, can you tell the jury about your deal with HBO? HBO meaning Home Box Office, please?"

"Well, you know about it," she said sullenly, realizing that she was trapped.

George poked. She admitted she'd "made a deal to do a second documentary."

"And how much money were you paid by HBO?"

Silence cloaked the courtroom before she answered. "I have been paid twenty thousand dollars," she said, acknowledging that she'd signed the contract two and a half years after Christa's death.

"Did you contribute any of *that* twenty thousand dollars to a trust fund for Ava? Or did you put it into the reward fund that the Worthington family put together?"

"It's not finished," she answered, referring to the film.

"The question is, ma'am, did you put any of the twenty thousand dollars—"

"No. No," she wailed.

Still, George wasn't through. Here was a principal commonwealth witness, exposed as an out-and-out opportunist, a fabricator, and he was going to maul her.

He resumed, shifting to another tack. While working on the second project, Jan's radio interview with Provincetown station WOMR was filmed by HBO; in addition to "writing" the documentary, she was *in* it. The interview was reproduced on the front page of the *Cape Cod Times*, and the reporter who interviewed her on air also wrote the print story.

She nodded, bracing for what might be next.

George stopped, glanced at the clock, then looked over at Nickerson. It was 3:56 P.M. The judge nodded and declared court recessed for the day. Leaving the witness box, Jan shot the attorney a look of pure hatred. George stifled a smile as he turned and ambled back to the defense table where McCowen continued to stare into space, as if he hadn't comprehended what had just taken place.

A half-dozen reporters, including Eric Williams, the *Cape Cod Times* man who'd conducted the WOMR interview, all but charged down the balcony stairs as the courtroom emptied. Rocking back and forth on the balls of his feet, George fielded their questions, never once using the word *lie* or *liar*. Instead, he said, it had been "a very good day for the defense."

Later, alone with the last reporter, Mike Iacuessa of the *Provincetown Banner*, the courtroom empty except for the court stenographer packing up his equipment out of earshot, the stout lawyer burst out laughing. "How'd you like my beginning? Not too bad for a seven-minute cross, eh?"

Day 5, Friday, October 20

On Fridays, lawyers, as a strategic matter, will try to implant testimony in jurors' brains as seeds to germinate over the weekend. Here, George again asked Jan when she started negotiating with Grossbart/Barnett. She admitted it was "probably" only a month after the murder. Her response ws significant. Besides suggesting that this woman had had no compunctions about capitalizing on her cousin's death, Jan's pitch to potential script buyers, George knew, didn't square with what she told police the night Christa's body was found and then again three days later. Nor with how she'd described her actions at the crime scene during her direct testimony on Thursday.

Rhetorically, he needed a runway, though, so he asked the obvious: her memory was "probably" fresher immediately after the incident than when she wrote the screenplay, correct? Jan admitted to sanitizing some of the story but only to "protect" her cousin. Without being asked, she added that she had accurately described her own actions at the crime scene.

Armed with police reports, George walked her through the disparaging comments she had made about her slain cousin: Christa was "neurotic" and "sometimes had spent a lot of time on one or two issues and not been able to let go of them." Christa was "troubled" about raising a child alone in Truro and considered moving back to Manhattan. She had "a difficult time with men" and had stalked Stan

Stokowski, Gloria Vanderbilt's son, before her move back to Truro. "She was looking for him in places so she could talk to him. She hadn't found the right guy in her life, and she was looking for that."

George moved on to Tim Arnold, another of her troubled relationships. Welsh objected. At sidebar, George argued "state of mind," that the defense centered on McCowen having consensual sex with the victim. Welsh disagreed, citing, of all things, the rape shield law.

"I don't mean to interrupt," George said. "I just want to say one thing—"

"No, I'm speaking now," Welsh insisted.

George went on anyway. "I'm impeaching her because . . . here's a woman who says that she was close to her cousin. Yet when she's talking to the police, she's impugning her."

Welsh repeated that Christa's "numerous relationships" should not be admitted. "Isn't that why we have a rape shield law?"

He was arguing from left field here, and Nickerson, the scholar, called him on it by expressing doubt that the rape shield law even applied. First, though, he questioned George. "I assume you're saying the sex was consensual between these two people?"

George nodded.

"Thereby you've got to distinguish why isn't this fellow the murderer? Because we've got the DNA. We've got the body . . ."

George nodded again. Nickerson continued, turning to the prosecutor.

"I don't see where the rape shield law is of any efficacy in this situation, quite frankly." He paused, looking down at the papers on his desk. "The issues are so riddled in this case with questions of consent and who else had a motive or opportunity to commit this crime, and who else despite the absence of DNA as to particular other individuals, the 'who else' basically boils down to her other sexual partners."

George nodded once more.

Welsh, sensing where this was going, said that his objection was "two-pronged, not just rape shield but also general relevance."

The judge thought for a moment, asked about the relevance of Gloria Vanderbilt's son. George said that when Jan spoke with

Trooper Mason, she volunteered Stokowski, "because she was saying that the reason Christa had come to Truro in the first place [was] because this relationship had shattered her. . . . I was only getting into it to establish that Worthington . . . was in a state of mind where, being troubled, she would have allowed a stranger into her home."

Nickerson nodded, motioning for him to go on with cross. George quickly asked Jan about the comments she'd made to police about Tony Jackett. When she hesitated, he barked, "It's an easy question."

Welsh jumped back in, objecting. Nickerson sustained. "Your function, sir, is to ask questions at this time and wait for the answer." He would admonish George to back off with other witnesses, too.

When Jan finally answered, she said her cousin had been seeking money from Jackett. She wanted Tony to put Ava on his Provincetown-employee medical insurance, which angered both Jacketts, husband and wife, insofar as they felt Christa "had tricked him because he, Tony, was led to believe Christa couldn't have a baby."

George moved on, forcing the witness to acknowledge that she and Christa were not as close as Jan originally portrayed. Although Christa attended Jan's wedding in 1998 and had come to dinner several times afterward, Jan had not called her cousin in six months. Although off-season Truro is a tiny, even hermetic town, Jan had been unable to tell police about Christa's wardrobe, the names of Ava's babysitters, or even whether her cousin owned a cell phone.

George now asked if she recalled telling Mason what she did when she arrived at the crime scene. He held in his upraised hand the detectives' reports, portions highlighted in bright yellow.

Jan admitted she told Mason that she'd run to the threshold of the doorway, looked inside, and saw Christa lying on her back, wearing a bathrobe, possibly green.

Hadn't she told Mason she "freaked out" at this sight and returned to Arnold, who had remained outside by the van?

"No, no," Worthington stammered.

"That's *not* what you told Trooper Mason?"

"Well, that's not what happened. But—"

"No, that's not the question," he snapped. *"Is that what you told Trooper Mason on January 6, 2002?"*

"I may have."

Asked if what she told Mason was factually incorrect, she said, "I don't know, I don't know," then corrected herself. "Part of it's correct, and part of it isn't."

"So, there is a mistake there in Trooper Mason's report?"

"I don't know," she repeated weakly, adding in response to the next question that Christa had been wearing a green bathrobe. Tim Arnold had said the same but recanted when shown photos to the contrary. Yet the green bathrobe had gone missing.

"Did you then tell Trooper Mason that you checked the inside of the van for Ava, and then you began to run toward your parents' house for a phone?" he continued.

"Not that I remember, no."

George handed her the detective's report, "Interview of Jan Worthington on 1/6/02," and instructed her to read the fifth paragraph. When she looked up, signaling that she was done, the courtroom took a collective breath, waiting.

He repeated the question: Did Worthington tell Mason that she ran toward her parents' house for a phone after checking on Ava?

"I . . . he must have heard that, but yeah," she said.

"Is it correct?"

"No."

"So, is it your testimony here today that Trooper Mason's report . . . is incorrect?"

Welsh objected. Nickerson sustained.

Asked whether the police report had failed to refresh her recollection, Jan balked. "My recollection . . . of what I did does not need refreshing."

George tried again. "Is what you just read in Trooper Mason's report about running toward your parents' house for a phone after checking on Ava in the van correct?"

"No," she replied.

The red-dot routine began again. He asked Jan to show where she parked, then to trace her movements. Four or five other people entered the house to check on the body, she said. Nine or ten arrived in the three or four cars parked along the driveway. Someone moved her car at some point, she added. George affixed the dots, playing with the witness by making minute adjustments to the right or left, per her directions.

He asked if she remembered what she told Mason during their second interview, on January 9, 2002, before she "signed any film and book deals."

"I . . . I don't understand your question," she stammered, suddenly realizing where the questions were headed.

As of January 9, 2002, she hadn't signed any film deals about the murder, she answered, nor had she composed any drafts or outlines. When she spoke to the trooper that day, she told the truth about her actions on January 6, 2002.

George came back. "Do you remember specifically discussing with the trooper going up the steps of Christa's house," he asked, "what you did when you got to the top of the steps? Do you recall telling him again on the ninth what you did?"

"I remember walking over to her body."

"Did you tell Trooper Mason that?"

"I don't remember."

George produced another Mason report, detailing the trooper's interview of Jan on January 9, 2002, and asked her to read the third paragraph to herself. After a moment, he prodded, "Do you remember telling him that you 'weren't prepared for the sight of a family member and lost all professional composure'? Did you say that?"

"I don't remember. But I may have."

"And did you then say that you began to scream and ran from the doorway down the driveway toward your parents' house on Depot Road? Do you remember saying that?"

"No."

For Jan, this was turning into a nightmare. When George asked if the account in Mason's second report was thus incorrect, she responded, "It's not what I remember."

George asked her to reread the third paragraph.

She complied, then said, "Yeah?" in her surliest tone yet. George was delighted.

"Did you tell Trooper Christopher Mason that you *never* entered the house?" he repeated. "That you 'did not enter into the house more than one or two steps, if at all'?"

"That's what this says. It's not what I remember."

"Is that what you told Trooper Mason?"

"I guess I must have, if it's there."

The noose was tightening. The Worthingtons, sitting with Francine Watson Randolph, the neighbor who'd helped with Ava the night Christa's body was found, strained forward in their seats. Only Toppy, Christa's father, stared at the floor.

George was not about to let go. He directed the witness to her interview with local reporter Eric Williams on his WOMR radio show on May 13, 2004, *after* she'd arranged for her HBO film and for the interview to be taped as part of it.

"Now, the story you told Eric Williams is not the same as what Trooper Mason recollects you telling him, right?"

"It may not be . . ."

"Well, you told Trooper Mason you never entered the house. That's what the report from January 9 says, as well as the report of January 6, right?"

Welsh objected. At sidebar, Nickerson shook his head, indicating his growing fatigue with Jan the chameleon. No question, she had told WOMR listeners a different tale: "I was in action," she'd said. "I felt for a pulse and knew she was not alive. And then I wanted a phone to call the police, because I wanted the police to get there before the rescue squad, because I knew it was a police matter at that point."

"You know, it's going to be a long trial," Nickerson intoned. "And I'm not trying to try this case for anybody. But the simple truth is yesterday, didn't she say she touched the carotid artery?"

George smiled. "Yes, and either way, it helps me. She's tampering with the crime scene, or she's lying about what she did."

Nickerson nodded in agreement. George returned to the witness, who had watched this exchange from the stand and was visibly angry, almost shaking. She *had looked* for a phone inside the kitchen, she insisted, her voice shrill now. Had she, or had she not, gone inside the house? he asked again.

She "may not have," she said, then quickly changed tack, saying she'd never told Mason she was inside the house.

"You told Trooper Mason on January 9, 2002, that from your vantage point at the doorway, you saw your cousin and that you entered the house perhaps one or two steps but no more? Didn't you say that to him?"

"I must have."

"Well, you were lying, then, ma'am, when you spoke to him? Or you were lying when you were speaking to HBO and the radio. Which is it?"

Welsh objected. Nickerson shook his head. "Overruled."

George pressed on. "When were you telling the truth?"

"I . . . I was telling the truth on the WOMR radio."

"Just to be clear, you were telling the truth to WOMR radio, but you were not telling the truth to the chief investigator in this case about your own actions at the scene?"

"The night of the interview, I was trying to protect . . . I was afraid, and I was . . ."

Again, George asked if her memory was fresher right after the murder. Jan stalled, saying she didn't understand the question.

"Is that too tough for you?" he snarled, crowding the stand in an attempt to invade Worthington's space. Nickerson waved him back.

Seated with the family in its reserved first row, Christa's aunt Diana's head had begun to jerk from side to side in regular spasms that might be confused with an attack of Parkinson's. Cousin Susan Worthington pulled Diana close. They were all ashen-faced, including Jan's mother, Cindy, as if witnessing the erosion of the lofty Worthington name after nearly a century's dominion.

George repeated the question, and Jan answered by saying that she told two other rescue workers, Lisa Silva and Jeff Francis, that she had checked Christa's pulse. When George reminded her that Francis was present, there in the courthouse, and could be called to the stand, she quickly backtracked. "I don't insist on anything about that night."

She said, "I might have said 'a few steps in the kitchen,' but I *was* in the kitchen." She didn't say how she managed to check the pulse from the doorway. Eventually, she said Mason never asked whether she went inside, again contradicting the detective's report.

Still, George wasn't satisfied. "Is it your testimony here today that Trooper Christopher Mason did not ask you less than four hours after this incident occurred what your actions were at the crime scene in the death of your own cousin?"

"I don't know."

George nodded magnanimously and returned to the money she made from her two film projects. When had Jan last held a full-time job?

"Two years . . . four years ago," she said, when she was "a dispatcher and a records clerk at the Provincetown Police Department."

"Madam, isn't it a fact that you have arranged with HBO here today to film your testimony through the Court TV cameras that are up in that balcony as part of your film project?" George rolled back on the balls of his feet, pointing up at the camera on the left side of the balcony, its bundle-of-snakes cables feeding this charade out to millions of astonished viewers. He waited impatiently for her answer.

"The HBO project is covering the entire trial. Yes, sir."

"They're filming your testimony right here today, aren't they?"

"They're filming everyone's testimony."

"Is it your belief that they will use your testimony during the making of your film?"

"Probably."

"Isn't it a fact, ma'am, right now as we stand here, you are profiting from the death of your cousin?"

Welsh objected. Nickerson overruled.

"Am I profiting?" Jan stalled. "Yes . . . it's part of the documentary, what happens here today."

Slowly, George did a little pirouette, contemptuously turning away from the witness to walk back to his table. His message was, *You're a liar, lady. Stop wasting our time.*

It might have been worse yet had he gone into the particulars of Jan's bankruptcies and her history of nonpayment of several years' worth of state and federal income taxes. Even worse, he could have mentioned how she and her late husband, a local Portuguese fisherman like Jackett, had overseen her mother-in-law's transfer into an old folks' home after the woman sold her West End Provincetown home and Jan and husband Billy subsequently erected a $1 million–plus residence along Depot Road, where Jan, a stone's throw from her parents' residence, resides today. The documentary was canceled shortly after Jan's testimony, when it became abundantly clear that HBO had an insurmountable credibility problem.

Welsh tried to rehabilitate his witness, but it was futile. Tim Arnold had told police that Jan went "partway in and then just started screaming, standing in the doorway." Trooper Massari reported that she told him "she kind of 'freaked out' [and] subsequently . . . did not perform any rescue measures on the body." And after the January 9 interview, Mason reported: "Worthington was not prepared for the sight of [a] family member . . . began to scream and ran from the doorway down the driveway towards her parents' house on Depot Rd."

All but two of the jurors had been riveted, transfixed by the drama, and Jan was visibly in pieces as she stepped down from the stand. Nickerson called the morning break, and outside in the lobby, she erupted, flailing at Welsh. "How could you let him do that to me?" she screamed. Normally a reserved man, the prosecutor snapped back, "Bet that sixty thousand looks real good to you now, eh?" Disgusted, he turned and walked away.

It was just before 11:15 when paramedic Jeff Francis of Provincetown's Lower Cape Ambulance and the Truro fire department took the stand. He had arrived at 50 Depot Road in his personal vehicle, he said, and Christa had a "fairly large pool of blood around her upper body." Her naked lower half lay inside the kitchen, her upper body in the hallway.

"Her head was tilted to the right, almost [so] that her right cheek was against the floor," he testified. The body was cool. The blood pattern on her abdomen looked like small handprints.

The dark hallway made it hard to read vital signs. He called in his Code 99: patient with no pulse but possibly savable, then when fellow paramedic Tim Rowell moved her leg away from the bookcase, "her knee . . . stayed bent [so] it was obvious rigor mortis had set in." Worthington's status changed to a Condition 13. George would use that call to undermine the basis of the commonwealth's posited time of death.

One of the men handed a brown blanket from the living-room couch to EMT Lisa Silva, who covered the body.

"Reflecting back," he would not have done so, Francis told Welsh.

For cross, George once more set up the crime-scene diagram and asked Francis to retrace his steps with the red dots. He also asked the witness to affix dots showing Rowell, EMTs Jeff Sturtevant and Lisa Silva, fire captain Leo Childs, and police officers Allen and Costa.

"It's going to get to be crowded," the witness joked lamely. The last dot represented Costa, the ninth person inside the cramped kitchen.

Francis didn't remember seeing every responder listed on the incident report, but George used the opportunity to read additional names into the record: deputy fire chief Brian Davis and EMTs Mike Benjamin, Zach Goldstein, and Malloy, whom Jan previously mentioned.

George asked Francis about rigor mortis and cyanosis, body discoloration caused by a lack of oxygenated blood flow. Francis said he didn't see signs of cyanosis or decomposition because of the bad lighting. But according to police interviews, EMT Sturtevant had turned on a light near the kitchen table, raising another inconsistency.

Next up was veteran Trooper Joe Condon, who was tall and physically imposing. Condon had been a state trooper since 1982, working forensics from 1990 until a year and a half before the trial. On the night of January 6, 2002, he videotaped and sketched the scene, collected evidence, and searched for fingerprints.

Upon entering the Worthington house, Condon noticed a lot of stuff inside, "more items than the house could hold." He'd seen Christa's chest wound immediately; he didn't need to pull her clothes back to document it. He also noticed that her fingers had begun to decompose. "Some of the skin had started to recede," he said, meaning the victim had been dead "for some time." He confirmed that a yellow rescue blanket had been added to the brown blanket over the body.

Condon's videotape was the high point of his testimony, the reason Welsh called him as a witness. George objected to the tape being shown in its entirety; the court had been careful to limit the number of still photos, and the tape included close-ups of the victim's vagina. Welsh acknowledged that he wanted to use seventeen additional stills of Christa's genitals, adding that it was unlikely he would get to take jurors to 50 Depot Road. The new owners, a lawyer couple from Boston who bought the property from the estate for nearly $1 million despite its gruesome pedigree, weren't keen on a viewing.

Nickerson, who'd already seen the tape when he considered the suppression motion back in July, ruled it relevant and "quite instructive."

The video, on TV ten feet from the jurors, opened with Christa's green Escort, doors shut, police flags nearby designating evidence-collection sites. Moving inside, the camera paused on the broken doorjamb, then on the kitchen table, a child's sippy cup and Christa's cell phone on top. "I believe there was one single digit visible on the display, the digit nine," Condon said. The camera panned to the far kitchen wall; the cordless landline was missing from its base.

The detail was chilling, suggesting that the victim had tried desperately to call for help, had lived through seconds knowing of her peril.

The seventeen-minute tape played out in silence. Jurors stared, frozen, taking in the evidence of two-and-a-half-year-old Ava's attempts to clean her dead mother's body: the bloodstained washcloth on the bathroom floor, a child's stepstool in front of the sink, covered with more blood. As EMT Francis had testified, the bloody prints on Christa's body were made by tiny hands. A child's broom rested against the hallway wall, near the body.

George realized that this was a critical prosecution moment: the visual of the crime scene would push some jurors past the point of no return. He sat quietly and forced McCowen to do the same, staring down at the defense table beforehand.

The camera moved toward the study, Condon noting bloodstains on the door frame. Moving back to the bathroom, it paused on a potty chair next to the toilet.

In the living room were two sofas, toys, and a lit Christmas tree. Back out in the hallway, the area near the stairs was cluttered with books and buckets of toys, but the staircase was "pretty much a free shot up to the top." At the top was a child's gate and another door covered with cobwebs. "It didn't look like anyone had been up there in a while," Condon said.

The downstairs bedroom held a couple of bureaus and a mattress on the floor, hippie-style. In the adjacent study, the camera picked up a laptop computer on Christa's desk, bookcases against the wall, and stacked file boxes. Condon reported that police found no evidence worth collecting from upstairs, from the living room, or from the bedroom.

In the reserved benches, the Worthington family watched in horror. Aunt Diana, still trembling, put her hand to her mouth and paled as she digested the sight of her niece's house covered with blood and cluttered with the detritus of Christa's screwed-up life, including her now motherless child's scattered toys. Amyra Chase, Ava's guardian, had not come to court this day; perhaps she'd been warned about the video.

The scene shifted to the day after Christa's body was discovered, when Condon returned to shoot outside in better light. Visible now were the toys in the yard, a Stop & Shop receipt dated January 4 in a window well, and an outdoor shower stall. It had rained lightly overnight, but the parallel marks on the ground were still clear.

Condon set the stage for an outside struggle that the prosecution would later link to McCowen's statement. From the ground, the trooper collected a set of car keys on the passenger side of Christa's Ford, crushed as if they'd been run over; a pair of eyeglasses; and a sock near the driver's side, its mate in a nearby flower bed. When Welsh moved to admit a barrette discovered in the driveway between the car and the house, a battle about relevance ensued.

Condon reported that the barrette was discovered between "two parallel disturbances" in the gravel driveway that appeared to have been made by a toy or by a person "being dragged." Welsh advocated the latter, naturally, and continued to do so as the trial advanced. Nickerson allowed the barrette into evidence. The prosecutor finished by bringing Condon back to the phone he'd found inside, the number 9 glowing hideously showing on its screen.

On cross, George focused on the thoroughly tainted crime scene, then asked Condon to explain how the items found outside came to be there. The trooper admitted that he couldn't. He also acknowledged having no idea how many people had walked through the house and the yard or what they might have touched. George showed him the police sign-in sheet: Condon was fourth on the list, Chief John Thomas first. Neither Costa nor Allen was listed, meaning that at least nine other people had entered before police established the sheet, twelve before MSP specialist Condon arrived to collect and videotape evidence.

The witness hedged when asked if McCowen's fingerprints had been found, saying that he no longer worked in the unit when McCowen was arrested. Yet McCowen's prints were not at the scene, George pointed out—not one, not even a partial. Of the ten finger- and palm prints taken from the house, four matched paramedic Francis; one matched Chief Thomas; one matched Truro police officer John Lundborn, and one matched Christa, found on the inside glass of the kitchen door. The rest were on the hallway door frame, too smudged for comparison.

Condon agreed with this summary. Had he mentioned how unusual it is to secure only ten prints from any crime scene, he might have raised the specter of someone wiping the place down, postmurder.

"Did the house appear to have been the scene of a struggle?" George asked.

"In my opinion, no."

"Did you find any sand or gravel or seashells or anything of that nature on the bottoms of her feet?"

Condon said he did not.

The next witness was Kimberly Squier, an eighteen-year veteran of the State Police, the last thirteen on plainclothes duty with CPAC. A tall, athletic blond woman with short bangs, she looked younger than her forty-plus years, and in his inimitable style, District Attorney O'Keefe had described the experienced police sergeant to me as "eye candy." She was indeed attractive, but more to the point, she was a professional; her performance proved it. Squier arrived at the crime scene after six P.M., specifically to interview Ava. The little girl was in Jan Worthington's parents' living room with neighbor Francine Watson Randolph, who had received the child from EMT Malloy.

Squier's steady testimony evidenced years of practice, her tone level and businesslike. She saw that Ava felt comfortable with Randolph, so the trooper decided that the three would read a book together. Soon Ava rallied. She gave Squier a stuffed bird, a cardinal. The officer started with easy questions.

How old was she?

"Two," Ava said, holding up two fingers.

Her birthday?

"May," the little girl said.

Squier asked her to identify colors, starting with the stuffed bird.

"Red," Ava replied. Her socks were purple, her pajamas pink and white.

"Do you have any dogs or cats?" Squier asked.

No.

Asked who lived at her house, Ava became animated.

"Mommy lying down. Mommy won't get up. Mommy lying down." She looked directly at Francine, then around the living room.

"Mommy won't get up. Tried to get Mommy up. Mommy dirty. Tried to clean Mommy. Those are my paints, not Mommy's paints."

Squier asked if anyone had come to visit. Ava said Tim and his dog Sammy, then "That's my mommy, not another mommy. *That's my mommy!*"

In the face of these heartbreaking answers, Squier somehow pressed on. But the trooper could not get anything more from her. The little girl was clearly tired, so the interview ended. Ava was taken to Cape Cod Hospital for evaluation. Other than diaper rash and an ear infection, there was no physical trauma.

The next day, Ava was interviewed at Children's Cove in Hyannis, a shelter for young crime victims. Squier observed through a one-way mirror. Ava repeated some phrases but said nothing new.

After that interview, Squier concluded that Ava "did not see or witness anything that happened to her mother that night."

Asked if she had obtained the buccal swab from defendant Christopher McCowen on May 26, 2006, after his arrest, Squier said she had.

"Do you see him here in the courtroom?" Welsh asked, waiting for her to point.

"Yes . . . he's in the blue suit next to attorney George."

Without segue, Welsh had leaped from Ava's tragic experience to McCowen, a deft move. McCowen had no choice but to meet Squier's gaze. With that, Welsh closed direct.

It was a heavy moment. George asked if Ava ever identified "any other person," besides Tim Arnold and his dog, who came to the house.

"No, she didn't," Squier replied.

Abruptly, George sat, ending cross-examination. McCowen, who'd been doodling on a yellow legal pad, did not look up. As with Condon, the idea was to move on, minimize Squier's air time before the jury.

Trooper Carol Harding, also assigned to CPAC, had observed the autopsy and was in court in lieu of the medical examiner, Dr. James Weiner, who, it turned out, was suffering from leukemia. It wasn't the ideal arrangement for the Commonwealth. George knew Welsh had no choice.

The twenty-four-year veteran started in by explaining that after a trace examination in Boston, the body had been transported to Weiner's office back in Pocasset, three miles from the Cape Cod Canal. The evidence collected was then sent to the crime lab in Sudbury, west of Boston, to be processed by criminalistics. Weiner had prepared a rape test kit, taking swabs and smears orally, rectally, vaginally, anorectally, and paravaginally. He'd also collected blood, head and pubic hair combings, and left and right fingernail clippings.

Welsh moved to admit the kit into evidence, then asked to display an autopsy photo on ELMO. Every eye in the courtroom strained. The Condon video had not been clearly visible from the backmost benches, but the awful image now flickering on-screen was.

George objected to the close-up of Christa's face, her mouth and one eye open, the other eye swollen shut completely. "It's a horrendous photo," he argued at sidebar, "a close-up of . . . a dead woman with her eyes open. It's inflammatory."

She looked like a dead fish, her mouth puckered open as if she'd gasped for a last breath. The open eye seemed to say she'd known she was dying.

Once more, Nickerson leafed through the prosecutor's pile of autopsy photos, eliminating some, allowing the rest. George was livid, as any defense attorney in his spot would be. It was Friday, and puppeteer O'Keefe had doubtless instructed Welsh to end the week with exhibits that would haunt the jurors all weekend.

But the judge had ruled. George shut up.

Welsh's first photo showed a one-and-a-half-inch abrasion to Christa's left forehead. It was a close-up. No juror looked away, but one of them, the middle-aged insurance claims analyst, seemed to let out a short gasp.

Welsh moved on, using the photos whenever possible. Harding detailed the wounds altogether calmly, like a salesperson enumerating the features of a large-screen TV: the three-eighths-inch contusion on Christa's upper left breast; the two-inch wound to her right eyelid; a one-and-a-quarter-inch abrasion on her left hip; a half-inch circular abrasion on her left knee; two circular wounds on her left forearm, one three-quarter-inch, the other one-inch; and the one-by-half-inch abrasion to her mid-chest. Clicking the remote for a new slide, Christa wound up with the small, seemingly innocuous incision beneath Christa's left breast, the wound that killed her.

It was four o'clock. Before she could get into describing the fatal stab wound, the bailiff intoned, "All rise." The jurors shuffled out of the courtroom, more than half with their heads bowed.

Day 6, Monday, October 23

Despite the graphic autopsy pictures, most jury members began the second week looking comfortable; they'd settled in. Men wore chinos and open-collared sport shirts or sweaters, only one or two in a sport jacket or necktie. A goodly number of the women sported mock turtlenecks and L.L. Bean boat shoes as if folksiness was the norm for a late-October Cape Cod murder trial.

Welsh picked up where he had left off, once more walking Harding through Worthington's gruesome wounds, using the same plodding, mechanical approach: hand the witness a photograph, ask what it depicts, move to admit the photo into evidence, utter a knee-jerk

"All right," then scan his notes for the next question. In contrast, George had rarely referred to notes; with two or three attacks planned for most witnesses, he'd struggle to ask just one question at a time. Not exactly employing the King's English, his technique nonetheless served to keep witnesses, and Judge Nickerson, off balance.

But sometimes the attorney could throw himself off balance, too.

Welsh proffered ten wound photos in all. Harding described Christa's hand contusions: one two and a quarter inches on her third left knuckle, another three-eighths inch on her third right knuckle, another half an inch on the outside base of her right thumb, and so forth. All were defense wounds, the results of the ex-fashion writer's futile attempts to save herself.

Welsh turned to the sexual-assault kit. Rape was key to the commonwealth's case, for it provided motive. Having sexually assaulted the victim, the predator had to silence her. But there was more to it still. Without rape, the state had no Mandingo, no King Kong, no dark-skinned beast to contrast with the fair-skinned victim, which was the motif that lay behind every turn in Welsh's rhetoric. As future events would show, the proceedings had begun to evoke the pattern of a classic American lynching, if for no other reason than that the rape charge had not been filed for three and a half years after the homicide, and then not until an African-American was arrested.

Welsh asked Harding about the savage knife wound that penetrated Christa's body to nick the floor beneath. George objected, the fifth time in a matter of minutes. Nickerson sustained.

Welsh asked for a sidebar: Harding had already testified about the stab wound. George hadn't objected. Why now?

George said the word *knife* made the difference. Previously, Harding testified to the wound, not to what caused it. A technicality, but he had to stop the lurid testimony.

Nickerson agreed. "It's not for this witness to say it's a knife."

Harding stepped down.

Because the medical examiner was ill, prosecutors also called a substitute physician, Dr. Henry Nields, a nerdish-looking technician who had performed 2,500 autopsies, 200 of them homicides, and had reviewed Weiner's notes, charts, and photographs only thirty days earlier. The two had never met.

According to Nields, Weiner arrived at the murder scene at 7:55 P.M. and found Christa wearing a black thermal shirt and black sweatshirt, both pushed up, exposing her breasts. As other witnesses had mentioned, the lower half of the body was naked.

Weiner noted a drip pattern across the right side of the victim's face; blood had leaked from her nose and mouth, then pooled on the floor. "The body is cool and in full rigor," he wrote.

The stab wound was the cause of death. Nields testified that the dying process took minutes. He could not give an exact number but acknowledged that the victim's death might have taken longer.

"The wound passed through her left second rib, perforated her left lung, and exited the left chest cavity through the back through the posterior aspect of the fifth intercostal space and perforated the skin on the left side of her back," he read from Weiner's notes.

The wound indicated that the murder weapon had a blunt edge and a sharp edge. "A semi-opaque grayish tan flake," approximately an eighth of an inch, was removed from the wound by Lieutenant Kenneth Martin, who would testify that it was dried flesh.

As with Harding, Welsh walked Nields through each injury, using photos on ELMO, plying jurors with another dose of nightmare material. Worthington's five hand bruises were consistent with attempts to block blows. The contusion to her left breast was consistent with blunt impact.

Nields went on to say that there was a small amount of blood in the victim's vagina, but he could not say whether or not a sexual assault occurred.

Weiner had estimated that Christa Worthington died between twenty-four and thirty-six hours before he observed the body at 50 Depot Road. Nields explained that medical examiners use body temperature, rigor mortis, and liver mortis to estimate time of death.

"And it's really only an estimate, isn't that fair to say?" Welsh queried, anticipating George's moves.

The witness agreed. Welsh returned to his seat. George, walking in an exaggerated lumber, moved in front of the witness stand. Nields had never talked to Weiner? Had never been to 50 Depot Road? Affecting the mien of an absent-minded professor, George stopped, noting with an exaggerated expression, that parts of the autopsy report seemed to contradict the Commonwealth's case. He asked Nields to explain rigor mortis.

The process involves three "twelve-hour windows," the witness said. It takes about twelve hours for rigor to form; full rigor lasts about twelve hours, then starts to dissipate "over the next twelve hours or so."

George reminded him that Worthington's body was in full rigor in Pocasset at one P.M. on January 7, just as it was when Weiner examined it at eight P.M. the night before in Truro.

"If Christa Worthington was not in full rigor two and a half hours before that, what would that mean to you as an expert witness?" he asked.

Nields had had little time to prepare. He said such evidence would indicate that "the time of death . . . was closer to when she was found than the twenty-four to thirty-six hours that he estimates."

According to EMTs, rigor had not fully set in when the body was discovered. Francis and Rowell straightened Christa's arm and leg, the same leg several prosecution witnesses testified was originally lodged in a bookcase. What did that mean? George asked.

The doctor was having trouble keeping up, but George wouldn't slow down. He interrupted the witness's answers several times. Flummoxed, Nields testified that science was "a subjective judgment," that time of death cannot always be established with certainty.

George looked at him dubiouly. After Christa Worthington's body was found at approximately 4:30 P.M. on January 6, 2002, he repeated, her arm and leg were straightened, and she was moved from the doorway. "Would that tell you that her time of death was shorter or longer than twenty-four to thirty-six hours, if [rigor is] setting in at four-thirty?"

It was "hard to be precise," Nields repeated. "But it would suggest that . . . it would be more consistent with it being less than the twenty-four to thirty-six hours."

"So, that means Christa Worthington died on Saturday or Sunday, doesn't it?"

"It actually doesn't mean that," Nields answered, trying to gather himself up. "It can't really tell that for sure. Again, it's an estimate. I could say that if rigor, in fact, is just setting in, then . . . then in all likelihood that death would have occurred at an earlier . . . or closer to the time that the body was observed than if rigor was full. But it's a subjective judgment as to what full rigor is. So, in all honesty, it would be hard to be very definitive about that."

"You all done, Doctor?" George might as well have given the witness a dope slap.

But he wasn't through. He asked about other methods used to determine time of death, such as examination of the vitreous humor, the gelatinous substance that fills the eyeball, and potassium levels. Nields said he didn't feel either method was useful. Asked whether Worthington's vitreous humor was tested, Nields consulted Weiner's notes, then acknowledged that he could find no reference to it.

George raised the issue of lividity, or liver mortis, discoloration of the body that becomes fixed after eight to twelve hours. Again, Nields was forced to admit that the issue was not mentioned in Weiner's January 6 notes. George asked what the omission might mean. Nields said he couldn't answer with scientific certainty. Undaunted, George, who'd used this line of attack in previous murder trials, posed the question as a hypothetical.

Telling the doctor to assume no mention of lividity on January 6 at eight P.M. and a report of fixed lividity eighteen hours later, did the doctor have an opinion as to whether lividity became fixed in that eighteen-hour period?

"I do not," Nields answered. "No."

"Doctor, if there was no lividity in Christa Worthington on January 6, 2002, at about eight P.M., what does that tell you?"

"If there was no lividity there, then there is lividity later, then that indicates . . . again, it varies from case to case, but . . . but . . ."

He was trapped, almost stammering.

"Lividity generally takes twenty minutes to . . . set in," he said. "So, it suggests that . . . if, in fact, there was no lividity . . . that the death would have occurred relatively recent to when the body was found."

George let the point sink in, rolling his eyes at the ceiling, then asked about body temperature. The witness testified that a dead body cools approximately two degrees during the first hour, one and a half degrees per hour after that. Generally, a rectal thermometer is used at crime scenes, but Weiner's notes stated only that the body was "cool." Nothing indicated that the victim's temperature had been taken.

George pointed out that the body was in full rigor mortis on January 7, when rigor should have been dissipating, according to the prosecution's timeline. The body was not in full rigor at 4:30 P.M. the day before, as it should have been if Christa's death occurred during the early hours of Saturday. "It does not appear that Christa Worthington died prior to eight A.M. on Saturday, does it?" he asked.

"I really . . . in all honesty, I can't say that. I . . . really can't say that, one way or the other."

George paused, then gave him another slap. "What are you here to testify about, then, Doctor?"

Welsh objected to the sarcasm, and Nickerson sustained, giving George a parental sideways glance. George didn't give a rat's ass. His point made, he moved on to the rape charge. Nields agreed that McCowen weighed 200 pounds at the time of the murder, Christa between 100 and 110. George asked if Nields knew the size of McCowen's private parts.

He didn't.

"Doctor, can you show this jury where on this diagram there is a sign of any sexual trauma to Christa Worthington's vaginal area?"

"The only thing . . . was described in the handwritten note; there was a small amount of blood in her vagina at the scene."

"Could you tell the jury how it got there?"

"No."

Nields conceded that he couldn't say whether Ava deposited that blood while wiping her mother, and he didn't know how deep into the vagina it was. Asked whether the blood was on top of the vagina or inside, he scoured Weiner's notes. Several sheets of typescript fell from the folder onto the floor. Awkwardly, he bent to pick them up.

"If I told you, Doctor, it doesn't say that, would that help you?"

"Let him look in his records," Nickerson admonished. "That's what the gentleman is doing."

"It says . . . small amount of blood in the vagina," Nields murmured.

George leaned on him. "Can you tell us *anything* about where that was located?"

"Only that it was in . . . only that in the report, it was in the vagina."

"Now, Doctor . . . other than that small droplet of blood . . . and you can't tell us where it came from or how it got there, can you tell us what indications there were of sexual trauma?"

"No," he answered.

George asked if Weiner's report indicated any tearing, bruising, or contusions in the vaginal area.

"It does not mention any. . . ."

The witness was now a near puppet, reading another physician's notes. George kept going, trying to build one success atop another. The medical examiner would have to acknowledge that there was no sign of rape, then, yes?

Nields admitted that Weiner did not report any scrapes, tears, or bruises in the vaginal area, the anal rectal area, or the labia. Nor did he document any damage, injury, or trauma of any kind to the vulva or perineum, the diamond-shaped area in front of the anus.

"So, there is no evidence of *any* violent sexual contact with the victim in this case in the form of injury, is there?"

"There's no report of injury, right . . . in those areas."

The prosecution had gone to great lengths to detail the body's many injuries. But none suggested rape. George walked back to the defense table and plopped down beside McCowen: nothing more need be said about the alleged rape.

Welsh rose and asked, "This business about time of death is not an exact science, is it, sir?"

Nields agreed, then volunteered that bruising or tearing of the vaginal area does not occur in every sexual assault.

"In fact, there are a good number of cases where there is no bruising, correct?"

George objected. Nickerson intervened, asking if Nields was aware of any studies to that effect. Nields said he was not.

Yet medical literature is replete with probability studies of injuries resulting from sexual assault, and the data would not have helped the Commonwealth's case in the least. For some in the audience—namely, the half dozen or so old-timey reporters, the experienced ones with years of rape or rape-murder trials under their belts—it was hard to believe that Welsh, the seasoned prosecutor, was so woefully uninformed.

The prosecutor now leapfrogged to the vaginal blood, and the charade continued. "It's consistent with trauma," the witness testified. "It's consistent with an infection. It's consistent with inflammation. It would be consistent with benign or malignant tumors. It would be . . . consistent with blood being deposited by some injury to a penis after . . . or during sexual intercourse."

George wasn't unhappy with this guessing, although he made a show of objecting. At sidebar, Nickerson said he would allow the testimony because George had opened the door during cross. Besides, Nields was "a doctor." George's shrug said, *So what?*

Welsh opined that the witness was "being fair" in his answer. When he tried to elaborate, George interrupted. "Well, if I could just finish, Bob," Welsh objected.

"Well, let *me* finish."

"No, I was talking," the assistant DA insisted.

"The answer was speculative."

"I was talking to the judge."

"The answer was speculative."

"Now, I'll control the sidebar," Nickerson admonished. "Is there anything else you'd like to say to me, Mr. George?"

George shook his head. Nickerson waved his hand in disgust; the defense should proceed with recross.

Nields testified that the blood taken from Christa's vagina had not even been preserved, leading George to ask whether the witness's answer to Welsh's last question about the source of the blood had been an expert opinion or a guess. At this point, George was suddenly yelling.

Nickerson glared down at him.

George ignored him. "Doctor, you realize a man is on trial for murder here, don't you?"

"Yes."

"And you realize what your testimony means here?"

"I testify as best I can to answer the questions that were asked. I'm not sure what you mean."

"But you're still willing to get up there and guess about these types of things with his life on the line?"

Welsh had objected halfway through the question. Nickerson, who'd heard enough, called morning recess. As the jurors filed out, he ordered the attorneys to sidebar and blasted George. "The next time you launch into a question that is so blatantly argumentative and so blatantly inappropriate, you will be thoroughly chastised in front of the jury. *Don't do it again.*"

With the jury back, George did his most contrived mea culpa to date: "I would like to apologize to the court for my behavior in asking that last question of Dr. . . . whatever his name was." He sneered. "Dr. Nields. It was inappropriate, and it was done in the heat of passion, and I apologize."

Nickerson glared again. "And the record doesn't even begin to tell us of your volume. I think we'll just simply leave it that the apology is accepted."

George nodded, knowing that the round was solidly his. But the white-haired judge was out of sorts for another reason. A Boston TV cameraman had inadvertently filmed a juror in the parking lot, violating the court's media order. Informing the courtroom of the incident, Nickerson declared that only Court TV's camera would operate henceforth. Tapping into the video and audio feeds would have to satisfy the media's needs.

At 11:45, State Police Lieutenant Monte Gilardi took the stand. Supervisor of the Bourne forensics unit, he photographed evidence and collected fingerprints at the Worthington murder scene. It was dark when he arrived, and Trooper Condon directed him to the items found in the sand-and-clamshell driveway. Gilardi testified that he thought a scuffle occurred there; on the passenger side of Christa's car, the sand and gravel seemed trampled.

"I also observed what looked to me to be two linear lines or marks emanating from that disturbed area of ground and moving toward the back of the vehicle. And in a curved sort of way from the back of the vehicle toward the front porch or the front stairs of the home," he added.

The lines were parallel but uneven, farthest apart near the car, closer together toward the porch.

Gilardi said he tried to duplicate the marks, using a plastic stroller found near the house, but it had four small fixed wheels and was not heavy enough. He tried a child's car, also found outside, but that didn't work, either.

Welsh walked him through the crime scene, using a chart. The trooper repeated the testimony of others, with a few additions. From the front door with the broken lock, a large piece of wood had splintered off. There were small red-brown stains on items on the kitchen table. In the bathroom, he saw the stains others described but also a bloodstain on a white rug and another on a hand-held carpet cleaner in the hallway.

Welsh asked about fingerprints, the trooper's specialty. Gilardi enumerated the prints found, adding that three others had no match.

McCowen's prints were never found at the scene. Nevertheless, Welsh asked the trooper to describe his encounter with the defendant when he fingerprinted him on the night of his arrest, anticipating George's claim that McCowen was not sober when questioned.

"I would say he was as sober as could be," Gilardi testified. He said McCowen wrote "Big Dog" and "Hammer" when asked about aliases.

Welsh finished by lunch break.

At two, George asked Gilardi whether he'd ever met McCowen previously, whether he knew the defendant's IQ, background, or medical history—specifically, whether he knew about his epilepsy. Gilardi did not. Nor did he ask McCowen whether he was taking any medications, even after McCowen requested painkillers for his knee.

He admitted that McCowen's fingerprints were not found at the crime scene. When George asked why Tony Jackett's prints were not on the report, the trooper appeared perplexed. He retrieved his lab sheet to double-check: no mention of Jackett. The prints of local drug dealer Shawn Mulvey hadn't been checked, either.

Robert Martin was the fifth cop to take the stand. Head of crime-scene services at the main lab in Sudbury, Martin had collected evidence from the body proper. His account was even more graphic than Gilardi's or Harding's.

"One could see that she had defecated, and one could also see her vaginal area as well because it was facing you," he said. "The victim had a shirt and vest on, which was pulled up to the area just below the breast. The shirt actually extended a little bit longer over the left side, and the right side was pulled up to just about the area just below the nipple. The victim's head was off to . . . the right side [and] blood was flowing from the victim's mouth and nose."

Grass was "not just on top of the hair but also entwined and matted into the hair itself," he added.

At the trace exam in Boston, the body was reexamined and photographed under controlled lighting, and the breasts were swabbed for saliva. In many sexual-assault cases, he said, suspects place their mouths on "the actual nipple of the victim . . . so, we'll swab those areas in the effort to retrieve any potential DNA which would have been left behind."

The neck was swabbed for the same reason.

Each layer of clothing was removed from the body and bagged for transport to the crime lab. Welsh moved for the admission of Christa's brown fleece zippered jacket, black long-sleeved shirt, and blue fleece vest. George objected, saying that the clothing had no forensic value. Nickerson admitted the items, partly because of the confusion over the green bathrobe.

Afternoon recess interrupted Martin's testimony.

Early on, in the course of idle hallway gossip, one court officer had mentioned Nickerson's propensity for getting stricter as his trials progressed; that pattern seemed to be emerging. The courtroom was particularly crowded this Monday; two criminal-justice classes from Cape Cod Community College were in attendance, adding to the density. Nickerson had welcomed the students and their teacher, but before afternoon recess, he repeated his dress and conduct codes: "A courtroom is surely a public place. All will observe some basic levels of decorum. Bare midriffs are not permitted on women. Bermuda shorts are not permitted on men. Holding hands and making lovey expressions one to the other are not permitted. Cell phones are absolutely barred."

It seemed a bit gratuitous. Who would show up in superior court so skimpily attired? Time would tell.

The prosecution's next witness was another Martin—Kenneth Martin, assistant technical manager for forensic biology at the MSP crime lab, who'd overseen the criminalistics and crime-scene response units. He was the CSI guy.

Martin got to 50 Depot Road at 10:30 P.M.

Both the sippy cup and a medicine dropper on the kitchen table, he said, tested positive for blood. The cell phone did not. A bloodstain was found on the wooden block holding kitchen knives; a knife found in the sink was clean.

The hallway wall was spattered, "probably from the movement of her arms." Additional stains were found on the other side of the body, toward the living room.

Loose hairs were found in the pool of blood around the victim's head. "Her hair apparently had stuck there, and it was pulled out," Martin explained, when paramedics moved her body. He corroborated vegetative material in the hair on her head.

Blood also was found on the handle of the child's broom, as well as in its straw "thistle." Medium to dark brown head hairs were found in the straw, too, as well as blue, clear, and yellow fibers.

In the bathroom, the bath mitt was stained, as others had previously testified. The Merrell clogs found next to the kitchen door also tested positive for human blood, a drop on the right toe and "transfer stains" on the left heel.

No blood was detected on the keys, the eyeglasses, or the socks found outside. The socks had brown animal hairs and soil on the bottoms, where they'd touch the ground if their owner were walking upright.

Christa's fleece vest was bloodstained and contained light and dark brown head hair and light brown pubic hair. Her T-shirt, a black J. Crew, had scattered bloodstains on the sleeve, a pea-sized cut on the back near the center waist. The brown jacket also had hairs, noteworthy in that some were white.

Ava's clothes tested positive for blood, saliva, and urine. Her socks were bloodstained.

Martin also found a medium brown head hair, eleven and three-quarters inches long, next to Christa's right breast. During the trace exam, he'd recovered medium and dark brown head hair from her torso, as well as red and gold fibers. Most were consistent with Christa, who had medium brown hair, or Ava, who had dark brown. The exception was the hair on the breast: Christa's hair was only six to eight inches long.

The breast swabs revealed "nothing on the right breast," he said. On the left, "there was no seminal fluid, but there was saliva."

Trace materials from Christa's pubic area revealed blue and white fibers, a light brown pubic hair, and more vegetative material. Vaginal swabs were positive for semen.

The investigator testified that shoes taken from Tim Arnold evidenced no blood. Likewise, a jacket, sweater, pants, and boots taken from Jeremy Frazier. A Minicci watch, taken from McCowen, had blood on its face and armband, though not enough to determine whether it was human blood.

At four, court recessed. All in all, it had not been an especially good day for the prosecution. Megan Tench of the *Boston Globe* wrote that not only had the ME failed to establish the time of death but the day's testimony "had raised more questions than answers" and that "the trial has thus far revealed that more than a dozen emergency workers trampled and possibly contaminated the crime scene." In addition, there were "no conclusive signs of rape, and investigators found no fingerprints, footprints, or hairs linking McCowen to the crime."

But one thing did work. As Martin described the blood-spatter patterns, jurors became aware of Christa's clothes in brown paper bags, sitting on the prosecution table. The bags were sealed with red tape. Exhibit 45 was her black top; 46 was her socks. Amyra Chase blinked back tears. Jurors, not a half-dozen feet away, couldn't help but notice.

Day 7, Tuesday, October 24

The ongoing George-Welsh head-butting was interrupted by the most precious of set pieces so far. One of the Cape Cod Community College students, either deaf to Nickerson's dress code or defying it, showed up just after 8:30 in, yes, the proscribed Bermuda shorts. A court officer told him to change. Instead, student John Kirwick tried to blend into the crowd, taking a seat in the back row of the press balcony. As jurors filed in, Nickerson spotted him and ordered the student brought before the bench. Bermuda shorts were prohibited, the judge boomed.

Kirwick stammered, "Well, like, I didn't know . . ."

"I'm considering summary contempt on you, young man."

"All right, I'll leave."

"I'm sorry?" Nickerson glared down at him. "*I'll* decide what I'm going to do with you in due course. Now you're in the custody of the sheriff."

The astonished crowd watched as Kirwick was cuffed, shackled, and led to the court's holding cell to join the county's most hard-core prisoners charged with rape, murder, and mayhem.

Nickerson then gestured for the proceedings to begin. When Robert Martin resumed the stand for cross-examination, George asked the crime-scene investigator about items not tested. Two suspects of particular interest were Arnold and Jeremy Frazier, McCowen's Wellfleet "bro." Keith Amato would soon join their ranks, along with Truro Police Sergeant David Costa and Tony Jackett.

Of greatest interest was Frazier, the prosecution's star grand-jury witness, identified by McCowen the night of his arrest and scheduled to take the stand. On June 17, 2005, two months after McCowen's arrest, Martin received Frazier's Tommy-brand size 36/32 wool pants, his black and gray Timberland boots, a large white-and-navy-blue Nautica sweater, and a leather jacket. George was most interested in the sweater but didn't say why. Instead, he focused on Tim Arnold and the brown blanket police had sent to the crime lab in spring 2002. Tests revealed semen on both sides, minute bloodstains, medium brown to light brown hairs, and several fibers. Was it scientifically possible for the semen on Christa's body to transfer to the blanket?

The witness said it was. He could not say whether the sperm on either side of the blanket had come from Christa Worthington's body.

Some semen found on Christa was never tested, but George didn't raise that issue. Instead, he had Martin address the difficulties inherent in determining the date of *any* semen deposit.

"If semen is deposited on a blanket or bedding," the witness said, "I can't account for people's laundry habits, how they wash their clothing. . . . It could stay there for a very, very long time."

The length of time semen remains on a human body "would [also] depend on hygiene." It could remain in the vagina for ninety-six hours—four days, the witness said, again calling into question the assertion that McCowen had sex with Christa on Saturday morning as opposed to earlier, possibly Thursday.

Martin said one of the first things to go on a sperm cell is the tail. Heads are more resilient. The sperm in this case, Martin said, had no tails.

The presence or absence of sperm tails has been used effectively by Peter Neufeld and Barry Scheck of the Innocence Project, the New York–based nonprofit responsible for freeing most of the nation's 242 convicted prisoners exonerated in recent years by DNA testing and other forensic analysis. Martin's sperm-tail testimony was thus critical. The state claimed that McCowen raped the victim during the early morning hours of Saturday, January 5. But its own experts testified that there was no physical evidence of rape and that tailless sperm collected from the victim's vagina indicated that intercourse, consensual or not, had occurred as early as Thursday afternoon, almost two days before. The Thursday in question was Worthington's regular garbage pickup day.

George knew what he was on to. He moved into a collateral area, forcing Martin to acknowledge that he was never given a hair sample from Arnold, Frazier, or even Jackett. Most hair tested matched Ava's dark, Christa's medium, or Arnold's light brown hair. Martin had no explanation for the lone, no-match hair found on the victim's breast. But even after Arnold's DNA matched the semen on the blanket, his hair was not DNA-tested. Moreover, Martin admitted that not one hair found at the scene matched that of an African-American.

As George turned to the vegetative material in Christa's hair, he was interrupted by the strange sounds of what seemed to be a juror's snoring; moments later, it seemed he'd fainted. It was "Mick Jagger," who'd earlier been admonished by Nickerson for wearing sunglasses until he explained that they were medically mandated.

The judge ordered the panel out of the courtroom; the man was removed on a stretcher and taken to Cape Cod Hospital, comatose. By 10:16, court was back in session. Nickerson formally released the juror from service, leaving fifteen of the sixteen seated; only twelve would deliberate, leaving three alternates still in reserve.

With Martin's testimony, the defense continued to rack up points. The crime lab never compared the grass on Christa's head with outside vegetation; soil samples from the driveway were never compared with dirt and debris found on her clothes. No pubic-hair samples had been taken from any of the suspects, nor were the loose pubic hairs "combed" from Christa's body compared with anyone's DNA. Martin acknowledged that he didn't even test the blood on the bath mitt, assuming that it was Christa's.

The bloodstains on the hallway wall were tested only to determine that the blood was human. It, too, was assumed to be Christa's.

Martin said that a male DNA profile was generated from the blood on the left heel of the clogs found near the kitchen door.

"At any time were you able to . . . connect Chris McCowen to this scene from the bloodstains or hair examined?"

"From the samples we had taken, no," Martin said.

George nodded and returned to the defense table.

Welsh had little to work with. "Which is better, having a hair or a DNA profile?" he asked lamely. And what did tailless sperm really mean? Couldn't it have been deposited Friday night, after all?

"It's possible," Martin said. It's "difficult to say."

On recross, George had only one question: Did Martin believe the sperm could have been deposited Thursday, Friday, or Saturday?

The answer was a reluctant affirmative.

The next witness took the stand and carefully introduced himself. "My name is Christopher Mason." The unhurried complete sentence hinted at what would soon become clear: the detective was special. The prosecution's star witness would testify for the next two days, earning the nicknames "Robo Cop" and "Golden Boy" among the courtroom's more cynical reporters. Mason had been an MSP trooper for thirteen years, the shortest tenure of any police witness thus far, yet one year after Christa's murder he'd been put in charge of the investigation, the biggest one anyone could remember. A tall, thinnish man in his late thirties, he was good-looking in a clean-cut, outdoorsy way, Nordic blond with keen blue eyes, and a runner who'd competed several times in the arduous Boston Marathon. Later, it would come to light that several female jurors found him sexually desirable and chatted about it. Such thoughts would not have crossed the detective's mind, putatively, given his cold, practiced professionalism.

Mason dressed carefully, too, more Nordstrom than Brioni, granted, but his gray suit, crisp white shirt, and fresh haircut were perfect for what he had to do. His testimony was to center on the interview he and his partner, Sergeant William Burke, conducted with McCowen on the night of the arrest, which Mason had reduced to a twenty-seven-page report. After the DNA match, this report was the sharpest arrow in the prosecutor's quiver.

Welsh began by producing a sales receipt from the Orleans Stop & Shop where Christa had shopped midday on Friday the fourth. He then played the store's surveillance videotape, with Mason pointing out Christa in a red jacket and black shirt. Ava, in a blue pullover, was visible, too. Together, they were pushing their cart through the store's vegetable section to the checkout counter. The receipt showed that they checked out at 12:14 P.M.

For the first time, jurors were seeing Christa alive, a walking, if not talking, creature, and the impact was tangible. Everyone—jurors, journalists, and spectators—knew she'd be dead in twelve to twenty hours, turned into the beaten, bloody corpse in the gruesome crime-scene photos and video just exhibited.

Mason had interviewed hundreds of people during the three-and-a-half-year investigation, but Welsh moved straight to McCowen. As Kimberly Squier had done, the detective identified the defendant. "He is wearing a white shirt and blue tie." Mason's outstretched hand was steady as he pointed. McCowen raised his chin to look back at him but otherwise sat motionless.

The detective's first interview with the defendant was at the Cape Cod Disposal yard on April 3, 2002, three months after the murder. When he and Burke asked owner Don Horton to identify the driver whose route included 50 Depot Road, McCowen, said Mason, told them that he did not know Christa Worthington, that he had "never spoken to her." He collected her trash on Thursdays, before noon, from the wooden bins outside the house, never from inside. Sometimes Christa would watch him and wave. On occasion, he'd see a small girl standing beside her.

McCowen said he learned of the murder on January 6 from his friend, Dave Amerault. He volunteered to provide DNA and fingerprints, but the officers didn't take him up on the offer.

As Welsh moved on to the second interview, on March 18, 2004, conducted in the office of McCowen's probation officer, George asked for a sidebar; the jury would speculate about why McCowen was on probation.

Nickerson instructed Welsh, "Don't give [the witness] a chance to come up with an oblique answer. Give him a leading question."

During the second interview, almost two years after the first, Mason and Burke wanted to retrace their steps, and this time, they did take McCowen's DNA, explaining that they wanted to "eliminate" him as a suspect.

McCowen told them that the information he'd previously provided was correct, "that he did not know Christa Worthington, had never spoken to her, and had never dealt with her other than to wave to her during his trash-pickup duties."

By now, Mason's style on the stand was everything it had promised. He recited answers from memory, almost word-perfect, volunteering nothing until asked, which may be the hardest thing of all for any witness. Often, he'd begin with a yes, then repeat Welsh's question aloud, as if to trigger some imprinted memory pattern, hands clasped at his waist, body swaying slightly, as if his trunk were the pendulum of a metronome. At times, he'd draw his right hand across the upward-flexed palm of his left or clasp his right wrist with his left hand, steadying actions both. Sometimes he'd unclench his hands and use each as a spatula, one moving one way, the other in the opposite direction; the overall effect, again, being one of smoothness, a rhythm that translated as unruffled poise. His suit jacket remained buttoned, his eyes unblinking; ninety percent of the time he focused on individual jurors, who were meant to feel privileged, indeed blessed, by the trooper's undivided attention.

McCowen's willingness to provide police with his DNA was to remain one of the great mysteries of the case, since it could so easily hang him. But that kind of cooperation isn't uncommon, even among the guilty. Experts call it an irrational need to postpone confrontation. Or perhaps, in McCowen's case, it was arrogance, a fear-driven insistence on winning; *he* could beat the odds.

The swab was taken according to protocol, Mason explained. "The right cheek is swabbed ten to fifteen times. The left cheek is swabbed ten to fifteen times. The swab is held beneath the subject's tongue for about a five count." McCowen did it himself.

The second interview raised nothing out of the ordinary, Mason testified. Thirteen months later, on April 7, 2005, they received verbal notification that his DNA was a match. Six days after that, a written report from the crime lab allowed the officers to obtain a search warrant for McCowen's residence at 63 Lafrance Avenue in Hyannis.

Welsh moved to show a second videotape, now of the arrest. George objected, not wanting jurors to see the defendant handcuffed. He was reaching. Welsh called him on it, telling Nickerson that the defense would likely claim that McCowen's statements to police were not voluntary as a result of ingestion of marijuana and Percocet. "The video," he said, "does clearly depict the defendant walking without any difficulty down some steps and into the cruiser."

This was where Welsh was good, anticipating the opposition's next move, and Nickerson agreed, offering to instruct the jurors that individuals are routinely handcuffed when taken into custody.

With the lawyers still at sidebar, the judge also returned to the Cape Cod Community College student in the courthouse holding pen. He ordered the student back into the courtroom. Viewers held their breath.

Asked what he had "learned," Kirwick, still in his silly Bermudas, could barely speak. He "just hadn't been thinking," he said. He "didn't realize it was a direct order."

Nickerson scrutinized the boy for a moment. "I'm at a loss to understand what sort of an education you've had, young man. But I think it's a lesson learned, and we'll go on from here."

The student stammered "Thanks," then was taken back to lockup and discharged, completing another valuable chapter in his education.

The five-minute videotape showed McCowen exiting 63 Lafrance Avenue in handcuffs, then being put into the rear seat of an unmarked cruiser. Mason pointed to himself, wearing a black jacket, sitting beside the prisoner after "making his weapon safe," then reading McCowen his Miranda rights. Burke drove. McCowen said he would cooperate. He also asked if someone would retrieve his house keys, believing he'd be going home soon. He'd never need those keys again.

Police entered 63 Lafrance at 7:05 P.M.; twenty-five minutes later, the prisoner was taken to a first-floor conference room at the barracks, uncuffed, and seated at a long table.

Mason gave him a printed copy of the Miranda declaration and a form that waived his right to an attorney, repeating the terms of each.

McCowen signed both.

He formally declined electronic recording of the interview, then asked Mason if that decision made him "look like an asshole."

It was a curious locution and Mason said he told McCowen that courts prefer that interviews be recorded "to ensure accuracy" but that it was his decision; Mason would not advise.

The answer was misleading. Under Massachusetts law, police must advise the suspect that they're taping but do *not* need consent. Cops, in general, do not want to tape interviews, however; a visual or audio record can impede their ability to get a suspect to talk. More than 250 towns and counties nationwide have adopted taping as protocol; the Massachusetts State Police on Cape Cod has not. Mason was covering himself. The SJC, Massachusetts's highest court, had recently expressed a strong preference for taping but stopped short of making it mandatory.

McCowen was told he had a right to medical attention and to one phone call. He wanted to call his girlfriend but first, "straighten everything out." At that point, Mason testified, "I began the interview by informing Mr. McCowen that he was at the State Police barracks, that he was under arrest [for] the murder of Christa Worthington."

McCowen was interrogated for the next six hours. During that time,

Mason said, the defendant gave eight different accounts of his actions on the night of January 4–5, 2002. They reviewed past conversations. Did McCowen recall what he said? Had he been truthful? The prisoner said he told the truth; he had never been inside Christa's house.

Mason told McCowen that some people described Christa Worthington as "flirtatious or giving off a vibe" and asked if she "ever flirted with him" or "led him to believe that she was interested in him in any way."

He said she had not, then added "that he knew what I was getting at . . . that he didn't think of Christa Worthington as 'a ho' . . . that he had never heard anything about Christa Worthington's reputation."

McCowen had "fucked around" with women on his trash route, but Christa, at 110 pounds, wasn't one of them. "She was not his type," Mason reported, "as he preferred 'big girls with meat on their bones.'"

McCowen denied knowing anything about Worthington, but he "thought" she dated Portuguese men, because he could tell that her daughter had a Portuguese father. Mason relayed McCowen's opinion of Christa as a "high-class lady" who "lived on a large wooded piece of land." He'd heard the Worthington family used to own all the land in that area.

McCowen said he had that information because "everybody had told him . . . just like how he knew about Tony Chop Chop." Mason recognized the nickname of Antone Costa, a Provincetown carpenter and drug dealer convicted of a series of grisly dismemberments in Provincetown-Truro during the late '60s. The Costa murder trial was held in the same courtroom as McCowen's; Costa was sentenced to life at Walpole penitentiary, where he hanged himself in 1974.

According to Mason, McCowen had picked up Worthington's trash on the Thursday before the murder. Asked if he had contact with Christa that day, he said, "I can honestly say seriously I didn't know her."

Mason said he told McCowen that the reason he was asking these questions was that McCowen was "young, in good shape, and he seemed to be charming," raising the possibility of a relationship with Christa Worthington. Mason then wondered aloud what the person who committed the crime had been thinking. McCowen said whoever did it must have been "drunk or stupid."

"His response was that if he had done it, he would make sure the kid did not see anything and that Christa Worthington was alone."

When Mason asked about DNA evidence left at the scene, McCowen added, "That's another thing that showed that this guy was stupid."

They were an hour into the interview. At that moment, the detective slid the DNA report across the table. McCowen looked at it for one minute, bowed his head, then said, "It could have been me."

"I asked Mr. McCowen to tell me, well, how is it that it could have been you?"

McCowen responded "that he had been extremely intoxicated that weekend but that he . . . could not recall having had sex or being in Truro."

Welsh walked the detective through each of McCowen's statements denying physical contact: April 2002, March 2004, and during the April 2005 interview. Here, too, the assistant DA was good at methodically piling up evidence. With most jurors transfixed by Mason's smooth delivery, Welsh made it clear that the defendant had lied three times before being told his DNA was found at the murder scene.

Returning to the interview, Mason explained that McCowen remembered being "piss-ass drunk" with his friend, Jeremy Frazier, at an open-mike rap contest that night at the Orleans Juice Bar, a nonprofit, under-twenty-one club. McCowen, twenty-nine at the time, was drinking outside in the parking lot. He and Frazier broke away from the contest to visit McCowen's former girlfriend, Pamela Maguire, and their daughter in Dennis, some ten miles away.

Welsh played a video of the rap contest on ELMO. McCowen could be seen in white pants and a red athletic top. Next to him was Shawn Mulvey, another Wellfleet-Eastham "gangsta," with a black-and-white bandanna around his head. To Mulvey's right stood Frazier, a blue baseball cap on backward.

McCowen was the first to raise Frazier's name in connection with the case. The two had stayed at Pam Maguire's for about a half-hour, then returned to the Juice Bar where McCowen continued to drink Alizé, a strong cognac-fruit concoction made famous by rappers such as Tupac Shakur and Notorious B.I.G. They'd purchased the Alizé at Windmill Liquors in Orleans en route to Maguire's.

Mason reported that McCowen said, "I don't remember having sex with this lady" as he tapped the DNA report in front of him. He indicated that Frazier had taken him home later that night and that they "drank to blackout, the second time in his life he'd done that."

Mason encouraged him to try to recall even "one small event" from that weekend, anything to trigger his memory. After a moment, McCowen bowed his head and said, "Yeah, fine, I had sex with her."

He said he couldn't remember clearly, though. "Anything could have happened, but I know I didn't kill her."

He was so "piss-ass drunk" he did not remember how he got home. Mason reminded him that he'd earlier said that Frazier drove him home. McCowen said, "That sounds right."

He went on to say, "If I was going to do some stupid shit, I'd be a smart criminal and make sure Christa was alone. And that her kid wouldn't be up to see this shit." He had read or heard that Christa's door had been kicked in, and "that wasn't something that he would do." His "forte," as he put it, was "sex, not kicking in doors."

Nickerson called the lunch recess at 12:59 P.M. Outside in the court-house parking lot and across the street at the Dolphin Restaurant, re-porters compared notes and recalculated the odds. Until Mason, the defense had been ahead. Not so now. Jurors seemed all but entranced.

At two P.M., Nickerson called the parties to sidebar, delivering an update on the hospitalized juror's status. Once more, he complained about the press. During the lunch hour, he'd learned that members of the media had turned up at Cape Cod Hospital, inquiring about the discharged juror's identity and medical condition, a clear viola-tion of the media order. The judge turned from the lawyers to the packed courtroom. "Let me be clear," he roared. "I do not take the breach of the court's orders lightly. Contempt is a remedy. Imprison-ment for the breach of an order is a remedy. Significant fines upon a corporate news organization is a remedy. . . . Offenders will be dealt with appropriately."

Having vented, he called for the jurors.

To maximize Mason's time on the stand, Welsh took the detective back over the first hour of the interview. At the one-hour mark, Mason said, he reminded McCowen that he could use the phone. The de-

fendant said he would make his call later. Instead, he requested cigarettes. As questioning resumed, he purportedly said, "Anyone who is
going to do a crime is going to do it all the way."

Asked to explain, he said, "It's black and white. I never kicked in
anyone's door. If I get turned away for sex, I just leave. I never took
her phone or wallet."

Mason informed the courtroom that he hadn't told McCowen those
items were missing. McCowen continued, saying that "if he had taken
her wallet, he would have used her credit cards and that credit cards
'can tell a lot.'" His friend Matthew Solomini, he explained, was in jail
for credit-card fraud. "A piece of ass is different. Stealing is bullshit."

It would be a waste of time, McCowen repeated, to try to recall
the events of that evening; detectives could check his alibis with Kelly
Tabor, Maguire, and Frazier. He played basketball with Dave Nichols and Dave Arsenault the next day, Saturday. Aside from that, he'd
hung around the house and spent the day smoking pot.

Lieutenant Robert Melia, who'd been in and out of the room
since the start of the interview, delivered McCowen's Newports. Another detective filled a cup from the water dispenser to serve as a
makeshift ashtray. As McCowen continued talking, Mason noticed he
spun the cup with his left hand, rotated the cigarette ember against
the rim with his right, sharpening it like a crayon.

McCowen went on, saying that he and Frazier had stopped to buy
cigarettes. He remembered riding in Frazier's car because of the stereo's thumping bass. Then he said, "If we went to that house, one of
us would have knocked on the door. If we were having sex, I wouldn't
know what Jeremy was doing."

Mason took him back to when he first heard about the murder.
McCowen stated that everybody was "up in arms because this was a
murder," and "murders don't occur in Truro."

When he went to work that Monday, his boss, Don Horton, asked
if he'd ever had sex with Christa Worthington. His response was, "You
fucking crazy?"

McCowen believed Horton asked the question because he knew
McCowen had sex with other women along his trash route.

He admitted that he had not had sex with Worthington at any

time other than that Friday night. Questioned again about how he came to be at Christa Worthington's house, McCowen said only that he had been at the Juice Bar and then "shit happened."

"I told Mr. McCowen that that 'shit happened' part was the part that I was interested in," Mason said. In response, McCowen speculated that if he had sex with Christa Worthington, "then maybe Jeremy would have gone back and done the same thing."

Mason asked, "Well, are you suggesting that Jeremy did the murder?" McCowen said, "No, I'm not suggesting that Jeremy did the murder." Mason said, "I informed him there was no evidence of Jeremy Frazier having had sex with Christa Worthington. In fact, it was his DNA, Mr. McCowen's, that was recovered from the body."

At a later point in the interview, McCowen would insist that Frazier did do the murder.

He told Mason he couldn't remember what happened after he had sex with Christa Worthington but that he knew Jeremy had been there with him and had driven him home.

Had he argued with Worthington? McCowen responded, "I wouldn't waste my time."

Mason testified that McCowen "stated that if somebody told him that they weren't interested in sex, that he was 'fine with that' [and] 'if we're going to have sex, we're going to do it, no ifs, ands, or buts. But if it's no sex, fine.'"

Mason pointed out that he was using the word "if." "I said, you know, we've already established that you had sex with Christa Worthington. And his response was, 'No way I can deny it.'"

"Is that a direct quote, sir?" Welsh asked.

"Yes."

Mason told McCowen it was "the other things . . . besides the sex" he wanted to know about. McCowen replied, "That's something beyond me."

The detective said McCowen knew he had sex that night because the next morning he woke up on the couch at the apartment he shared with Kelly Tabor. His girlfriend "can smell sex," he said, and if he hadn't slept with another woman, he would have climbed into bed with her, not crashed on the couch.

McCowen was talking around the detectives' questions. He said the DNA report was jogging his memory, that Frazier took him to Worthington's and then back home; he wouldn't have driven through Wellfleet for fear of getting busted for OUI. It was probably his idea to go to Worthington's; he didn't think Jeremy knew Christa. McCowen said he'd told his friend, "I know this bitch in Truro who will give up some ass."

"Is that a direct quote, sir?" Welsh asked.

"That is."

From Mason's account, McCowen seemed to alternate between hypotheticals and reality. He said he would have directed Frazier how to park, then said he was too "fucked up" when they arrived and didn't know what time it was. Asked if Christa's daughter was awake, he replied, "No. What kind of person would have a kid up at that time of night?"

For the first time, he admitted he'd been inside the home, telling Mason, "There was a lot of shit everywhere. If I remember correctly, when I walked in the house, I was staggering and weaving and all of that. I guess we had sex right there."

"Right there" was off the kitchen, in the hallway where Christa was later found dead. "He then added that they may have had sex in either a room he described as an office or in the living room," Mason said.

McCowen's vagueness raised questions about his state of mind during the interrogation. He claimed he wanted to clear everything up but Mason had to pry each detail from him; at other times, he seemed reluctant to answer questions at all. One explanation is that he was wasted, as George would repeatedly argue.

When Mason provided the tableau of sex on the kitchen floor, one juror couldn't help herself; she blinked and rolled her eyes toward the ceiling to communicate disgust, perhaps to the Worthington family, perhaps to the other jurors. What she didn't know was that Christa Worthington had a history not simply of promiscuity but of sexual antics. She wrote in her diary of Jackett, "What makes the passion go on like a switch? Facing each other, I do nothing but look at him. I don't make a move. And he comes to me, on me and then down taking off my clothes. . . . He rolls my legs back. . . . I'm helpless . . . exposed with my knees to my chest. And he's at me and there's nothing I can do about it."

She and Jackett had sex outdoors on the dunes near Pilgrim Lake, at Corn Hill, inside the Honda Civic with Christa straddling Tony in the bucket seat, even atop the hood of his car. They squeezed in boat rides up the Pamet River, finding spots to do what they needed to do, both onshore and aboard Tony's tiny skiff amid the tall marsh grass. Jackett liked this sort of thing; he once got pulled over on Route 6 with another woman's head buried in his lap. Christa and McCowen screwing on the floor could not be ruled out.

Unfortunately, George was in a bind defense attorneys often face: bash the victim, you risk losing jurors; fail to bash the victim, you give away points, maybe undo your case.

At Mason's urging, McCowen then sketched a floor plan of the house, correctly locating the kitchen, the hallway, Christa's office to the right of the hallway, and what he described as "some table" to the left. He also wrote the word *door* on the sketch twice, explaining that he did not know what was behind either. Welsh entered the sketch into evidence, then tried to pin down the date McCowen had been inside 50 Depot Road.

"Mr. McCowen stated that he was unsure of the exact date," Mason testified, "but that he knew that it was a Friday and that he knew that it was a Friday after Christmas. And I asked him, 'Well, how is it that you knew those two things?' Mr. McCowen explained to me that he had had a discussion with Christa Worthington that evening . . . about getting rid of the Christmas tree. . . . I then asked Mr. McCowen what happened after he had this discussion with Christa Worthington about the Christmas tree. . . . His response was, 'I fucked the shit out of her.'"

"Is that a direct quote, sir?"

"Yes, it is."

McCowen went on to say that "if Jeremy Frazier went back later in the evening, then that was on him."

For the moment, Mason ignored the comment. He asked again where the sex had occurred. McCowen reportedly stated, "One or the other; office or living room. It had to be on the floor."

"So, in this second rendering of where the sex was," Welsh asked, "he didn't mention that little hallway right off of the kitchen; is that correct?"

"That's correct."

The juror rolled her eyes again; she was going to carry this one right into deliberations, you could tell. None of the Worthingtons stirred.

Mason said the defendant then told him that "if Worthington had wanted him to use a condom, he would have . . . because Christa Worthington was not a 'chicken head.'" The detective paused. "Mr. McCowen then pantomimed oral sex and explained to me that a 'chicken head' was a female that was willing to climb up into the cab of his truck and perform oral sex on him."

He stated that if he had sex with her, it would have been late and that he wouldn't have stayed at the house but would have gone home instead.

When Mason balked at the use of the word *if*, McCowen laughed and said, "After I had sex with her, I went home." Everything had been "cool," he added. He had even given Christa Worthington his phone number as he left.

McCowen admitted he'd arrived in Truro at 1:15 or 1:45 A.M., having stopped for cigarettes at the Eastham Mobil station. When Frazier started going through "her shit," he told Mason, everything stopped being "cool."

Later in the interview, McCowen would identify specific items Jeremy attempted to steal, but now the detective asked him to remember what he could about the actual sex act with Worthington. McCowen answered that "they had had 'straight sex' [which he] described for me as penal-vaginal sex, and indicated that he was on top." McCowen went on to describe it as "masonry style," adding, " 'It didn't take me long to bust a nut.'"

"Masonry style" drew a few titters from spectators that quickly died off as Mason continued. Christa, McCowen reportedly claimed, hadn't been wearing underwear. Also, during the time the two were in the living room, Frazier had been talking on his cell phone.

Asked what led up to sex with Christa, McCowen said, "Whatever, whatever . . . one thing led to another. You can say some clever shit when you're drunk."

Pressed to be more specific, he stated that he "probably said, 'I won't say nothing if you don't say nothing,'" adding he would have said that "because that's the easiest way to get pussy."

Mason appeared tired for the first time, perfectly understandable. His near-robotic memory of the six-hour interview was remarkable; he'd been on the stand most of the day. Welsh showed him the April 14 report to prompt his recollection of McCowen saying he and Frazier left the residence at that point, Frazier driving him home.

Mason's follow-up questions yielded yet another version of the evening's events. Jeremy, McCowen said, was "probably going through her shit" while he and Christa were in the living room. They'd been in the house for one and a half to two hours. As they left, Jeremy's car almost lost its muffler on the bumpy, high-crowned driveway.

"My recollection of what he said is, 'I do have regrets of fucking her, and I'm sorry she's dead. But I don't go around killing people, especially with kids there. If I would have killed her, why would I still be on the Cape?'"

Maybe McCowen, the master spinner who once convinced counselors at a school for troubled youth that he had been raised in a ghetto, not blue-collar, lower middle-class, had started to crack. Or, as George would argue, maybe McCowen was near-retarded, stoned, an eager-to-please man-child.

Mason constantly brought McCowen back to his arrival at the Worthington home. Each time, the suspect revealed more. This time, he said Christa was "startled" when she came to the door, but she knew his name, and he introduced Jeremy. Again, everything was "cool." Maybe Jeremy went back later looking for sex, he said, and she turned him down, leading to the violence.

"He explained to me that . . . he doesn't go crazy if he gets turned down for sex. He told me that 'if she pissed me off, I'd say, "Fuck you, you sorry piece of shit." I never let it get to a point where I would kill.'"

Knowing that Christa had once pulled a knife on former boyfriend Thomas Churchwell, Mason suggested that maybe Christa had attacked McCowen, a mitigating, maybe even exonerating, circumstance.

McCowen said that "wasn't a possibility. . . . If she had come at me with a knife, I would have beat her ass. . . . How would it look if you just had sex with this lady, and she just came at you with a knife?"

Mason asked what items were taken from the house. McCowen repeated that he'd either read or heard that a phone or a wallet was missing. Mason pressed the confrontation angle: perhaps there'd been a misunderstanding between McCowen and Worthington; the FBI believed that such a scenario between Christa and her killer was likely. McCowen said the FBI was "totally wrong."

George requested a sidebar, sensing that Welsh was heading toward McCowen's domestic-violence history. Welsh agreed to skip portions of the report, but George wanted another line excluded: McCowen's alleged statement, "Women are always getting me into trouble."

Welsh argued that it went to the defendant's state of mind: "I think that that does have some bearing, Judge. If he gets rebuffed or rejected, he loses his cool, and then he faults the woman for it."

Nickerson agreed.

Resuming, Mason said that McCowen tried to end his story at that point by once more saying he didn't remember having sex with Christa. The DNA report again brought him back, with Mason commenting that based on everything the detective knew from the scene and from what McCowen had said, he didn't believe he was being truthful.

McCowen protested, saying he wasn't "that kind of person," that he realized this made him "look like a bad guy." Then he stopped, didn't finish the thought. Mason paused, then told McCowen that other troopers were speaking to Jeremy Frazier at that very moment.

"I asked what would he say if those troopers and I determined that Jeremy Frazier was somewhere other than Truro on that evening?"

McCowen replied, "Then it's all on me if Jeremy can account for his time."

The line resonated in the domed courtroom; even the bronzed codfish seemed to be listening. Welsh paused, then had Mason resume his account. Police could obtain cell-phone records, he'd explained, that would show whether Frazier had been in Truro or somewhere else that night. It was a manipulative, skillful move. Dolefully, McCowen answered, "Then there is nothing I can say."

Mason said he asked him "to just tell me the truth, that I wasn't there to judge him." McCowen then told the detective that if Worthington had come at him with a knife, he would have sat on her; he was that much bigger. If he had been really mad, he'd have pushed back. But "none of that happened," he said.

The interview was at the three-hour mark. Again, both detectives told McCowen that they didn't believe he was being truthful.

"Mr. McCowen then informed us that he didn't rape anyone," Mason testified. George interrupted, saying he wanted the answer repeated.

"He didn't rape anyone," Nickerson said forcefully, irritated with the defense attorney's age-old trick.

Mason continued. "Mr. McCowen at that point said, 'She flipped out on Jeremy and did whatever.' He stated that Jeremy Frazier had been going through Christa Worthington's—he described it as 'her shit'—during the period of time that he was having sex, and as they left the residence, Christa Worthington followed them outside, screaming at them . . . about the phone or a wallet or something. . . . Jeremy Frazier turned around suddenly and 'started drilling her.'"

McCowen said he started "yelling at Jeremy Frazier, you know . . . I think it was, 'Fuck it. Let's go.' Or words to that effect." When Christa ran back to her house, Frazier followed.

"So," said the prosecutor, "that's the first version of the story he told you, with a confrontation where one of the two of them does something to Christa Worthington?"

George objected to the form of the question. Nickerson sustained.

Mason explained that McCowen said he asked Frazier whether he'd taken anything, and Jeremy said he hadn't. "Mr. McCowen stated that he then told Christa Worthington, 'This is my boy. If he says he didn't take anything, he didn't take anything.'"

"And did he indicate what he and Jeremy did then?" Welsh asked.

He indicated that he and Frazier left the residence, Christa following. She yelled at Frazier, called him "an asshole." Frazier turned and "punched Christa Worthington twice in the face." She screamed and ran back inside the house.

"Mr. McCowen stated that he and Jeremy then began to make their way toward Jeremy Frazier's vehicle. Mr. McCowen observed Christa Worthington at that time at her front door with a phone to her ear [and] he informed Jeremy Frazier that she was calling the police. And he stated that Jeremy Frazier said, 'Fuck that,' [and] then ran back up to the residence and kicked in the front door."

McCowen claimed he saw all this from the front seat of Frazier's vehicle, where he remained, without going back inside the house. When Frazier returned, McCowen asked what had happened. "He indicated to me that he . . . told Jeremy Frazier at that point, 'Tell me you didn't do anything stupid.'"

At eleven P.M., three and a half hours into the interrogation, pizza and sodas were delivered to the conference room. McCowen took a soda, leaving the pie to Burke and Mason.

Mason again confronted McCowen, saying he was blaming Jeremy Frazier for things he had done and that he had gone to Christa's alone. McCowen denied it. Christa had followed them outside, McCowen in front as he and Jeremy walked toward Frazier's car. Behind him, Christa and Jeremy were arguing. He told them, "Knock it off." But Frazier turned and punched her. "I think his words were 'dead in the face, twice,'" Mason said. She then ran back to her front door, "bitching at them." Frazier, according to McCowen, said, "Fuck this, I'm just going to do her," and went inside "for about ten minutes." When he came out, he stopped, turned around, walked back to the door, and kicked it in.

The day's testimony ended.

For the first time in seven days of trial, jurors had heard evidence linking Christopher McCowen to Christa Worthington's murder— hard, concrete, and persuasive, if Mason's report of the nonrecorded interview could be taken at face value. But they hadn't heard anything about the defendant's record, his stint in a Florida prison for theft, or the five restraining orders taken out against him by frightened, angry girlfriends during his seven years on the Cape. That was about to change.

Day 8, Wednesday, October 25

The ludicrous incident that kicked off trial day eight exceeded any occurrence to date, including the Bermuda-shorts-clad student dragged away in leg irons, the ill juror carted out on a stretcher, even the bizarre panoply of the bereaved, justice-seeking Worthingtons dressed for a J. Crew catalogue photo shoot.

No sooner had Nickerson made his entrance than Welsh approached the bench to report that he and Detective Mason had been stopped by a juror the preceding afternoon outside the district attorney's office. The juror wanted to ask Mason a question; Welsh told her that would be improper, and the two men walked on. The encounter occurred during lunch break, after Mason's first hour of testimony.

No defense attorney wants a juror approaching the prosecution's strongest witness. George reminded Nickerson that the court had instructed jurors twice daily to avoid such contact.

When the jury filed in at 9:10 A.M., Welsh identified the woman. Ever mindful of the record, Nickerson agreed with the defense; an inquiry was warranted. He sent the panel back to the jury room and had the woman brought to the lobby, his private office just outside the courtroom. George said he'd waive McCowen's attendance, but Nickerson refused, believing that McCowen should be at the conference.

Welsh, George, the defendant, the court stenographer, and a bailiff gathered in the judge's lawbook-lined quarters at 9:22 A.M. The room was dimly lit and small, and Nickerson seemed bigger than ever. He urged the juror to take a seat on the couch, the only piece of furniture in the office apart from the judge's desk and chair. The meeting was about to turn into another exercise in something close on imbecility.

"Good morning, Mrs. Tuttle. Thank you for joining us. Don't be upset, please," he said in his most genteel voice. "It's alleged that you had said apparently to the witness who is now on the witness stand, 'Can I ask you a question?' Something to that effect?"

The juror was obviously uncomfortable in such proximity to McCowen, who was standing a half-dozen feet away. There and then, George wanted her ousted.

"That's true, yes," the woman said.

"All right. If you don't mind my asking, what was on your mind at that time? What were you doing?"

"It was so innocent. I had forgotten, honest to God, that my . . . I have a cousin whose husband is a detective on the state troopers over in Framingham. I never thought of it when I was filling out the form, because I don't think I've seen him since maybe his mother-in-law's— my aunt's—funeral, which was ten or fifteen years ago. And what I was going . . . I was just intrigued by the fact he was a detective. And I was going to ask him if he knew him."

"Have you discussed this particular incident at all with your fellow jurors in any way?"

"I don't think I did . . . I was shook enough that I had done it that . . ."

"All right. Were you shook enough that you may not be sure if you talked to your fellow jurors?"

"I'm not sure. I don't . . . if . . . oh, my God, if I did, there's been no . . . no one questioned . . . gave me, asked me anything about. And I apologize to everyone if . . . it was a bad decision or whatever."

A juror, a state trooper's relative, trying to buddy up with the commonwealth's number one witness? But Nickerson didn't discharge the woman on the spot there and then; he continued the inquiry. Had the contact with Mason affected her ability to be "fair and impartial"?

"Absolutely not."

The juror was asked to leave the lobby. George conferred with Mc-Cowen in the secretary's office next door; when the two came back, George reported that the defense wanted the woman dismissed.

Truth be told, he had wanted to bounce her before. Eight days earlier, he'd asked Nickerson to excuse her for cause. A religious conservative, she said during voir dire that she could never be impartial about abortion, cloning, or child abuse, then hesitatingly added that she would feel compassion toward any child whose mother was murdered. Nickerson saw her hesitation as thoughtfulness, not guile, and called her "the salt of the earth."

Welsh asked the judge to retain her, downplaying the juror's disregard of the court's instructions. George said she had lied on her juror questionnaire, then again during voir dire, when asked if she was related to a police officer. "She forgot that she had this relation but suddenly remembered when Mason was testifying?" He was prepared to fight.

"If I were to excuse her," Nickerson said, "I take it you're not asking me to make individual inquiry of each juror as to whether they know anything about this incident?"

"I have to determine whether this case will become undone by the ripple effect of this juror," George replied.

Nickerson paused, thinking, then said, "I'm going to excuse her . . .

as a matter of discretion. We had fifteen jurors. Now we're down to fourteen . . . But that moves us to another concern, which is whether this juror spoke in any way about any of this to her fellow jurors."

George said it wasn't a major issue but that it would do no harm to push a little harder. The juror was summoned again.

The judge asked, "Mrs. Tuttle, I gather this happened somewhere around the noon hour yesterday, did it?"

"Yes."

"OK. I know that jurors as a matter of course tend to form friendships. Did you talk to any of your lunch friends or anybody at all on the jury about this matter?"

"I don't believe I did. I think it was like an instant thing, and then I went, oh, God. And that was it."

Smiling, Nickerson sugar coated the pill: "I can see by looking at you now that you're upset that you did it, Mrs. Tuttle. Don't worry. OK, dear? Please. Now, I am going to excuse you from the jury. Do not discuss this case or the reasons for your dismissal with anybody until after the jury has finished its work."

Mrs. Tuttle looked confused. "Can I tell my husband? He's going to want to know why I'm home."

"Tell your husband that you were excused. And beyond that, you really can't talk about it yet."

"I can't tell him why? I'm just asking so I won't do the wrong thing."

"Just tell your husband that something was said in passing in the hallways . . . and that you'll be sure to fill him in on every single detail as soon as this jury is done with its work."

"Every single detail" could well have included Nickerson's citing the woman for contempt, if not perjury. But the ever-courteous jurist bid Mrs. Tuttle a good day instead.

Nothing was mentioned as to why prosecutor Welsh hadn't reported the incident earlier, right after lunch, before Mason had resumed his testimony.

At 10:14 A.M., with the remaining jurors back in the courtroom, Welsh returned to McCowen volunteering a DNA swab when he knew it would match. Mason repeated McCowen's response: "At first, I didn't remember having sex with that lady; and then I just hoped it would go away."

"And did Sergeant Burke ask the defendant, Christopher Mc-Cowen, something at that point, sir?"

"Yes. Sergeant Burke then asked Mr. McCowen if he felt better having told the police about his involvement. . . . Mr. McCowen's response was that he had been hiding what he referred to as 'this shit' since it happened and [that] it had been an 'up and down battle.'"

"And did he indicate anything about how he was feeling at that point, sir?"

"Yes, he informed Sergeant Burke that he did feel better but that he also felt he was going to be 'screwed.'"

Welsh asked if the defendant explained why Frazier would kill Christa Worthington when he didn't even know her.

"His response, as I recall it, was, 'Probably pissed him off because she was calling nine-one-one. He's got to stop her from talking on the phone.' Mr. McCowen stated that he did not want to be blamed for what had happened. He indicated to me, 'Jeremy did do it. Jeremy is the one who done this.'"

"Did he state something further?"

"Yes, he stated, 'I got my piece of ass, I'm fine. That's on him. I'm the innocent one here.'"

"Did he state something further?"

"Yes, he predicted that Jeremy Frazier would say that he wasn't there and . . . that he didn't do it."

He said he had also seen Jeremy Frazier take something from the house, "a black T-shirt wrapped around something. And indicated to us that he didn't know what was in the T-shirt [or] where it went."

Mason paused, looking away from the jurors and back to Welsh. "He said he felt bad about what had happened to Christa Worthington but also felt that he was in a . . . in his words, 'a Catch-22.' So, I asked Mr. McCowen, 'Well, what was the Catch-22 as he understood it?' And he replied to me that if he had sex, then Jeremy can say he wasn't there."

"That term, the Catch-22, did you supply that to him in your questioning, or did he give you that?" the prosecutor asked.

"He gave that to me."

Roy McCowen, the defendant's father, who was seated in the front row, muttered, "Chris don't know any 'Catch-22.' That man's lying." Several people in the area turned. Welsh, not ten feet away, went on as if he hadn't heard. How did the defendant know Jeremy committed the crime? he asked.

"McCowen told me, 'This is what happened,'" Mason replied. Once more, the defendant said that he and Christa went into the living room and had sex on the floor; then she noticed Frazier coming out of her office and confronted him. Frazier said he was just "checking out" the house. But Christa followed him outside, "yelling and bitching." That's when Frazier "gave her two quick pops." McCowen claimed he said, "Fuck it, let's go," but instead, Frazier hit Christa a few more times, then followed as she ran back to the house.

"Mr. McCowen informed me that he had remained outside and that from his vantage point, he could 'hear a lot of things knocked over inside,'" Mason explained. When Frazier exited the house, McCowen said he saw Christa at the front door, dialing police. He told Frazier, who ran back and kicked in the door.

Mason once more told McCowen that this version of events didn't explain how McCowen knew that Frazier killed Worthington. "His response, as I recall it, was, 'No, I didn't do it. I got kids of my own. There were two people there. I'm not the killer.'"

At that point, Mason said, McCowen told the detectives it was "understandable" that they thought he killed Christa, "but [he] wanted to assure us that he had only had sex. . . . I told Mr. McCowen, as did Sergeant Burke, that we felt that he still had more to say."

Mason shifted from one foot to the other, pacing himself as a Method actor would, pausing to convey thought, emphasis. When he resumed, casting his gaze from one juror to the next, his tone remained steady as he let the cat jump from the bag: "Mr. McCowen stated, 'It was a mistake.' . . . I then asked Mr. McCowen, 'Well, what was a mistake?' . . . His response was, 'I never meant for us to go up there and do what I did.'"

"And *do what I did*?" Welsh repeated.

"That's correct."

"Is that a quote, sir?"

"Yes."

The prosecutor asked the detective to continue. McCowen's story, Mason said, shifted once more. After Jeremy hit Worthington, Mc-Cowen started "firing into her." If his friend was in a fight, he'd alleg-edly explained, he would fight alongside him.

"He stated that Jeremy Frazier then grabbed Christa Worthington under the arms and dragged her inside the residence. . . . He indi-cated that he had to help Jeremy Frazier get Christa Worthington into the kitchen."

Next, according to the witness, the defendant and Frazier wiped down Worthington's body with dishtowels from the kitchen. Mc-Cowen said Frazier pulled a knife from the butcher block on the kitchen stove.

The sequence of events was askew—the wipe-down had to follow the stabbing, not vice versa—but Welsh wasn't concerned. His strut had a new spring to it. He crowded the witness box and urged Mason to supply additional details.

"He stated that he, Mr. McCowen, had stood in the kitchen and watched as Jeremy stabbed Christa Worthington once in the chest. And as he told me," Mason said, raising his arm, "he motioned to his chest, saying, 'The knife came out clean. It wasn't like we got blood all over us.'"

Mason the interviewer did not pounce. He asked McCowen to tell him about the moment when *he* hit Christa; the defendant said he punched her once in the face and gave her "one quick poke to the chest." The dishtowels, he said, were rags from the stove. He didn't know why they wiped the body.

"I asked Mr. McCowen to also tell me more about the knife. Mr. McCowen went on to describe the knife as having a blade length of approximately eight inches, and he described the knife as a 'regular kitchen knife.'"

"And did Mr. McCowen tell you something at that point?" Welsh asked.

"Mr. McCowen stated, 'I never meant for that lady to get killed. It's a nightmare after nightmare. And not a day goes by that I don't think about it.'"

"Did he say anything further?"

"He stated, 'Yeah, I had sex with her. Yeah, I beat her ass, but it was Jeremy that stabbed her.'"

The testimony was rapierlike in its effect on the jurors. Several had turned into zombies, slack-jawed, transfixed by the witness. Even as they questioned McCowen, Mason explained, he and Burke had been picking up notes slipped under the door of the interview room, updates from an interview being conducted simultaneously with Frazier thirty miles away at the Truro police station. Based on this information, Mason told McCowen that neither he nor Burke believed Frazier was at Worthington's residence that evening.

McCowen didn't respond. Mason asked him to review the timeline once more. Again, McCowen recited the sequence of events, this time indicating that when Christa confronted him, Frazier denied being in her office, claiming he had been in the kitchen all the while. McCowen told Mason he had to take Frazier's side. "This is my boy." Christa was "just somebody I'm fucking." When the two left, Christa yelled after them, calling Frazier a "fucking asshole." Frazier yelled back, "Fuck you, bitch. Stupid cunt." Then Jeremy lost it, and, McCowen explained, "we put the boots to her."

McCowen told the detective he was wrong about Christa having grass in her hair; her head didn't hit the grass. Her head hit the gravel driveway "so hard," he said, "that he could still hear it to this day."

Then they dragged her inside the house.

"At that point," Mason testified, "Mr. McCowen stated, 'The next thing I know, he grabs a knife from the block.'"

After the stabbing, McCowen noticed Frazier carrying the black T-shirt. In a previous account, he'd said he didn't know what was wrapped in the shirt, but this time, he said it covered a phone, a wallet, and the knife. Frazier tossed the items into the backseat. McCowen said he didn't know why he'd taken them.

It was just past midnight, almost five hours into the interview. According to Mason, McCowen had begun the evening saying he had never been inside Christa's house. He'd since admitted he had sex with her, witnessed Frazier strike her, helped his friend beat her and drag her inside, then stood by as Frazier stabbed her with a kitchen knife. The detectives pressed on.

McCowen told them he watched *CSI* and *NYPD Blue*, and he knew that "the shitheads that do these things always call for a lawyer." He hadn't done that; he was cooperating. "And he wanted to assure me," Mason said, "he had not committed this murder. . . . I told Mr. McCowen that while I appreciated his cooperation, I didn't believe him."

With this, McCowen decided he should call his lawyer. At 12:09 A.M., Mason escorted him to the phone in the booking area. McCowen got attorney Nicholas Grefe's voice mail and left a message.

Police had retrieved the attorney's office number for him; it's unlikely anyone looked up Grefe's home number. Arguably, the interrogation should have stopped at that point. But as McCowen was fingerprinted, he told police he was not done talking, that he wanted to clear everything up. "It beats being in a cold cell," he allegedly said. The detectives were happy to oblige.

Back in the conference room, Sergeant Robert Knott took over alongside Burke, while Mason spoke by phone with the troopers grilling Frazier. Fifteen minutes later, Mason returned to the conference room and hurled another hand grenade.

"I informed Mr. McCowen that I had spoken with the troopers that were speaking with Jeremy Frazier and that it sounded like Jeremy Frazier had people that were going to be able to verify his whereabouts . . . somewhere other than Truro that evening."

It was 12:40 A.M. Protocol dictated an additional advisory as the interview's six-hour mark approached. McCowen was advised of his rights to prompt arraignment, to an attorney, and to a probable-cause hearing before a judge or magistrate within twenty-four hours. "No statement I make six hours or more after my arrest will be accepted by court unless I waive my right to prompt arraignment," the form stated. McCowen waived it.

Welsh jumped ahead to 1:15 A.M., when McCowen asked to phone a girlfriend, Callie Duryea. Mason recalled, "I heard him say, 'Hey, they got me for that murder.' And then there was a pause. And he added, 'In Truro.'"

The detectives again pressed McCowen to say more. He "responded that he had told us everything and encouraged us to go ahead and test the knives that we recovered at his house and to test his vehicle," Mason declared.

The knives proved benign. And McCowen's white Nissan 240SX, long since junked and "parted out," provided nothing. The green Ford Escort belonging to his then-girlfriend Kelly Tabor was traced to a Middleboro salvage yard, but it, too, had been sold for parts.

The interview ended at 1:35 A.M., after McCowen said they could stay there all night, his story wouldn't change. He was booked and photographed. On the mandatory suicide-watch form, he indicated that he'd taken two Percocets that afternoon for knee pain. Mason stressed that McCowen did not appear to be under the influence of alcohol or narcotics.

After morning recess, Welsh revisited the impairment issue. In addition to the Percocets, marijuana was recovered from McCowen's bedside table at 63 Lafrance. Again, Mason stressed that the defendant was lucid and sober.

The twenty-seven-page statement was not all the prosecution had to offer. McCowen drew sketches that night, and Welsh produced the one that showed where McCowen customarily parked his garbage truck outside the Worthington residence. On the back side, another sketch depicted where Frazier lived.

Welsh also was armed with taped phone conversations between McCowen and girlfriends Callie Duryea and Catherine Cisneros while awaiting trial at the Barnstable County House of Corrections, a period of more than a year and a half. Conversations between prisoners and visitors are routinely recorded, and ever-diligent Mason had retrieved three: May 7, 2005; May 31, 2005; and July 16, 2006. In the July 16 tape, McCowen, in a thick Southern accent, revealed that he had Tabor's car that evening at the Juice Bar and later at an after-party in nearby Eastham. Throughout the twenty-seven-page statement, Mason had him saying he had been in Frazier's vehicle.

Welsh turned away from the witness stand, leaving the detective to the energies of George's cross. Those in the courtroom knew the twenty-seven-page statement was critical. But which parts were true? George needed to make small, important points, not tear the likable Mason apart.

No version of events recited in the typed statement was entirely plausible. The prosecution's theory that McCowen raped Christa in the hallway where she was stabbed simply didn't jibe with any account. Nor was the thesis tenable that Christa was dragged, presumably unconscious, to the hallway; it was unlikely that the perpetrator would have bothered. Moreover, the ground outside was frozen and embedded with shards of pulverized Cape Cod clamshell, but Christa's lower extremities weren't cut or abraded, as they would have been if she'd been dragged, presumably.

Harriet Ryan, reporting for Court TV's website, called the statement "a complicated piece of evidence" and said that "neither the prosecution nor the defense believes what McCowen told the trooper is the truth." George intended to use the statement's inconsistencies to negate its credibility: McCowen had been steered through it by a police officer desperate to solve the case. What neither George nor Ryan could have known is that within a year, Mason would be promoted to the rank of sergeant and, fifteen months later, to lieutenant.

"Is it fair to say that Mr. McCowen told you twelve different versions of events?" George began.

"I think in my count it's eight, but . . ." Every version contained portions the detective believed and portions he did not believe, he explained. No single version was plausible in its entirety. He'd come to this view based on "my common sense, my experience and training, and what I know about the crime scene."

An outside struggle was plausible, as was the theory that Christa was dragged into the house. But "I can't say what the exact mechanism of the crime was or what the exact chronology of the crime is. I can only say that I'm aware that Christa Worthington was beaten, that she was stabbed."

Citing the autopsy report, George asked if the investigator knew there was no debris in Christa's hair other than grass, that her feet were clean, that there was no bruising about her ankles or lower legs. Other than the bruise to the knee, Mason agreed.

George asked if he found it plausible that Christa Worthington "had come out of the house while Ava was sleeping inside to confront a two-hundred-pound black man and his associate in the dead of night?"

Mason said he had "no way of knowing."

Was it plausible that she came outside "bitching at McCowen or bitching at Frazier?"

"Well, I would only point out that those aren't my words."

"I was trying to straighten that out," George said, an edge to his voice. When McCowen said that Christa Worthington had come out of the house bitching at them, did the detective find *that* claim believable?

Welsh objected. Nickerson let George continue.

Question after question, Mason skirted the plausibility issue, saying he had no way of knowing how Christa would react to a late-night visitor. He admitted that her going outside to confront two men wasn't all that likely.

George needed to nail down the fact that the DNA match proved only that McCowen had sex with the victim. Sex. Not rape.

Mason acknowledged that the only thing that changed between McCowen's first two interviews and the last was the DNA report. McCowen's denials of any physical contact contributed to his arrest.

"So the lie alone about not knowing Christa Worthington and the DNA report is what caused you to arrest him?" George asked.

"That's correct."

"Then you went right out and arrested him for murder the next day?"

"Based upon that information, the DNA hit, and the previous two interviews, we sought and applied for a murder warrant for Christopher McCowen, which was issued by this court," Mason replied, in a tone he might have used to describe his annual tax return.

George would return to that issue later. He asked the detective about Tim Arnold, Keith Amato, Thomas Churchwell, and the Jackett family.

At the time of McCowen's arrest, Mason was aware that Arnold's semen had been found on the brown blanket. Asked if hairs found on Christa's body were consistent with Arnold as well, he said only that hairs were recovered at the scene; their origin was uncertain.

Other factors pointed to Arnold: the ranting, addled messages he'd left on Christa's voice mail, the pair's rocky relationship, his comment to Burke and Mason demonstrating that he knew where

Christa had been stabbed, the blanket sperm and possible hair matches. George walked Mason through each.

"Did you ask Arnold if he killed Christa Worthington?"

"Yes, I did."

"And did he say to you, as Mr. McCowen did seventeen or eighteen times, 'I did not kill Christa Worthington'? Did he tell you that?"

"Mr. Arnold claimed that he did not kill Christa Worthington, yes."

Had Mason or Burke raised their voices with either Arnold or McCowen? Mason said they had not. Hadn't they told Arnold that his actions and statements were consistent with someone involved in the murder? Hadn't they encouraged Arnold, as they had McCowen, to "just be truthful" about his involvement?

"That's correct," Mason answered. "I told him if he was involved in her death that this was the time to be truthful."

"Did Arnold then deny any involvement?"

"Yes."

"Did you believe him?"

"No."

When the detective acknowledged that he had not arrested Tim Arnold, George roared back at him, "Well, his DNA was at the scene, wasn't it? Actually, his semen was at the scene, wasn't it?"

"His semen was at the scene," Mason answered dryly.

"And his hair was at the scene, wasn't it?"

"He had a prior relationship with Miss Worthington and actually had lived in the home, yes."

George asked him to pinpoint the moment when Arnold was eliminated as a suspect.

The witness was as formidable as ever. Arnold was ruled out, Mason said, only after McCowen admitted that he had sex with Christa, "beat her ass," and tried to finger Jeremy Frazier.

George continued to probe the double standard. "Did Tim Arnold ever admit to having sex with Christa Worthington?"

"Yes, he did."

"Did he say it was consensual sex?"

"He indicated it was consensual sex on the couch in the residence."

"Did you believe him?"

"Yes."

"How come when Chris McCowen told you he had consensual sex with her, you didn't believe him?"

"Well, I found the circumstances of his coming to have consensual sex with Christa Worthington to be unbelievable." Christa was beaten and stabbed, her legs spread, the witness continued. "I was concerned about his story that he had never known Christa Worthington, had never spoken to Christa Worthington, but yet went to her house at two in the morning, a stranger in a drunken condition with another stranger, knocked on her door, and said something like, 'I'm tipsy. I just wanted to get some ass real quick.' And that her body would be found in that condition later. Those things didn't lead me to believe that the sex was consensual. That and his track record for having lied throughout the course of not only the first two interviews but the third."

It was a good answer. But it didn't address the dilemma faced by any black man being grilled by two cops in the middle of the night about sexual congress with a white woman: the sure, atavistic, passed-from-father-to-son knowledge that the blood-drenched history of American lynchings has always rested on the subtext of black "rape."

The reply also ignored Frazier, how investigators looked the other way and discarded "Wu's" presence at the murder scene.

"And you were also aware that there was no evidence whatsoever, physical evidence, of rape in this case, weren't you?" George asked.

"Well, rape or sexual trauma?"

"Was there *any* evidence of tearing, bruising, anything of that nature in this case?"

"No," Mason conceded.

"Was there any physical evidence in the autopsy report that she had been violently assaulted, vaginally?"

"Strictly vaginally?"

"Yes, sir."

"No."

After the break, George reminded Mason that Dr. Weiner, the medical examiner, placed the time of death at twenty-four to thirty-six hours before the body was found. He asked if the detective had investigated Saturday's events. Mason said they interviewed Tony

Jackett, who'd driven by the house that morning, and also talked to Truro resident Girard Smith. George would return to Smith later.

Mason acknowledged that police never inquired about McCowen's whereabouts on Saturday.

"Is that because you believed Mr. McCowen was guilty and you didn't need to do that?" George asked.

Mason said he felt that McCowen's Saturday activities weren't relevant.

George shifted gears abruptly, a tactic he thought might throw hyperorganized Mason off balance. He moved away from the witness box, repositioning himself behind McCowen's chair at the defense table, forcing Mason to look away from the jurors.

"Trooper," he said, "Mr. McCowen was telling you a story that was different from the medical evidence in the case, wasn't he?"

"No, I think Mr. McCowen's version of the events was in some ways consistent with the medical examiner's report insofar as he indicated that he had punched Christa Worthington once in the face. And I noted that the autopsy report showed abrasions and contusions to the face."

Mason conceded that the medical examiner placed the time of death at about eight A.M. on Saturday the fifth.

"Mr. McCowen was telling you about an event that occurred much earlier than that, wasn't he?" George asked.

"Hours earlier."

"Were you aware of the condition of the sperm found on Christa Worthington at the time you interviewed Mr. McCowen?"

"Yes."

Asked if he'd researched how long sperm might be present in a human body after sex, Mason replied, "No, I relied upon Mr. McCowen's statement as to when that sperm was deposited."

George slapped back. At the time, did the detective know anything about McCowen's educational background, his upbringing, his retarded mother, or his epilepsy, causing grand-mal seizures to the age of fifteen?

No, Mason said. He took McCowen at his word when he said he understood his rights during arrest and interrogation.

Mason acknowledged that no audio or videotape was made of the interview and that the twenty-seven-page report took eight days to put together. He'd typed it himself, he said, based on his notes from the interview.

"And it contains exact quotes, doesn't it?"

"Yes, it does."

"And the exact quotes were from your memory, just as you testified here today from your memory without notes?"

"The exact quotes are contained in the notes."

George knew the claim was questionable. Even the most experienced news reporters, several he'd checked with, say that taking accurate, complete notes while simultaneously conducting a six-and-a-half-hour interview is nearly impossible without a tape recorder. But he let it go, moving on to McCowen's sobriety. At the motions hearings in July, Catherine Cisneros testified that on the day of the arrest, her boyfriend had nothing to eat until she took him to Burger King after one P.M. There was no food in his house for dinner that evening, either. Cisneros was scheduled to testify later.

Mason said police had McCowen under surveillance for three days before the arrest. During the first two, he worked at Allied Moving in Hyannis; the day of arrest, he went to Burger King with Cisneros, returning at around two P.M. He did not leave his building again. McCowen was watching the cartoon channel, wearing headphones, at the time of his arrest.

George produced photos of McCowen's room, prodding the witness to point out three or four marijuana roaches and a pipe in the ashtray on the bedside table, alongside a Percocet bottle. According to police inventory, a bag of pot was found elsewhere in the room.

Did McCowen understand his situation? George asked. Mason admitted that he did not know whether McCowen could read or write but insisted that he'd told the defendant he was under arrest for murder inside the cruiser and then again when they arrived at State Police barracks.

Yet McCowen had wanted "to clear things up," even five and a half hours into the interview? George asked rhetorically. Had McCowen ever wavered from his statement that sex with Christa was consensual, that she was "cool with it"?

Mason conceded that he had not.

George suggested that McCowen actually had sex with Christa the day before, Thursday, while on his trash route. He asked Mason to recall the defendant's statement about hauling her Christmas tree. "He said he actually was sitting with her in her living room talking about it before they had consensual sex in his version of events?"

"Yes, that they had a discussion about the Christmas tree."

George knew McCowen had been at 50 Depot Road on January 3. He showed Mason time cards obtained from Don Horton, the defendant's boss at Cape Cod Disposal.

The courtroom audience listened intently, as if the next question or two would prove dispositive.

"And if McCowen was at Christa Worthington's house on Thursday picking up the garbage and called in for the Christmas tree, that wouldn't affect your opinion of this case, would it? In terms of his involvement in the death. Would it?"

Welsh objected.

At sidebar, George told the judge he had learned through Horton's attorney that Horton had received a call that week about picking up a Christmas tree but could not recall the specific address. The call mostly likely came in during McCowen's shift, supporting his claim that he'd been inside the house and, ultimately, the Thursday sex scenario.

Welsh called it "totem-pole hearsay," one person's story atop another's. Nickerson gave George latitude.

The defense lawyer asked whether McCowen told the detective he discussed picking up the Christmas tree on Thursday, January 3, or that he had sex with Worthington that afternoon.

Mason shook his head.

"But he did tell you that he had consensual sex with Christa Worthington on the living-room floor after a conversation with her about her Christmas tree on Friday, January 4, going into the fifth?"

"Yes," Mason conceded. Although he didn't acknowledge it, he knew that McCowen's peccadilloes along his garbage route had made him something of a legend.

After recess, George got the detective to admit that McCowen often backtracked through the interview. The idea was to plant the notion that perhaps the Christmas-tree tryst was off by a day and that Mason and Burke intentionally got McCowen to tell a different version of events by saying that they didn't believe him.

He asked the witness to consider a hypothetical: McCowen came to 50 Depot Road at 2:30 P.M. to pick up garbage, then conversed with Christa about the tree.

Welsh objected. Nickerson called a sidebar. He wanted to know the rest.

George posited Thursday afternoon as the time McCowen and Worthington had consensual sex; he wanted to know if Mason could find this consistent with the version of events that he believed was true.

"How would you establish that he had sex with her on Thursday?" Nickerson asked.

That's what McCowen told Eric Brown, a defense psychologist, George explained, a statement admissible under the "state of mind" exception to the hearsay rule.

Nickerson wasn't so sure. "I see problems in that area . . . so, I'm not going to let you just fly into this. If you've got some cases you want me to read, I'd be happy to look at them."

George temporarily abandoned this topic and instead got Mason to agree that no sperm or DNA from McCowen was found in the living room, nor was there any sign of a struggle inside the house. No murder weapon was recovered, no fingerprints from McCowen, no wallet or purse, no black T-shirt, no black fleece pants. In the last version of McCowen's statement, Frazier knocked Christa unconscious outside, dragged her inside the kitchen, and stabbed her. In the next-to-last version, Frazier kicked in the door and walked out with the items. Had the defendant ever described the purse or the phone? Mason said he had not.

Did Mason ask McCowen what he'd heard or read about the case?

Yes, the detective answered, "when I asked him how did he know the phone and wallet were taken from the house, he indicated that he had read or heard it."

George mentioned a press release issued by the DA's office more than a year after the murder; it never mentioned rape. "And at that time, did you have any evidence that Christa Worthington had been sexually traumatized? In other words, was there any physical evidence of rape?"

"Physical evidence, no."

George asked how concerned investigators were about the time of death. Her last known contact, Mason reported, was at eight P.M. on January 3, when she spoke to a babysitter named Linda Schlecter. Asked whether or not Christa was alive on Saturday, Mason answered that she'd missed her noon hair appointment.

"And missing a hair appointment doesn't necessarily mean she was dead at that time, does it?"

"That's correct."

George reminded Mason that the autopsy report suggested a later time of death and that the condition of the sperm indicated an earlier sexual encounter.

Then he moved on to evidence that would have turned the tide in almost any other case in any other county. He directed Mason's attention to Girard Smith, the local who saw a vehicle pull out of Christa's driveway on Saturday afternoon, January 5.

Welsh objected: hearsay. George rephrased the question.

Mason explained that Trooper Squier had done a registry check on all black trucks between Orleans and Provincetown. Smith claimed that the vehicle was "dark," and its license plate began with "16," "17," or "18." Some of the people they'd already interviewed owned black vehicles. Keith Amato was one, Mason said. And Tony Jackett's pickup was dark purple.

"Now, based upon your theory of the case, Christa Worthington was dead at that time, wasn't she?"

"Well, my theory of the case is based upon Mr. McCowen's statement that he saw Jeremy Frazier stab Christa Worthington on that evening. So . . ."

"So, based on the theory of the case you're proposing to the jury, Christa Worthington was dead Saturday afternoon? She was lying on the floor of her kitchen?"

"On Saturday afternoon?"

"Right."

"Possible, yes."

Mason agreed that he had not gone back to review the trucks after McCowen's arrest. George asked if investigators knew that "a vehicle registered to Jeremy Frazier's father or his company" was on the list.

Mason did not.

George directed his attention to a 1988 GMC truck registered to Matthew A. Frazier Enterprises Inc. on the DMV list and asked, mistakenly, if Matthew was Jeremy's father.

Mason knew the father as "Froggy."

George asked whether Frazier's parents sat in on the first interview.

Mason claimed he didn't know. He hadn't conducted that interview; he'd been busy at the time with McCowen.

When George moved the list into evidence, Welsh objected, calling it hearsay. At sidebar, Nickerson scoffed, wondering if the prosecutor would require the registry's keeper of records to testify. Welsh said he wasn't worried about authenticity; he was worried about relevance. George hadn't laid a proper foundation.

At that point, just before calling it a day, the wily old defense lawyer in Gary Nickerson came to the fore. "Well, I would tend to think that we're going to have Mr. Frazier on the stand himself, aren't we?" he said, sending a knowing smile George's way.

"Yes, Your Honor."

"So, mark it for identification," he said, glancing back at Welsh, "and we'll see if he can tie it in."

Day 9, Thursday, October 26

The twinkle in Nickerson's eye was gone. Overnight, the judge learned a *48 Hours* cameraman had filmed a juror at the front door of the courthouse at lunch on Wednesday, another "transgression" that offended both the judge's pride and his granitelike Yankee sense of order. He summoned a CBS representative to the dock.

"You are?" he asked the middle-aged producer of the network tabloid.

"Martin Zyde," the man answered. In a New York accent, Zyde explained that his cameraman was shooting general footage of people exiting the courthouse when he mistakenly filmed the juror. The cameraman had arrived just the day before, unaware of the court's media restrictions.

Nickerson paused, then advised Zyde to contact the CBS legal department and ordered the producer and his cameraman to appear in court at three P.M. the next day. "The court will be considering contempt proceedings," he announced. "Contempt proceedings may include punitive measures such as incarceration or fines and other appropriate remedies." In the interim, all camera equipment connected to CBS and its affiliates was to be removed from courthouse premises.

Zyde was, as they say, in deep shit.

At 9:10 A.M., jurors were back in their seats, and George picked up where he left off: the black truck. Mason had testified that he was aware that Amato owned a black Ford Bronco, and Tony Jackett had a dark Toyota pickup. George asked the detective to scan the list for those names. Mason struggled.

"I know you don't have to take my word for it, Trooper, but if I told you that Jackett's and Amato's names aren't on that list, would you take my word for it?"

Courtroom spectators laughed when Mason responded, "Yeah. Sure, I'll take your word for it, sir."

The Bronco didn't qualify as a truck, and the Toyota was dark purple; neither had come up in the search. But Smith would later testify that he wasn't certain the vehicle leaving Christa's driveway was actually a truck.

George asked whether the black trucks on the DMV list were investigated further, whether any names jumped out at the detective. Mason said investigators kept the list in mind as they interviewed people. "We were aware of whether they did or did not have a black vehicle."

"So, after Jeremy Frazier's name came to your attention in April of 2005, did you go back to the list and check it out again?"

"No, we did not go back to this list. We would have run a registry check on Jeremy Frazier to see if he had had a black vehicle at that time. . . . We didn't conduct checks of his extended family."

George returned to the truck registered to Matthew Frazier Enterprises. Both men had done their homework the night before. George now knew that Matthew Frazier was Jeremy's uncle, known locally as "Bubba." Mason knew that Matthew was the uncle, a landscaper who ran a septic and porta-potty business. Jeremy's father, "Froggy," was in landscaping, too.

The nicknames bounced around the courtroom as if the trial was taking place on some backwoods bayou on Lake Pontchartrain in Louisiana, not Yankee Cape Cod. Even Nickerson smiled despite his lingering displeasure with CBS.

George was visibly delighted at this state of affairs. "Just so the jury is clear," he repeated, "Froggy Frazier is Michael Frazier, Jeremy Frazier's father, right? That's his nickname, *Froggy*?"

Mason testified that he spoke to "Bubba" after court the day before and was told that Jeremy would not have had access to his uncle's vehicles. The 1988 GMC truck in question was currently at a repair shop in Orleans.

"Do you plan to do any forensic testing on it today or before Jeremy Frazier testifies?" George asked. Mason said no.

Asked whether he knew of Jeremy Frazier before McCowen's April 14 interview, Mason replied, "I can only say that Jeremy Frazier was not known to me personally."

His answer was less than candid. Frazier had a record, and police incident reports of January 2002 showed that McCowen had fingered Jeremy as a Wellfleet dealer. Mason had to know about him. It was vital to the prosecution.

"Was he connected in any way with any member of the investigation team in terms of having been arrested before?" George asked. "Or was he an informant of any kind?"

Welsh objected. "Sidebar, gentlemen," Nickerson ordered.

George pounced. "I could word it differently, Your Honor, but I have documents . . . that suggest that Frazier was an informant on the arrest of Shawn Mulvey that occurred in May of 2002. Now, Shawn Mulvey was arrested for selling Ecstasy . . . I think that's a Class C . . . as a result of an undercover operation. . . . When Mulvey was interviewed in this case in May of '05 and then again in July of '05 . . . one of the things Mulvey says to the police is . . . 'I feel awfully strange about alibi-ing Frazier, since he's the one that set me up on that drug bust that I got arrested for before I left for Florida' . . . and I don't want to tip my hand at sidebar, but I can tell you as an officer of the court . . . that Frazier did have a connection with the State Police in South Yarmouth prior to McCowen bringing up his name. And therefore, that is why he would have been cleared in this so easily on basically his word alone. So you know, Frazier was put into the grand jury on this case on June 14, 2005."

At that point, George explained, police already knew that Mulvey had refused to back up Frazier's alibi. A month later, after Frazier testified before the grand jury, Mulvey did a U-turn, giving Frazier the alibi he needed.

"Listen," George went on, brandishing a copy of one of the police reports naming Frazier as a dealer, "it's a very powerful argument for the defense—that they have tailored their case to make sure that Mc-Cowen is the one and only one that committed this crime. But I'm just asking general questions. I don't intend to go very far down this road. I just want him to say what I believe he will say: No, there was no connection between Frazier and this investigation prior."

Welsh countered that George's reference to Frazier's arrests was "an attempt to start a smear campaign" and that "the business of Frazier being an informant" was privileged.

But the privilege is not absolute, the judge pointed out.

"Right," Welsh said weakly.

It's subject to breach, "depending upon a defendant's need—"

"Certainly," Welsh said.

"—for the information in the course of his defense," the judge finished.

Welsh's interruptions suggested that the commonwealth's case was in meltdown. If George could prove that Frazier lied before the grand jury, the indictment against McCowen was void. Without a valid indictment, the trial was over.

Welsh tried to regroup. "I don't have a problem with it if the court takes that position. It's been said a couple of times, the commonwealth . . . wants to be fair to Mr. George. But what is given in discovery does not necessarily make it admissible. I mean, that's just so that he has all the information about the case."

The commonwealth's compliance with the rules of discovery was another land mine, and it was ready to blow. Hurriedly, Welsh insisted that Frazier was "not a drug guy." But he was. George knew it. And so did the prosecutor.

"I want you to understand, Your Honor," George snapped, "I knew what I could get in through this witness because I know what reports he's signed and what reports he hasn't signed."

Nickerson nodded, ending the discussion. George went back to Mason, who said he was unaware of any connection between the Massachusetts State Police and Frazier before McCowen named him on April 14 and that he was "not aware that Jeremy Frazier has ever been in contact with any of the investigators connected to this investigation."

There was a long pause. "Would that be an important factor in determining whether or not Frazier was telling the truth when he was first interviewed in this case?" George asked.

"That would all be subject to what the level of contact was."

"Well, say the contact was on the night of January 5 in the early morning hours, say about 12:03 A.M. on January 5, which is about the time McCowen said he and Frazier were up at the house. Would that be important?"

"If he had contact with one of the investigators?" Mason stalled, repeating the question.

"With the Massachusetts State Police?"

"With the Massachusetts State Police or the investigators?"

"Yes," George said.

"Including both those groups, yes, that would be important to know," Mason replied, looking George directly in the eye.

Courtroom spectators were riveted, straining forward in their seats. George took a temporary detour, going to the Truro DNA dragnet that took place on the third anniversary of the murder. Investigators swabbed 150 to 200 men, Mason testified. But it wasn't until three months later, on April 7, 2005, that authorities met with the crime lab to discuss processing. McCowen's match came back that very day.

Mason also acknowledged that he had gone through hundreds of pages of phone records and traced a dozen people's calls, among them Christa, Tim Arnold, Tony Jackett, and Keith Amato. When an unfamiliar number came to light, police tried to identify it. An unfamiliar number in Jackett's records led police to seize the business and personal phone records of this author, for example.

George moved back to the DNA report connecting McCowen to Christa: "You didn't know whether the deposit of DNA on Christa Worthington's body was the result of consensual sex or forcible sex, did you?"

"That's correct," Mason responded, adding that McCowen's repeated denial that he'd known her led to his suspicions.

George asked why Chris McCowen wasn't afforded "the luxury" of being interviewed, as were Tim Arnold and others, as opposed to being arrested.

"I would say that there were other things that I considered," Mason answered cagily.

"And yesterday you told us that the three . . . well, actually, the two lies about knowing Christa Worthington and the DNA report caused you to have him arrested? Isn't that what you told us yesterday?"

"Those items and the items that were contained in my arrest affidavit caused me to seek an arrest warrant for Mr. McCowen."

Mason was at his very best. He couldn't go anywhere near McCowen's "prior bad acts," the court had ruled, but he could wait and hope that George would ask a question that would "open the door."

George turned back to Mason's twenty-seven-page report, completed eight days after McCowen's interview. "Was it ever brought back to Chris McCowen for him to read to see if he agreed with what you were reporting?"

"No," Mason said. "At that point, Chris McCowen had been appointed counsel."

"And during the course of the interview, you told us that he told you a great many different versions of events? You say eight, I say twelve."

"That's correct."

"Approximately how many times during that interview did he tell you he did not kill Christa Worthington?"

"I would have to look at the report to actually count them up."

"If I told you it was sixteen times, would that be more than your memory recalls? Or less?"

"That would be more."

"And how many times did Chris McCowen tell you that he may have had sex with Christa Worthington but he didn't rape her?"

"He indicated that once."

Abruptly, Nickerson interrupted, his eyes on George, beckoning the attorneys to sidebar.

"Did you hear someone in the audience say something?" the judge asked.

George said he heard someone in the gallery say, "Object! Object!"

"That's what I heard," Nickerson replied. "I'm going to send the jury out, and I will address the audience—"

Welsh stopped him, holding up his hand. By insinuating that all Mason had on McCowen were the two denials about knowing Christa and the DNA report, Welsh said, George had opened the door to prior-bad-acts evidence. Mason had testified that there was more in his affidavit.

George shook his head, flailing against the prospect of Welsh delving into McCowen's record.

Nickerson paused, then agreed with the prosecutor. "He gets the question on redirect as to what this officer knew as his basis for going forward to take this man in without interviewing him."

There it was. A defense catastrophe.

The restraining orders against McCowen and all of the evidence supporting them had become fair game: the defendant's slapping women, his screaming, his smashing girlfriends' furniture in the middle of the night. Nickerson's call appeared just, although George would later assert that he'd been set up.

Worse, the cluster was twofold. As the defense attorney asked the question of Mason, he had been rummaging through his file in search of a letter Christa Worthington had written, but hadn't sent, to Tony Jackett's wife. George wanted it and Mason's response to it firmly on the record. It read:

"Dear Mrs. Jackett,
      From Sept to the day your mother in law died I was sleeping

with your husband. I just thought you should know . . . he stopped
by after dropping Luke off in Hyannis . . . We went to bed . . . He
would say he was going roller blading on a Sat. He was gone for
four hours—he was with me having sex. He would say he was just
going to check the boat and he'd be checking/fucking me. I saw
him 4 to 5 times a week . . . He fell in love with me. The first day we
slept together we were in bed from 11 AM to 7 PM. He said he'd
never spent the entire day in bed with a woman before. There
is a curve to his anatomy. And when he comes he makes a sweet
whimper . . ."

Christa then added, "Early on he gave me your phone number.
I was surprised he would do that. 'You can call me. There's nobody
home in the day.' I never called."

The letter was something of a shocker, but George had failed to
bring it to court that morning, forgotten it, with the result that the
jury never got a glimpse of this side of Worthington. Later, the grav-
ity of the omission would become apparent. Now Nickerson's ruling
opened the door to damning evidence.

The judge took up the matter of the outburst. It had come not from
some anonymous nut case but from Toppy Worthington, Christa's
seventy-year-old father. Peering down, Nickerson asked Worthington
how he was connected to the case; whether the judge was feigning or
not was unclear.

"I'm Christopher Worthington, father of the victim," Toppy answered pompously, as if oblivious to the dirt that had been published
about him and his heroin-addicted girlfriend. To his left, family members sat shoulder-to-shoulder, like birds perched nervously on a wire.
None had made the slightest gesture toward McCowen's father and
stepmother, fellow victims in this tragedy, seated not ten feet away. It
was difficult to tell whether the clan was with Toppy or saw him as an
unpardonable embarrassment.

"All right. Let me be clear to you, sir. You have no right to speak out
during this trial," Nickerson chastised. "You have no right as a question

is being made to say 'Objection, objection.' It was audible. I heard it. One of the counsel heard it. If you repeat that conduct, sir, you will be forfeiting your right to attend this trial. Do you understand?"

Worthington, chopped down to size, sat down as the judge called a brief recess. Throughout his career, Nickerson had carefully protected his record, and when he came back from chambers ten minutes later he backpedaled on the restraining orders; he would admit them on a limited basis only, to allow the prosecution "appropriate inquiry" into Mason's reasons for proceeding to arrest without interviewing first.

George objected to *any* mention of the restraining orders. The judge shook his head. "Unfortunately, you've made your own bed, Mr. George."

At 10:41 A.M., the jury was back. With slightly less spring in his step, George moved forward with a new line of attack, one he'd adopted during pretrial motions in July. At the time of McCowen's arrest, was Trooper Mason aware that the thirty-three-year-old garbage collector had been an informant for the Cape Cod Drug Task Force?

Mason, again shifting from foot to foot with an almost uncanny rhythm, said he was not. Since that time, he'd learned "that on one occasion, Mr. McCowen met with officers from the Wellfleet Police Department and a Mashpee officer that was assigned to the Cape Cod Drug Task Force."

George knew the answer was nonsense. McCowen had been snitching to the Wellfleet police, then to the Cape Cod Drug Task Force (a State Police unit) since the late 1990s. Mason knew that George knew that he knew. It was part of the game. But who could prove what?

Mason acknowledged that the Cape Cod Drug Task Force was headquartered in Barnstable County, led by his own commanding officer, Detective Lieutenant John Allen. He also admitted that Officer John Santangelo "is known to me as a Mashpee police officer" and that he was now aware that Santangelo met with McCowen on January 7, 2002, at approximately six P.M., about twenty-four hours after Christa Worthington's body was discovered.

McCowen never mentioned the meeting during his interrogation, Mason said. When he later obtained the report, the detective became aware that McCowen had fingered three locals selling narcotics. One was Frazier.

The report was written by Wellfleet police officer Michael Mazzone, who had since moved on to the Barnstable County Sheriff's Office, then relocated to Florida.

George returned to the six-hour interview. When his client's memory failed, perhaps police filled in the gaps? And when the grand jury indicted in June 2005, Mulvey had not yet provided an alibi for Frazier, correct?

Mason demurred.

George repeated the question: Had Mulvey backed up the alibi on May 13, 2005, when the detective interviewed him?

Mason shook his head. "Mr. Mulvey had relocated to Florida. I contacted him via phone. . . . I asked him, did he have a recollection of the night at the Juice Bar? And he indicated that he had not been to any function at the Juice Bar. I asked him if he had a recollection of being at a party, an after-party, in Eastham . . . January 5, 2002. And he indicated that he did not have a recollection of being at that party. . . . The only recollections he had of that time period were that Jeremy Frazier had spent the night at his house before and that Jeremy Frazier and he had gone out drinking on numerous occasions."

Mason said he got in touch with Mulvey by contacting his father, telling him "that I was investigating an important case on the Cape." Asked whether he'd queried Mulvey Sr. about whether Frazier spent the night of January 4–5, 2002, at his home, Mason couldn't recall. Nor could he recall whether Frazier told the grand jury he had. "I would have to see the grand-jury testimony to say what he said exactly."

Mason was in the grand-jury room at the same hearing. In fact, he'd prepped Frazier's testimony. He needed to rebut McCowen's assertion that Frazier was at Christa's the night of the murder; the Mulvey alibi was intended to prove that Frazier could not have been there. To make McCowen the murderer, Frazier had to be out of the picture. But this was the fundamental weakness of the prosecution's case: it wanted to cherry-pick from McCowen's statement, to rely on some portions, dismiss others.

George showed the witness the grand-jury minutes and asked whether Jeremy Frazier testified under oath that he had slept at Mulvey's house that night.

Welsh objected. "He's asking this witness to say what Frazier said in front of a grand jury."

Nickerson sustained. Sacrificing truth for protocol, the prosecution was invoking the sanctity of grand-jury proceedings in American jurisprudence, which was an object joke, since every trial lawyer knows a prosecutor can induce a grand jury to indict pretty much at will.

George pressed on, asking whether Frazier told Mason before his grand-jury testimony that he'd slept at Mulvey's that night.

"I would have to . . . I have to look at the reports of the interviews of Jeremy Frazier."

This was hard to believe but Mason's demeanor again carried him through; jurors were taking notes, writing furiously.

"And is it fair for me to say that you believed Jeremy Frazier prior to putting him into the grand jury . . . you believed his version of events?"

"Well, I can only say that we continued to conduct the investigation in order to confirm or dispel what Jeremy Frazier was saying. . . ."

"But at the time you put him into the grand jury, you believed he was telling the truth about not being at Christa Worthington's house; isn't that so?"

Mason said he wouldn't "couch it as a belief." His team continued to investigate "in an attempt to corroborate or dispel" Frazier's version of the events of that evening.

"But it was your belief when you talked to McCowen that he was not telling you the truth about Jeremy Frazier."

"That's correct."

George established that Mason questioned Frazier after subpoenaing his phone records to confirm his whereabouts. "And he was actually carrying his cell phone at the time . . . in January of 2002, that was in the name of someone else, wasn't he?"

"That's correct."

That phone was "in the name of David Murphy?" George asked. Mason concurred.

This name hadn't surfaced before; the press stirred. Murphy, who worked with Frazier at Magnum Movers in Eastham, was an ex-con who had served twelve years in state prison for manslaughter. Jurors were unaware of his record, just as they were unaware of the criminal histories of Frazier's other coworkers who were on the prosecution's witness list, waiting outside in the hallway to be called to the stand.

George entered the phone records into evidence, put them up on ELMO, then turned back to Mason.

"Now, did you and Sergeant Burke ask Frazier about this 978 number that was being dialed on the fourth? Say 11:50, 11:56? See it there . . . 978-585-0217? And is it fair to say that Frazier used to call that page number quite a bit, right?"

"Yes, I believe he did."

"In fact, I know you're not going to agree with me, but if I told you that Frazier called that 978 number approximately twenty-five times on the fourth and fifth of [January] 2002, would that refresh your memory?"

"I would say that number appears a number of times on Jeremy Frazier's phone bill."

"Is there a State Police barracks in Concord, Massachusetts?"

"Yes, there is." Mason knew what was coming.

"You asked Frazier about that number, didn't you?"

Mason explained that Frazier told him the number went to a pager "from that time period," but he didn't know whose pager.

George pressed harder. "Did you ever run these numbers to find out who was carrying that pager?"

"I don't believe a subpoena was done for that pager number, no."

"Well, I direct your attention to 12:03, where it says incoming."

"Yes."

Phone records don't lie. George gestured toward ELMO. "Did you ask Frazier about who was calling him from this number or who this number represented to him after calling the pager a couple of times just before that?"

"That was one of the numbers that Mr. Frazier could not recall . . ."

"Trooper, did you ever run that number, 394-3410, to find out where it came from?"

"No, I have never submitted a subpoena for that subscriber information."

"Does that number look familiar to you?"

"I don't know."

"If I told you that that's the phone at the Commonwealth of Massachusetts State Police barracks in South Yarmouth, would that refresh your memory?"

"I don't know that to be a number at the barracks."

George handed Mason the Verizon phone records, highlighted. "Does that appear to be the number that's on Jeremy Frazier's cellphone bill at 12:03 A.M. on January 5, '02?"

"Yes, it lists 508-394-3410."

"I would like to show you the cover sheet for that batch of phone records. Could you tell us who that phone is assigned to, according to Verizon?"

Mason stalled, but there was no way out. "This phone is assigned to the Commonwealth of Massachusetts State Police, 1172 State Road, which is the barracks' address in South Yarmouth."

"Now, that's the barracks where Chris McCowen was interrogated in this case, right?"

"The conference room is at that barracks, yes."

After establishing that the number was an auxiliary line, George asked, "Can you tell us why Frazier, who was never known to you or any of the investigators in this case, was receiving a phone call from the State Police barracks at the very time that McCowen says he was on his way up to kill Christa Worthington?"

"I do not know."

"Trooper, is this the first time it's ever come to your attention that Frazier was getting a phone call from someone at the State Police barracks at 12:03 A.M. on January 5, 2002, while he is supposedly getting ready to kill Christa Worthington?"

Many spectators believed the defense had prevailed there and then. The commonwealth's key witness, an acknowledged drug dealer McCowen had fingered as the real killer, was playing phone tag with State Police at the very time of Christa's murder.

Mason asked George to repeat the question.

"Did Frazier ever bring it to your attention that he had received a phone call from the State Police barracks in South Yarmouth right at the very time that McCowen says they were on their way up to Truro, or actually at 50 Depot Road in the process of committing the crimes in this case?"

"No, he did not."

George asked Mason if he ever questioned Frazier about that incoming call.

"He identified it only as a pager."

"Did you follow up that question with 'Who did the pager belong to? Does it belong to a state trooper? Does it belong to your mother or your father or anyone of the sort?'"

"No, we didn't ask him if it belonged to a state trooper or his mother. We only asked him if he could identify who was the subscriber to that pager. He indicated he could only recall that that number was a pager."

George asked if Mason would have arrested Frazier had he known Frazier was in contact with police barracks the night he allegedly was involved in the murder.

Mason, stuck, said no.

George was happy. The answer confirmed what many suspected: Frazier's covert relationship with police insulated him from arrest.

"And it was your testimony earlier, wasn't it, sir, that Frazier was not known to you or known to anyone connected to you in this investigation?"

"That's correct. Mr. Frazier was not known to me prior to Mr. McCowen mentioning Mr. Frazier during the interview."

After recess, Welsh began damage control. It was obvious the prosecutor and the detective had rehearsed during break, cobbling up improvs, and now Mason reiterated that Tim Arnold had been treated altogether professionally when interviewed at the psychiatric hospital. Asked about his decision to seek an arrest warrant, he explained that he was aware that five different women had taken out restraining orders against McCowen, who also faced a number of charges in Barnstable District Court.

Judge Nickerson interrupted, repeating his "limiting" instruction: jurors were to consider the information only to assess Mason's thought process when he initiated the arrest, nothing more.

Beginning recross, George again stood back from the witness, one hand grasping the back of McCowen's chair. Most of his maneuvers were staged, of course, but his affection for his client struck most press people as real. Moreover, the attorney's posture sent a powerful message: he wasn't wired to accept defeat.

Again showing the witness Verizon phone records, George singled out a call from the South Yarmouth State Police barracks at 12:03 A.M. "Whose phone number is that?"

"I do not know."

Using a second set of records, George established that the number was Jeremy Frazier's, the cell phone he was using under Dave Murphy's name. "And that's the phone number I just showed you on the ELMO, right, that's on the State Police phone records, isn't it?"

"Yes."

Abruptly, he walked away. He was done. Mason stepped down, leaving the Murphy connection dangling.

The next witness was Jeremy Frazier, whose phone calls to and from the cops stood as the defense's biggest score of the day. Welsh's witness had been damaged ahead of time and the prosecutor had no time to prep him. George was about to turn Frazier into the trial's major laughingstock.

Many Outer Cape locals knew Frazier, while others had only heard about his reputation in the aftermath of the murder. All but the most jaded in the courtroom gallery leaned forward, eager for a closer look at the beefy twenty-three-year-old who swaggered to the stand in a brand-new suit, a gold earring in one ear, sporting a fuzzy goatee meant to mask his recessive chin. The pea-green suit was set off by a yellow tie atop a matching yellow shirt. Despite his youth, Frazier was overweight and nearly bald.

From the get-go, his attitude announced that he was used to being in trouble, adept at denial. He stared blankly out over the packed courtroom, answering questions in a bored, dispassionate tone, "Yup" with a nod or a clipped "Nope." He and McCowen did not look at each other; the defendant stared at police reports on the defense table. Mason and Squier listened from the last row of the spectator gallery.

Asked to spell his name, the witness did so slowly, F-R-A-Z-I-E-R. He worked driving "roll-off trucks." In January 2002, he was nineteen and worked at Magnum Movers. Home schooling enabled him to graduate. Asked about the age difference between McCowen and himself, he responded, "At the time or right now?" Laughter rumbled through the courtroom.

"Well, wouldn't it be the same, sir?" Welsh prodded.

"Oh, yeah, of course. Seven, eight years, I would say."

Done with introductions, Welsh ran the Juice Bar video, giving Frazier a pointer. The bumbling witness stood between jurors and the TV monitor, forcing Welsh to move him so jurors could see.

"That's me," Frazier said, pointing at the screen. "That's Christopher. And that's Shawn . . . Shawn Mulvey."

No one had asked him to ID Mulvey, but the name reminded everyone in the room that Frazier's testimony had been carefully coached; some said rehearsals began back in August.

Welsh pointed out the video's time stamp, 6:36 P.M., and asked Frazier to recount his activities that evening.

Frazier drove his Cougar to the Juice Bar in Orleans with friend Eli Auch, hung out there with Mulvey and Chris Bearse, and then, about two hours into the rap show, left with McCowen to go to Dennis, where Chris's "baby's mother" lived. His account differed from McCowen's in that he said they took McCowen's car, the green Ford Escort belonging to the defendant's then-girlfriend, Kelly Tabor.

They stopped at Windmill Liquors, and McCowen bought the Alizé, Frazier being underage. He described it as a fruit punch, about 12 percent alcohol; he didn't mention that it's a favorite among rappers. They drank it in the car on the way to Dennis, where they stayed for forty-five minutes to an hour before returning to the Juice Bar, just before a fight broke out between two girls. He didn't remember what time they left Orleans for Tom Bilbo's after-party; they must have arrived between ten and eleven P.M.

With "a little buzz" going, he rode to the party in Mulvey's Honda, McCowen following in the green Escort, two or three other cars in the convoy. Asked if anyone rode with McCowen, the ever-articulate Frazier replied, "He went by his self."

Shortly after they arrived, another fight broke out. "A kid pushed my friend's girlfriend," he explained, identifying the culprit as Artie DuBois. "I hit him in the face once, and that was it." Eight to fifteen people jumped in; DuBois's side was outnumbered. When a vase and an easel got destroyed, Bilbo kicked everybody out. Again, Frazier did not know what time it was.

Welsh asked what McCowen did at the party, where he was inside the house. The witness said he remembered McCowen being there at first but didn't know whether he had already left by the time the party ended.

Welsh asked again; Frazier again said he didn't remember. He left with Mulvey, planning to go back to Mulvey's place, "call some females, hang out, drink a little bit more."

"Was there anybody else around, if you recall?" Welsh asked.

"Chris," Frazier responded, referring to Chris Bearse. "He was leaving when we were leaving. He was going to come back to Shawn's house, but he just ended up taking off."

Frazier admitted that he was intoxicated but knew he was in Mulvey's Honda low-rider because he remembered looking out the sunroof and listening to the deep bass of its custom sound system. Mulvey lived in Eastham, a two-to-five-minute shot from Bilbo's. They were alone at the house, Mulvey's father being in Connecticut. Frazier tried to call some females, "but then I got passed out," he said.

When Welsh asked him to be more specific, he recalled making one call, without connecting. "It was pretty late."

Welsh knew that Frazier's cell phone records proved otherwise, so he rephrased the question, asking if the witness remembered receiving calls at any time that evening. Frazier soft-pedaled, saying he didn't remember. He slept on Mulvey's couch, woke up at nine or ten the next morning. He'd spoken with McCowen by phone two or three times since that night and visited once at his Hyannis apartment. The encounters were "just, like, what have you been up to, kind of conversation. You know what I mean?"

The night of McCowen's arrest, Frazier was wakened at his Wellfleet home, where he lived with his parents and brother. Police talked with him at the kitchen table, then later at the Truro police station, where he was swabbed for DNA. Had he been involved with marijuana? Welsh asked, trying to defuse his witness's liabilities ahead of time. Frazier answered, "That's correct."

Then Welsh asked directly, "Did you get to Truro that night? Did you kill Christa Worthington?"

Frazier shook his head. "I did not." He had been to Worthington's only once, to deliver furniture while working for Magnum Movers.

Welsh kept direct simple, needing Frazier to testify only that he wasn't at Worthington's home the night of the murder. But during cross, the self-acknowledged doper's memory shriveled.

George began by asking, "That was the night you were accused of killing someone, you know that, right?"

Frazier couldn't or wouldn't recall how many times he'd been arrested. "Some got dropped. I don't really know my record," he said.

Frustrated with Frazier's selective memory, George asked if he might be "wrong about a lot of things."

"Yeah," Frazier answered, snarling.

George asked the witness where he was the day after the Bilbo party, Saturday, between noon and five P.M., hoping the information would tie in with Girard Smith's testimony about the black truck leaving Christa's driveway.

Frazier said he was home all day with his mom. "I was a little hungover but I was relaxing because I had a hard week at work." He'd gotten home at ten or eleven that morning, after Mulvey drove him back to his car at the Juice Bar.

"You don't remember major parts of Friday, do you?" George asked.

"Going to the Juice Bar."

"When you were interviewed by the police for the first time, you told them you didn't remember where you were that night, didn't you?"

"No, until they, you know, told me."

"What did they 'tell you'?"

"Well, explaining what happened, where I was that night, you know; and then it started coming back to my mind."

"They were explaining to you where you were?"

"No, they were explaining, like, what happened and what I did that night. So, I started remembering it."

The transparency of his words was extraordinary, hard to believe. Then again, this was the "new" Cape Cod. Even after Mason the audience was all ears.

"Did you tell them what you were doing that night? Or were they telling you what you were doing that night based on their having spoken with witnesses?"

"They were mentioning things, and I started remembering what I was doing that night."

George threw more bait. "You've talked to the police before, haven't you?"

"Yes, I have."

"You know how to talk to police, don't you?"

"Yeah . . . yes."

"How many times have you been arrested and not prosecuted?"

"What does 'prosecuted' mean?"

"How old are you? *Twenty-three?*"

"Twenty-three."

"You can't tell us how many times you've been arrested?"

"Arrested, like, three, four times," he answered.

"And all three or four times you were arrested, you weren't prosecuted?"

"No."

"They just dropped the charges?"

"Well, some of them got dropped, yes. I don't really know my record."

George, not yet aware of Frazier's arrest for threatening two British tourists at knifepoint in July 2004, continued in the same vein. "You don't know your own record? Twenty-three years old? You don't remember what you were arrested for?"

"I remember what I have gotten arrested for, but . . ."

"What did you get arrested for?"

Welsh objected. As the three men huddled, Nickerson asked for Frazier's rap sheet. Cross was about to get interesting.

The judge didn't see any drug offenses in Frazier's history, only two vandalism convictions as a juvenile. Was George suggesting that Frazier had "walked off" offenses by providing information? Welsh interrupted. He said he didn't have a copy of Frazier's full record but thought it included only minor in-possession-of-alcohol and traffic violations. Items found in his car suggested drugs but offered nothing to support charges.

George had relied on the prosecution to produce the witness's record as required by discovery rules. This was a mistake. The knife incident that would later come to light should have been admitted. The facts weren't negligible.

On July 2, 2003, nineteen months after the Worthington murder, Wellfleet teen Andrew Parent and soon-to-be-busted cocaine dealer Jesse Pecoraro were driving by the Wellfleet pier when, they said, two British men spit on Parent's car. The incident was random; those involved had never met. Joined by Frazier, Frazier's brother Jason, and another man, Parent and Pecoraro later located the Brits in front of Mac's Seafood at the pier. Instead of being intimidated, Keir Kennedy-Mitchell and Blake Fisher called the group "pussies." According to the Wellfleet police report, Kennedy-Mitchell said "the shortest person of the group, who was wearing a white ball cap on backwards, reacted . . . by pulling a knife out of his back pocket and 'flicking' it open in a threatening manner."

National Seashore employee Rebecca Savin witnessed the event. The "local boys" asked what the men were doing on their "fucking turf." Both Parent and Jason Frazier later confirmed that Jeremy held the knife.

Three days passed before Kennedy-Mitchell reported the incident to police; he told them he was worried about retaliation. Frazier was charged with assault with a dangerous weapon, a felony. But the following year, when neither Englishman appeared to testify, charges were dropped.

That was then. Now, still at sidebar, George tried again to establish that Frazier had an ongoing relationship with police before he was questioned about the murder.

Welsh said he didn't "have a problem with that," adding, "I'm not sure we're dealing with a real Learned Hand here. I mean, he just said a minute ago, 'I don't know what *prosecuted* means.'"

George nodded and went back to work on one-earringed Frazier, who said he'd been arrested three or four times; each time, the charges were dropped. Asked if he had a special arrangement with police, he said, "Nope." He could not recall whether he'd had any incidents during 2002. Frustrated anew, George asked whether the witness's non-functional memory was the result of his being "drug wasted."

Welsh objected, but Nickerson allowed the question. Frazier admitted he used pot in 2002 but denied using cocaine or other drugs. He also said he had not been drinking.

"You've told the jury you have a pretty specific memory of Friday night but not Thursday, not Saturday, not Sunday? Is that your testimony here today?"

"No, sir."

George made light of Frazier's sudden etiquette. *"No, sir?"* he mimicked. "You have no memory of Friday?"

"I mean, I remember what I did that night, yes. I remember. But . . ."

"But you don't remember what you did Thursday?"

"Nope."

He recalled only lying around the house on Saturday, nothing at all about Sunday.

"When the police first came to talk to you in April of 2005, you had no memory of what you did on Friday night, either, did you, other than the Juice Bar?"

"No."

"Does that no mean I'm right, or you have no memory?"

"I have a memory of what I did that night, yeah."

"But on April 14, when the police surprised you and woke you up out of your sleep, you had no memory then?"

"No memory."

"Did you need time to collect yourself before you talked to the police again?"

"No."

"You didn't talk to them again till May 5, right?"

"Yeah."

"Do you know whether it's May 5? Or are you just saying May 5 because I'm saying so?"

"I don't know. I don't know. I don't know," he wailed. Pressed again, he said he was sure he told police during the first interview that he went to Mulvey's. George showed him the April 14 police report, asking him to read the last paragraph silently.

Frazier took a moment to look over the report, then said he was surprised when police showed up at his door that night. George asked if he'd beaten Artie DuBois into semiconsciousness at the Bilbo party. Frazier admitted breaking Bilbo's mother's vase but not over DuBois's head.

George returned to the first police interview. The report quoted Frazier saying he had gone home with either Auch or Mulvey; he had been drinking and couldn't remember which. George asked when he remembered.

"Then it finally came to my attention that I did go to Shawn Mulvey's house."

"OK. That's what I'm getting at. It came to your attention. Who told you?"

"No, I finally remembered."

"Who brought it to your attention?"

"I remembered."

The lunch break intervened. Jurors returned at 2:23.

Frazier's confusion grew as cross continued. Asked again if he was unable to remember whom he'd left the party with when police first asked, he said that was correct. George asked, "Is that correct today, too?"

Frazier answered, "Yeah," then caught himself, saying he remembered spending the night at Mulvey's. He said he didn't speak with Mulvey between the interviews of April 14 and May 5.

George paused. He walked back to the defense table, leafed through a file, cleared his throat loudly, then returned to the witness with several sheets of paper in hand. Quietly, he reminded Frazier that his cell-phone calls were a matter of record.

Frazier amended the answer. He couldn't recall whether they'd spoken or not.

George was incredulous. Frazier had not called his friend, the person providing his alibi?

Welsh objected, but Nickerson overruled.

George moved on to David Murphy. "In 2005, when you met with the police, were you carrying a cell phone in someone else's name? Dave Murphy?"

"Yes."

"Who is Dave Murphy? Another friend of yours?"

"Yes."

"Now, why would you use the name of another for a cell phone?"

Frazier sighed, then explained that the bill had been too high, his mom wouldn't get him a cell phone, so he'd turned to Murphy, a coworker at Magnum Movers.

George switched back to Mulvey. Had Frazier talked to him between the two interviews? Mulvey had moved to Clearwater, Florida, Frazier explained. He did not recall the last time he'd talked to him before the first interview, either.

George asked if police ever told him Mulvey initially denied that Frazier had spent the night. No, Frazier said.

"None of [the] police officers in this case told you that Shawn Mulvey had told them on May 13, 2005, that you weren't at his house?"

"No."

"When did you become aware that Shawn Mulvey had told the police that you were not at his house?"

"They never told me that."

In truth, investigators had ignored Mulvey's denial of Frazier's alibi, fueling widespread gossip about Frazier's cozy police connections. George took Frazier back to January 4, 2002. "Were you using drugs that day?"

"No."

"You understand . . . that this is a very important day, right?"

"Yup."

"And did the police ask you where you had been that day?"

"Yes."

"And did you remember?"

"No."

"In fact, you didn't even remember where you had been after the Juice Bar the first time they talked to you, right?"

"Yup. Until they fed me pieces of information where I was that night."

It was a Perry Mason moment. Police had "fed" Frazier information? One former prosecutor in the audience muttered he'd never seen anything quite like it.

"So, they were feeding you pieces of information? You just said *fed you pieces of information*, right?" George pressed.

"Yeah."

"OK. Who was *feeding* you pieces of information?"

"The two officers that showed up at my house. I don't recall their names . . ."

"Well, you're telling us you were being fed pieces of information. How were they being fed to you? By telephone?"

"No, by persons. By face-to-face from what Christopher McCowen said we did that night. He was telling me, and I was starting to remember. Slowly, little pieces of information."

"But on April 14, 2005, you didn't have that memory when they came to see you at your house, right?"

"Yes."

"And . . . you told us that you had gone back and thought about it and come up with what had happened that night on your own. Do you remember testifying to that?"

"Yes."

"Were you being fed information between the fourteenth and the fifth?"

"No."

"So, you talked to nobody on the State Police between the fourteenth and the fifth, the second interview?"

"I don't recall."

"Did you have a handler at that point? Someone that you used to speak to in this case that would give you information about the case so you would be able to talk to them?"

"Yes."

"Who was that?"

"Christopher Mason."

So overwhelming was this revelation that the entire courtroom seemed to sigh. People seated side by side on the benches looked at each other, eyebrows lifted quizzically. Only the Worthingtons remained unmoved, unresponsive, and George could barely believe his luck. Frazier went on, describing how Trooper Mason and Sergeant Burke came to his house, triggered his memory.

He again said they supplied him with information about where he had been the night of the murder. Before the interview, he said, police talked to him off the record for twenty to thirty minutes, and after this prepping, he had been able to "put the pieces together." He'd had trouble remembering, he explained, because he was intoxicated.

George passed him a copy of the police report of this second interview and asked him to read the highlighted portion to himself. After doing so, Frazier said he could not recall, even during the interview, whether he woke up at Mulvey's house on Saturday or Sunday. The report said he'd had to be corrected, prompted.

"I wasn't sure at first," he explained. "They had to feed me pieces of information to remember that night because it was three years ago."

The odds of a guilty verdict seemed to fall with each minute Frazier spent on the stand. His mother, Darlene, was at the rear of the courtroom in a baby-blue cardigan, black stretch pants, and boots straight from Wal-Mart. Her expression announced that this was but one of many ordeals she'd suffered with her son and that it might turn out to be the last.

"You've been in Christa Worthington's house, haven't you?"

"Nope."

"Well, that's not true, is it?"

"No, I have not been."

"That's not true, is it?" George repeated.

"No, it's not true . . ."

"You helped move things out of her house, you told the police?"

"Yes, I have, actually," he admitted, his face slack despite George's slight mix-up over whether they were delivering or picking up.

George asked if he had scraped his muffler on Christa's driveway.

Here, Frazier didn't bite. Inside the house, he said, he went only as far as the living room. "I dropped all of her stuff there. That's where she wanted all of her stuff, and we took off."

George pounced. Worthington was *present?* Frazier corrected and said the delivery occurred after the murder.

"Were you using drugs throughout all of 2002?"

"No," Frazier responded.

When Frazier had said *she,* many in the courtroom thought he might fall apart. But he'd slipped back into the shoddy-memory routine. Asked if he had been in Christa Worthington's house in January 2002, Frazier actually said he didn't know.

George asked again; Frazier repeated his answer.

Irritated, George said, "Is that because you were using drugs then, and you don't remember?"

Frazier acknowledged that he'd given police the clothes he was seen wearing at Bilbo's but then wondered aloud whether he had washed them during the three-plus-year hiatus since the murder. George asked if the blood wouldn't get washed out over time, and Welsh objected. Nickerson said the witness could answer if he knew.

"That gets them clean, yes," replied Jeremy Einstein Frazier.

The garments were a leather jacket and a Nautica blue and white sweater, Frazier said. Like most spectators in the courtroom, he had no idea where this information would lead. George knew that blue and white fibers had been found in the victim's vaginal area and not tested, one more fact that might contribute to an acquittal or a hung jury.

Frazier named Mulvey, Bearse, and Auch as his closest friends. Later testimony would show that two of the three had criminal records—more points, potentially, for the defense.

He denied setting Mulvey up for an Ecstasy bust, denied that Mulvey ever accused him of it. George knew Mulvey would contradict this, buttressing the theory that Frazier's special relationship with police earned him a pass at McCowen's expense.

Frazier confirmed that shortly after Mulvey's May 2002 marijuana arrest, his friend moved off-Cape. He could not remember whether they spoke before or after the June 2005 grand-jury date. He believed it was close to that time.

George asked if Chris Bearse had seen Jeremy leave the party on the evening of January 4, 2002. Frazier said he had.

"Could you be wrong about that?"

"Could be, yes."

George moved on to the police barracks phone calls. He established that the number on Frazier's bill was his own pager, then focused on the 12:03 A.M. call. Frazier had already testified that he was unsure how close it was to midnight when the Bilbo party broke up. Again, he could not recall where he was just after midnight. George handed him the police report detailing his phone calls. It didn't help. Frazier said he couldn't remember.

George asked about Frazier's nickname, "Wu." He'd earned the moniker wearing a Wu-Tang necklace in high school, a salute to the Wu-Tang Clan rap group, he said, adding that he'd also belonged to the Sun Devil Clique, a social group, "not a gang." The Sun Devil group included Auch and Josh Santos.

George came back to the cell-phone calls through a series of questions about Eric Kinton, known to Frazier as Chris Bearse's mom's boyfriend. Frazier denied speaking with Kinton in 2005 or 2002. George was setting a trap. Kinton would testify that Frazier once called him seeking help breaking into "a rich woman's" house in Truro, where there was "lots of money, rare coins, and jewelry." Mason had also interviewed Kinton. In one interview, Frazier's overture occurred before the murder; in the other, it was after.

Frazier said he did not recall the last time he spoke to Kinton.

George showed him his phone records again. "It says that someone dialed [your number] on January 5, 2002, at about 12:03 A.M. Do you see that?"

"Yes."

"Well, if I told you that the orange line I just showed you was a phone call that you received from South Yarmouth State Police barracks at 12:03 A.M., can you tell us what that conversation was about?"

"I didn't talk to nobody from the State Police on that phone."

"It's your phone record, isn't it?"

"Yes . . ."

"You told us that you don't remember where you were at 12:03 because you were so drunk, right?"

"Yeah."

"So, you don't have any idea who called you from the State Police barracks, do you?"

"Nobody called me from the state barracks . . ."

"OK. I'm asking you today, sir, do you have any memory whatsoever of talking to a State Police trooper—"

"No, I did not talk to no State Police," Frazier interrupted.

"—on the evening that you're supposedly killing Christa Worthington?"

"No, I did not talk to State Police officers."

George stopped.

All along, his voice had been rising steadily toward a climax, filling the courtroom, and now he turned away from the witness and walked back to the defense table with a contemptuous flick of his hand. His message: Frazier, a chief prosecution witness who'd testified before the grand jury, a rapper wannabe with a criminal past, had chatted with State Police in the middle of the night at the time Worthington was supposedly murdered.

At 3:40, Mulvey was sworn. In stark contrast to Frazier, he seemed relaxed, above it all, even here in the grand courtroom with its thickly varnished portraits of judges emeriti, its phony Greek columns, and the iconic codfish. In response to Welsh's questions about his background, he waxed prolific about his former life on Cape Cod. At the Bilbo party, he was the helper, trying to protect people during the fight, telling Frazier not to drive because he was too drunk. He assisted Bilbo with cleanup; the house-shattering debacle had overturned couches and smashed furniture. Mulvey's role was to back up Frazier's alibi, yet his corroborating testimony was not without discrepancies. And he took pains to distance himself from the friend he was bailing out.

At the time of the murder, Mulvey lived in Eastham; he moved to Clearwater, Florida, six months later, in June 2002. He and Frazier had been friends for three years, but he'd met McCowen only a couple of times. "You know, there's not too many people on Cape Cod," he explained, "so after a while, I just ended up being friends."

His account of the evening of January 4, 2002, differed from Frazier's. Frazier had testified that he went to the Juice Bar with Eli Auch; Mulvey said he and Josh Santos rode there in Frazier's car. They arrived early to help set up for the rap show.

Mulvey and Jeremy performed that night. Afterward, Frazier and McCowen went to Dennis in McCowen's car and were gone about an hour. Mulvey was drinking his own bottle of Alizé. After a fight broke out between two girls, everyone cleared out "pretty quick."

They arrived at the Bilbo party at about 10:30. "I believe Jeremy parked quite a walk away and I parked a few cars behind him," Mulvey testified.

He explained the fight as Jeremy had; it erupted after Artie DuBois bumped into Eli Auch's girlfriend. Bearse decided to say something but ended up letting fly. Mulvey admitted striking DuBois as well. Then others jumped in. Frazier knocked over an armoire, a vase, a lamp, and other stuff.

Mulvey's account turned saccharine: he could see DuBois was going to get hurt, so he decided to help push him outside, through either the window or the door.

Bilbo ordered everyone to leave. Mulvey, Frazier, and Bearse were the last to exit. They stood outside for about fifteen minutes as cars cleared, deciding what to do next. "Jeremy was probably the most intoxicated, so I told him to come with me," Mulvey recalled. With Jeremy in the Accord, Mulvey drove, and Bearse followed. When they reached Brackett Road, the turnoff to Mulvey's father's house, Bearse drove home to Yarmouth instead.

At the Mulvey home, they drank rum and called several girls, but none would join them. The two were alone at the house. Mulvey believed his father was on vacation. "I don't really keep tabs on him," he answered testily. They got to sleep between 2:00 and 2:30 A.M., Frazier on the living-room sofa, and they woke around ten, when he took Jeremy back to his car at Bilbo's.

Welsh asked if Frazier remained at Mulvey's all night. "The whole night. Yes, he did," Mulvey replied. Welsh repeated the question twice. Mulvey said he was 100 percent certain.

Welsh tried to clear up the inconsistencies. During the May 13 phone interview, Mulvey told police he didn't remember the after-party, that he had never been to the Juice Bar. During the subsequent interview, in July 2005, he gave the account he delivered in court. Why the discrepancy? Welsh asked.

At first, Mulvey explained, he had followed his father's advice: *Don't get involved, don't talk to police.* Later, he took it upon himself to admit what he knew.

He said nothing about his interaction with the police, and Welsh nodded, as though it all made perfect sense, that the witness's reluctance to cooperate was understandable.

George was already at the witness-box rail, face-to-face with Mulvey, before the prosecutor sat back down at the prosecution table. But court was about to adjourn for the day within minutes. George was able to establish only that Mulvey moved from the Cape in June 2002. "It was a family move," the witness said.

The defense lawyer requested a sidebar. He'd received a criminal complaint regarding Mulvey, via discovery, that morning. He wanted the probation department records before continuing.

"Do you have them?" Judge Nickerson turned to Welsh.

The prosecutor hedged. "It's not in my—it's not readily accessible."

Nickerson agreed to order the records, suspecting nothing.

This was a decisive moment. Facts that emerged later demonstrated that Welsh and his mentor, DA Michael O'Keefe, were sitting on these very records, and had been sitting on them all along. The documents impugned Mulvey, Frazier, and a half-dozen other commonwealth witnesses. Nickerson didn't know it, George didn't know it, but Welsh had just lied to the court.

Day 10, Friday, October 27

The trial of the man accused of murdering a Vassar-educated *New York Times* fashion writer had spilled over into the hall-of-mirrors drug world of Outer Cape Cod. The prior day's testimony about dealers, snitches, police "controls," and gangs was about to reach a crescendo, unraveling before a national TV audience.

Robert George opened with yet another request for a sidebar. "Your Honor, I typed this myself, and it got wet in my briefcase," he explained. It was a motion for a view of the Juice Bar; the homes of Tabor, McGuire, Bilbo, and Mulvey; and 50 Depot Road.

The soggy document was pathetic but showed how much the defense was outgunned, outmanned, outperimetered. In the attorneys' box opposite the jury there sat seven assistant DAs, a handful of secretaries, and a crew of interns; additional staffers stood at the ready across the courthouse parking lot in the DA's office. Here George was typing his own documents at his vacation cottage several miles up the road in Dennis. The night before, he'd slogged through case law pertinent to Nickerson's admission of the restraining orders, cutting heavily into his customary four-hour sleep.

He was court-appointed, being paid $100 an hour by the state, one-fifth his normal rate; McCowen's family had promised to pay him from the proceeds of the sale of the family's Oklahoma farm, but those funds were tied up in probate. His "staff" consisted of two part-time private investigators and a secretary. This author was reading case law, scouring courthouse records, and interviewing locals about Frazier's Wu-Tang crew. But rightly or wrongly, George was pleased with his underdog status, and whatever the inequality at hand, he didn't want outside help. Some trial analysts might frown on such a stubbornly solo approach, but the defense lawyer didn't care about the opinions of academics. He was not a "white shoe" lawyer, never had been, never could be. He loved the publicity but his ego was precisely what he offered to his client, unconditionally. His energy might sometimes blind him to detail, but the man wasn't built for defeat. He worked alone. Period.

Ironically, in the aftermath of the McCowen case, he would be offered a sweetheart partnership at a large Boston law firm; he stayed at the job, with its many perks, less than eight months.

George intended to use Mulvey's drug bust to discredit him, to show that the twenty-seven-year-old was a user and a dealer. Most important, he intended to prove that Mulvey had received favorable treatment from the DA's office in exchange for corroborating Frazier's alibi.

He outlined the dates, indicating that the timeline was not coincidental. At the end of the previous day's testimony, Mulvey had said he left the Cape in June 2002. He moved with his family, wanting to attend an electronics school in Florida. George asked if there might be another reason. Mulvey replied, "Nope."

George moved to January 4, 2002. The witness repeated his earlier testimony. After the Bilbo party, Bearse followed his car down Route 6; when Mulvey turned onto Brackett Road, Bearse didn't. Later, Bearse's memory would differ.

George asked whether Mulvey had any contact with Cape courts during the three years between his departure and his May 13, 2005, police interview regarding the Worthington murder. Welsh objected, voicing concern about inferences that might be drawn from the witness's criminal past.

At sidebar, the prosecutor pointed out that the drug charges against Mulvey had been continued without a finding; absent a conviction, George couldn't use those charges to impeach the witness.

George said he wasn't concerned with the charges per se but with how they were handled. His limited information indicated that Mulvey sold marijuana to an undercover agent on May 8, 2002, and conversed with the agent about selling Ecstasy. Mulvey then left the state. George was about to explain that the warrant was not issued until sometime later, when Welsh interrupted, saying that he wanted to be excused so he could grab his own files on the matter. Suddenly, the documents not "readily accessible" the day before, were on hand.

When the prosecutor and his file returned to the huddle, George explained that the warrant was not issued until March 20, 2005, two months before Mulvey's first police interview about the Worthington case, one month before McCowen's arrest. But the warrant was not served until May 31, eighteen days *after* Mulvey's first Worthington interview. The date was important, George said; the warrant seemed material to his subsequent interview, on July 1. "I'm talking about all of the maneuvering that was done to get him to change his story, or at least the inference that something was done for him in return for him to change his story."

"His original story was, 'I don't know nothing'?" Nickerson queried. George nodded.

"Yeah, [but] there's a reason for that, Judge," Welsh put in. "He's saying his father told him, 'Don't get involved.'"

"Well, are we required to accept his reason," the judge asked, "or can we draw some inferences about the rest of his track record?"

Welsh was undaunted. "Are we required to accept Mr. George's reason as to that's why he left for Florida, Judge?"

"Absolutely not," Nickerson said. "That's the point. It's up to the jury to make a decision."

"Thank you, Judge," George said, turning back to the witness.

Mulvey admitted that he sold marijuana to the undercover agent at his father's house on May 8, 2002. The police report indicated that a "confidential informant" was also present. George wondered if Frazier was the CI. Mulvey said no, but Frazier had probably set him up; he'd called Frazier for the drugs.

"I had contacted him because another so-called friend came by and said he wanted something and with another kid I had never met before. And I don't sell drugs. So, I went and called Jeremy Frazier and got it from him, I went and drove up the road and met him and brought it back to the house, and that's how it manifested."

George reminded the self-described nondealer that he had sold drugs in this case to an undercover agent. He handed the witness an Orleans PD report headed "Undercover Negotiations with Shawn Mulvey Regarding the Purchase of Ecstasy." It verified that Mulvey had contact with the undercover officer on May 9, 2002, the day after the marijuana sale.

Mulvey admitted to the conversation but insisted that the report was wrong. He had not talked with a cop but with the "so-called friend" who had been with the undercover officer. The friend, the CI, was Charlie Whitcomb, a six-foot-five-inch Orleans man in his mid-twenties. Regarding Whitcomb, Mulvey added, "I don't like a lot of people up here. Everybody is back stabbers."

Mulvey said Whitcomb offered money for Ecstasy. He advised the would-be purchaser to call the next week; he'd look in Provincetown, see what he could do.

On May 13, Whitcomb called back to check on progress. Mulvey said his source would not have the Ecstasy until the end of the week; Whitcomb should call again on Tuesday. But that was just an excuse, Mulvey testified; he didn't want to get the Ecstasy, didn't want to be involved.

George again accused him of being a dealer. Mulvey snapped back, saying the charge had been dismissed. George ticked off five phone calls about the Ecstasy, but Mulvey held his ground: "You'll see every phone call, I said I cannot get it. And I never got it for him."

George was butting heads with a mastodon; the lanky, self-assured kid wouldn't quit. George again tried to establish that Frazier was Mulvey's pot supplier. "And the undercover agent and Charlie Whitcomb were calling you to buy drugs from you, which you were buying . . . from Frazier?"

"Which is funny," Mulvey said, "because Charlie Whitcomb knows that I don't get that. And everybody knows . . . where to go."

"But Frazier is your source? And you are the source for the people calling you on the telephone?"

"No, sir. Not at all."

"You're the middleman?"

"I was only the middleman in that instant [sic]. That's why I thought it was funny. Everybody knows where to go."

"What do you mean, 'everyone knows where to go'? What are you talking about?"

"Because the Cape Cod community is very small. Everybody knows everybody's business. That's why I thought it was funny that he kept calling me over and over again. Because they know where to go. They don't come to me. I am nobody in this big puzzle." He added that the serial caller "was good friends with Jeremy."

"You said you told . . . Charlie Whitcomb or the undercover policeman . . . to call you when you were finished with your work, and you would bring the agent to your source of supply? Do you remember saying that? On May 22, 2002, at ten-fifteen?"

"I may have."

"Were you a drug user at this time in May of 2002?"

"Recreational weed, pot. I really didn't smoke all the time."

"Where would you get it?"

"Jeremy."

"So, is it fair to say that your relationship with Jeremy Frazier revolved not only around friendship, but it also revolved around drug use?"

"Like I stated before, there is not too many people to hang out with up there."

Mulvey agreed that he'd left the Cape after selling drugs to an undercover officer but denied that was his reason for leaving.

Almost three years passed before March 2005, when Cape Cod resurfaced in Mulvey's life. His father had been told about the warrant issued for his son during a return trip to Eastham; less than two months later, on May 13, police called. They didn't ask about the warrant; they asked whether Jeremy had spent the night at his house. As George had indicated earlier, Mulvey denied it, saying he did not remember.

On May 31, 2005, the warrant was actually printed. The timing here, George repeated himself, wasn't coincidental. Mulvey waffled, saying he was unaware of the exact date.

George showed him the date as listed on police documents, then went on to Mulvey's second chat with police, on July 1, 2005. Burke and Mason actually showed up at Mulvey's door in Florida, unannounced. The warrant hadn't been cleared up; Mulvey was in default in Orleans District Court. Were the detectives concerned about the outstanding warrant?

"They didn't say they weren't concerned. . . . We didn't talk about it very much," the witness answered.

The testimony, once more, strained credibility. Mason and Burke traveled to Florida—ever diligent, hyperorganized Mason, who toiled overtime throughout the three-and-a-half-year investigation—without knowing of the outstanding warrant for Mulvey's arrest? Mason, who'd even brought with him the videotape showing Mulvey at the Juice Bar?

The witness went on, explaining that he later appeared in Orleans District Court for a "regular misdemeanor charge." He didn't know the exact date, not even the month, but said the case was resolved on August 24 with a $252 fine, court costs, a $50 witness fee, and a continuance without a finding for one year.

But having sold drugs directly to a cop and having discussed selling Ecstasy, Mulvey easily could have faced more serious charges: traf-
ficking or possession with intent to distribute. George asked whether
Mulvey ever talked to Frazier before his second interview in July 2005.
Again, the witness said he wasn't sure. They had spoken two or three
times. He'd chosen not to confront Frazier about the setup, he said,
because "what was the point?"

George turned to Frazier's alibi, the prosecution's primary reason
for calling Mulvey to the stand. Mulvey's father didn't allow his son to
have houseguests, correct? "He doesn't like my friends staying over,
yes," Mulvey agreed, adding that Frazier had never been there when
his father was home.

Next, George got the witness to repeat that he'd taken Frazier
back to Bilbo's house on Saturday morning to retrieve his car. Frazier
had testified that he left his car at the Juice Bar; Mulvey drove him
from there to the party. Mulvey said he never drove his low-rider to
the Juice Bar because the dirt parking lot was too uneven. He also testified that his car had never undergone forensic testing. Police never
asked him for fingerprints, a DNA sample, clothes, or phone records.

Asked if Elaine Gambrazzio, his father's girlfriend in 2002 and an
upcoming witness, had stayed at the Eastham house that Friday night,
Mulvey said no.

On redirect, Welsh did what he could. Frazier had been tainted, and
Mulvey had to keep Jeremy out of Worthington's house the night of the
murder. If Jeremy went down, the prosecution's case went with him.

On recross, George asked about Mulvey's court appearance—who
represented him, whether he'd dealt with a clerk-magistrate. These
were the setup questions, leading to the punch: "Do you remember
what the judge looked like?"

No one was surprised when Welsh objected. His father, the presiding judge in Orleans District Court, had handled Mulvey's case.
Robert Welsh Jr. also had a hand in processing Frazier's Wellfleet pier
knife case.

Score another point for the defense.

The commonwealth called Chris Bearse, who testified that he'd
seen Frazier and Mulvey leave the Bilbo party together. George had

Bearse repeat previous testimony: Mulvey's father didn't allow his son to have houseguests. Bearse had been to Mulvey's "a lot" but never when the elder Mulvey was there.

Next, Welsh called Thomas Bilbo, who contributed nothing more than the time his party ended.

After recess, it was back to the cops. Mashpee Police Sergeant John Santangelo had served with the Cape Cod Drug Task Force, an amalgam of town, state, and federal police, and he testified that some of his informants were paid, some were just good citizens, and some were looking to cut a deal. He met with McCowen on Tuesday, January 8, 2002, at six P.M., a little more than forty-eight hours after Worthington's body was discovered. Wellfleet Police Detective Michael Mazzone arranged the meeting, and Wellfleet patrolman Lloyd Oja was there, too. Oja was expected to testify, but Mazzone was not. Welsh needed to explain why the officer who had been McCowen's "handler" since the late '90s would not appear at trial.

Mazzone had left the Cape, Santangelo said, and lived "somewhere in Florida." The prosecutor asked why McCowen had become a snitch and got the answer he expected: McCowen had been caught with contraband, a parole violation that could have sent him back to the Florida State Penitentiary. George interrupted. He wanted the contraband excluded—McCowen had never been charged.

Asked the question again, Santangelo admitted that Mazzone gave McCowen a break. Nickerson stopped him, telling jurors that they were not to hold Santangelo's words, a "break on a small marijuana matter," against McCowen. Instead, they were to regard the statement as merely "foundation" explaining Santangelo's contact with the defendant.

Welsh elicited details. The meeting took place behind the Orleans Stop & Shop in an unmarked police car used for drug purchases. McCowen named three local dealers, including Frazier. The Worthington murder was never discussed.

On cross, George established that state cops outnumbered locals on the drug task force, that it was headquartered in Dennis, and that Lieutenant John Allen was in charge—the same John Allen who led the CPAC unit and supervised the Worthington homicide investigation. In addition, Allen's daughter, then a Truro cop, had been at the Worthington crime scene.

He then delved into McCowen's comments about Frazier. Santangelo agreed that McCowen had been clear: Jeremy was "a large-scale" dealer.

"You're selling pounds at a thousand a pound, you're a large-scale drug dealer on Cape Cod, aren't you?" he asked.

George's figures were off; the going rate for a pound of grass was closer to $2,800. But no matter. The sergeant testified it was "fair to say" that Mazzone hadn't followed up on Frazier, that Frazier had never been investigated. He denied that "Wu" was one of his own informants, said he didn't know if Frazier was handled by Mazzone or Oja.

Santangelo's testimony did more for the defense than the prosecution. McCowen's status as a denizen of the Cape drug world paled in comparison with the data that Frazier and Mulvey were known dealers who were never bothered by the cops. Again, the most plausible conclusion was that the duo had been "bought off" in exchange for their testimony against McCowen.

When Lloyd Oja took the stand, George objected; the officer's testimony could only be cumulative. Nickerson seized the opportunity. "So, your cross-examination, I suspect, will be quite short, then, eh?"

"Or it might be repetitive," George shot back, doing another Joe Pesci "So what?" impersonation.

And it was.

Welsh next called Christine Lemire, a DNA analyst at the State Police crime lab, a tall, austere woman in a dark business suit. Lemire had been employed at the lab for eleven years, processing crime scenes for the criminalistics unit before rising to the rank of supervisor.

She examined twenty-three samples from the Worthington crime scene, including those from Christa's body, then cross-referenced them with samples taken from forty-nine other individuals. Her testimony was mind-numbing. Calling the genetic profile "a blueprint for our very identities," she said the chances of an African-American man other than McCowen matching the swab taken from Christa's right breast were 199.80 billion to one. McCowen had been a minor match in the vaginal swab, meaning that his DNA was less than Christa's; the odds of another African-American matching that swab were 1.17 billion to one, 7.20 billion to one for Caucasians, and 10.20 billion to one for Hispanics.

DNA samples taken from Christa's fingernails were less conclusive. Genetic material from three males was found in the clippings. Lemire testified that one in twelve African-Americans and one in six Caucasians would match those samples.

Frazier did not match any.

On cross, Lemire admitted that the fingernail clippings were never compared with Arnold and that neither McCowen nor anyone else matched the bloodstain on the heel of Christa's left clog. As the day drew to a close, jurors' eyes glazed over, as if the rehash of crime-scene evidence, followed by lab reports and statistical analyses, was about to induce a coma. When the bailiff sang "All rise," they sprinted to the door with an alacrity not seen before.

Day 11, Tuesday, October 31

If public opinion was shifting toward McCowen, the defendant's demeanor didn't reflect it. He sat at the defense table staring into space. Sometimes he wrote notes to George, who'd come up with a routine to prevent him from ogling two young, well-endowed jurors: George passed him sourball candies; unwrapping them took concentration. McCowen didn't look happy or scared. He looked bored, a fact that enforced the defense claim that he was a limited individual. The hardest thing about representing someone like McCowen, George explained, "is that you care more than he cares about the nuances and the weaknesses in the case against him. I fight them harder than he does . . . which in itself came to convince me that he certainly was taken advantage of.

"McCowen is the classic prototypical black defendant. I shouldn't say all black defendants are the same. I'm talking about the ways people have stereotyped black defendants in the past, going back to *To*

Kill a Mockingbird. They bring in this guy who clearly doesn't understand the situation he's in, whether it's because of drugs, alcohol, or
his intellectual limitations, and they interview him for six or seven
hours, which is no different than the rubber hose, really. They don't
feed him or give him any rest, and they continue to jerk him around
in fifteen different directions.

"And it really wasn't good cop/bad cop, here. It was just basically
cop/cop. Every time Burke talked to him, he was saying, 'You know,
Chris, we don't believe you.' Or 'That's not true' . . . and if Chris is
aiming to please, which is who Chris is, he's unhappy that he's not
pleasing them. 'What do I need to do? What do I need to change in
my story to please you fellas?' They're saying to him, 'You haven't told
us the whole story,' and every time they say it, he gives them a little
more. As his lawyer, what I have to do is hold a mirror up to the jury
and make them say, 'Am I giving this guy a fair shake? Am I looking
at every piece of evidence the way I should, or am I just accepting it
because Chris Mason and the prosecution's giving it to me?'"

Chemist Christine Lemire didn't help. Having given her hours-long,
brain-deadening set piece on the particulars of DNA, her point was
simple: McCowen's DNA matched.

George raised the Thursday sex scenario, the idea that McCowen
and Worthington indeed had sex, consensual sex, a day earlier. He
dealt with the vaginal swab first, offering evidence that sperm could
have been deposited *before* the time of the murder. Lemire conceded
that sperm cells can last in the vaginal cavity three to five days, sometimes longer, echoing the medical examiner's testimony.

George asked where and how the sample had been stored. Hadn't
the state withheld the results of four outside audits showing problems
with supervisor Robert Pino's conduct at the lab? Wasn't Pino's name
on one report that linked McCowen's DNA to the crime? And wasn't
it also the case that McCowen's sample had not been sent to the lab
until July 7, 2004, where it remained untested until January 2005?
Lemire insisted that the sample had been stored under "appropriate
conditions" but couldn't be specific.

The DNA analyst frequently referred to her notes; she had not tested McCowen's sample, hadn't even seen it, which was an echo of the medical examiner situation. She did test the brown blanket, making the match to Tim Arnold, and most of the other items found at the crime scene: keys, eyeglasses, clogs. McCowen's DNA was not found on any of these items.

George wrapped up Lemire's cross with Jeremy Frazier. Previous testimony revealed that blue and white fibers had been obtained from Worthington's pubic hair and that Friday evening, Frazier was wearing a blue and white Nautica sweatshirt. Lemire admitted that she had not been aware of the threads found in the pubic hair, nor was she asked to do DNA testing on Frazier's blue and white sweatshirt.

On redirect, Welsh went back to the right-breast swab, the vaginal swab, the minor profiles, and the like, connecting McCowen to the victim's battered body. The low sperm count, Lemire volunteered, could be explained in several ways, including the possibility that the donor's sperm, per se, was weak—a suggestion lacking credibility, given that twenty-nine-year-old McCowen had already fathered three known children on the Cape alone.

George closed by noting how difficult it was to pin down the time of McCowen's sex with Christa. His message to the jury: the prosecution's case would be far more difficult if it had to rely exclusively on the DNA sample. It desperately needed McCowen's April 14 statement to go with it.

Jeremy's uncle, Matthew Frazier, was the commonwealth's next witness. Not on the original witness list, he'd been added to negate, in advance, testimony about the black truck seen leaving 50 Depot Road on Saturday afternoon, January 5.

Welsh next called Scott McCabe, a state trooper assigned to the narcotics section of the Cape Cod Drug Task Force. In his early thirties, long-haired McCabe almost could have passed for Colin Farrell in *Miami Vice*, his overstylized appearance fairly screaming that he was a narc. But his role in the Worthington case was limited; he'd executed the search warrant at 63 Lafrance Avenue, no more.

On direct, McCabe laid out the particulars of McCowen's arrest. Eight to ten officers entered the building around seven P.M. to find him sitting up in bed, arms stretched out in front, sheets down near his feet, watching cartoons on TV, while simultaneously listening to music through headphones. The room was a mess. McCabe and a uniformed trooper put McCowen against the wall, handcuffed him, and told him he was under arrest. They held him there until the residence was secured, then brought him into the dining room, where they sat him in a chair.

Knowing that the defense would argue that McCowen was wasted when his statement was taken, Welsh asked whether the defendant had difficulty walking or understanding what was being said. McCabe said he did not, although he acknowledged finding the previously mentioned roaches and Percocet bottle. The room did not smell of pot, he said. Noticing that McCowen wore only socks, sweatpants, and a tank top, he asked if the suspect wanted shoes or a sweatshirt. McCowen did; McCabe retrieved them.

About twenty minutes after the search warrant was executed, the trooper testified, Mason and Burke entered the residence and walked McCowen out.

George went at the ponytailed witness hard, asking McCabe if he was capable of determining McCowen's sobriety. "If I told you he had a seventy-four or seventy-five IQ, that would be news to you today, wouldn't it?"

Welsh objected, asked for a sidebar, then railed against George's repeated "underreporting" of McCowen's IQ scores. "There need be a good-faith basis to ask the question," he groused.

"I have a tremendous good-faith basis, Your Honor," George said, rocking from one foot to the other.

"Is it a seventy-four or seventy-five?" Nickerson asked. "It does seem like the figure keeps creeping lower."

After a heated back-and-forth about the results of eleven different IQ tests administered to McCowen, Nickerson said he'd take care of it with another limiting instruction. Welsh still objected. After a few more volleys, the Boston street kid in George flared; it was oddly humanizing, the pomp and circumstance of superior court reduced to two guys butting heads like stags in the bush.

"Wait a minute, wait a minute," George said. "Mr. Welsh needs to study his materials more closely . . ."

"Well, here's where we are," Nickerson said. "I keep hearing different figures."

"That's because there *are* different figures."

"And I'm going to tell the jury that any of these figures contained in a question are not part of their evidence," the judge repeated.

After the instruction was given (although half of the jurors looked genuinely wasted), George put the question to McCabe again. The trooper had not been aware of McCowen's IQ, he acknowledged.

McCabe's testimony took all of ten minutes. He was followed by the commonwealth's last witness, Detective William Burke, Mason's partner, the ranking officer of the investigative team. Burke was older, fifty-two, and forlorn-looking, with the sallow complexion of an Irish drinker. His dialect was pure Boston: "caarr," not "car." He moved with a slight stoop, his body language announcing that he lacked Mason's intelligence and charisma. The younger detective was the Swiftian spider, the Dionysian borne aloft by native will and talent; the other was the plodding bee who'd been schooled by years of practice, in the field and in court.

Burke first encountered *his* boss, Michael O'Keefe, when he was a Dennis cop, before his twenty-four-year stint with the "Staties." Now, attached to the Cape and Islands District Attorney's Office full-time, some saw him as the DA's shadow, accompanying his boss between the courthouse and the district attorney's office, walking in lockstep, almost.

Sergeant Burke's testimony so mirrored Mason's that George questioned the point directly, as he had with Oja, but Nickerson allowed the prosecutor to plow on. George was right, though. Burke's answers were repetitions, a waste of time, although there were exceptions. When Mason left the April 14, 2005, McCowen interrogation to check in with officers interviewing Frazier, Sergeant Knott took his place. Knott showed McCowen a black-and-white Polaroid of a woman and a girl that had been found during the arrest, wrapped in a T-shirt. McCowen said the photo fell out of a bureau during a moving job; he retrieved it, intending to give it back to the owner. Knott asked McCowen about several pairs of women's thong underwear; McCowen said they were "trophies" from women he had sex with. Detectives also found a stash of older-women, "hot groins" porn mags in a battered suitcase.

None of this did the defense any good, certainly, and George, when he took over, focused on Jeremy Frazier. Mason's testimony had established that Frazier's cellphone was registered to the ex-con Dave Murphy; Burke concurred that police were aware of Murphy's ten-to-fifteen-year stint at Walpole State Prison but yet they'd never spoken to him in person.

Weren't police troubled by nineteen-year-old Frazier carrying the cell phone of a convicted killer during the weekend of Christa Worthington's murder? No, Burke said, "because Mr. Murphy worked with him at Magnum Movers."

"Christa Worthington's belongings were in storage at Magnum Movers before she died, isn't that so?"

"I believe they were . . ."

Burke didn't know whether Murphy and Frazier kept in touch on that cell phone prior to Christa Worthington's death. Nor did he know that Murphy was arrested for assault and battery with a dangerous weapon on his wife in December 2001, days before Worthington's murder.

Welsh objected. Nickerson sustained.

George asked whether investigators tried to flesh out the connections among Murphy, Mulvey, Frazier, or any other Magnum Movers employee. As for Murphy, Burke said, "I believe I ran a Board of Probation check," then acknowledged that he'd never asked Frazier about his relationship with the convicted killer.

"And despite the fact that we have this State Police phone call coming into his phone on the very night that McCowen alleges that [Frazier] was killing Christa Worthington, have you been able to flesh out whether or not Frazier had any connection whatsoever with the State Police at South Yarmouth?"

"I am being told that he has no connection with the State Police."

This was patently ridiculous, and there was more. George handed him paperwork from Magnum Movers showing that Christa Worthington stored her belongings there in 1999, as well as a photocopy of the murder indictment against Murphy from Cambridge Superior Court.

Welsh objected. Nickerson sustained but revised his ruling after examining the documents. It was clear that the police had been sitting on this information, notwithstanding Burke's repeated "I am being tolds," "I had been informeds," and "I don't remembers." In plainspeak, Burke, too, was lying.

Not fibbing. Not waffling. Lying.

George displayed the murder indictment on ELMO. "Now, Trooper . . . when you interviewed David Murphy about the cell phone that Jeremy Frazier was carrying . . . you were aware that Mr. Murphy had been charged . . . with murder in Cambridge?"

Burke answered affirmatively but said he didn't know how many years Murphy served or his release date.

The witness zigzagged all over. First, he claimed he was unfamiliar with Dave Murphy's history. Now, he openly acknowledged that at the time he interviewed Murphy, he knew that Frazier's pal had been charged with murder.

George had another surprise. He took Burke back to the crime scene and got him to acknowledge that Truro Police Sergeant David Costa had initially been in charge of keeping people out of the house. Referring to the green bathrobe that Arnold and Jan Worthington had seen, George asked whether Costa was ever alone in the house. Burke was uncertain. David Perry, another Truro officer, was assigned to work with CPAC a few days after the murder, he said. Perry was the ranking superior. Costa would have been expected to report anything he came across to the investigative team, but he wasn't authorized to act without permission.

Costa's unofficial role in the investigation had long fed the rumor mill. At one point, it was widely believed that he was a suspect. And locals relished the memory of Costa's wife, Cheryl, confronting Jan Worthington outside the Blacksmith Shop, a Truro restaurant where Worthington was a barmaid, accusing her of having an affair with Costa. Cheryl was a volatile personality who allegedly went after a female park ranger who'd also dallied with her husband. Costa denied even knowing Jan, and Jan drove off in tears. The episode, witnessed through an open door by locals at the bar, was a highlight of the season, dovetailing, as it did, with the story of the two locked inside Costa's cruiser.

Day 12, Wednesday, November 1

George called for an umpteenth sidebar as court opened on the day the defense was expected to begin. He had been digging for evidence to prove that Mulvey's father was home the weekend of the murder, to quash the idea that Frazier was welcome to spend the night. The phone records of Elaine Gambrazzio, the elder Mulvey's ex-girlfriend, filled the bill. But Gambrazzio did not want to testify.

"Last night, I received the phone records which you ordered produced," George explained to Nickerson. "They indicate that Gambrazzio was not at the house on Brackett Road that weekend, but—"

"So, it's exactly the opposite of what you said the other day?" Welsh interrupted. The judge smiled slightly.

"Maybe you'll let me finish, Mr. Wonderful," George snapped. "She was on the phone all weekend with William Mulvey, who *was* at the house. . . . I'm not going to get into the stalking stuff. But I have been able to establish that Mulvey was home that weekend, which is a direct contradiction to both Frazier and Mulvey's testimony that their [*sic*] father was in Connecticut."

George had asked Gambrazzio to be in court that morning, but she hadn't shown up. Another witness, Frazier's would-be partner in crime, Eric Kinton, was also a no-show. George said Kinton had been served with a summons; he was uncertain about Gambrazzio. Nickerson indicated that he needed a return of service in hand to issue a warrant, tsk-tsk-ing at George again.

Jurors filed in at 9:05 A.M., and Burke returned to the stand. George got the investigator to repeat that he had never spoken to David Murphy after their phone interview, nor had he contacted Magnum Movers to verify who worked there, even though he knew that several members of Frazier's crew had weighty criminal histories.

George asked whether anyone looked into Christa's stored items. Burke said other troopers did that; he'd cleared it.

"And what was the purpose of checking on her storage facility? . . . To determine whether there was anything missing . . . or whether there was anything of any evidentiary value in this case?"

"I believe so, yes."

George handed him the Magnum Movers document showing that Sergeant Costa had signed in before going through Christa's locker. Burke testified again that after the first few days following the murder, David Perry was assigned to work with the MSP team, not Costa.

"And have you ever become aware of what Sergeant Costa removed from her storage facility?"

"No, I didn't know he removed anything." Burke added that Costa assisted on the first night "when we spoke with the Worthington family," but he had not been assigned to look for the murder weapon. "We were looking for the weapon," he said.

"And are you aware of whether or not Sergeant Costa conducted his own search for the weapon?"

"I'm not aware of that." Burke said he didn't know that Sergeant David Costa had been seen in the woods near Christa Worthington's house with a metal detector on January 7, 2006, at seven A.M.

Two or three local reporters knew absolutely where George was headed. Costa and another man had been spotted using a metal detector to search a culvert on Mill Pond Road, one-eighth of a mile west of 50 Depot Road, looking for "anything that might have been taken from Christa Worthington's residence," according to the MSP's report on the incident. Burke, the head investigator, had now forgotten about it. Costa first injected himself into the investigation after the discovery of Christa's body, unilaterally briefing the family, resulting in public disclosure of crime-scene details. He contacted Cape Cab and Mercedes Cab on January 12, ostensibly to determine if either had Depot Road area fares over the weekend of January 4–6. He took the liberty of interviewing Truro harbormaster Warren Roderick nine days later, on January 21. Roderick, a friend and confidant of the victim and her go-between with Tony Jackett, mentioned being quizzed by Costa when he was subsequently interviewed by Burke and Mason on April 30.

Was Costa bucking for a promotion, fantasizing that he would bag the killer single-handedly? Or was something else at work? Either way, Costa was part of George's strategy to muddy the waters, to upset the simple rape-murder scenario being thrown at McCowen.

He moved back to Tim Arnold's hospital interview, then spoke of Keith Amato, who would be the lead-off defense witness. At issue was the double standard investigators applied to these suspects, as opposed to McCowen. The only common thread was that no interview was recorded.

George reminded the detective that McCowen had been handed a recording waiver within minutes of signing his Miranda waiver, then asked if the defendant had sought advice. Burke said police were prohibited from offering advice.

Was McCowen ever provided with a written copy of his statement? Ever asked to initial the pages?

"No, he wasn't," Burke answered.

"Was Tim Arnold allowed to read his interviews?"

"I believe he looked at them prior to his testimony here."

Burke wasn't sure how many days it took Mason to transcribe his notes, because he'd been on vacation. He knew the report was not produced that evening. After examining it, the detective admitted that it had taken eight days to produce. He conceded again that Mc-Cowen was never given a copy to review.

George pointed to McCowen dropping Frazier's name two days after the body was discovered, when he met with his handlers at the Orleans Stop & Shop. Like Mason, Burke said he was not aware that the defendant had been a cooperating informant on January 8, 2002.

George asked when, exactly, the DNA report was slid across the table.

Echoing Mason, Burke said it was about an hour into the interview when McCowen looked down for a minute before saying, "It could have been me."

Burke admitted only that McCowen mentioned his past blackouts "around the same time." Mason had testified that the blackout discussion occurred just after McCowen was shown the DNA report. It was a small discrepancy, but the defense lawyer's goal was to illustrate that there was disagreement even between the two experienced detectives who conducted the unrecorded interrogation.

Sensing this, Burke reiterated that McCowen said he did not kill Christa and did not remember how he got home that evening and suggested that police check his alibis. Two and a half hours in, he still said he didn't remember how he got home that night. The pizza hadn't arrived yet, nor had McCowen taken a bathroom break. Even after he got his cigarettes, he said he was having a hard time remembering.

George pointed out that the defendant had used the word *if* in his explanations. "Was he corrected that he shouldn't be saying *if*?"

"Yes, he was." Burke explained that McCowen already had told them he had sex with Worthington, then changed his account.

"Did you pursue the fact . . . that he was now saying he was uncertain? Or did you just get him back on track?" George asked.

Later in the interview, McCowen continued to say "probably" and "would have" when suggesting that he went to Truro for sex. As late as the fourth or fifth version, Burke said, he was still using "if." He was told that the word was "no longer an option" for him.

"So, you needed him to give you a statement that matched up with the physical evidence, didn't you?" George asked.

"No, we needed him to tell us the truth," Burke responded, more adamant than he'd been so far.

George backed up to previous interviews, pointing out that McCowen offered to assist both times. Fourteen months passed before detectives collected his fingerprints and DNA, but McCowen hadn't quit his trash job. By the time of his arrest almost three and a half years after the murder, he had never once left Cape Cod.

McCowen "had never told you at any time that he had killed Christa Worthington, had he?"

"No, he hadn't," Burke said.

"He had actually given you a pretty detailed explanation, at least in his mind, of how Jeremy Frazier killed Christa Worthington, didn't he?"

"He said that Jeremy Frazier killed her, yes."

Burke conceded that McCowen told them Jeremy would claim he wasn't there and that McCowen was right. "Jeremy told us he wasn't there. Shawn Mulvey told us that he was with Jeremy at his house.

Chris Bearse said that he saw them leave the party and head toward Mulvey's."

"Shawn Mulvey told you he didn't know what you were talking about the first time you went to meet him, when you talked to him about Jeremy's alibi, isn't that true?"

The reference to the Mulvey interview of May 13, 2005, brought cross-examination back to McCowen's interview the night of his arrest. At 12:15 A.M., five hours in, he was still cooperating. At the five-and-a-half-hour mark, when he was notified of his right to a prompt arraignment, McCowen once more waived his right to remain silent, wanting to clear matters up.

Taking a slight detour, George asked if Burke had come across a letter McCowen wrote to Catherine Cisneros indicating that he had sex with Christa the day before. Welsh objected, and after another heated debate at sidebar, Nickerson ruled the letter inadmissible "hearsay."

Stymied, George huffed and puffed, saying that he'd take the matter up again with Cisneros on the stand. Nickerson nodded indulgently, the magisterial father figure. It was inescapable: George and Nickerson were channeling Joe Pesci and the tall, graying character actor Fred Gwynne in *My Cousin Vinny*, the 1992 comedy pitting an unstoppable (and unlicensed) defense attorney against a patriarchal small-town Southern judge. Was this trial a comedy also? Given all the byplay, at times it seemed so. McCowen didn't help; he rarely raised his head from doodling to take an interest in events that would define the rest of his life.

On redirect, Welsh yo-yoed back to Costa. Burke changed his tune, saying that the Truro Police sergeant answered to his chief, not the MSP, and would not have needed Burke's permission to follow a lead. Locals, in the gallery and at home glued to Court TV's live coverage, wondered why George didn't come back for another shot at the pug-nosed career sergeant over his 1999 conviction for lobster scrubbing. Blatantly lying under oath, Costa had so discredited himself and his department that Burke's boss, DA O'Keefe, declared to the press that his office wouldn't call Truro's number two to the stand unless he was "the sole witness in an ax murder."

Welsh's damage-control efforts exhausted, George asked Burke about Frazier's clothes, the Timberland boots, wool pants, leather jacket, and all-important blue and white Nautica sweater. Burke said he was aware of certain lab reports tied to Jeremy Frazier but did not know anything about blue and white fibers.

George produced Robert Martin's July 26, 2002, report and asked if blue and white fibers had been found on Worthington's body.

"That's what the document says, yes," Burke replied, blinking.

"Could you tell us where they were found?"

"Trace material was covered [*sic*] from Christa Worthington's pubic area."

"Do you know whether or not Martin ever compared the fibers from Jeremy Frazier's blue and white Nautica sweater to the blue and white fibers found in Christa Worthington's vaginal area?"

"I don't know that."

"Thank you, Sergeant," George said.

Wanting the last word, Welsh asked one question: Didn't the DNA swabs from Christa Worthington's body match Christopher Mc-Cowen? After Burke dutifully replied, "That's correct," the commonwealth rested.

George moved to dismiss the indictment. Motion denied.

He moved for a required finding of not guilty on aggravated rape and murder. Motion denied.

No one was surprised.

George began the defense with Keith Amato. Because the burden of proof in criminal cases rests on the prosecution, many defense lawyers keep their presentation of evidence to a minimum. George felt this case was different, with too many serious issues in play to run through quickly. He spotlighted police misconduct immediately.

"Mr. Amato, when is the first time we met, you and I?" Amato answered that it was just the previous Thursday evening, when George picked him up at the Hyannis airport.

Amato lived in New York City, his nine-year marriage to Braunwyn Jackett dead almost a half-dozen years. His work life, even before

Braunwyn, was jumbled, ranging from blue-collar construction to culinary school to minor acting gigs; at present, he was in the running for a part with Manhattan's Living Theater, working part-time as a chef and tugboat deck hand. The handsome forty-one-year-old had lived in Atlanta, Los Angeles, Florida, Hawaii, and Huntington, Long Island, where he'd grown up in an upper-middle-class family.

He'd first come to Cape Cod at age sixteen, during the summer of 1981, with a girl who would become his first wife. He returned in 1995 and met and married Tony Jackett's daughter. Their daughter, Etel, was born a year later. At the time of the Worthington murder, Keith worked construction by day and had his cooking job at High Toss Pizza in Wellfleet by night.

Strategically, George was using Amato to buttress the claim that Mc-Cowen, pressured by the cops, had falsely confessed. Like Tim Arnold, he had been a major suspect who was subjected to a grueling police interview pursuant to rumors that he'd had an affair with Christa, had substance-abuse issues, and abused women. George wanted the jury to see that even a self-assured cosmopolitan like Amato could buckle under police badgering. He was the first witness who knew Christa Worthington personally since the victim's cousin took the stand eight days earlier. He would also testify about the Jackett family, and here he had a lot to say. It was no coincidence that his ex-father-in-law, dressed in jeans and a fashionably beat-up leather bomber jacket, was now esconced in the press balcony, having driven the fifty miles from Provincetown to take in Keith's testimony. Perhaps he was worried.

More than any suspect on the radar screen during the long investigation, Jackett had motive to commit the crime: Christa had pressed him for child support and for health insurance for their daughter. When they'd met to discuss the issues behind St. Mary's of the Harbor in the East End of Provincetown, Tony refused, telling Christa that she'd "tricked" him and gotten pregnant intentionally. Christa had come away from the June 2001 meeting convinced she'd have to file a paternity suit. Friends advised against it. When she argued that she and Ava needed "maintenance money," Melik Kaylan, an old friend from Vassar, told her the Cape was "a small community" and "that's how people get hurt."

Jackett would soon be escorted out of the courtroom, though, as he was still a potential witness.

George jumped right in, asking for Keith's IQ. Amato replied that he had tested at 140 in eighth grade, adding, "Hopefully, it went up a little bit since then."

Next topic: the Jacketts. Amato said he and the rest of the family did not learn until May 2001, some two years after the child's birth, that Tony had fathered Ava. The news caused great turmoil. "It was really hard to fathom that Tony had a child for that long and nobody knew about it," he explained. "Everybody felt sort of betrayed, and it took a while for things to kind of—what's the right word?—kind of smooth out."

At the time, Keith was recovering from another family trauma, one that caused a rift between him and his father-in-law more than a year earlier. Etel, age four in the spring of 2000, was cruelly assaulted by a next-door neighbor's older child. Tony tried to hush the matter; his wife's father owned the apartment Amato and Braunwyn were occupying. Amato saw his father-in-law as an opportunist unwilling to seek justice for his granddaughter. When the two came close to blows, Amato called authorities. George asked if the incident caused problems within his marriage. Amato responded, "To say the least, sir."

Amato had never heard of Christa Worthington until Tony, pressured by his ex-mistress's threats of exposure, came clean about Ava. Keith met Christa for the first time at a break-the-ice get-together at the Jackett home during that summer of 2001.

"We had a little dinner party, and I cooked fajitas for everybody. Things had smoothed over a little bit, and everybody was trying to make the situation amicable for the baby."

He would see Christa just four more times, starting with an encounter at Pamet River, adjacent to the several Worthington properties on Depot Road. Tim Arnold was with Christa when Amato arrived with Etel for a swim, and, offering a common Cape Cod courtesy, Christa said that if he ever needed to shower when coming off the beach, he should feel free to use her outdoor shower at nearby 50 Depot.

Later that summer, he took her up on the offer, a move that piqued investigators' interest.

Several weeks after that, he saw Christa on the green at Truro

Center during a concert; he was with Etel, Christa with Ava. Their last encounter was on her birthday, in December, at High Toss Pizza while he was at work.

"She was a little bit depressed," he recalled.

Amato said his anger with Tony over the assault on Etel had never waned, but the murder threw the family into further turmoil. Tony's relationship with Braunwyn, quietly described by some locals as "too close," caused additional strain, especially after Braunwyn confronted Christa and accused her of "fleecing" Tony by demanding that Ava be put on his health insurance. When the incident with Etel forced Keith and Braunwyn to move, they were thrust into the Cape's insane summer housing market. Keith boarded with another man; Braunwyn and Etel moved in with the Jacketts. Amato explained that the idea was to "get a little money together and not pay ten thousand dollars for a two-month rental in the middle of the summer." Whether or not the separation accurately reflected the state of their marriage, police would use it against Amato later.

Amato characterized his first meeting with police, three weeks after the murder, as "very uneventful." At that point, it was common knowledge that his father-in-law was a prime suspect.

Amato was asked to come to the Truro station again on February 6 to speak with Mason and Trooper Jim Massari. Again, Amato said, the tone was friendly, so the request for a DNA sample caught him by surprise. "It kind of came out of nowhere. But my reaction was, by all means. If it helps in the investigation, take it." A month later, investigators contacted Amato's son from his first marriage, who was nineteen and lived on Long Island with his mother. "My son actually called me up crying. *Why are police asking questions about me?* It shook him up," Amato testified. The call, he added, caused a spat with his ex-wife.

A short time later, Amato attempted suicide. The attempt was half-hearted, but stemmed from a piling up of things, none of which, he said, had anything to do with the Worthington murder. But investigators grew more suspicious. A third interview was conducted on June 13 after Bill Burke, who had handled the incident involving Etel two years earlier, called and said investigators wanted to "review phone records."

Amato knew that police had asked around about his alibi: working construction from seven to five on Friday, January 4, then cooking at High Toss from 5:30 to ten that evening. He had assumed they were satisfied. He didn't know investigators had collected his son's DNA, as they had so many others', from a discarded soda can.

Mason and John Mawn met him in the lobby as soon as he arrived at the Truro police station, then escorted him upstairs. It was early afternoon. As they settled into the interview room, Mason pulled out a four-inch-thick ring binder of phone records. Keith, of course, was unaware that investigators had gathered hundreds of pages of such records, starting the day after Christa's body was found.

Right off, the officers accused him of lying. Mawn noted the inconsistencies in his previous statements about his marriage. Braunwyn had recently left for Colorado with her brother Luke; hadn't she found out about his affair with Christa? It was the same technique that would be used on McCowen.

Amato said he did not feel comfortable talking with them about his marriage. "It got very loud," he testified. "Trooper Mawn slammed his hand down on the table and said, 'This is a murder investigation. And if we so choose, we will turn your life inside out.' . . . I was starting to realize that the interview was not going in the way that I expected it . . . they were kind of looking at me in a different light. . . .

"I'm discussing with Trooper Mawn one thing and trying to defend myself . . . and Trooper Mason was interjecting, which was confusing me; and I wasn't really able to hold a thought together . . . I was starting to sweat . . . my heart was starting to race."

The detectives were particularly interested in Amato's shower at Christa's. Again, they insinuated that he lied. During the first two interviews, he hadn't mentioned that his friend Gino Monteiro was with him. Amato pointed out that they hadn't asked whether or not he was alone; besides, he'd forgotten Monteiro was there. The two were involved in theater. "We had been down at the Pamet swimming. And we had a play that night in Eastham. We were running a little bit late, so we used Christa's facilities to shower," Amato told the packed courtroom. Mawn, he said, saw that as a lie.

"What was his tone of voice when he said that to you?"

"His tone of voice was very aggressive. I was having a hard time . . . like I was turning into a suspect, it felt like. I was no longer just being asked innocuous questions . . . they were trying to establish something about me that was not true."

"At some point . . . did you end up agreeing with them?" George asked.

"Yes, I did, as a matter of fact. I agreed with Trooper Mawn that I had been lying because I was getting nowhere trying to explain to him that I wasn't lying, and it was draining me. . . . I was feeling very nervous at this point. I was without counsel. I was with these two state troopers that were kind of badgering me. And I was hoping that it would slow things down so maybe I could even catch a minute of clarity."

"And what did Trooper Mason say to you in the middle of all this?"

"Trooper Mason said to me, 'What has your mental state been throughout this winter?' And I said, 'Well, to be completely honest with you, I've been a little bit depressed.' And Trooper Mason said, 'Well, that's a bunch of BS. I'd call being a little bit depressed underrating it, because we know that you tried to commit suicide.' . . . I felt like somebody came up from behind me and hit me in the head with a stick. I was floored," Amato said, stopping to catch his breath. "There had only been three people, one of which was my therapist on Cape Cod, that knew about it," he added. "The other two were my ex-wife, who at the time was in Colorado, and my ex-wife's father, whom I had told this to two days earlier."

"That's Tony Jackett?"

"That's Tony Jackett, yes. It was appearing that people were saying things about me, like I was kind of being fed to the State Police to possibly take the onus off of other people."

Again, the witness told the courtroom his head was spinning; his body was covered in sweat. It was at this point, with Mason looking "directly in my eyes," that Burke came into the interrogation room, excusing the other two detectives. "I thought Sergeant Burke was a gift from God at that point, like he was going to rescue me from these guys," Amato explained. Instead, Burke said he'd been telling the officers that Amato was a stand-up guy, but now it was time for Amato to "tell the truth." This was the moment for him to choose: twenty-five years or life without parole.

It had been less than an hour since the same benign-looking Burke told the courtroom how fair and considerate, how professional and thoughtful, he and Mason had been when interviewing McCowen. Leaning forward, his hands on the witness-box rail, Amato went on, his voice firm. Burke, he said, posed the ultimatum, "Cop a plea, son, or we're going to send you away forever."

"My reaction to that was I felt like throwing up right there on the spot. I was devastated. I gathered myself and [said] I was a person [who] knew how the system works at times and that . . . my family would leverage and sell everything that they owned in order to get me the best defense possible. And that you're not going to pin this murder on me, is basically what I said."

After that, "I excused myself. I said, 'This is the end of this interview, and have a nice day.'" No one tried to stop him. Outside in the parking lot, "I threw up in the bushes across from my car."

When he looked at his watch, Amato realized he'd been in the room with the policemen for three and a half hours. "I had lost complete conception of time," he said.

Five months later, during a chance meeting at the Orleans courthouse on November 26, he asked Mawn if he was still a suspect. The trooper answered, "Keith, after we got through with you on that interview, we knew you didn't do it."

On cross, Welsh's goal was to show that the detectives' third degree had been justified, that police had good reason to suspect the witness. Welsh's efforts were fruitless. Right off, the articulate Amato took charge of the questions, correcting and adding to his answers. He stood up to the prosecutor as no witness had done so far.

Welsh dwelled on the shower at Christa's, leading Keith through information he'd given police. He had gone into the house after the shower; Christa was home with the baby, had soup on the stove. Later, he told Braunwyn he'd been there; his wife had no problem with it.

During the first two interviews, Welsh charged, Amato had told police he'd been alone, which was a lie. Self-possessed, Amato asked for a glass of water, then answered with a simple "Yes."

Welsh had him repeat that Mason never raised his voice during the third interview. He then asked if Amato hadn't been cleared on the basis of the DNA he surrendered.

Amato balked. "I was never told that. *Ever.*"

"You were cleared, were you not?"

"I was never told that, sir."

The "sir" was resonant, indistinguishable from *Screw you.*

"All right. Well, you weren't arrested, were you, sir?" the prosecutor pressed.

"No, I wasn't arrested," Amato fired back. "But I was also never told that my DNA was cleared by anybody in the state, no."

Welsh moved to Gino Monteiro. Had Amato lied about his being at Christa's to get the police to stop badgering?

"No, I was not lying, sir. As I explained earlier in my testimony to the defense, I had honestly and inadvertently forgot that Gino came with me. There was a lot on my mind at that point in my life concerning situations with my daughter, concerning being homeless, concerning the fact that the family was embroiled in this murder investigation."

Welsh agreed to call it a slip but asked if Amato realized that police had to reinterview countless people because of his little slip.

George objected. Nickerson said the witness could answer if he knew.

Amato remained defiant. "I'm aware that they would probably have to go over it if somebody inadvertently forgot something, yes. But I am not a liar, sir."

Welsh again insinuated that the interview got off to a bad start because police thought he was lying.

Amato interrupted. "This is reminiscent of the interview, sir. I did not lie to the State Police. I had inadvertently forgot to tell them this."

"My questioning of you here today is reminiscent of the interview?" Welsh asked, his tone surprised.

"Yes, the way you're questioning me right now."

"All right. And did you tell the police that you had lied about the third visit with Christa that took place at her residence?"

"At that point in the interview, sir, the way it was being conducted and the hostility that I felt and the fear that I was feeling, I would have told the State Police that I was the king of Alaska, sir."

Prosecutors like Welsh bank on scaring witnesses, but he couldn't scare this one. Amato's "king of Alaska" statement would be quoted in full in the national press the next day. If a strong-willed man with a 140 IQ would have told Mason he was "the king of Alaska," what about the undereducated, eager-to-please McCowen?

The prosecutor did not back off, though. He rehashed the shower details, asking if Amato recalled Trooper Mawn inquiring "what you did for underwear and things of that nature."

"I recall Trooper Mawn being very aggressive and not . . ."

"Sir . . ."

". . . not believing that I had put my pants on over my bathing suit, saying that was definitely a lie. I tried to explain that it was a Speedo bathing suit, which is a suit professional swimmers use. And at that point, Trooper Mawn said, 'Oh, are you a fag wearing a Speedo?' He then asked me if I had had sex with men. And I asked him, 'What relevance does that have to what's going on here?'"

A fag wearing a Speedo? Reporters buzzed. A witness besting a prosecutor can be entertaining enough, but the cheeky Amato had truly come into his own here. Welsh was drowning, eliciting answers that bolstered the defense.

The prosecutor argued that Amato knew he was a suspect before the interview that made him throw up; he'd made a comment to that effect beforehand that got back to police.

Amato interrupted him. "I think what they were referring to is when Peter Manso [this author] came to High Toss Pizza at one point during the winter. And jokingly, I said, 'Peter, if something happens to me, you'll get me Alan Dershowitz, right?'"

"And that was a lighthearted comment?"

"That was absolutely a lighthearted comment."

Welsh shook his head skeptically for the jury's benefit, then moved back to the suicide attempt. "It happened, didn't it?"

"That was a cry for help, sir," the witness answered. "Yes, you're absolutely right."

"But I mean Detective Burke didn't manufacture some story about a suicide and put it in front of you?"

"No, he did not, sir."

"And at the end of the interview, sir, are you saying that Burke threatened you with a jail sentence?"

"Absolutely."

Welsh's harsh questions did indeed echo the interview Amato had described, and one of the few black spectators in the courtroom, a short, middle-aged woman who would later befriend Catherine Cisneros, couldn't suppress her grin. At a Celtics or Socks game, the woman would have been cheering her brains out.

Welsh's final question was whether Amato had ever been charged with the murder.

Obstinate to the end, Amato replied coldly, "No, I believe we established that already."

He'd dismissed the prosecutor like a pesky bug.

On redirect, George stayed with the suicide attempt, asking if it was manufactured. "What was manufactured was its connection to the Christa Worthington case, isn't that so?"

"Yes. Trooper Mason stated that it looked very suspicious . . . that it might be in connection with Christa's murder, me being involved . . ."

George returned to the pressure put on Amato during the interview.

"I would have told them anything at that point," Amato said. "I was feeling really intimidated. I was without counsel . . . in the throes of a panic attack."

According to the police, he said, someone had reported that he was seen kissing Christa, that he'd taken multiple showers at her house, not just one, and that he'd been at a Provincetown Inn rendezvous with Christa and Ava, drinking. "And this was all not true."

Brandishing the police report of the June 13 interview, George noted that it did not reflect the threats and accusations Amato had endured, then established that it was Mason who wrote it, just as it was Mason who wrote the report on McCowen's interrogation after the arrest. The same supervisor (father of Truro patrolman Meredith Allen), Detective Lieutenant John Allen, signed off on both reports.

"Did they ask you if you wanted to be taped?"

"No, they never asked me if I wanted to be taped. They never asked me if I wanted a lawyer present."

"Were any of your interviews taped?"

Amato shook his head. "No."

"Thank you. Nothing further of this witness."

As intended, the abrupt wrap-up left Welsh scrambling. On recross, he tried to cast doubt on Amato's account of the June 13 interview, reminding the witness that he'd compared that hostile experience to their exchange there in the courtroom. "Would you have told this jury anything just to stop my questioning?" he asked weightily.

"Absolutely not, sir. I'm in a court of law under oath in front of the movie cameras and press."

An edge of sarcasm in his voice, Amato was hamming it up aplenty, enjoying himself on national TV.

"And you can tell the truth, sir, even when you are under pressure and they're asking you the tough questions, can't you, sir?" the prosecutor went on.

"I told them the truth the whole time, yes, sir."

"You're not going to just agree with what the police ask you because the questions are tough, are you?"

"No, I'm not."

"You're going to tell the truth?" Welsh repeated.

"That is what I did throughout."

"As you have here today?"

"That is true."

New York City had battled small-town Cape Cod, and New York was the victor, hands down. Stepping away from the witness, the frustrated prosecutor spat, weakly, "That's all I have. Thank you," and retreated to the prosecution table.

George next called Russell Redgate, Tim Arnold's lawyer. Before he could proceed, Welsh complained: George would likely introduce the four letters Redgate wrote to the DA's office, which would violate the attorney-client privilege.

Nickerson rolled his eyes. The commonwealth was not the client; it was up to Redgate, not Welsh, to raise the issue. The objection wasn't just misplaced, it made no sense.

Redgate, a tall, deliberate man, testified that Arnold hired him on June 16, 2002. That same day, he sent the first of four letters to Michael O'Keefe, then still the first assistant DA. George wanted to address the second letter, dated January 20, 2003. Responding to Mason and Burke's interrogation of the pajama-clad Arnold in Hyannis two days earlier, Redgate drew the parameters for future police contact with his client: all interviews were to be recorded, Redgate was to be present, and all past statements attributed to his client were to be produced in full.

Redgate never received any statements, largely because O'Keefe's office resisted document production, mandatory or not. Redgate had also explained that he wanted the interviews recorded "so that there would be an accurate record, not subject to people's memories" and "to eliminate questions about the way in which things were said."

None of the subsequent interviews was recorded, however. And until McCowen was arrested, Redgate was never, not once, told that his client had been cleared.

The witness's testimony was interrupted by the lunch break. Trial resumed with a brief, inconsequential cross, after which George called Don Horton, the owner of Cape Cod Disposal. Horton had employed McCowen from June 2000 to November 2002, eleven months after the murder. His company provided trash service from Harwich to Provincetown, and 50 Depot Road was one of about 100 stops on McCowen's Thursday route. His job also included painting dumpsters, vehicle maintenance, and yard chores.

Horton testified that the defendant was a good, if not model, employee. He showed up for work on time, completed his route on schedule. The only feedback ever received about McCowen was positive: "They liked him. In fact, they still ask about him. Elderly ladies even baked him cookies."

McCowen's pot smoking caught up with him at one point. After a drug test confirmed Horton's suspicion, he had another employee travel with Chris; it was a safety issue. When McCowen's driver's license was suspended, Horton reluctantly let him go.

The defense attorney asked about Christmas trees. Horton explained that trees, wood products in general, had to be separated from garbage. Drivers often stuffed them behind the cab, then threw them into the woods behind his building. Some customers were charged extra, some not. He remembered McCowen calling in that week about a tree but wasn't sure which day.

On cross, Welsh addressed the pot smoking—"So, he was not a model employee, was he?"—before focusing on McCowen's intelligence. The prosecutor established that the defendant learned his route in two to three weeks, the same as any other driver.

After Horton acknowledged that he could not recall asking Mc-Cowen if he'd had sex with Christa, the prosecutor quickly segued to the $10 million lawsuit Toppy Worthington had filed against the trash company, seeking to saddle Horton with civil liability for his employee's alleged crimes. Welsh asked Horton if his prospects would be better if McCowen was acquitted.

George objected. Nickerson overruled, earning a big laugh from the packed courtroom by adding, "Overruled means go ahead. It would be easier if I said stop and go, but I say overruled and sustained."

The laughter was telling. By now, the two attorneys had become irreconcilable siblings. Everything was an issue. Every point won or lost had become potentially decisive.

Horton agreed that McCowen's acquittal would help with the civil suit. He denied that this fact affected his memory.

When George took over, Horton confirmed that he had not been sued when he gave a statement to troopers on April 19, 2005.

"How much do you make a year, Mr. Horton?"

"Well, some years are good, some years are bad. But I would say around sixty thousand dollars."

"You'd have to work about two hundred years to pay this off if they get that, right?"

"It would be a while," the short, rumpled man answered, old-fashioned New England humor intact. Many in the audience laughed again. The Worthington clan, like figures in a Grant Wood painting, remained starchily stony-faced, although most had known Don Horton, their Truro neighbor, for more than fifty years.

George's fourth witness was seventy-six-year-old, bearded Girard Smith, the epitome of the respectable elderly citizen, a relief from the parade of low-life dopers, rappers, cops, and snitches who had testified for the commonwealth. Smith was the son of another old-time Truro family and returned in 1998 after a career selling office furniture. He worked summers at Highland Light in North Truro, one of Cape Cod's oldest lighthouses, educating visitors about the area's history. He also served on the board of directors for Truro's Council on Aging, the Truro Neighborhood Association, and Elder Services for the Cape and Islands.

On January 16, 2002, ten days after Tim Arnold discovered Christa's body, Smith ran into Chief John Thomas at a town selectmen's meeting and described seeing a car shoot down the driveway of 50 Depot Road on Saturday, January 5. He testified that he had detoured from his normal walking route that day. It was Saturday; he was unable to get to the post office by the noon closing.

At the time, he did not know where Christa Worthington lived, but he was walking on Depot, "not far from the harbor," when he heard the car coming down the long driveway. He turned and observed a large dark vehicle turn right at the bottom of the drive and disappear, heading east toward Route 6. His focus was more on the driver than on the vehicle, he said. George asked him to describe the person.

"He was Caucasian. He was a little dark, but he was not black. And he did not—the thing that surprised me, he didn't look left or right. He just came right out. So, all I saw was a profile."

"How old was the person, if you know, sir?"

"I thought he was in his late thirties, in that general area."

Three days after his conversation with Chief Thomas, Smith, who was puzzled that police hadn't gotten in touch with him, came across Mason and Mawn while taking another neighborhood walk. The two detectives were canvassing the area, checking its many unoccupied summer homes. George asked about the encounter.

"Well, to start with, they asked me who I was. And they had a file that they went through. 'Oh, you're the walker?' They started asking me questions [about] what I had told the police chief."

Smith told them that the vehicle could have been a van or a truck; it was large, possibly a work truck. He believed the number 16, 17, or 18 appeared on the license plate. He had stood about fifteen feet from the vehicle, he said, close enough to see clearly.

After that chance meeting, police brought Smith photographs of vehicles, but he couldn't identify the exact type. He knew only that it was big and dark. He was never shown photographs of possible drivers.

George showed the witness a picture of Matthew Frazier's orange truck and asked him to imagine it black. He also got Smith to acknowledge that police called him just the previous week, on Thursday, wanting to talk to him; before then, he hadn't heard from investigators since February 2002. Their call came the day after the truck issue was raised in court, during George's cross-examination of Mason.

It was clear that investigators had never taken Smith's account seriously. But why? And why did police take an interest only when they learned that Smith was on George's witness list? Because he had told them that the driver of the runaway vehicle was Caucasian, not African-American? What did they need now?

On cross, Welsh addressed the delay between the murder and Smith's report. He'd first heard about the murder at the post office, where reporters and police gathered the day after the body was found, yet he had only spoken up at the selectmen's meeting almost two weeks later; he hadn't gone directly to the police station.

The prosecutor also tried to confuse Smith, suggesting that he had seen the vehicle closer to two P.M. and wondering how Smith picked up his mail before the post office closed. Smith corrected him quickly: he never told police it was two P.M., and he had decided not to go to the post office.

Smith's testimony established that a young, nonblack driver had peeled out of the victim's driveway less than a dozen hours after the estimated time of the murder. Welsh's frustration at not being able to poke holes in this story was evident. His voice had grown harsher; he was careless about attacking the geriatric gentleman. Smith was the day's second witness to contradict police reports. Like Amato, Smith wouldn't budge.

During a follow-up interview, Smith was shown a bunch of Sunday newspaper auto ads in an attempt to ID the rogue vehicle. "All right. Did it look like this van, sir?" Welsh asked as he pointed to one.

"Could it have looked like that van?" Smith answered. "Four and a half years later, I'm not going to tell you yes or no. I have no idea."

Was it an SUV? A Chevy Suburban? A Ford Explorer? Smith could not say.

The elderly Truroite testified that he did not see a snowplow, eliminating Matthew Frazier's truck. Welsh suggested that he had fabricated the story to sell to Jan Worthington's TV crew. Again, the prosecution strategy failed. Smith had been splitting wood at Jack's Gas—the Route 6 filling station made legendary by Edward Hopper's painting—when the HBO crew pulled in, asking him to appear on camera. Eight or nine other locals, in addition to Worthington, had been paid to tell their stories, so he asked to be paid as well, he admitted. But when the crew asked him to sign off on his story, he refused. He was never paid.

When Welsh sat down, George returned to the cops' sudden interest in Smith the previous Thursday. The witness told them he had an appointment that afternoon but could meet later, at 3:30 P.M.

Cape prosecutors shy away from jurors from Provincetown, Truro, and Wellfleet, where people tend to vote Democratic, are traditionally "artsier" and think for themselves. George was determined to exploit these qualities in Smith.

"And last Thursday at about four, when you showed up at the Truro police station after four years to talk to the police again about this case, who was there to interview you?"

"Nobody. They'd left."

When the jury was dismissed at 3:48 P.M. two matters remained before the court. First, a capias for Eric Kinton, the African-American boyfriend of Chris Bearse's mother, who ignored his subpoena. George wanted Kinton held overnight, so he would be available to testify in the morning.

Nickerson ordered a probation check on the ex-con. While waiting for the report, he turned to the second issue: George's request for a jury view of 50 Depot Road. Suddenly, the judge looked up, aware of a disruption in the courtroom. It was not Toppy Worthington this time. He focused on Catherine Cisneros, the defendant's girlfriend, seated in the front row.

"Now, Mrs. Zernos," he boomed, getting the name wrong, "you have been engaging in running conversations during the course of this trial. Frankly, I'm not going to tolerate it any longer. Do you understand, ma'am?"

Meekly, Cisneros replied, "Yeah."

"*Yes?*"

"Yes, sir."

"All right. Let's stop with the chitchat, please."

Returning to George's request, he said he'd had a peculiar encounter with the woman who now owned the Depot Road property. She refused even to state her name. Her attorney had intervened. The owners were opposed to the view but would not contest it as long as the press was held at bay.

The view, said the judge, would likely not take place until Friday or Monday.

Nickerson turned back to Kinton, but George had changed his mind. He didn't need a warrant after all. Nickerson sighed, then rose. They were done for the day.

Day 13, Thursday, November 2

The morning's first witness, Elaine Gambrazzio, was in her mid- to late thirties, hard-looking, and she had been dating Shawn Mulvey's father, William, at the time of the murder. George hoped her testimony would prove that William Mulvey had been at home the Friday night of the murder, when Frazier claimed he slept there. Shawn Mulvey, Frazier, and Bearse all testified that no one ever spent the night at Shawn's when his father was home. If William Mulvey was there, Frazier was not.

There were a few problems. First of all, Gambrazzio had not been on-Cape that night but at her home in Abington, south of Boston. George planned to use telephone records to prove that several lengthy calls were made from her phone to William Mulvey's, but even so, the records were far from conclusive. Moreover, Gambrazzio was a reluctant witness. She had dated "Terry" Mulvey for two and a half years, and the relationship had not ended well; her former boyfriend had intimidated her, making her loath to appear at trial. His past lent credence to her fear.

The story was not pretty, but it was useful to the defense. After thirty-three years as a firefighter in West Haven, Connecticut, "Terry" Mulvey was chosen from sixty applicants to become Eastham's fire chief in April 1999. Then, in January 2000, he was arrested in West Haven, charged with stalking a former girlfriend. Eastham suspended Mulvey and, in May of that year, fired him.

The phone records showed that between Thursday, January 3, and Sunday, January 6, Gambrazzio made ten calls to the Mulvey residence. On January 3, her 5:07 P.M. call lasted 2 minutes, 39 seconds; her 5:19 P.M. call was 45 minutes, 11 seconds. She could not recall the conversations, but she testified that she lived alone; Terry and Shawn were the only residents of the Mulvey household. Conversations with Shawn would have been short. Pushed by George about the longer call, she said, "It would have to be Terry."

She called the Mulvey home twice more that night. At 10:26 P.M., the call lasted 5 minutes; at 10:58 P.M., 65 minutes.

The only two calls made on January 4, the night the prosecution claimed Christa Worthington was murdered, were short: one at 10:51 P.M. lasted 7 seconds; another at 11:00 P.M. lasted 11 seconds. Maybe someone in the Mulvey residence picked up the phone, then hung up. Or perhaps she reached an answering machine.

The next morning, the fifth, Gambrazzio called again, three times in rapid succession: at 11:27 A.M., the call lasted 23 seconds; at 11:28, just 8 seconds. The third, placed at 11:29, went on for 37 minutes, 50 seconds. She called once more after noon, at 12:47 P.M., and was on for 4 minutes, 30 seconds.

None of these calls was placed during the time Frazier and Shawn Mulvey claimed they were at the house together. On cross, Welsh suggested that the two calls late Friday night had gone into voice mail. He wondered if she ever had conversations that short with her former boyfriend. Gambrazzio said no, adding, "I usually hung up on him once he became annoying."

Welsh tried to suggest that the two short Saturday calls were picked up by a machine. But it was clear that within two minutes of the first call, a lengthy conversation ensued.

The back-and-forth between witness and prosecutor went on for almost ten minutes. At one point, Gambrazzio stopped, anxious about identifying her town. On redirect, George wanted her to elaborate.

Welsh objected. George explained at sidebar that she lived in "deathly fear of Bill Mulvey."

Nickerson was skeptical. He deemed Gambrazzio's testimony "minimally relevant" and said he had concerns about why George had called her.

"It's not my role to reach the factual conclusion in that, and I will not," he explained as if addressing a law-school class, astute and over-bearing. "Likewise, it's not my role to determine relevancy based on the weight of evidence. The parsing out of weight is strictly up to the jury. . . . I will allow you to inquire in this regard. She has shown some obvious tension and reluctance to testify in the matter."

George did his little bob and weave, which by now most of the reporters had come to see for what it was. He then asked why the witness was reluctant to name her hometown. Was it Mulvey?

"Most definitely. . . . He harasses me on the telephone."

Mulvey had called her a few days after George's investigator visited. She told him to stay out of her life and hung up. He kept calling. She didn't answer.

Welsh objected to the line of questioning, and Nickerson sustained; the court had heard enough.

Still, the question hung in the air: if William Mulvey had returned to the house within an hour or two after Frazier left on Saturday, why wouldn't Shawn remember? His claim that his father had not been home at all that weekend did not seem credible. Coupled with the confusion about which cars the two young men were driving, Gambrazzio's testimony seemed more relevant than Nickerson allowed. It didn't blast a hole in Frazier's alibi, but it was another brick in the growing wall of reasonable doubt.

*   *   *

Eric Kinton, a lean, almost gaunt black man wearing a Black Panther–
type leather jacket over Levi's, proved not nearly as reluctant a witness
as George had assumed. Once on the stand, he admitted his check-
ered past, explaining that he came to the Cape in 1999 from Boston
to "change his life." He had a child with Chris Bearse's mother, although they were no longer together.

George was interested in the conversation Kinton had with Jeremy Frazier. The witness knew Frazier because he came to the house
with Chris Bearse "all the time." Frazier seemed polite enough, always removing his hat when he came inside. One day, Bearse gave
Kinton Jeremy's phone number and asked him to call.

"Jeremy said he had a pickup. He mentioned there was a house—
jewelry, coins, money. And it got kind of abrasive when he explained
to me that it was a woman. Because I asked him who it was. You know,
was it somebody local, a local drug dealer? You know, what are you
getting into? And he explained that it was a woman. And that's when
I got kind of irate with him."

A "pickup," Kinton explained, was "street lingo . . . just something
[that was] quick money, easy money."

"Did he go on to explain that the pickup involved some type of
breaking and entering or robbing someone's house?"

"Yes."

"Now, after he made this proposition to you on the phone, did
you take him up on it?"

"Absolutely not. I'm not a B and E artist. I've never broken into
anyone's house."

Burke and Mason had questioned Kinton just before the start
of the trial. Jared Bearse, Chris's brother, had told them about the
phone call. Kinton told the officers that the conversation occurred
before the murder. He repeated that assertion when questioned
by defense investigators and again when he spoke with George.

"I know for a fact without anyone saying anything to me that the
conversation took place *before* the murder," he testified.

George was done. In this instance, less was more.

Welsh tried to establish that Frazier could have been referring to *any* house, in *any* town on the Lower Cape. Likewise, Kinton had never assigned a year to the Frazier call. Couldn't it have been 2003? 2004? Kinton shook his head, it happened before the murder.

Welsh pointed out that Frazier never actually told Kinton, "I did this or I didn't do this thing."

"No, I didn't speak to him anymore. The only other occasion that I spoke about him was when it all came out. I told Christopher and his mother, if he did have any involvement, I didn't want him in my house or around my house no more."

George's next witness was probably more reluctant than even the last two. Pamela Worthington Franklin, like Girard Smith and Keith Amato, would blatantly contradict police reports. But her testimony would work against the defense, so much so that many wondered why George called her to the stand.

Pam, the second oldest of Christa's cousins, and her husband, Teddy, lived at 49 Depot Road, directly opposite Christa's driveway. She and her aunt Diana, Toppy's sister, were closest to Christa of all the Cape family members. Pam had been interviewed by Burke the night the body was discovered, then again by Burke and Mason three months later on April 8. George held the reports generated by these interviews.

Ever the fashion plate, Pam had outdone herself for her appearance on the stand. As she settled into the witness chair, one female reporter catalogued her outfit aloud: a tailored Vera Wang suit, bracelets, bangles, studded gold earrings, and a pale Hermès-logo scarf. Her makeup was nearly perfect: thick blush, lip gloss, and mascara a skosh too dark for her highlighted strawberry-blond hair. Her footwear and matching handbag, per the reporter, were "either Jimmy Choo or Christian Louboutin."

For years, Pam's passion for clothes had been the subject of talk among friends who benefited from her annual castoffs. She was totally into her appearance and its effect on men, even Nickerson. Too smart to give any indication of lasciviousness, the judge nonetheless did nothing to hide his admiration. As Pam made herself comfortable in the witness chair, she smiled back at him a tad nervously, then testified that she was close to her cousin at the time of the murder.

George asked if she spoke with detectives about whether Christa had been in a relationship at the time. She said she didn't recall. This was her first misstatement. During the April 8 interview, Mason reported, Pam told the officers she "would not be surprised if Christa was in a relationship at the time of her death." Further, she was on record as saying that Christa "would entertain a possible relationship with any type of man regardless of status, looks, personality, or marital status."

This latter admission was critical, given the defendant's color and claim of consensual sex, but when George tried to show Franklin the pertinent paragraph in Mason's report, Welsh objected. The victim's past relationships were not relevant, he said.

The parties would learn later that jurors had a hard time imagining the wellborn victim in an affair with a black garbageman or even that Christa had affairs with multiple men. But Pam had told police that her cousin's past relationships had been "intense and tended to involve conflict," that there was a "slyness" to Christa, that she played everything "close to the vest" and, most weightily, was "looking for love through sex."

Welsh knew the contents of the reports, just as he knew what police had been told by Christa's psychiatrist. He also knew that his boss, Mike O'Keefe, had famously called the victim "an equal opportunity employer" who would bed "the husbands of her female friends, the butcher, or the baker," which coincided at least partly with Pam's statements to police. Even so, the prosecutor was determined to shut down George's questioning.

Nickerson turned to his computer, reviewing the transcript, then asked for the police report again. "It's the sort of thing that's right on the cusp of what should or should not be admitted. I'm going to allow it."

Asked to explain the disparities between her statements to police and what she was saying now, Pam affected the same woeful, family-of-victim body language her sister Jan displayed earlier and put a spin on her comment about Christa's "intense" relationships: her cousin's involvements tended to be intense because she so cared for the other person. Pam denied using the word *conflict* altogether and claimed not to remember saying that her cousin would entertain "any man," regardless of class or color. "I'm sure I didn't say those words," she insisted. Christa's boyfriends were limited to "the two that I knew of in the last five years."

She added that Christa "would have been interested or attracted to certain men that were writers, artists, somewhere along the line of the way she viewed the world."

This was the kind of fabrication people think they can get away with on off-season Cape Cod, where norms of plausibility are not part of the everyday foliage, even for those not afflicted with Worthington hubris. Tony Jackett, the father of Christa's baby, an artist? A poet? Jackett's greatest talent was the art of self-promotion, the gift of gab. Cousin Pam's claim that Christa had only two boyfriends during the last five years of her life was equally absurd; ID-ing her various lovers had become a popular, all but ubiquitous, local Truro pastime.

But jurors sat rapt, enamored of the witness, as though Martha Stewart herself were on the witness stand. Call it class envy. The teachers, social workers, and food wholesalers who held McCowen's fate in their hands were a little starstruck, gazing across at those yards of Hermès that seemed to speak to them of truth and virtue.

George asked if it was possible that Christa had been in a relationship that Pam didn't know about, given her "slyness," her tendency to play everything "close to the vest"?

"I believe that had she been in a relationship at the time of her death, she would have told me," the witness answered, looking at the lawyer directly.

George asked about her telling police she sometimes heard voices and cars in Christa's driveway and that she'd heard something that very Sunday afternoon when the body was found.

"I took my dog outside approximately one to one-thirty and was sitting on my porch and heard what I thought was a woman's voice, yelling, 'Stop it. Stop it.'" Pam didn't think it was Christa. Maybe someone farther down Old County Road was yelling at a dog, she suggested.

From the defense table, George retrieved a large aerial photo of
the area and asked Pam to locate Old County. The sandy lane was
barely wide enough for two cars to pass and well past Christa's cottage, with nothing but woods and a few houses in between. Burke's
report quoted Pam on January 6 saying she heard a vehicle go up
Christa's driveway that Sunday. Now she testified she didn't hear a
vehicle at all. When George showed her the report, she again shook
her head and said she didn't remember making the comment.

She admitted telling Sergeant Burke that the voice she heard
didn't sound like Christa's and that it came from "somewhere" on
Old County "between one and one-thirty, I believe."

Afterward, she said, she went inside and continued making a stew.
George ended direct.

Welsh asked if the voice she'd heard was even a woman's. Pam
hedged, said it could have been a man's. She testified that Tim Arnold
treated Christa "very well," not what she reported to Burke following
the murder. Back then, she said Christa was nervous because Tim was
such a handful, with his brain surgery, depression, and financial woes.

On redirect, she again denied telling Mason and Burke that
Christa might have had a lover at the time of her death. George
folded, cutting his losses. He'd gotten pretty much nowhere. The witness later thanked him for being so nice to her.

After morning recess, George asked for a sidebar. His next witness,
Matthew Salamone, a Cape Cod Disposal employee, would testify that
McCowen told him during fall 2001 that he was having a relation-
ship with "a rich woman from Truro" who was on his garbage route.
The conversation allegedly occurred at Rick's Outer Bar. Christa
Worthington was not named.

Welsh argued that the conversation was hearsay. Nickerson
agreed. Salamone was out.

George had expected Pam to testify that Christa had relationships
with many different kinds of men, then have Salamone testify to Mc-
Cowen's mention of an affair with the wealthy woman in Truro. His
plan had failed. He moved on to the first of his several defense experts.

No one knew why he wasn't calling Christa's shrink, Dr. John Livingston, or Trooper James Massari, who'd interviewed Livingston. The Provincetown-based Livingston had spoken of Christa as a woman who "always seemed dissatisfied." She had quit therapy following her rapprochement with the Jacketts in 2001, and the doctor said he "would not be surprised" if she had thrown herself into another relationship, which more than passingly echoed Pam's statement to Detective Burke that Christa "did not want to be alone" and was "looking for love through sex."

At the very least, testimony from Livingston would have presented jurors with a Christa who was more complex than they wanted to acknowledge.

The first defense expert was Dr. Richard Saferstein, who had spent twenty-one years as chief forensic scientist for the New Jersey State Police. As a professional witness, Saferstein had testified in 1,500 to 2,000 trials, and here his testimony began with investigators' mistakes while testing evidence, the most damaging being the semen swabbed from Christa's outer genital area, never analyzed for DNA.

"There is a very important piece of evidence that's sitting on a shelf in the Massachusetts State Crime Lab right now," he said. "We have a big question mark here that could have readily been solved with that one specimen."

Saferstein reiterated that the semen found inside Worthington's vagina had a low sperm count, consistent with being deposited several days before the body was found. He noted that investigators overlooked the eleven-and-three-quarter-inch hair found on Christa's breast; her hair was similar in color but several inches shorter. Again, no microscopic testing was conducted. No testing was done on any of the hairs found at the crime scene.

Investigators also ignored various bloodstains, including those found on the broom handle, the hand mitt, the bathroom rug, the towel, and the bathroom sink, all assumed to be the results of Ava's attempts to clean her mother. The wash towels should have undergone additional testing to determine if anyone wiped their hands after mopping up.

Investigators wasted the cast police made of a footprint outside near Christa's car. No attempt was made even to determine the shoe size, Saferstein observed.

Finally, he chastised, blue and white fibers found on the body were never compared to Frazier's blue and white Nautica sweater.

With the jury back from lunch at 2:11 P.M., George called Catherine Cisneros to testify that McCowen had been stoned at the time of his arrest and had barely eaten all day. But George was worried; with Cisneros fidgeting in the witness box, he asked Nickerson at sidebar to set parameters for her testimony. He'd steer clear of questions about her relationship with McCowen, he said, but would that keep the door closed on prior domestics per the judge's earlier limiting instruction?

Nickerson shook his head; he'd rule on those issues as they arose. George nodded, then declared that he had no questions for the witness and gestured for Cisneros to step down. Nickerson immediately called him back.

"I'm not quite sure what sort of stunt was just played out in front of the court," he hissed, "but let me be very clear. My last ruling was simply a ruling that would take things question by question. I in no way foreclosed evidence of any kind here at the sidebar."

It was impossible to know whether this performance was strictly for the record or if it came from some deeper place in the judge's Yankee soul. But with different approaches to the law and vastly disparate personalities, Nickerson and George had been going at each other for almost two weeks now, and it was clear that their slow simmer was likely about to reach a boil.

The two stared at each other for a moment. Then, in a low, throaty voice, George raised another issue: the next witness, Dr. Eric Brown, was due to arrive in the courtroom at three P.M. Right now he wasn't here. The afternoon's testimony hadn't taken as long as anticipated. It was only 2:15.

Nickerson sent the jurors to the jury room. No sooner were they gone than Welsh jumped in, arguing again that Brown should be precluded from telling jurors what McCowen told him: that he had sex with Christa Worthington on Thursday. The comment was hearsay, he said. George, happy not to have to deal with another "tardiness" lecture from the bench, countered that the statement fell within the state-of-mind exception to the hearsay rule.

Furrowing his brow, the judge expressed skepticism about sex with Worthington being a state-of-mind issue. "It's much more than that, Your Honor," George said, rebounding. McCowen spoke with Worthington about removing the ornaments before he hauled her Christmas tree. But instead of hauling it after calling Horton, he had sex with Christa on the living-room floor. Mason testified that the sex between McCowen and Christa occurred on Friday. McCowen told Brown he confused the two days during the interview; he'd been wasted and tired.

"If the jury can't hear what McCowen was thinking during the interview," George said, "and if the sex on Thursday is part and parcel of what he was thinking and why he was saying the things he was saying, they can't get a full picture of whether or not this was a voluntary statement."

After once more reviewing case law, the judge ruled: Brown was precluded from testifying about McCowen's state of mind. The defendant had not described what he felt while talking to Brown but what he felt earlier during the police interview.

The ruling made it impossible for Brown to refer to the Thursday sex scenario, unless Welsh opened the door on cross. George could only hope.

Later events proved that the setback was major.

At 3:22 P.M., Dr. Eric Brown took the stand and described himself as a PhD with twenty-three years of experience as a licensed clinical psychologist. He'd served on staff at Boston's Community Mental Health Center, taught in the psychology department at Beth Israel Hospital, a branch of Harvard Medical School, and in 1987 became chief of mental health at the Suffolk County House of Correction. He was now in private practice, seeing fifteen psychotherapy patients weekly.

He had been an expert witness in 150 trials and was being paid $200 an hour to testify at this one.

Brown had reviewed McCowen's pediatric records, as well as his three police interviews, then met with the defendant for a total of fourteen hours, during which he administered two standardized tests: the Wechsler Adult Intelligence Scale, "the gold measure," and the Wechsler Memory Scale. Among the areas he evaluated were McCowen's understanding and use of language.

McCowen scored a 78 on the verbal IQ test, placing him in the lowest seventh percentile. A score of 100 is average, Brown said.

The witness next testified that he believed McCowen was under the influence of marijuana and Percocet on the day of his arrest, that stress and these drugs had definitely affected his performance. Fatigue would have been a negative factor, too; his interview with police began at 7:30 P.M. and ended at 1:35 A.M.

George asked how, specifically, a 78 IQ could have affected McCowen's performance.

Welsh objected. At sidebar, Nickerson ordered the attorneys to bring him case law by the next morning, not to leave him "in the lurch to do my own work the way I was on the last issue."

George rephrased the question: "Dr. Brown, how does an IQ of this level affect a person's performance in an interview such as that on April 14, 2005?"

Welsh objected again. Nickerson, fed up, turned to the witness. "Doctor, when an individual is faced with a lengthy interview, something in excess of, say, four or perhaps five, maybe even six hours, where the issue at hand is one of great import, do you have an opinion, sir, as to whether a score of 78 on the verbal IQ would impact on that individual's ability to perform in an appropriate fashion in that interview setting?"

"Yes, I do, Your Honor."

"All right."

George jumped in. "Can you answer His Honor, please?"

Brown said he could and turned to the judge. Nickerson shook his head, instructing him to speak to the jury.

Brown said that a low verbal IQ would "severely compromise one's ability to participate in a meaningful, optimal way."

"Tell us how, Doctor," George said.

"Well, first of all . . . under the best of conditions, Mr. McCowen lacks a good understanding of language and conversation. So, he's likely to misinterpret what he hears . . . Having a low IQ makes him also very susceptible to manipulation, susceptible to eventually agreeing to what others want him to think and state. People such as Mr. McCowen who have that kind of verbal deficiency often compensate by trying to be agreeable, by trying to go along with the situation."

This testimony zeroed in on whether the defendant had been coerced, albeit "nicely," during the April 14 interview, and Welsh knew it. He moved to strike.

Nickerson intervened, asking the witness whether this was his opinion to a reasonable degree of medical certainty. Brown said that it was. The judge overruled.

Brown resumed. Someone with a 78 IQ would have difficulty remembering a prior question if it was asked in a slightly different way later, he said. The person's responses would get twisted. He'd have difficulty concentrating for that long a period.

The large Ingersoll clock on the west wall of the courtroom said it was almost four P.M. Nickerson called a halt to the day's testimony.

"Tomorrow, we're going to continue with the evidence, and we may finish," he told jurors. "If we do not, we certainly will be within striking distance." Closing arguments, he added, could be expected on Monday.

As jurors filed out, Nickerson turned to the defense table. "I have in no way excluded the type of questioning you're seeking, Mr. George. All I have said is, show me the case that says you're right."

George gathered his papers, fuming over the judge's potential— and likely—exclusion of the Thursday sex scenario. "It represented a double standard," he later opined. "I knew he was going to drop the ball here. It was OK to let in McCowen's priors but not the relationship between the precious Vassar girl and the black trash man."

Day 14, Friday, November 3

When court resumed on Friday morning, Nickerson called for the case law he'd requested. Neither attorney had it.

In that case, the judge ruled, Brown would not be permitted to go into the Thursday sex scenario. Were he to do so, he would be relying on the truth of McCowen's statement; since McCowen was not testifying, his out-of-court statement was hearsay.

"The defendant would have all the benefits of getting his side of the story in . . . and the commonwealth would be at the distinct disadvantage of not being able to cross-examine. To this jurist, that's fundamentally unfair."

If Brown had "an opinion" about McCowen's mental state, including how he felt during the Mason interview, the judge would allow him to state it. But regarding the ultimate question, whether the information McCowen gave during the interview amounted to a "false" confession, the judge ruled, "That is left to the jury."

Nickerson ordered Brown's reports sealed and marked for identification in case an appellate court called for them.

When jurors returned, Brown again explained that stress, exacerbated by the interview's length and the defendant's use of marijuana and Percocet, affected his ability to think clearly. Brown did not believe McCowen would "consciously fabricate and fake; but in an effort to come up with answers, in an effort to appease the people who are interviewing him, he [would] furnish answers and responses to satisfy their demand for information."

McCowen's history of epilepsy, Brown said, "seemed to be related to a head injury sustained at the age of four months after having been hit in the head with an iron" by his mother. The injury led to seizures, and McCowen took anticonvulsant medication, Dilantin and phenobarbital, until he was thirteen. These drugs, the phenobarb in particular, contributed to his memory deficits and bad school performance. He was enrolled in special-education classes but never finished high school, dropping out in eleventh grade. And his mother was mentally retarded, "so there's possibly a genetic explanation as well for Mr. McCowen's low verbal abilities."

Citing McCowen's verbal IQ score of 78, George asked what a mentally retarded person would score. Seventy and under, Brown answered. Six tests make up the verbal IQ, but Brown believed that three in particular—vocabulary, similarities, and general information—most accurately reflect how someone might function in the kind of interview McCowen faced on April 14. On those three tests, the verbal comprehensive index, McCowen scored 76.

Brown explained how the vocabulary subtest is administered. For the next five minutes, the witness droned on, one example after another, until George was forced to interrupt.

"The questions were just too difficult for him," Brown said.

George wondered about McCowen's performance in an interrogation like that of April 14.

"He would be intellectually overwhelmed. . . . And over time . . . begin to just either confabulate, say things that weren't true or go along with what he thinks that he's expected to say."

If the police had taped the interview, Brown added, it would be easier to determine where his attention lapsed, where he appeared distracted, dazed, or restless.

"Also, we have no idea of the sequence of questions. We don't know how they were posed, how they were phrased, and we don't know his response. All we have is a twenty-seven-page carefully crafted and edited account."

Welsh objected, and Nickerson sustained. But the deficiencies of Mason's effort, his compression of a six-hour interview into twenty-seven pages of two-, three-, and even one-sentence paragraphs, were evident. There could be no doubt that the report had been carefully crafted by a gifted investigator trying to wrap up the biggest case of his career.

George moved to the Wechsler Memory Scale. Brown said that McCowen was able to recall only about 50 percent of a short story he was asked to read. "Right off the top, half is lost," the doctor testified. In a stressful situation like the April 14 interview, McCowen would function on an even lower level.

Like most expert-witness testimony, Brown's repetitious answers provided more fluff than fact. But during cross-examination, according to *Cape Cod Times* reporter Hilary Russ, "the normally mild-mannered assistant district attorney, Robert Welsh III, raised his voice louder than any other day of the three-week trial." Using Brown's notes against him, Welsh challenged his scoring of McCowen's test, even his qualifications as a psychologist. He tried to dumb down the witness's scientific evaluations, invoking a "common-sense" contempt for education and analytic reasoning. It's said that Welsh listens to Rush Limbaugh every day while driving to work; Rush would have been proud.

The prosecutor continued with a series of quick jabs. A psychologist, Brown did not hold a medical degree. His test results were inconsistent. He'd written that McCowen had no memory of signing either the Miranda waiver or the electronic recording form on April 14, but the psychologist had warned him that anything they discussed could be used in open court. Had McCowen understood *that* warning? Brown replied that the defendant understood the warnings only "in a limited way."

Welsh's questions were coming *bang, bang, bang,* and Brown started to unravel. He'd noted that McCowen had abused marijuana since late adolescence, Percocet more recently, and the prosecutor demanded to know if the psychologist understood the concept of tolerance. Brown agreed that tolerance could diminish a high but maintained that the drugs still impaired cognitive abilities. Welsh asked about the alcoholic who has five beers every night versus someone who has five beers for the first time. Would the two function at the same cognitive level?

Brown had referred to McCowen's intelligence as marginal, but the prosecutor observed that the defendant was able to drive a garbage truck, keep to a route, cash his paycheck, and support himself. He'd also played football in high school, learning and memorizing plays.

Welsh reminded the courtroom that McCowen's overall IQ was 81, not 76. He'd scored 89 on his performance index. The 76 was not an IQ level but an index score; 78 was the actual verbal IQ.

The prosecutor was splitting hairs, but he walked Brown through the test results again. In the word-association test, the word "Sentence" elicited "Guilty, been to jail" from McCowen. Technically correct, it scored only one point. Why?

Brown explained that the test was looking for the other definition of the word. In any case, McCowen didn't explain a jail sentence, "guilty" being only part of the concept.

Welsh continued. To the word "Remorse," McCowen responded, "Feel sorry," scoring just one point; an element of guilt was needed to receive two. McCowen scored a zero for answering "Cry, show emotions" for the word "Pout." The manual required a comment about emotional expression to earn a point.

McCowen never finished the test. He failed six in a row, and scoring criteria called for ending the exam at that point. The prosecutor pointed out that in the information section of the test, McCowen correctly associated the theory of relativity with Einstein, and he knew that the main theme of the Book of Genesis was that God created heaven and earth.

Welsh pressed on, sometimes rewording an exam question to make the answers fit. Brown tried to correct him, but the psychologist's tepid responses only confused matters further.

To refute the assertion that McCowen's interview responses were driven by fatigue, Welsh reminded Brown that breaks had been taken. Brown responded, "Yes, but he didn't eat anything," rather than attack the question as simplistic.

Welsh continued. "Are you aware that he had several different girlfriends at the same time? Did he ever tell you that?"

"Yes."

"And he was able to juggle that?"

Welsh seemed to imply that promiscuity and juggling girlfriends took a high IQ. Nickerson, as fatigued as everyone else, called for morning break.

Welsh had eviscerated Brown, that was obvious. Not once had the psychologist countered that the defendant, a slow-witted black man with a history of involvements with white women, had simply been scared shitless during the interview. Not once had the witness opined about how *any* person of color would likely respond while being interrogated into the wee hours by a team of determined cops or that there were cultural issues ingrained in the black psyche that no psychologist, no historian or academic, could talk away as "color-blind."

It was as if the good doctor had never read Richard Wright or, better, James Baldwin, who, upon first visiting Georgia in the '60s, couldn't help but wonder if the Southern soil he walked on wasn't its deep red color because it had been stained with the blood of so many young black men, lynched and burned to death because of their alleged attraction to white women.

Something was missing from the whole discussion, and Brown simply did not get it.

When court reconvened, the assistant DA moved suddenly into the area George had been waiting for: McCowen's two drawings of 50 Depot Road, one showing where he stopped his garbage truck, the other the interior of the house. Here was the link. The psychiatrist now had the opportunity to say that McCowen told him he'd seen the inside of the house not early Saturday morning but on Thursday, when he had sex with Worthington. Instead, the witness said he hadn't discussed the outside drawing with the defendant. The second sketch offered another opening, but again, the witness failed. George had "spring-loaded" him to respond to either drawing with the Thursday sex scenario. But Brown bombed.

Jurors later insisted that they were turned off by all of the expert witnesses, prosecution and defense alike. George still hoped that the drawings would open the door to the Thursday sex visit. When he tried on redirect, Nickerson sustained Welsh's objection.

Refusing to accept what he called the "collusion between the two of them," George asked Brown what McCowen had *said* about drawing the picture.

Welsh objected. Nickerson sustained.

George asked how Brown understood the prosecutor's question when the drawing was put in front of him moments ago.

Welsh objected. Nickerson sustained.

Changing tack again, George asked if the drawing had changed Brown's opinion about the case. When the doctor said it had not, the defense attorney asked why. Before Brown could answer, Welsh objected.

It was hopeless. Nickerson intervened, asking whether the witness could answer the question within his prior guidelines. Brown doubted he could.

The judge disallowed the question, and George balked, bouncing his head from side to side, a gesture of frustration and loss. Nickerson responded, "There is an obvious way for the Thursday event to come into evidence, Mr. George"—he meant that McCowen could testify—"and you have elected not to follow that obvious route."

But George couldn't put McCowen on the stand. It would be a virtual repeat of the April 14 police interview. McCowen would agree with his interrogators, including Welsh. He'd need to please.

George explained later, "It's like he doesn't even want to talk about the case. Ordinarily, I'd say ninety percent of the time, I'm used to representing guys who are proactive in their own defenses, guys who want to know what you're doing. Most of those guys, if not all of them, are people who, something happens in court if you don't fight hard enough for them or they think you're sneaking something by them or being quiet, they want to know *why*. They monitor you constantly. This guy, he sits there, and he's more concerned about whether his girlfriend's going to get to visit him that night than he is as to whether a witness has just sunk him on the witness stand.

"Maybe it's denial. But funny thing is, I will tell you this—he's never said to me he did it.

"I've gone through the statement with him paragraph by paragraph. This is how he deals with it: 'I did not say that,' or 'I don't remember saying that.' You push him, and he'll deny having said something the cops say he said. Then, when you ask him what he did say, he'll say, 'I can't remember.'

"He takes the easy way out. If I put him on the witness stand, he'll sink himself."

At 12:09, the jury filed back in after the morning break, and George addressed Welsh's insinuation that the IQ test scoring was subjective. Brown said the manual was clear in its scoring directives.

He returned to the Miranda issue, Welsh having established that McCowen understood Brown's written warning. "What I meant by that answer," Brown said, "is that he doesn't understand necessarily the full implications of, let's say, waiving Miranda or of agreeing with me that whatever he tells me could be used as evidence."

The answer was complete fluff. McCowen had been on the street all his life; if he had any problem comprehending the impact of a signature, it was the result of his outsized ego, his hustler's faith that he could talk his way out of most anything, not limited IQ. Ironically, Mason and Burke understood the dynamics of what had gone on inside that interview room better than the PhD. Why hadn't McCowen balked, told the investigators to go fuck themselves and

clammed up until he had a lawyer at his side? George called it denial. Roy McCowen, the defendant's father, said it was showboating.
Whatever it was, it sprang from Chris's misbegotten belief that he
could stop what was happening by yakking—that talk, then more
talk, was the magic elixir that could get him out of there as well as
contain his dread.

George asked whether McCowen would have understood the significance of the DNA report. "I don't think he understood what his
exposure was, what his vulnerability was," the doctor answered.

Perhaps not even what DNA is, in fact.

Earlier in the day McCowen had leaned in close at the defense
table and said, "Bring the DNA stuff to the jail so I can look at it."
George had replied, "What, so you can show it to everybody in the
fucking lunchroom?"

Funny? Pathetic? Simply impossible.

On recross, Welsh reiterated that the psychologist was merely
giving his opinion of whether McCowen understood the waivers.
George came back to try one last time to get the earlier consensual-
sex scenario in. He asked Brown if McCowen said what went through
his mind when shown the DNA report on April 14. Brown began to
answer; Welsh objected.

Back to sidebar.

Welsh seemed jumpy, despite the witness's poor performance.
"Judge, I object to this attempt to elicit the Thursday interview. Further, I think that in the future, if Mr. George thinks that the door has
been opened, he shouldn't just simply start asking the questions. He
should come to sidebar, and then we can address it here."

George countered that the prosecutor had raised his voice to the
witness "about this very document. . . . I am asking to explore it. . . .
The commonwealth has dealt with it now two or three times on recross alone."

He was right. Welsh had done more than just skirt the issue.

Nickerson turned to his computer for the real-time transcript.
After a moment, he ruled. "In terms of opening the door, I don't
think he's done it. But he'd be well advised to stay the heck away from
it further."

George shrugged, announced that he had no further questions, then called Dr. Richard Ofshe. Irritation aside, George knew he'd just landed a major appealable issue.

Bearded and wearing a tailored suit, Ofshe held a doctorate in social psychology from Stanford and had been a professor at UC Berkeley for thirty-eight years. But his credentials ranged far beyond academia. Even Nickerson acknowledged that Ofshe was "probably *the* authority on false confessions in North America."

The witness's résumé included a Guggenheim Fellowship and a Pulitzer Prize for public service that he earned as a member of the tiny Northern California *Point Reyes Light* newspaper team, reporting on Synanon, the onetime drug-rehab program whose members attempted to murder a local attorney who'd won a lawsuit against the cult.

Ofshe had been a consultant to the Marin County Sheriff's Department, the California and Arizona attorney general offices, the U.S. Attorney's office in Los Angeles, where he assisted on the John DeLorean case; and the U.S. Department of Justice tax and criminal divisions. The list rolled on and on, and when he cited the work he'd done for the Canadian government's commission of inquiry on the CIA's reported torture of chemist and suspected terrorist Maher Arar, Welsh complained that the information was too far afield. Nickerson agreed, asking the witness to "tailor it down."

Ofshe was visibly annoyed. His stiff posture demanded, *What gives? I've been profiled in the* New York Times *and the* New Yorker. He was just getting started.

The professor explained that the bulk of his work dealt with people being psychologically coerced into confessing to crimes they did not commit. Police interrogations were of particular interest; he had penned forty to fifty articles and a half-dozen books on the subject. Of the 300 times he had testified in court, 275 focused on police custodial interviews. His work was cited by the Massachusetts Supreme Judicial Court in the recent *DiGiambattista* decision, he added, aware that George would use that case to challenge Nickerson's likely attempt to brand Ofshe's testimony "unscientific." Before appearing to testify, the witness reviewed prior trial testimony, motion hearings, discovery material, and Dr. Brown's reports. He had not met with Mc-Cowen face-to-face, though.

The resume and the acknowledgment of his $250 hourly fee went on until lunch. Before the jury returned, Welsh called for a discussion about Ofshe's testimony. The long, frequent sidebars were taking a toll; for the past weeks, those in the gallery had been sentenced to watch a pantomime: two men in suits, another in a long dark robe. This one was out in the open, though. The bumptious personality of defense attorney George made it more than bearable.

He was dead serious now, anticipating another one-two from Nickerson-Welsh.

"He'll talk about applying his methodology, about what a persuaded false confession is," George explained at sidebar. "Also about recording and what it means and what it doesn't mean. This has been accepted by Judge Grabau in Norfolk Superior Court; and I ask Your Honor to please, please let him testify in this case within the standards and guidelines that we have been talking about for the past week, because all of a sudden, I'm hearing Mr. Welsh has problems with the report."

Nickerson asked if any available data correlated the frequency of "false" confessions with police ploys. George referred to a large body of literature on the subject but couldn't be more specific. Nickerson nodded, meaning for him to proceed. The question was left unanswered; George guessed it would be addressed on an issue-by-issue basis.

"Doctor, have you reviewed the interrogation in this case? Could you tell His Honor how many different instances of it you see?"

Nickerson interrupted. "What do you call these things? Are they elements? Are these factors? What are they?"

"I would call them *indicia*." Ofshe seemed to relish the sound of the word.

"*Indicia?*" the judge repeated. "OK. What are the indicia that you found?"

"There are indicia of the use of motivational tactics that are typically associated with the communication of psychologically coercive and, therefore, dangerous motivators," Ofshe said. "There is substantial evidence that a statement may have evolved that would generally be classified as a persuaded statement, if not a persuaded false statement. . . . There is clearly evidence of the use of a major tactic that I would refer to as a witness-role strategy. That's the biggest of the dangerous tactics, and that's a tactic in which someone is offered the opportunity to take the role of a witness, place themselves at the crime scene, and speak about the actions of another person. The motivator for doing that is the communication of the idea that should you do that, if you were merely a witness, you would not have any problems in the future. In other words, a communication of an offer of leniency and avoidance of being charged with a serious crime. That suggestion is often not honored, but nevertheless, that is the way in which it's done."

A structural linguist couldn't have parsed these sentences. But Nickerson tried. "Were there any offers of leniency in this case?" he asked.

Sensing a trap, Ofshe dropped the jargon. "There is evidence in the record. The problem is that because we do not have a recording, we don't know what is under the tip of the iceberg. The tips of the icebergs are very clear."

Nickerson asked if he had any sense of how often these indicia led to false confessions.

Ofshe could not answer. "I think what you're asking is, is there a way of getting a number? And my opinion would be at this point in time, there's no way to do it. . . . What has been done is the demonstration time after time after time that these things are associated with when we have a full record, a very clear track to show how it occurs, so that—"

"In known false confessions?"

"In known false confessions. So we know that this is the only viable explanation. Also in this particular interrogation, we have not only these problems . . . we have the fact that this interrogation failed."

"Because there is no ultimate admission?"

"As important as that, there is no corroboration. The purpose in doing interrogation is not just to get somebody to say, 'I did it.' The purpose . . . is to develop additional evidence that links the person to the crime. . . . Absent that, you have nothing."

Nickerson nodded. Ofshe continued, mentioning studies in both the United States and England where people came to believe they had committed crimes that they had not. Welsh interrupted and asked for statistics.

"No one in their right mind would try to associate a number with it," Ofshe replied. "That it happens is without dispute."

Welsh asked whether experimental verification existed. Ofshe, unintimidated, said that such experiments were simply not possible, at least not "since the collapse of Nazi Germany."

George stepped in, citing the *DiGiambattista* case, where the Supreme Judicial Court of Massachusetts warned prosecutors that failure to tape defendants' statements in felony cases would henceforth be at their own peril. Waiver forms notwithstanding, taping statements was the *only* way to satisfy the legal standards set by that case.

Ofshe jumped in. His paper, "The Decision to Confess Falsely," "arguably the clearest statement about how interrogation can produce confession and false confession," was relied on by the Supreme Court of Massachusetts, the Supreme Court of Canada, and the Supreme Court of Utah, "which makes me acceptable in the reddest of the red and the bluest of the blue."

"Well, wait, wait, *wait*," Nickerson railed. "The bluest of the blue here hasn't given you carte blanche yet in *DiGiambattista*, have they?"

"They have relied on my work."

"They *reference* your work, sir."

Nickerson had done his homework. Ofshe's work was quoted in *DiGiambattista*; he hadn't actually testified. Looking up from his papers, the judge referred to Professor Saul Kassin's research; he suspected that Ofshe didn't look favorably upon Kassin.

Ofshe deemed Kassin's research "terrible." The judge then mentioned Ofshe's protégé, Richard Leo. Looking down with a smile, he asked if Ofshe's student had surpassed him yet.

Nickerson was at his hot-dog best, adding a lively scene to the show. But it was mere foreplay. Abruptly, he lowered the boom: if anyone was going to identify Dr. Ofshe's "indicia" in the twenty-seven-page report of McCowen's interrogation, it would be the jurors, not an expert witness.

"Counsel," he announced, looking at George, "at this stage, I'm ready to let him go halfway, to what Judge Grabau had in front of the Norfolk Superior Court back in January. As we progress, I may be moved further. But I think we start with that."

His reference was to the January 2006 Dedham, Massachusetts, "Dominatrix" case, where Ofshe testified on behalf of a defendant found not guilty after confessing to cutting off a client's head. In the eyes of many, his theories had emerged victorious in the highly publicized trial.

With the jury back in, the witness gave a thumbnail history of police-interrogation methods over the past 100 years, going well past the good cop/bad cop tag-team interrogation. The Wickersham Commission of 1931 uncovered rampant police use of "the third degree": breaking bones, throwing suspects down stairs, truncheon thrashings. After the Wickersham report, police needed different tools to manipulate suspects, even more so after the U.S. Supreme Court's *Miranda* decision in 1966.

George asked the witness to explain, and Ofshe requested an easel. Nickerson shook his head, instructing the witness to "just tell" the court.

Denied his visual aid, Ofshe started by describing modern inter-rogation as a "multivariant process that moves through time."

This, too, bugged the judge. But Ofshe didn't fabricate the wooden-sounding phrase. In law-enforcement circles, it's known as the Reid method. John Reid, inventor of the multifaceted interview, is responsible for a curriculum that has schooled thousands of law-enforcement officials since the late 1940s. According to the website www.reid.com, the method has been used by police departments in San Francisco, Pittsburgh, New York, Miami, Boston, and other cities; by the Department of Defense, CIA, Secret Service, Army, Navy, IRS, and so forth. The Bush Defense Department was especially receptive, using the method to train interrogators for Abu Ghraib and Guantá-namo Bay during the early 2000s. The Reid course is headquartered in Chicago; its bible is *Criminal Interrogation and Confessions.*

According to the program's literature, graduates report an im-proved confession rate of more than 25 percent; a quarter claim as much as 50 percent. These results are based on the method's patented Nine Steps. George wanted Ofshe to demonstrate that almost all were used to secure McCowen's April 14 statement:

1. *Positive confrontation:* The suspect is left alone for a short period before the investigator enters, carrying a folder. He informs the suspect that it contains evidence of his guilt.

2. *Theme development:* The investigator presents a moral justification for the suspect's actions, placing the blame on another person's influence or on unfortunate circumstances.

3. *Handling denials:* The investigator interrupts the suspect when he denies guilt, because "the more often a suspect denies his involvement in an act, the more difficult it becomes for him to eventually tell the truth."

4. *Overcoming objections:* "The suspect's objections clearly indicate the investigator is making substantial progress," says the website. Through the Looking Glass: If you say you didn't do it, you confirm you did.

5. *Procure and retain the suspect's attention:* "At this stage of the interrogation we are dealing with guilty suspects—the innocent or truthful suspect will not move past Step Three." Here, the suspect will often become withdrawn, tuning out; the appropriate response is to invade his personal space, so he feels threatened and continues playing the game.

6. *Handle the suspect's passive mood:* Most suspects begin to feel defeated and often cry. Basically, the suspect has "resigned himself to the fact that telling the truth seems inevitable."

7. *Present an alternative question:* "Did you plan this thing out, or did it just happen on the spur of the moment?" An answer to either is an admission of guilt.

8. *Elicit verbal details of the offense:* The investigator immediately reinforces the confession with praise; then, maintaining eye contact and close physical proximity, he elicits details "to de-

velop information that can be corroborated by subsequent investigation." Investigators are warned against taking notes, as doing so "may dissuade some suspects from continuing with their verbal statements."

9. *Convert the oral confession to writing:* If the investigator is alone, a witness should be brought in to hear the oral confession, which should then be reduced to writing or, alternatively, audio or videotaped. The suspect should read the confession, initial any changes, add the date and time, and sign it.

Ofshe's work has earned a multipage response on the Reid website, designating him as Reid's number one enemy. Now, without his graph, he asked the courtroom to imagine as he tracked a person's perception during an interrogation. He likened it to "doing calculus in one's head without a pen and paper."

Part academic, part moralist, and decidedly contentious, Berkeley-style, Ofshe knew his phraseology would irk Nickerson. He was right. The judge called another sidebar.

"You've got to be kidding," Nickerson chided George. Ofshe sat ten feet away in the witness box, doing nothing to hide his eavesdropping efforts.

"That's what he testified in front of Judge Grabau," George replied.

"Well, that's not how he's going to testify here. He's not going to lecture . . ."

"You've made that clear to the jury, Your Honor . . ."

"He's not going to lecture on and on and on."

George wanted a rise from the judge, again hoping to trigger judicial error. "With all due respect, Your Honor," he goaded, "your treatment of this witness is communicating to the jury that you have a disrespect for him."

"My treatment of him *how?*"

"Now, without an objection, you've interrupted his testimony. And I understand you may be concerned, but it's pretty clear that this witness—and I think it's being communicated—doesn't meet your standards—to the jury."

"Well, if you can document it, you're welcome to record it. I've invited you to the sidebar in the hopes that this can be tightened up by some appropriate questioning. He appears to be launching into a lecture."

"He's a professor," George said, affecting an air of befuddlement.

"And he's not going to launch into an explanation of 'three-dimensional calculus' because he's piqued that I've denied him his board."

There it was. Nickerson, a theatrical personality, was a control freak to boot, competitive to the core. But Ofshe had irritated the jurors, too, those charged with determining guilt or innocence; most of their faces reflected not boredom but a marked distaste for this rude outsider challenging the charming white-haired judge. Jurors could now justify rejecting anything Ofshe said; he was a snob, a pointy-headed, effete intellectual who'd come to the Cape from, of all places, *Berkeley*.

Sidebar over, George again asked the witness to explain psychological interrogation, step by step. Ofshe outlined the Reid method, describing the tactics as fairly subtle. "What the interrogator does . . . is to introduce scenarios for the crime. And it's in the very nature of the scenario that the leniency offer is communicated." An interrogator might point out the difference between premeditated versus accidental killing, for example, noting that the former could carry a death sentence. The objective is to convince the suspect that his situation is hopeless; he should confess.

Ofshe had already referred to the tactic known as witness-role strategy, where police claim to have evidence that places the suspect at the scene but suggest that perhaps he was not alone. Police then solicit a confession by claiming that they're really after someone else. When Ofshe referred to the Central Park jogger case, perhaps the most infamous of false confessions, Welsh, who'd come down with a cold, could not help himself. "I didn't know he was going to be permitted to get into specific cases," he wheezed.

"Well, only some of them," the judge said.

"Doctor," George continued before Nickerson or Welsh could say anything further, "I have to ask you a question before you go on to the Central Park case."

"Sure," Ofshe said. "You're in charge."

Nickerson couldn't let the remark stand. "No, no, no. Close. Close, but not quite."

Ofshe refused to back down. "He's in charge of the questions that get asked to me," he said, smiling at the judge provocatively.

"Not even that, Doctor." George tried to keep the peace.

But the professor had to have the last word. "I can't do it alone," he said, shrugging.

In a matter of minutes, the courtroom had turned into a school-yard. Nickerson waved, gesturing for Ofshe to stop. George interposed himself between the two as much as the courtroom layout permitted and resumed questioning.

Ofshe said that taping custodial interrogations was the only way to establish whether the Reid tactics were employed. "Stenographic record would be fine. Audiovideo would be better. But you would still need the transcript to really work on it. You need to know exactly what was said and done."

It was the last hour of the last day of the third week of the trial. Whatever his skepticism, it might have been obvious to Nickerson that the process Ofshe described was evident in Mason's report: the stage-by-stage erosion of the defendant's confidence, the cops' insistence that McCowen was lying, the emergence of details about Christa's living room and events at the Juice Bar. It was all there. But few jurors were paying attention; Welsh must have been encouraged. Michael Iacuessa wrote in the *Provincetown Banner*: "Brown's analysis was often overly academic . . . and the jury seemed fatigued at times, especially as both attorneys tried to dance around the admissible areas resulting in vague questions and answers. Dr. Richard Ofshe, who followed Brown, also proved academic and," Iacuessa added gently, "a tad long-winded."

Day 15, Monday, November 6

After thirty-three witnesses, more than 100 exhibits, and testimony that would run to nearly 4,000 pages of transcript, the McCowen trial was coming to a close. But Ofshe had not yet completed testifying, and this morning, he was like a batter on deck, eager to step up to the plate. At a weekend party packed with trial journalists, he had railed against the judge: "That sonofabitch! I've testified all over the country, and this guy thinks he can throw his weight around in his little jerkoff backwater called Cape Cod? *How dare he curtail my lecture!*"

The diatribe was a wonderful set piece, especially "curtail my lecture!" George had spent most of the weekend trying to soften his witness's attitude. Now, as the bailiff intoned "Hear ye! Hear ye!" Ofshe appeared calm. But appearances can deceive.

Right off, the professor testified that false confessions are not "that" rare, explaining again that he couldn't and wouldn't cite a percentage, since determining the number of interrogations taking place in a given year is impossible. Although the suspect's age, personality, and intelligence are factors, "every case I've ever worked on involves situations in which the interrogator chooses to introduce tactics that are prohibited."

George returned to investigators' failure to tape McCowen's interview, an issue that could prove decisive on appeal. Taping was vital, Ofshe said, "recording the entirety of an interrogation allows anyone who needs to get to the truth—not to win, not to make a case, not to be successful, but to get to the truth—to know exactly what happened."

For the first time, the purpose of recording interrogations had been stated simply: *"Not to win, not to make a case . . . but to get to the truth."*

Ofshe defined three kinds of false confessions. Voluntary confessions, where someone independently claims responsibility for a crime, occur most often in high-profile cases (three unrelated people confessed to the JonBenét Ramsey murder). Compliant confessions occur when the confessor admits guilt after an interrogator convinces him that overwhelming evidence damns him. Such claims, Ofshe pointed out, "don't have to be true. Police are free to invent evidence that simply doesn't exist for the purpose of making someone feel hopeless."

The third type of false confession is persuaded, where the suspect actually comes to believe he's committed the crime, although he has no memory of it. An interrogator might say, "Tom, you used to be an alcoholic. What happened was you had a dry blackout." Once a black-

out has been suggested, "all the interrogator has to do . . . is to introduce information that supposedly is reliable." In some cases, Ofshe
explained, interrogators will ask a suspect to visualize himself at the
scene and just say what comes to mind first, telling him that will most
likely be the truth "because their subconscious knows what they did."

The bearded professor was prohibited from discussing Mason's
report, but the inference was clear. Time and again, the two detectives prompted McCowen to fall back on the fact that he was drunk
and couldn't remember what happened at Christa's. They also played
on the subject's fatigue, as Reid recommends.

George reiterated: no accurate record existed of what the defendant actually said or how the interviewers got him to say it. "Is that
why the recording is so important to have?"

"The recording tells you how the result came about," Ofshe said.
"Without the recording, how can you really know how someone was
convinced to make the decision to confess?"

George asked how many pages of transcript Ofshe would expect a
six-hour interrogation to generate. Welsh objected. Nickerson inter-
jected: Did George mean one taken down by a stenographer? George
said yes. The judge claimed he didn't believe Ofshe ever had worked
as a stenographer.

An audible groan emanated from many of the reporters in the
balcony. Ofshe had testified at hundreds of trials, conducted countless interviews as a social scientist and Pulitzer Prize–winning journalist. His familiarity with transcripts could be assumed, no?

Nickerson asked for a range: how many pages would a six-and-a-
half-hour interrogation generate?

"Three hundred fifty to 500 pages would probably be a reasonable estimate."

"Have you ever seen twenty-seven pages for that amount of time?"

"No," Ofshe answered, definitively.

He returned to the indicia of "persuaded" confessions, focusing
on McCowen's tentative words. "All that conditional stuff in there
is actually reflective of the fact that the person does not have actual
memory but has been gotten to participate in making up a story. It
starts out tentative, and if the person is made to repeat the story often

enough, the tentative elements of it will tend to drop out. . . . The interrogator tells the person in no uncertain terms, 'Stop using *probably*. Stop using *if*. Stop using *maybe*. Just tell me that this happened.'"

Having gotten the suspect to discuss a hypothetical crime, Ofshe continued, the interrogator then pulls the rug out from under him. George asked if Ofshe had formed an opinion about McCowen's case. Welsh leaped from his seat, reminding the judge of his prior ruling: the witness could speak only in generalities.

Nickerson knew he was treading a fine line. He agreed to hear George's proposed inquiry but not before the jury. Once more, the jurors were led out.

George's first "hypothetical" was less a question than a defense summary. Assume a six-hour interrogation, not taped but memorialized in a statement composed several days later from a police detective's notes; also assume the defendant's IQ was 76 to 78, and he'd used marijuana and Percocet before the interview. Further, assume police suggested that the defendant might have committed the crime in self-defense, that it might have been accidental, not premeditated, that the victim might have been the aggressor. Last, assume that as the interview progressed, the statements of the accused evolved: first he knew nothing, then was a standby witness, then participated, although another person committed the crime.

"Based upon a professional degree of certainty," George asked, "was such an interview consistent with a compliant false confession?"

"Yes," Ofshe answered. The only available record, Mason's twenty-seven-page report, failed to reveal the dynamics of the interview.

Posing his second "hypothetical," George asked the witness to assume the circumstances detailed in the previous question but to add a defendant who stated eighteen times that he had no memory of events before the crime because of drinking; then, when he began to describe himself at the crime scene, he used the words *possibly, if,* and other uncertain qualifiers until interrogators told him directly to stop using those terms. What would that scenario suggest?

Predictably, Ofshe answered that these were indicia consistent with a persuaded false confession.

George turned back to the judge. Nickerson asked if that was all. George quickly coughed up another question, prompting the judge to chide, "I'm not suggesting you need more, Mr. George."

Welsh took pains to establish that Ofshe was neither a clinical psychologist nor a psychiatrist, then posed his own test questions. Was the witness an expert in assessing the performance of people with a 78 IQ? Ofshe shot back: he knew such a person was 22 points below average, more than one standard deviation below the mean. "There is a substantial literature on that," he offered helpfully. "You might want to look at Gudjonsson's *The Psychology of Interrogations, Confessions, and Testimony,* which has an entire section devoted to reviewing the literature on intelligence and vulnerability to interrogation."

Again, Nickerson held up his hand, signaling *enough.* But he had to taunt Ofshe, saying, "The real problem is the nature of the science—if we want to call it a science."

He then issued his edict. Ofshe could not draw conclusions about McCowen's confession. That task was within the sole province of the jury, which "must make its judgment on the totality of the circumstances. And perhaps there is some danger that Dr. Ofshe's lens or viewpoint is a bit narrower than that."

Ofshe, in other words, should keep his "indicia" to himself.

When jurors returned, they heard statistics from three studies on false confessions. One, published in the *Stanford Law Review,* analyzed miscarriages of justice in 350 capital cases and found that 14 percent were caused by an innocent person falsely confessing. A second, from the Center on Wrongful Convictions at Northwestern University Law School, where Ofshe was once a fellow, looked at Illinois homicide cases during the last forty-five to fifty years, finding that 50 percent involved false confessions. The third, issued by the Innocence Project in New York City, reviewed 130 exonerations via DNA during the past fifteen years; 25 percent of those wrongfully convicted had falsely confessed.

The numbers were powerful. But were jurors listening? Or were they prepared to convict on the basis of a "confession" neither taped nor transcribed, created from memory and notes a week later? Six and a half hours condensed into twenty-seven pages, never read or signed by the defendant?

On cross, Welsh returned to the Innocence Project. Didn't DNA, in the hands of project directors Scheck and Neufeld, prove that the suspects did *not* commit the crimes? His point: DNA tied McCowen to the victim, not the other way around.

It's unclear whether Ofshe was aware of Welsh's recent appointment to the district court bench by Republican Governor Mitt Romney or whether he knew of the young prosecutor's privileged lineage, which many saw as the source of his bumpkin arrogance. It did not matter. Ofshe wasn't about to back down. A remnant of the '60s counterculture, the once-poor Brooklyn Jew drove a blood-red 348 Ferrari, inhabited a San Francisco–Pacific Heights townhouse filled with French antiques, had a pied-à-terre in Paris, and wore $3,000 Zegna suits. More, his credentials as a scholar aligned him with the angels, at least as he and many of his colleagues saw it. Everything about the man, especially his antiestablishment thinking, was at one with his hubris. He might as well have told the prosecutor, "I've been around and read the books, hick. You haven't. Learn your place."

Welsh wasn't ready to throw in the towel. He asked if it was "possible to say with certainty whether a confession is false or whether the person might be just lying?"

"It's possible to say with a certain degree of confidence. It depends on the strength of the evidence."

Welsh wondered whether the fact finder should examine the type of questioning—raised voices, offers of leniency. Ofshe used the question to return to the importance of taping, the only way to know how coercive an interrogator's tactics might have been. When Welsh began to nitpick, Ofshe exploded. "I am not here to tell American society how to interrogate."

"Doctor, Doctor, try his question," Nickerson admonished, an intrusion from the bench second only to the judge's open critique of George's decision not to put McCowen on the stand.

Welsh asked if Ofshe was critical of the police practice of bluffing suspects with nonexistent evidence "connecting them to the crime," adding, "You don't think it's dangerous for the police to lie to suspects?"

"No, I don't think that will elicit a false confession."

Police lie, Ofshe went on, pointing out that his testimony would have been quite unnecessary had Mason and Burke taped McCowen's interview. That comment, his last, prompted Beth Karas of Court TV to make a prediction. The Worthington trial, Karas told her audience of millions, might well become the seminal case on the issue and eventually mandate the recording of all felony interviews in Massachusetts.

As Ofshe stepped down, Welsh announced that he intended to call five rebuttal witnesses. Two were reporters, an unusual twist. News outlets don't cotton to their news gatherers testifying in court, a practice that threatens both journalistic integrity and First Amendment protections. Again, members of the out-of-town press had to remind themselves that they were on Cape Cod.

The first was Eric Williams of the *Cape Cod Times*, who was perhaps best known for his morning show, *The Eric Williams Radio Experience*, which aired on WOMR out of Provincetown. Williams was more personality than reporter; the *Times* had tapped into his trademark goofiness and had him compile a running blog about the trial, while coworker Hilary Russ wrote the straight news stories. His name had already come up in connection with Jan Worthington, but Welsh was calling Williams to blunt Keith Amato's testimony. The reporter had interviewed Amato on air in July 2002, a month after Amato's contentious interview with police. During the show, Williams asked Amato what a police interview was like. Amato told him that "they behaved in a professional manner." At Welsh's urging, Williams quoted Amato again: "Did they beat me with a phone book? No, they did not."

On cross, George established that Williams did not really remember the details of the interview. "It's my job . . . to push the truth across as I see it at the time," the reporter asserted, one of the more interesting takes on journalistic responsibility to surface during the trial. "Once that happens, I'm on to another story," he said.

Welsh's next rebuttal witness was Truro police chief John Thomas. Known locally as "Popcorn" for his unremarkable intelligence, Thomas nervously recalled Girard Smith approaching him on January 16, 2002, to report the dark truck coming out of the driveway at 50 Depot Road. Smith had not been able to remember any distinguishing marks, said the chief. "He described the operator as a white male, in his late thirties to early forties, with a day's growth of beard."

Mason testified next, principally about Smith. When the detective accidentally encountered him while canvassing the Worthington neighborhood, Smith said the truck was black, like the detective's cruiser. When Mason pointed out that his cruiser was actually dark blue, Smith said it would be more accurate to say the vehicle was "a dark color." As for the driver, Mason testified that Smith "could only say white male, oval face, due to the fact that the vehicle was traveling at a high rate of speed and was turning away from him."

Again, nothing new.

Next up was Marilyn Miller, a reporter for the *Cape Codder*, a once stalwart weekly that had fallen on hard times. In her fifties, Miller was known as a conscientious, community-minded Truro local. Her appearance on the stand drove home the fundamental inappropriateness of journalists testifying. The *Cape Cod Times*, at least, initially fought the subpoena served on Williams, but the *Cape Codder* had just been sold by the *Boston Herald* to a bunch of bean counters, it was rumored, who didn't understand the basics of running a viable newspaper.

Miller had interviewed Smith and quoted him saying that the mystery driver might have been "high as a kite." He'd speculated that perhaps some druggie had made a pass at Worthington, then killed her when she rejected him. Smith's scenario wasn't all that different from McCowen's, nor was Smith alone in suggesting that drugs had played a role in the murder.

What was more interesting was that Miller quoted Smith saying he had seen someone searching in the weeds a short distance from the Worthington residence shortly after the murder. He'd been unable to ID the searcher but said the person's vehicle, with a fishing vessel insignia on the door, was parked nearby.

The prosecutor was not through dissing Smith's vehicle sighting. He next called Trooper Kimberly Squier, who had run the DMV list and brought Smith the back-page auto ads from the Sunday newspaper. According to Squier, Smith chose three that might match the vehicle he'd seen: a Ford Expedition, a Ford Excursion, and a Ford

Econovan. Welsh marked the section as an exhibit and put the ads up on ELMO. Squier testified that Smith said it could have been an Expedition or an Excursion but only if it had blacked-out windows.

George made one point on cross: police had not gone back to Smith with more photos, either of vehicles or of suspect white males.

The commonwealth finally rested, as did the defense. Testimony was over. As the jury filed out for the lunch break, George, Welsh, and Nickerson began negotiating jury instructions, the legal framework the jurors would use to reach their verdict. Of paramount concern was whether jurors could use the "joint-venture" theory: McCowen committed the murder with someone else. George objected; the commonwealth's entire case rested on the assumption that McCowen alone was guilty. Welsh maintained that a joint-venture instruction was warranted.

The sudden shift in the prosecution's strategy was, and also was not, surprising. Admitting that McCowen might have had an accomplice was an affirmation of the defense's contention that someone else committed the crime. It had been the ticking time bomb all along, the Achilles' heel of the commonwealth's case. It was why the cops protected, and continued to protect, their witness; the slightest proof that Frazier was at 50 Depot Road on the night of the murder would invalidate his grand-jury testimony and undo the entire trial.

On the other hand, joint venture offered the commonwealth insurance, a bargaining chip, if one or more of the jurors couldn't quite buy the April 14 "confession."

Welsh also asked that the jury be instructed on all three theories of first-degree murder, including felony murder, which meant that McCowen could be found guilty if, for instance, Worthington was killed while he'd been burglarizing her house or during her rape, giving the prosecution an additional shot at him, still.

George argued for instructions on second-degree murder and voluntary manslaughter, also on provocation, including heat-of-passion and sudden-combat, all mitigating circumstances. Nickerson agreed to give an alternative voluntary-manslaughter instruction in both subcategories, heat-of-passion and sudden-combat, but nixed self-defense.

Nickerson returned to joint venture. Would that issue raise the possibility of battery manslaughter, intent to harm but not to kill? If the jury was to be instructed on joint venture, shouldn't it be instructed on battery manslaughter as well?

It was a good call, and the judge added he would have the verdict slip ready for the attorneys to review after lunch; he had to think further about battery manslaughter. George moved for a required finding of not guilty, a pro forma motion he knew was futile. Nickerson denied the motion outright.

George began closing argument at 1:12 P.M., sans notes. Waving his eyeglasses, he outlined alternative scenarios, any one of which, taken seriously, he thought, would raise reasonable doubt.

First: Christa Worthington was alive on Saturday morning, January 5, 2002, dressed in her black fleece sweatsuit and a green bathrobe. The light in the study might have been on, but other lights in the house were out; it was daytime. She heard someone come up the driveway, went outside to greet the arrival, found herself in a scuffle, ran inside, and bolted the door. The intruder broke into the kitchen, punched her, knocked her to the floor. Maybe she had a knife, maybe not. The assailant was so angry, or so panicked, he stabbed her through the lung. Maybe he had sex with her, maybe not, but afterward, he pulled off her sweatpants, her socks coming off at the same time. Grabbing the house phone, he ran out to his vehicle, carrying the sweatpants and the knife but dropping the socks on the way. As he fled, he nearly ran over Girard Smith at the bottom of the driveway.

"Now, if that story makes any sense based on what's happened in this case, that's reasonable doubt," George said. "That story makes more sense than any crock of bull that's going to be put before you during the commonwealth's . . . closing statement."

"Excuse me, counsel. *Sidebar*," Nickerson barked, obviously in response to George's language.

"I am loath to interrupt counsel during closing argument, but I will not sit by and see the prosecution's case addressed as 'a crock of bull'—"

"Sorry, Your Honor."

"—versus your case or anybody else's case," the judge went on. "We will use appropriate respect to our fellow counsel and their positions in the matter."

"Absolutely, Your Honor."

Back at the jury box, George asked the panel to imagine Tim Arnold sitting in the defense chair, with his history of mental illness, his anger-management problems, and his unrequited love. George reminded jurors that Christa had broken up with Arnold, and he had remained a pest. He'd peeked into her bedroom window. He'd tried to break in through the kitchen door. His diary entries were "off the wall." His semen was found on a brown blanket in Christa's living room. Forensic testing proved that his hairs were all over her body.

"Would you have convicted anyone the Commonwealth put before you?"

George paused before thanking the jury for three long weeks of service, then apologized if he had done anything to offend them. He thanked the judge and the prosecutor. "There are things that he has done that I didn't like," George said of Welsh. "It doesn't mean I don't like *him*." Finally, he expressed sympathy for Christa Worthington's father and Ava, pointedly excluding Jan and her sisters. Returning to the defense theme, he attacked the police for mishandling the investigation. He would now deal with issues he raised during his opening statement.

First, jurors had learned about police tactics from Arnold and Amato. And despite the cops' best efforts, McCowen never confessed. His eyes filled with tears at the interrogation table not because of guilt but "because he realized they didn't believe him. They weren't his pals. They were trying to pin this thing on him." Nothing prevented police from using a stenographer or running a tape, or even asking McCowen to initial the report. McCowen had offered no new facts to investigators, no "inside" information. George attacked the second most damning piece of prosecution evidence: the DNA match. The defense hinged on the theory that McCowen had consensual sex with Christa on Thursday, the day before the murder. Jurors could not speculate about the victim's hygiene; no one knew when she'd last showered. Dr. Saferstein testified that saliva could stay on a woman's

breast for an "extended time." All that mattered was that she had not
showered between Thursday and the time she was murdered.

He focused on the Thursday sex scenario, invoking the Christmas
tree conversation, reminding jurors of Horton's testimony: McCowen
had been at Christa's house on Thursday as part of his regular route;
he'd called in about a Christmas tree sometime that week.

"He didn't rape her, because there's no evidence of rape. And the
sperm in her vagina was placed there, deposited there right about the
time that he says."

George cited McCowen's low IQ, his history of epilepsy, his use
of alcohol and marijuana, his enjoyment of women. Police needed
a statement from him; if the DNA could be attributed to consensual
sex, their case disintegrated.

He listed the flaws in the DA's investigation: nineteen or twenty
people tramped through the crime scene; not one hair found on the
victim's body was McCowen's; semen found on the victim's breast had
not been tested; and the blue and white fibers found in her pubic hair
were never compared with Jeremy Frazier's clothes. DNA from three
unidentified men was found under Christa Worthington's fingernails.
Not one fingerprint tied the defendant to the scene, not one.

Given all of these discrepancies, should a human being be on trial
for his life? "Is it fair? Is it reasonable doubt?" he asked. "Of course,
it's reasonable doubt. It can't be anything else."

Police ignored the black truck, ignored the call made to Frazier
on a phone registered to David Murphy, a convicted killer.

"And Mulvey," he continued. "Mulvey would have you believe that
he went to Florida to pursue his electronics career . . . when you now
know he was running from the police. . . . You know he lied about his
father being home for the weekend. Why? Why are they lying?"

McCowen, he said, had remained on the Cape for thirty-nine
months after the murder, police knew where he lived, where he worked;
they knew his pals. They talked to him several times after the murder,
including a conversation just two days after the body was found.

"He didn't run. And when they put him in the police car, he
wanted them to get his keys, because he thought he was going home
later," George bellowed, stabbing the air with his eyeglasses.

"The guy had no idea, absolutely no idea. . . . And the reason these police believed the word of a Jeremy Frazier over Christopher McCowen, it can only be one reason—because he's white and McCowen is black. They couldn't accept that McCowen could have had some kind of relationship with Christa Worthington, because he wasn't up to her standards. . . . He didn't fit their game plan.

"He's a man with nothing to hide." George wound down, asking the panel to do the right thing, not because his client was the victim of a false statement, not because he had sex with Christa Worthington, but because the government's case was "based on nothing but reasonable doubt . . . on incorrect and ignored evidence."

The defense lawyer's syntax had become garbled at times during his forty-five-minute address. And he'd pointed his finger in too many directions instead of telling a single coherent story, which probably should have been the same story his client told over and over again during his interrogation: Jeremy Frazier killed Christa Worthington.

But there was no denying that George had been a machine gun, blasting rapid-fire holes through the body of the prosecution's case. Reasonable doubt, reasonable doubt, reasonable doubt. A few jurors had looked away, but reporters and spectators were riveted.

Welsh appealed again to common sense, basing his case on the DNA evidence that proved McCowen had sex with the victim. The April 14 statement was, he said, even more compelling. He read from notes and never looked up.

Neither did Christopher McCowen. He stared down at the defense table as he had throughout the trial. A bump on a log. A cipher. A child among adults.

Welsh surprised the courtroom when he offered a new scenario, trying to plug the holes in his case. When McCowen arrived at Christa's house, the victim went outside, locking the door behind her to protect her daughter. She approached the intruder's car in the dark or maybe went to her own car to get her cell phone from the glove compartment. McCowen got angry and, trying to stop her from calling police, kicked and beat her into helplessness, broke down the door, dragged her inside to the hallway off the kitchen, removed her pants, and had sex with her.

"While doing that, he reaches up under her shirt and grabs her breasts," he surmised, reminding jurors that the DNA on her right breast was not saliva but skin cells.

When the defendant realized that he was on the hook for rape and burglary if he left Worthington alive, he took a knife from the nearby butcher block and stabbed her.

It was, indeed, your basic black-beast scenario, McCowen the predatory ape, dragging his victim through the jungle.

Welsh reminded jurors that McCowen, the informant, gave Jeremy Frazier's name to narcotics officers on January 6. "And what's interesting about that interview is when the defendant can throw someone under the bus, he chooses his friend Jeremy Frazier. What does he say to the police about being able to make a controlled buy from Jeremy Frazier? 'I can buy drugs from Jeremy easy.' In other words, ladies and gentlemen, Jeremy Frazier is the perfect patsy in this case. . . ."

"As you are probably aware," he continued, "the commonwealth doesn't get to pick its witnesses. If we did . . . we would pick productive members of society, people like you on the jury. But those are not the people who are in the periphery of these types of crimes. It's people like Jeremy Frazier . . . and while you may not like Jeremy Frazier, those are the kind of people that Chris McCowen associated with."

McCowen didn't want to be recorded in the third, fateful interview, hoping it wouldn't make him look like "an asshole," proving that he knew how to say no. He told Mason at the beginning, "I can honestly say I don't know her." Later, after admitting he punched her once in the face and once in the chest, this became, "I could still hear her hit the ground" and "we put the boots to her."

Welsh paused, looking at his notes. Then recalled McCowen telling Mason he helped wipe the body down with dishtowels.

"What innocent man says those things?" he asked. "If someone were pulled off the street and showed DNA results matching them to a crime, wouldn't that person say those results must be wrong? Not 'It could have been me'? An innocent man would not say those things."

The defense, he said, wanted jurors to believe that Frazier got a pass on marijuana and murder because he was an informant. But "none of those things change the statement to Mason and Burke [or] the DNA match. And none of these things unfortunately make Christa Worthington any less dead."

Turning to crime-scene blunders, he admitted that the brown blanket was placed over the victim, but it was done "in the interest of decency." However, "in a scene like that, I suggest to you the most important piece of evidence is the DNA." The notion that the untested external genital swab might have shown a different person's DNA should be rejected for what it was, "utter nonsense."

"Ladies and gentlemen, we're not going to charge Jeremy Frazier on the strength of an individual who has changed his story nine times."

He didn't mention that a charge against Frazier would make the prosecution's case evaporate, nullify the indictment and the trial itself. Instead, he shrugged off questions about time of death, saying that the precise time was "impossible" to determine. He dismissed the absence of rape evidence, suggesting that Christa Worthington might have been unconscious, not struggling, when the alleged act occurred, as if that would preclude vaginal injury.

McCowen killed Christa so she wouldn't report the rape, he said. "The intercourse came, I suggest to you, after she was dragged back inside."

Winding down, the prosecutor outlined the different charges and the theories supporting them. Under the joint-venture theory, the defendant was guilty even if jurors believed that Frazier was with him, because he aided in the murder; he need not be the stabber, as long as he intended to commit the crime.

Christa's battered kitchen door was evidence of aggravated burglary under the law, he said, just as the aggravated-assault charge was justified by McCowen's use of a knife.

As for the ultimate charge, all three theories of first-degree murder applied: the crime was premeditated, the defendant intended to inflict bodily injury and was indifferent to the victim's suffering. Christa's death, Welsh reminded them, was not instantaneous. No one could say how long she lay on the floor, bleeding, before she died.

The third theory, felony murder, he added, was supported by *either* the rape or burglary.

Finally, George was guilty of "playing the race card." He claimed that police couldn't accept the idea of consensual sex between the victim and the defendant because of bigotry and bias. Nonsense. "I would still be asking you to convict if the defendant were white and facing the same evidence."

When he stepped down at three P.M., the courtroom's atmosphere changed, decompressed, as if the air had been let out of a balloon. The jousting was over. Nickerson would instruct the jury tomorrow.

Day 16, Tuesday, November 7

Against all odds, the judge had managed to maintain a semblance of order throughout the proceedings. Now, with the new day, he advised the packed courtroom that the public was welcome to sit through jury instructions, but it would be tedious. Once he began, no one would be allowed to leave. Those not wanting to sit through the instructions should exit at once. A few did. A greater number surged toward the newly vacant seats.

Once more, Nickerson and the lawyers haggled at sidebar, this time over the content and wording of instructions. Spectators might have felt that all the good stuff was taking place out of earshot, but the posttrial transcript would reveal that "the good stuff" was arcane case law.

"Members of the jury, please rise," Nickerson began. "Long has been the tradition in the courts of this commonwealth that when a jury receives its charge in a case alleging murder, the jury stands. The jury stands in recognition of the solemnity of the occasion. . . . But in this modern day and age, where charges have grown well beyond twenty minutes, I will allow you to be seated. Please be seated, jurors."

The instructions that followed were inscribed in the jury instruction handbook issued to every superior court jurist; there was nothing new or innovative: the jury should judge the case solely on the evidence, put aside bias, prejudice, and sympathy. Evidence and testimony should be accepted only if credible. "Simply because someone is an expert does not immediately give them credibility. . . . You decide if you believe all that the expert says, some of it, or none of it."

"If you find that any of the omissions in the investigation were significant . . . you may consider whether the omissions tend to affect the quality or reliability of the evidence presented by the commonwealth. Alternatively, you may consider whether the omissions tend to show the existence of police bias against the defendant."

McCowen's police record, the judge said, was "not a substitute for proof that the defendant committed the crime, nor . . . as proof [of] a criminal personality or bad character." It should be considered only in assessing Trooper Mason's request for an arrest warrant.

It was the commonwealth's job to prove that the defendant made the twenty-seven-page statement voluntarily, freely, and rationally, and "was not coerced, tricked, or cajoled." Per DiGiambattista, the jury must determine whether taping was practicable, and if it was, "then you should weigh evidence of the alleged statement with great caution and care. The absence of a recording . . . where a recording was practicable permits, but does not compel, a jury to conclude that the commonwealth has failed to prove voluntariness beyond a reasonable doubt."

This instruction did not address most law-enforcement officers' predilection *not* to record, but the message was clear: the commonwealth's strongest piece of evidence was to be viewed "with great caution and care."

Again, the judge emphasized the importance of the presumption of innocence and the necessity of proof "beyond a reasonable doubt."

He paused and gestured toward the three-foot bust to his left, displayed atop the bench. "I am not really positive as to Henry Scudder's claim to fame. But I am quite sure, ladies and gentlemen, as to why the statue occupying the niche at the other end of my bench is enshrined here."

The bust was of Lemuel Shaw, who, he explained, was born in "a yellow house on Parker Road here in West Barnstable" and became chief justice of the Massachusetts Supreme Judicial Court.

"The words of Chief Justice Shaw, usually dressed up for modern syntax, are echoed in every criminal case in this country today. What is proof beyond a reasonable doubt?"

To be free of reasonable doubt, the evidence must be strong enough to convince them of the defendant's guilt to "a reasonable and moral certainty."

The speech was another of Judge Nickerson's standard set pieces, given only God knows how many times in the past, but unbeknownst to Nickerson, Lemuel Shaw contributed more to American jurisprudence than the standard of reasonable doubt; the late local celebrity espoused the "separate but equal" principle used to justify segregation in the nation's schools for more than a century.

The story is told in the celebrated study of the 1967 busing crisis, *Common Ground*, by journalist J. Anthony Lukas, who depicted a Boston that was never as progressive about slavery and black rights as it pretended. When black parent Benjamin Roberts, in league with the New England Anti-Slavery Society, sued the city on behalf of his daughter in 1849, Chief Justice Shaw, he of Barnstable, wrote the opinion of the Supreme Judicial Court, ruling that segregated schools did *not* deny blacks equal protection of the law.

"Justice Shaw's ruling," Lukas concluded, "was to have a profound effect on the nation's history. The Roberts case was the chief precedent cited by the [U.S.] Supreme Court when it enshrined the doctrine in *Plessy v. Ferguson* (1896) and, thus, the genesis of the legal principle which was to govern the country's race relations until 1954."

In other words, Shaw was a racist. And for all his erudition, the Honorable Gary A. Nickerson needed a history lesson. Likewise, the custodians of Barnstable Superior Court, or perhaps the county's legal overseers, whoever they might be, needed to reconsider the courtroom's statuary.

Done with Shaw, Nickerson pointed to Dan Patenaude, the tall, Lincolnesque high school guidance counselor, and appointed him jury foreman. He had not just given Patenaude "a raise," the judge quipped; no juror had a greater vote than any other. The verdict must be unanimous.

He then launched into the three elements of aggravated rape: sexual intercourse, via force or threat of force, resulting in serious injury.

For aggravated burglary, the Commonwealth had to prove six elements, a mind-numbing list. Nickerson parsed each one as he'd discussed with the attorneys at sidebar. But tedium wasn't the only problem. Although mandatory by law, much of what was said was nonsensical. "Extreme atrocity or cruelty," for example, exists when "the defendant caused the person's death by a method that surpassed the cruelty inherent in the taking of human life" or, alternatively, is "an act that is extremely wicked or brutal, appalling, horrifying, or utterly revolting."

Intended to clarify, these explanations came across as gobbledygook. The list of "qualifications" only fogged things further: whether the defendant was indifferent to, or took pleasure in, the victim's suffering; the consciousness and degree of suffering of the deceased; the extent of the injuries atop the number of blows delivered atop the manner, degree, and severity of force used . . . it went on and on. Finally, the judge reached "the disproportion between the means needed to cause death and those employed."

It was nonsense. How could any layperson divine "the disproportion between means needed to cause death and those employed"? How could the defendant be anything but "indifferent to . . . the sufferings of the deceased" if, as the commonwealth charged, he stabbed Christa through and through after beating her to a bloody pulp?

A man's life was at stake. What did the law assume about the average juror's ability to rule intelligently, competently? Clarence Darrow once said it's "not the law alone or the facts that determine the results," and argued that any lawyer representing the poor would be well advised to avoid a trial at any cost. Now it was clear why.

Nickerson turned to the third first-degree murder theory: felony murder, a killing during the commission of a felony punishable by a maximum sentence of life imprisonment or during an "inherently dangerous" felony, that is, aggravated rape and aggravated burglary.

Second-degree murder was also an option, he said. It hinged on the commonwealth proving the absence of mitigating circumstances; the presence of mitigating circumstances allowed for the lesser charge of voluntary manslaughter. The defendant's mental impairment or intoxication could be considered, whether he thought before he acted, whether he intended to kill or was aware that his conduct created "a strong likelihood" of death, whether he acted in "a cruel or atrocious manner," and whether he intended to commit the aggravated burglary or aggravated rape.

Nickerson had been at it for close to an hour when he reached joint venture, a theory that had haunted the defense from the outset. In July, four months before trial, George decided that this was where McCowen was most vulnerable; he'd ducked it at every turn, maybe mistakenly.

The commonwealth had proceeded on two theories, Nickerson explained. In one, the defendant was the principal actor in the crime. In the other, he acted in consort with someone else. "A person may be found guilty of an offense on a theory of joint venture even if he or she did not personally do the act, but instead aided and abetted its commission as part of a joint venture with another person or persons."

To establish joint venture, the commonwealth had to prove that the defendant had knowledge that another person intended to commit the crime, shared that intent, and aided or agreed to aid in its commission.

This last was critical, the element of foreknowledge.

But how could the prosecution proceed on sole *and* joint venture simultaneously? McCowen either killed Worthington on his own or he was at Christa's house with Frazier, as he insisted to police. It could not be both. At the very least, the joint-venture scenario proved Frazier a liar, his grand-jury testimony a fairy tale and a sham. It didn't take Felix Frankfurter, or even a Johnnie Cochran, to connect the dots.

Every jury instruction must be based on evidence rooted in the record. But trial judges have broad discretion, and Nickerson had delivered a smorgasbord. Maybe he was playing it safe, covering all his bases. Or maybe for extralegal reasons, just maybe, he was offering McCowen the possibility of something short of life in prison.

The judge turned to the logistics of the jury room: the Dolphin Restaurant would provide lunch, smoking breaks would be allowed, but jurors were not to deliberate while apart. If jurors had a question, the foreman should write it down, and a court officer would deliver it to the judge. Court officers would also help with video machinery, but jurors were to stop deliberations when any court officer entered the room. Jurors should advise a court officer when they reached a verdict.

"There is no minimum and there is no maximum time for a jury's deliberation," Nickerson told them. "I take no role in determining the length of your deliberation. It's left solely to you."

He conferred with the attorneys. George had waived the joint venture, knowledge-of-a-weapon instruction but changed his mind. Nickerson reinstructed the jurors, telling them that the commonwealth had to prove that the defendant knew that "the joint venturer had a weapon." But mere knowledge "that the joint venturer was armed once inside the house was not sufficient to hold the defendant liable for the acts of that joint venturer. It must be proved that the defendant intentionally assisted that joint venturer in the commission of the underlying felony."

He paused to look at his papers, then went on. "If the commonwealth has not proved beyond a reasonable doubt that the defendant knew that the joint venturer had a weapon and that the defendant shared the mental intent for aggravated burglary or armed burglary, as we have called it, then you must find the defendant not guilty of felony murder under that theory and not guilty of armed burglary under that theory as a joint venturer."

There it was: to be convicted, McCowen had to have known that his co-venturer had a weapon, had to have knowingly participated in the planning and commission of the "underlying" burglary. If McCowen "put the boots" to Christa, as he allegedly told police, but was surprised when Frazier brandished a knife, jurors would be left in a gray area, a maze of legal qualifications and circumstantial exceptions.

Knowledge and intent both were necessary to convict.

In the "well," the depressed area in front of the judge's bench, the court clerk stood and pulled two poker chips from a wooden box to designate the alternates: Robert Lyon, the bow-tied dandy antique dealer, and Mary O'Prey, the graying Maureen Stapleton look-alike. They would have the most difficult task of all, Nickerson told them. Segregated from the rest of the panel, they could not discuss the case even with each other.

Nickerson turned to the defendant. McCowen looked up with his perennial blank stare. He had no idea what was coming.

"Mr. McCowen," Nickerson said, his tone extra soft and syrupy now, nearly that of a pediatrician talking to a young child, "you certainly have comported yourself as a gentleman in every respect in the course of the trial. So, my following comments are not in any way directed at you individually. However, in every case where I take a verdict, I have the defendant in the dock, [and] you will be shackled on the legs. The reason for that is security purposes. The jurors cannot see your legs. You will not be handcuffed, for they may see your hands. . . . Your lawyer certainly can stand next to you during the reading of the verdict."

"Yes, sir," McCowen said flatly.

"Thank you. Now, with regard to the row that is immediately behind the dock . . . that row will be vacant, because it will be occupied by court officers during the taking of a verdict."

The number of court officers would more than double, but the judge didn't mention that.

It was election day, 3:55 P.M., and the jurors had asked to be dismissed in order to vote. Among local candidates on the ballot was Republican District Attorney Michael O'Keefe. Out-of-town reporters couldn't help but note that O'Keefe's bid for reelection was unopposed.

Days 17–19, November 8–10

To spice up the stew, on Wednesday, Governor Mitt Romney formally nominated Welsh to the district court bench, his timing curious, to say the least. On Thursday, the tedium was uninterrupted. But on Friday, jurors sent a written query: "What is the legal definition for *beyond a reasonable doubt?* What is [*sic*] the parameters for which *beyond reasonable doubt* would apply?"

Nickerson clarified: the prosecution did not have to prove guilt beyond *all* doubt but must establish an "abiding conviction to a moral certainty that the charge is true."

When jurors returned to deliberations, a reporter proposed a verdict betting pool. His colleagues weren't interested, one because it was "disrespectful." It was a sudden spate of propriety for the Fourth Estate. In the past few days journalists had filled the news void with glam profiles of Welsh and Nickerson, as well as a feature on native son Lemuel Shaw; like Nickerson, they were clueless about Shaw's actual legacy. They were even mining the dregs, re-interviewing Tony Jackett. Like Jan Worthington, Jackett had snagged his own film deal. Never timid, he shared his thoughts on casting: daughter Braunwyn could be portrayed by Britney Spears, wife Susan by Madonna, and only the smoldering Antonio Banderas could fill the lead, Tony himself.

Day 20, Monday, November 13

With the utmost sternness, Judge Gary Nickerson dropped heavily into his swivel chair and ordered the courtroom closed to address "a vital matter that affects deliberating jurors." It was the beginning of the day. With only the lawyers, the court clerk, the DA's staff, several bailiffs, and the court reporter present, he briefed counsel on the weekend's events: a narcotics-related shooting had occurred in Falmouth, at the heel of the Cape. Local and state police, including Mason, had come to believe that a black man named Kyle Hicks was involved; Hicks was juror Rachel Huffman's boyfriend and the father of her two-year-old girl. Police had gone to Huffman's home, where Hicks was found sitting on the couch. A second man, hiding in a rear bedroom, had an outstanding warrant for assault. Huffman identified herself as a Worthington juror and told police that Hicks had used her vehicle earlier that evening. When investigators found 306 unused Massachusetts auto-inspection stickers in the trunk that were registered to a dealership in Dartmouth, she claimed they'd been left in the vehicle when she bought it; the dealership planned to retrieve them. Detectives had been unable to verify her story over the weekend. Huffman had no criminal record.

The night of the shooting, Friday, Huffman was interviewed at the police station, Nickerson continued, videotaped and audiotaped with her consent. (Rumor had it she insisted on being taped, having been exposed to the ins and outs of police interrogations during jury service.)

Nickerson had not yet viewed the tape but had been informed that Huffman again identified herself as a juror during the interview.

The judge explained that he needed to question each member of the panel. The matter was serious; a court officer had reported that a second juror learned of the weekend's events and told him that four or five other jurors also knew. In the meantime, Huffman had been sequestered.

The juror who'd spoken to the court officer was Taryn O'Connell, the young, amply endowed mother of two whom McCowen had ogled throughout the trial, much to George's frustration. The judge called her in first, reminding her that she was still under oath.

O'Connell explained that her husband had fallen asleep with the TV on Friday night. At about midnight, an attempted murder in Falmouth was reported, and she recognized one of the men on-screen as the father of Rachel Huffman's child. Rachel had shown her pictures of her girl, and Hicks was in one of the photos.

O'Connell acknowledged that she called Rachel's cell phone and, unable to reach her, called juror Eric Gomes, a bartender who was available at that hour. Gomes confirmed Hicks as the father but knew nothing about the incident. O'Connell said she then called foreman Patenaude, who'd also seen the news and tried to reach Rachel.

Nickerson next called Gomes, one of two blacks on the panel. Gomes said he'd heard about the incident from a customer.

"You didn't hear by telephone from Miss O'Connell?"

"From?"

"Miss O'Connell, one of your fellow jurors?"

"She called me and asked me if I knew the person."

"OK. And you had some conversation with her?"

"Not much. Not really."

"But you did have telephone contact?"

Gomes nodded. "Yeah," he said, lowering his eyes to the floor, evasively.

"And?"

"I told her I was busy and I couldn't talk." He added that jurors had talked about the incident that morning.

MSP detectives survey the desolate murder scene at 50 Depot Road, Truro, after the discovery of Christa Worthington's body. (Photo by Kevin Mingora/*Cape Cod Times*)

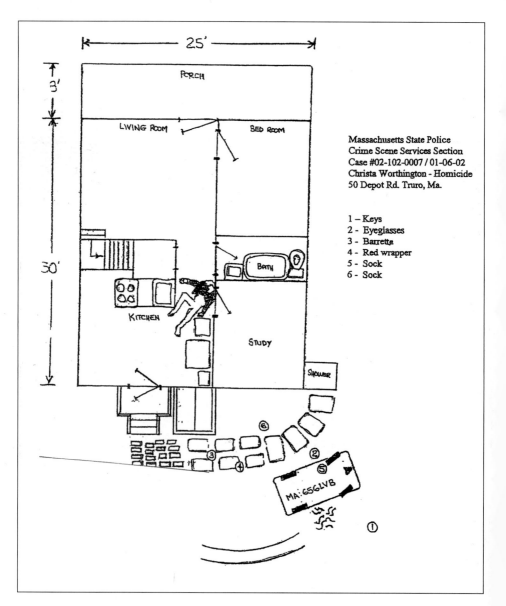

25'

3'

30'

PORCH

LIVING ROOM

BED ROOM

KITCHEN

BATH

STUDY

SHOWER

MA: 656LV8

Massachusetts State Police
Crime Scene Services Section
Case #02-102-0007 / 01-06-02
Christa Worthington - Homicide
50 Depot Rd. Truro, Ma.

1 – Keys
2 - Eyeglasses
3 - Barrette
4 - Red wrapper
5 - Sock
6 - Sock

MSP Crime Scene Services schematic of the interior of 50 Depot Road, showing the location of the body, and, outside, the location of various bits of evidence introduced at trial.

Historic Barnstable Superior Courthouse as the jury deliberates late into the evening after the dismissal of juror Rachel Huffman. (Photo by Steve Heaslip/*Cape Cod Times*)

Christa Worthington with her daughter, Ava, on Pamet Beach in Truro, the summer before her death in January 2002.

Dear Mrs. Jackett,

From Sept to the day your mother in law died I was sleeping with your husband. I just thought you should know.

Christa Worthington

On that day, he stopped by after dropping Luke off in Hyannis at the bus stop. We went to bed. He told me how early on you said you

Christa Worthington's affair with Tony Jackett lasted until she became pregnant and Tony abandoned her. Seething, she threatened to expose him to his wife, Susan, as indicated in this letter, which was never mailed. Along with Worthington's diaries that characterized Jackett as weak, opportunistic, and prone to self-pity, the letter was not introduced at trial for evidentiary reasons.

Tony Jackett: ex-fisherman, ex-garbageman, ex–dope smuggler, local shellfish warden, and lover. Tony appeared at the courthouse, sporting several days' growth, eager to make himself available to the media with his opinions on the trial and the evidence. During the three-and-a-half-year investigation, he'd signed a movie deal and boasted to Provincetown cronies of his many invitations to appear on TV. (Photo by Paul Blackmore/ *Cape Cod Times*)

Christopher McCowen was eighty pounds lighter when arraigned in Orleans District Court on April 15, 2005, and still in a state of shock after his arrest and six-and-a-half-hour interrogation the night before. The good looks that made him popular with women were still obvious even in the prisoners' dock. (Photo by Vincent DeWitt/ *Cape Cod Times*)

Worthington boyfriend Tim Arnold discovered the body and a suckling Ava. Here he testifies alongside the crime scene diagram and a photograph of the smashed door lock after the defense had confronted him with the fact that he once kicked open the same door during a heated lovers' quarrel. (Photo by Steve Heaslip/*Cape Cod Times*)

Jeremy Frazier, 23, the drug dealer who was called by the prosecution to plug a major hole in the Commonwealth's case. Throughout the trial, the DA's office withheld Frazier's unsavory reputation as well as his informant status for the Massachusetts State Police. (Photo by Steve Heaslip/*Cape Cod Times*)

Jan Worthington, the victim's cousin, showed herself to be a self-promoting, greedy, and untruthful witness. According to Jan, who marketed a screenplay about the murder while privately calling her cousin a troublesome "neurotic," the loss of Christa was almost more than she could handle. (Photo by Steve Heaslip/*Cape Cod Times*)

Defense attorney Robert George tries to rattle the unflappable (and sartorially perfect) MSP detective Christopher Mason with evidence of a cell phone call to State Police by Jeremy Frazier shortly after the estimated time of the murder. (Photo by Steve Heaslip/*Cape Cod Times*)

Keith Amato, the first witness to be called by the defense, commandingly describes his treatment by police interrogators that left him vomiting in the bushes outside the Truro police station. (Photo by Kevin Mingora/*Cape Cod Times*)

Superior Court judge Gary Nickerson's folksy manner made him a favorite of the jurors. Here he instructs them before deliberations with a history lesson featuring Cape Cod native and Massachusetts Supreme Judicial Court justice Lemuel Shaw, the father of "reasonable doubt." Unfortunately, Nickerson ignored Shaw's other achievement as the architect of the "separate but equal" doctrine that was used to justify American public school segregation for nearly a full century. (Photo by Kevin Mingora/*Cape Cod Times*)

Defense attorney Robert George helps the defendant with his tie
before the jury returned to the courtroom to be sequestered, and
even the seasoned court bailiff seemed to take notice of the personal
connection between the two. (Photo by Steve Heaslip/*Cape Cod Times*)

Pre-trial, District Attorney Michael
O'Keefe announces the Worthington
family's reward for information
leading to an arrest. O'Keefe was
forced to remove himself from the
case after making inappropriate
remarks about the victim as a
sexually promiscuous "equal
opportunity employer." (Photo by
Kevin Mingora/*Cape Cod Times*)

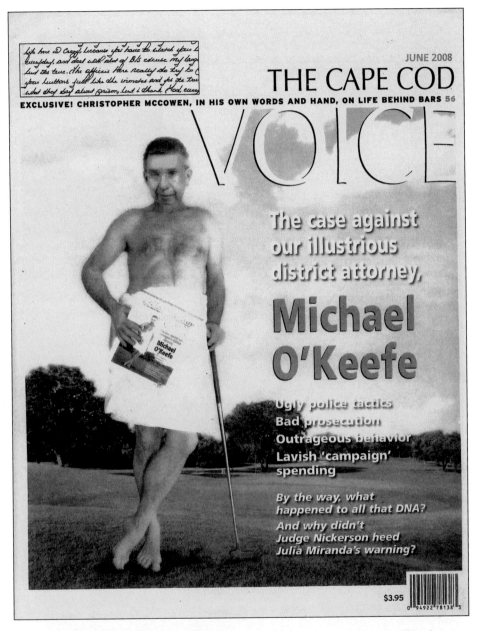

JUNE 2008

THE CAPE COD

EXCLUSIVE! CHRISTOPHER MCCOWEN, IN HIS OWN WORDS AND HAND, ON LIFE BEHIND BARS 56

VOICE

The case against
our illustrious
district attorney,

Michael
O'Keefe

Ugly police tactics
Bad prosecution
Outrageous behavior
Lavish 'campaign'
spending

By the way, what
happened to all that DNA?
And why didn't
Judge Nickerson heed
Julia Miranda's warning?

$3.95

0 94922 78138 3

Most Cape Codders were enthralled with the trial but many were turned off by the behavior of their DA. The *Cape Cod Voice*, since shuttered, mounted an up-front campaign against O'Keefe, mocking him for making a pass at a female writer while wearing only a towel, and for his well-known penchant for golf outings paid for with campaign funds. (Photo courtesy of *Cape Cod Voice*)

The relationship between Robert George and the author was well-known: the defense used Manso's research and his knowledge of the Cape Cod community in its examination of witnesses and in motions to dismiss, including its appeal to the SJC. The author, who was indicted after the verdict by the Cape Cod DA (along with two dissenting jurors), labored for seventeen months until the prison charges against him were dismissed—in the very courtroom where McCowen was tried. (Photo by Merrily Lunsford/*Cape Cod Times*)

Before juror Rachel Huffman was ousted, the McCowen jury poses for an unknown photographer, possibly a bailiff using a cell phone camera, inside the sanctity of the jury room. Back row, left to right: Sally Powers, Mary O'Prey, Robert Lyon, Charles Ivers, Eric Gomes, Roshena Bohanna, and Normand Audet; front row, left to right: Matthew Maltby, Laura Stacey, Taryn O'Connell, Marlo George, Rachel Huffman, and Carol Cahill. Lying playfully on the table (or is it in the laps of female jurors?) is the jury foreman, Dan Patenaude.

McCowen, who had been described as a heartless, cold-blooded, ex-con murderer and rapist by the prosecution, weeps at the moment of hearing the guilty verdicts on November 16, 2006. (Photo by Steve Heaslip/*Cape Cod Times*)

Catherine Cisnernos, upon hearing the verdict, is comforted by strangers and newfound friends. (Photo by Steve Heaslip/*Cape Cod Times*)

McCowen is led out of court after receiving three life sentences. (Photo by Robert Scott Button/Cape Cod Media Network)

Prosecutor Robert Welsh III, who is the son, grandson, and great-grandson of Cape Cod judges going back to the turn of the last century, stands at the news podium outside Barnstable Superior Court after the verdicts, surrounded by (l. to r.): MSP sergeant William Burke; MSP detective Christopher Mason; the victim's cousin, Pam Worthington; and Ava's legal guardian, Amyra Chase. (Photo by Paul Blackmore/*Cape Cod Times*)

The jury's social director, Matt Maltby, bids farewell to the judge's chief court officer, but not for long—a few weeks after the verdict, this court officer, and the chief jury court officer, attended the jurors' *gemütlich* get-together with prosecutor Welsh at Wimpy's, a local Osterville restaurant. (Photo by Paul Blackmore/*Cape Cod Times*)

"If it walks like a duck and talks like a duck and smells like a duck, then to me, it's a duck!" Robert George vows to find out what went wrong in the jury room and what really led to Judge Nickerson's removal of juror Rachel Huffman. (Photo by Paul Blackmore/*Cape Cod Times*)

Judge Nickerson's chief court officer and the chief jury court officer party with jurors and prosecutor Welsh at Wimpy's. (Photo by Robert Scott Button/Cape Cod Media Network)

The post-trial dinner at Wimpy's, minus the dissenting jurors, Rachel Huffman, Roshena Bohanna, and Normand Audet. Prosecutor Welsh sits with Charles Ivers, Daniel Patenaude, and Robert Lyon at the far table while Matthew Maltby faces the window, speaking with Laura Stacy (r) and Marlo George (l). (Photo by Robert Scott Button/Cape Cod Media Network)

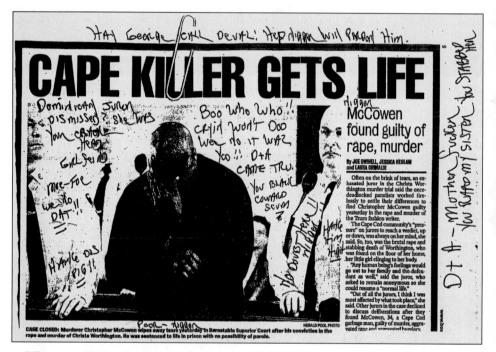

Whoever said New England was "enlightened?" Or that the McCowen trial didn't center on race? Attorney Robert George received hate mail during and after the trial, including this annotated clipping from *The Boston Herald*. The reference to Deval is to Massachusetts governor Deval Patrick, like McCowen an African American. (Photo from the collection of Robert George)

Foreman Dan Patenaude soon fessed up, too, which made George roll his eyes. The foreman listening to the news? Patenaude acknowledged that he'd tried to reach Huffman, then told O'Connell they'd deal with it on Monday.

Nickerson called Marlo George, who said she was completely unaware of the events. Sally Ann Powers, the Braintree High School employee, followed, saying she had learned of the arrest over the weekend and had noticed Rachel missing that morning while the group waited to be called to the courtroom. Asked if she could still be fair and impartial, a question the judge put to each juror as wrap-up, Powers was less than certain. "Once I settle down—right now, I'm very nervous. But once I get that behind me, I'm sure," she said.

George couldn't contain himself any longer. He told Nickerson he wanted further inquiry. Asked again whether she could be fair and impartial, Powers gave a firm "Yes, sir."

The judge moved on.

Norman Audet had learned that something was wrong with Rachel that morning; he hadn't watched the news. Carol Cahill also denied watching TV. Roshena Bohanna, the group's sole African-American female, said a friend who knew Huffman told her about the incident on Sunday. Charles "Chuck" Ivers claimed nothing was discussed in the jury room but then admitted that he'd overheard that one of the jurors' boyfriend "might have been arrested."

The four remaining jurors acknowledged that they had learned of the incident that morning; Laura Stacy, Matthew Maltby and Robert Lyon heard that Huffman's boyfriend was arrested but didn't know the details. Mary O'Prey, one of the two alternates, admitted that she'd heard something but didn't know which juror was involved.

With the jurors out of the courtroom, Nickerson quickly declared the panel "free of any taint arising from this incident." He didn't mention that four jurors had admitted violating the court's orders by watching TV, listening to news radio, and discussing the trial with outside parties.

Before calling Huffman, he turned to Michael O'Keefe. The shadowy DA had been calling the shots for the past three weeks from his office across the parking lot but was now in the courtroom, making his first appearance before the bench, ostensibly to answer questions about the inspection stickers in Huffman's car. Nothing new had come to light, O'Keefe growled; he was not inclined to press the matter.

But O'Keefe was not to be relied on. Huffman soon would be charged with possession of stolen motor-vehicle stickers, being an accessory after the fact to attempted murder, and possession of marijuana. Social services would threaten to take her child. For nearly two years, the matter would drag on, prosecuted by the O'Keefe office until all charges were dropped without imposition of criminal penalties.

Now, the twenty-two-year-old brunette was brought into the courtroom and asked the same questions put to the others. She said she could continue to serve despite the weekend's events and bore no prejudice toward the Commonwealth. Nickerson pronounced her kosher.

A visibly agitated Robert George moved to sequester the jury. The move was abrupt, major, and fraught with risk. Nickerson reminded him that sequestration could impose extreme hardship on at least one juror, a single mother of three with no relatives nearby. He postponed ruling.

O'Keefe, who'd been standing by, piped up. "I would ask that the videotape be marked for identification and that the record reflect that the officers from the State Police detectives unit who interacted with this juror . . . are available for the court to make inquiry of."

He admitted that several were his own MSP detectives. Nickerson nodded, unsurprised, then called the jurors back. Something in the judge's body language suggested that he was not in any way in awe of the DA. The two had a history, a past that was near baroque and offered another glimpse info the Cape's tangled legal world.

It started in the early '80s, when both men worked for the Rollins office and Gary Nickerson was appointed special assistant to the U.S. Attorney because of his expertise with the Massachusetts Wiretapping Statute, G.L. c. 272, sec. 99. But Nickerson had earlier failed to clear the FBI security check because of FBI knowledge of drug use among certain prosecutors in the Rollins office; only after personal intercession by Rollins and, reportedly, then–U.S. Attorney William

Weld, who would later become the Commonwealth's governor, was Nickerson cleared for his assignment.

His initial failure to clear the security check was unacceptable to the high-toned Nickerson and led to his departure from the district attorney's office. Rollins managed to keep him on as appellate counsel for a few years, but Nickerson prospered in private practice and eventually was offered several opportunities to serve on the district court bench. These he turned down, his eye on a superior court appointment. When a spot opened in the region, Nickerson and O'Keefe, it turned out, were the primary candidates. Rollins openly supported O'Keefe, rather than remain neutral between his top assistants. Nickerson, reportedly, was not only taken aback but responded with hardball tactics of his own, calling in due bills up and down the Cape as well as in Boston. O'Keefe had often boasted of being the ultimate politico, but, Nickerson outfoxed him, winning the coveted robe.

There was a fundamental difference in style between the two men as well, but the Superior Court judgeship jelled it. Ever since, according to local lore, the two had skirted each other like lions trapped in the same cage. Not even with all the glam of the Worthington trial did the local press dare to go near the subject.

Deliberations resumed. Two hours passed, then three. Shortly after two o'clock, the jury reported that it was deadlocked. Welsh opposed giving the dynamite charge, the Tuey-Rodriguez instruction that directs jurors to try again. George renewed his request that the panel be sequestered. Nickerson urged the jurors to agree on a verdict if they could "conscientiously do so." The alternative was to declare a hung jury.

With the panel back out at 2:36 P.M., Nickerson turned to George. "If I sequester I will not sequester . . . in the hopes that sequestration forces a decision. That would be using sequestration as a coercive measure."

George was having second thoughts, though. If jurors realized that he was responsible for locking them up, the move could backfire. "Your Honor, at this point in the game, I don't want to cause Mr. McCowen any damage. . . . We don't want to lose any jurors."

"I'm not in a position of making your tactical decisions," the judge said. "I need to know if you're moving for sequestration or you're not. . . . Do you wish more time?"

George thought for a moment. "Your Honor, I am moving for sequestration only if you don't let any jurors go who claim hardship. I'll be very honest with you. I'm not looking to change the composition of this jury at this point, not knowing how the votes are going."

Nickerson decided to sequester. "I will tell them that I am not sequestering them in any way to coerce a verdict. This is not the product of their . . . pronouncing a deadlock."

Every effort would be made to ensure jurors' comfort. Each would be allowed to contact a friend or a relative, have clothes and toiletries brought to the hotel. If child care was an issue, transportation and adjoining rooms would be arranged.

At four P.M., Nickerson gave jurors the news: they would be transported to the local Radisson under the supervision of bailiffs. Breakfast, dinner, and two alcoholic beverages would be provided. "You get two, and that's all you get," he told them, grinning; as always, he needed to cultivate friends and allies.

Juror Roshena Bohanna had a hardship. She'd had a root canal before reporting for jury duty and postponed her follow-up, and part of her tooth had fallen out only moments ago. Since it was already late afternoon and Bohanna's dentist was likely closed, Nickerson volunteered a court officer to take her to Cape Cod Hospital. Bohanna was the sole black female among the jurors; the judge had gone out of his way to empanel her, and he didn't want to lose her.

"Jurors," he said to those headed for the hotel, "I know it's an imposition. I know you have been patient. I know you have worked hard. I apologize. I must do this . . . to ensure a fair trial."

Day 21, Tuesday, November 14

Reporters milled about outside the courthouse, including many new arrivals, recalculating the odds. In anticipation of the verdict, *People* had sent a representative from New York. So did *Vogue*, whose well-dressed emissary was rumored to be writing a story about Jan Worthington, of all people. Jackett continued to dole out the same eager sound bites he'd been recycling since Christa's death; despite the transparency of his hypocritical chatter, there seemed to be no shortage of interest, especially on the part of several fortyish female TV reporters whose once vaulting careers had settled on personality profiles and human interest stories.

Upstairs in the courtroom, Welsh was agitated anew. He'd learned of several conversations juror Huffman had with her boyfriend in jail. The day before, while Huffman was in the jury room making arrangements for the move to the hotel, court officers allowed her to receive the calls; they should not have. That Hicks was allowed to place the calls was even more unorthodox; outgoing calls from the Barnstable County House of Corrections are always collect, never to a cell phone, always monitored.

Welsh, arguing that Huffman should be removed from the jury, asked to play the audio tape of the phone conversations for the court's consideration. There were three calls in all. He was concerned about two, one lasting seven minutes, the other six, made at 4:43 and 4:52 P.M.

Nickerson had already heard the tape but agreed to play it. Sound quality was marginal, but it was definitely Huffman, discussing their daughter, Hicks's attorneys' fees, and the sequestration—all reaching a national audience now via the Court TV feed.

"They just sequestered us, so I can't go home," she said, her voice breaking as she discussed caring for their child, who was with her mother. "There's so much going on. I am so freakin' upset."

Hicks asked how much longer deliberations were likely to take. "Do they think they're going to make you deliberate until you can make a [expletive] decision?"

"I guess so. I don't know."

During the second call, Huffman informed Hicks that the media had gone wild, "blowing you up" with a lot of coverage. The police who came to her house, she said, were "so friggin' dumb. . . . I told them, 'If you're going to harass me and talk to my neighbors, get a warrant.'"

As the sound died, Welsh announced that Mason had prepared a written transcript, highlighting relevant portions. "If it aids the court, I would hand that up," he said eagerly. "I'm not asking that it be marked."

The ever industrious Mason had apparently stayed up most of the night, transcribing. One Cape lawyer in the audience declared that the detective had set a record for the fastest Massachusetts State Police transcript production in history. Yet it took Mason eight days to craft McCowen's April 14 "statement."

"My argument, Judge, under Massachusetts General Laws 234, Section 26B," Welsh said, is that "a deliberating juror may be discharged when for specified personal reasons or 'other good cause shown' the juror is unable to perform his or her duty. . . . With respect to the conversations from Kyle Hicks [and] the juror in question, there is . . . evidence that she is either watching news coverage of this trial in violation of the court order or receiving information from others who have watched it. Specifically, I think there's a reference made to Court TV."

Court TV hadn't been broadcasting the trial at night, but that didn't matter. Nor did it matter that Patenaude, O'Connell, Bohanna, and Gomes were guilty of the same infractions.

"Additionally, the calls indicate a bias against the police," Welsh went on, adding that Huffman had lied by indicating that her relationship with Hicks was distant, not the "much closer relationship . . . disclosed to the court." He asked that she be removed.

Only later would the prosecutor learn that Huffman had been torn, not holding out for acquittal, as he believed.

George reminded the judge that after the extended hearing the day before, the court concluded that Huffman could go forward, that there was no sign of outside interference or bias. The prosecution's move to eject Huffman came directly on the heels of the deadlock; *that*, George said, was what had changed.

"Your Honor, we're going into the sixth day of deliberations, [and] to take her out now . . . would destroy the defendant's right to a fair trial in this case, and I object."

But Nickerson had already made up his mind. Huffman was out. She had earlier suggested that she was breaking up with Hicks, but the telephone conversations indicated otherwise.

George made no attempt to disguise his disgust. He asked the judge to reconsider. Welsh cut him off, citing *Commonwealth v. Tennison,* a case in which a juror was removed after a deadlock; in that case, the removed juror was the lone holdout, suspected of being on the take.

"I'm asking for a stay of these proceedings, Your Honor," George said.

"Yes, I'm denying the stay."

"Please note my objection."

"That's noted, sir."

Brought into the courtroom, Huffman stood in the jurors' box, expressionless, as Nickerson announced his decision. She would be escorted to the jury room to collect her belongings; then she was to leave the premises. She was not to speak to other jurors until they were discharged.

She nodded, saying nothing.

The courtroom had fallen into a hush. Even the handful of winos and dysfunctional court junkies sprinkled through the gallery seemed to get it: this was major. How it would affect the verdict was anybody's guess. Welsh was not the only one who believed Huffman had been poised to vote "black."

George was reluctant to move for a mistrial; conventional wisdom gives the prosecution the edge in a retrial. But he had never faced a situation like this. It was more than just another tortured twist in a trial fraught with weirdness, beginning with a superior court judge who'd run himself over with his own golf cart.

He had no choice.

"Your Honor . . . based on the defendant's right to a fair and full jury deliberation in this case and based on his right to a fair and full determination of the charges against him pursuant to the Massachusetts and United States Constitution, I would move for a mistrial in order to perfect the record."

"Let me ask you this, Mr. George, do you genuinely want a mistrial, or is this something to, as you say, 'perfect a record'?" Nickerson added ominously, "Be careful what you wish for . . ."

"I am moving for a mistrial."

Nickerson denied the motion forthwith and called in the jury. Alternate Mary O'Prey took Huffman's seat. Jurors were to begin deliberations anew, as required by law, Nickerson explained. The eleven carryovers were to set aside their work, all diagrams and charts were to be destroyed, all evidence reconsidered. One female juror mouthed, "Oh, my God," and hung her head, trying not to cry.

The jury filed out of the courtroom at 10:37 A.M. Outside the courthouse, where the fall leaves were still golden but the wind noticeably colder than several weeks ago, George took McCowen's girlfriend aside. "I want you to stop crying," he told her. "You cry, Chris cries. No good."

After an hour, Nickerson summoned the media back upstairs. He'd been told that Huffman had been set upon by reporters and photographers at the far end of the parking lot. Additionally, Boston's Channel 5 had aired a video of the jurors' bus leaving for the hotel the night before. Had any juror been visible? A woman from the station said no, but Nickerson had already morphed into Judge Roy Bean.

"If I say, 'Don't take pictures of the jurors' and you're taking pictures of the bus . . . the opportunity to run afoul of my order is enormous. However, if the media wishes to split hairs with me, get a picture of a juror and see what this court thinks of it. . . . There's already been one cameraman sent packing back to New Jersey. . . . If everybody thinks this is a light lark, perhaps the next one should be sent to jail. *Leave the jurors alone.*"

After lunch, he called the press back again. This time, his target was the *Cape Cod Times*; Huffman's name had appeared on the paper's website. The *Times*'s two beat reporters said they hadn't called that information in; perhaps an editor added it after listening to Court TV. A Court TV representative volunteered that its New York office had tried to bleep the name, but he wasn't sure it had succeeded.

Nickerson announced that he'd hold a contempt hearing at ten the following morning, then banned all cameras from the premises; the only exceptions were the Court TV camera and the two pool photographers approved for work inside the courtroom.

After twenty-one days and nearly as many crises, Nickerson was determined not to lose control of his trial.

Every reporter would lead the day's story with the Huffman-Hicks phone calls, quoting George saying something was rotten in the state of Denmark. "All this was known yesterday; all that changed was the phone calls. They spent more time investigating her than they did some of the more important issues in this case."

George wasn't alone. A number of Cape attorneys could not recall a single case where a juror's phone calls had been monitored. Elliot Weinstein, the highly regarded Boston attorney known for low-key, meticulous defenses, put a sharper point on it, telling the *Provincetown Banner* that "it sounds to me like the prosecution had misgivings about how the juror was leaning in her deliberations."

Day 22, Wednesday, November 15

Overnight, George had read the case Welsh cited. At sidebar, he argued that it was inapplicable to the Huffman situation. Nickerson wasn't buying. Instead, he called for the jury, then sent them back to continue deliberating. It was 9:09 A.M. In less than an hour, another written question reached the judge; referring to the appellate court's preference that police record interviews, the jury asked, "Do police officers have the option of recording a statement when practicable even though an individual has signed off his right to be recorded?"

It was a critical question. Nickerson turned to counsel for input. Welsh and George clashed again, each edgier than ever before, believing that he was losing the case. Welsh declared the answer a decisive no, citing *Commonwealth v. Sutherland.* George disagreed: the prosecutor was hanging his hat on a case that dealt with *secret* recordings; the issue wasn't consent, it was knowledge that the conversation was being taped.

"Mr. McCowen, much as when he calls from the jail, could have been told that he would be recorded whether or not he signed a waiver. They do not need his consent to record," George explained. "They simply need his knowledge that he is being recorded."

Again, he was thinking of the record. If McCowen was convicted, the appeal might bring *DiGiambattista* all the way home, make taping mandatory in felony interrogations.

Nickerson told Welsh that he would stick with the instruction he'd already given.

"'Do police officers have the option of recording a statement when practicable even though an individual has signed off his right to be recorded?' The answer is a qualified yes," he stated. "The wiretap statute requires only making a person aware of the recording."

The judge was at his best. He knew what was at stake.

"Now, as a practical matter," he added, "if somebody says, 'I don't want to be recorded,' and they're told, 'Everything you say is going to be recorded,' will they continue to speak? Probably not. But that's not my problem, is it?"

Jurors filed back in at 2:18 P.M., and the court's answer took but three minutes. Back out they went, a bailiff in front, another bringing up the rear.

According to Megan Tench of the *Boston Globe*, the only black newsperson at the trial, the clarification caused some raised eyebrows among jurors. Even so, it was a hands-down win for the defense. Many thought it would prove decisive.

Members of the press were weary, and one or two had turned outright goofy. One reporter suggested that the courtroom's statue of the iconic Lemuel Shaw be replaced with one of Alfred E. Neuman, the zany, grinning "What Me Worry?" figure of *Mad* magazine. "Let's steal the damn thing," the newsman ranted. "Fuck 'em. That'll shake 'em up."

So worn out were most that they'd stopped taking notes, even, not that there was much to write about. Eric Williams, scraping the bottom of the barrel for his daily *Cape Cod Times* podcast, went so far as to bring his videographer inside the courtroom at the end of the day to query George on his favorite alcoholic beverage, a play on Nickerson's two-drinks-per-juror limit. "A Negroni," the stout lawyer snapped, then strode away. George was a teetotaler, in fact, and did not know what a Negroni was. But he'd recently seen an old flick on TV where a young, handsome Warren Beatty, playing a gigolo, drank . . . what else? Negronis.

Day 23, Thursday, November 16

No one knew what impact the new juror was having on deliberations, but it was obvious from the delay that Huffman hadn't been the lone holdout. The press corps continued to mill about the courthouse, fidgeting, mingling with spectators, chatting with security guards at the metal detector in the lobby. One group of a half-dozen reporters got the clerk's office to agree to a fifteen-minute delay in reading the verdict once the jury came back, then fled across the street for coffee at the Piccadilly Deli. It was too early for the bar to be open at the Dolphin.

Upstairs, Nickerson was dealing with yet another media issue. Several Boston outlets moved for relief from the court's order regarding Rachel Huffman, and the *Cape Cod Times* was preparing a motion on the same issue. Huffman's identity was newsworthy, and the paper had already run two front-page stories about her. Neither George nor Welsh gave a damn. But George took the opportunity to request Hicks's phone number, as well as the visitor records from the Barnstable County jail where Huffman's boyfriend was still being held.

The wait continued. At 11:33, word finally reached the courtroom: "We have a verdict."

Reporters and spectators scrambled for the stairs, crowding the first-floor landing before bailiffs let them go up. Many press people were on cell phones, reserving space in the next edition. A stringer for the *New York Post* was heard above the hubbub, yelling at his editor, "All right, all right! I'm calling from the Worthington trial. . . . *Yes, on the Cape!*"

Inside the courtroom, Nickerson had never looked more authoritarian—tall, regal, and emotionless—a white-haired king presiding over his domain. Four or five female jurors, including the matronly Mary O'Prey, did not look up as they filed in, seeming to find their seats by radar. Traditional wisdom teaches that downcast eyes are not good for the defense. The lone black woman, Roshena Bohanna, was ashen-faced and almost stumbled. Her eyes were red-rimmed, as if she'd been crying.

"Mr. Clerk, you may proceed," the judge intoned. Courtroom doors were locked. Every pew was filled. O'Keefe's team filled the lawyers' box. It was easy to be cynical about the young black staffer who'd been put on display only two days earlier.

"Mr. Foreman, ladies and gentlemen of the jury, have you agreed upon your verdicts?" the court clerk asked.

"Yes, we have."

Time stood still. In the dock, the closely guarded defendant shifted from one foot to the other, his leg irons clanking in the silence. George stood at his side.

"What say you, Mr. Foreman, as to indictment number 05-109-01? Is the defendant, Christopher M. McCowen, guilty or not guilty of any offense?"

"We, the jury, unanimously return the following verdict of guilty of murder in the first degree," foreman Daniel Patenaude announced. "We, the jury, find him guilty, offense as charged," of both aggravated rape and aggravated burglary.

George swayed on the balls of his feet. "I would ask that the jury be polled, Your Honor," he called out in a tone no one had heard before. With heartbreaking tenderness, he reached up and wiped a tear from Chris McCowen's cheek with the cuff of his expensive suit. The four bailiffs moved in, squeezing them.

"I would ask that the verdict be recorded," Welsh said.

"All right. Mr. Clerk," Nickerson boomed, "please poll the jury."

Daniel Patenaude, the high school guidance counselor, rose once more. The clerk read each of the three charges, and Patenaude answered, "Guilty," "Guilty," "Guilty." Asked for the subcategories of murder one, he said, "Extreme atrocity" and "Cruelty and felony murder."

The clerk repeated the grim process with each juror. Two looked deeply shaken, as if the enormity of what they'd done had just hit home.

"If all the jurors would please stand," the clerk directed. "Members of the jury . . . you upon your oaths do say that the defendant is guilty on indictment number 05-109-01, guilty of murder in the first degree by extreme atrocity or cruelty and by reason of felony murder. So say you, Mr. Foreman?"

"Yes."

"So, ladies and gentlemen, say you all?"

The jurors chorused, "Yes."

It was over.

Nickerson announced that McCowen would be sentenced at two P.M.

The return of the verdict had taken fourteen minutes and ten seconds, an eternity. McCowen looked limp, broken. He couldn't lift his eyes from the ground to look at his girlfriend Catherine Cisneros, whose face was buried in her lap as she sobbed. The bailiffs, two on each side, took the prisoner's arms and hurried him out, his head bowed.

The sentencing phase of murder trials is particularly unpleasant. Victim-impact statements showcase not only pain but, often, vengeance, pure and low-minded, parading as pity for the deceased. Welsh had asked the court to allow two statements before McCowen's sentencing. Mary Worthington, the most preppie of the cousins, stood to read both in a surprisingly even voice.

"This is a case about the brutal rape and murder of Christa Worthington and nothing else," she began. "This is about a little girl losing her mother in the most heinous way imaginable. It's about the bravery Christa showed that night as she battled for her life and tried to protect her daughter. It's about the profound sadness and devastation that this has caused Ava, Christa's family, and her friends. . . . People ask about closure, but there will never be closure, because Christa is never coming back to us. Christa's greatest dream was realized when she had Ava, and we feel blessed to have her in our lives. She is, indeed, a gift from God. We will do everything in our power to remember Christa to her daughter, to remind her how lucky we all were to have Christa in our lives, how deeply we loved her, and how much we will always miss her."

George wasn't thinking about Christa or Ava. He was concerned about the sentencing even though here it was a mere formality. Life imprisonment without parole is mandated for all first-degree murder convictions in the Commonwealth of Massachusetts; the trial judge has no discretion.

Mary moved on to the statement from Amyra Chase, Christa's high
school friend and now Ava's guardian, later to become the child's
adoptive parent: "It has been our decision as a family to protect Ava
from the public, and so it is with tremendous trepidation that I allow
any knowledge of Ava to the public. But to those who have persevered so hard on Christa's and Ava's behalf, I want to assure you all
that Ava Gloria Worthington has emerged from that night as a very
bright, confident, and engaging child . . . And it is Christa who I
believe is the real victim . . . robbed of the privilege and delight of
raising her daughter."

When she finished, Welsh stood. "Your Honor," he announced,
"the court has heard the facts in the case. The jury has spoken. I
would ask the court to impose a sentence of life without the possibility of parole on the first-degree murder charge. . . . And on the
aggravated rape . . . a sentence of life to run concurrent with the
sentence on the murder indictment. And with respect to the aggravated burglary . . . a sentence of life on that indictment as well, to run
concurrent with the life sentence on the murder indictment."

"Attorney George?" Nickerson asked.

"I was going to ask you to sentence Mr. McCowen to concurrent
sentences. Whether or not the concurrent sentences need to be life
really is academic. . . . the life without parole would trump that."

George then said that McCowen would like to be heard.

"I would hear from the gentleman," Nickerson replied, adopting
a distant subjunctive. Spectators were riveted. The suit and tie Mc-
Cowen had worn throughout the trial was gone, replaced by plain
sweats that George had picked up at the Hyannis Mall during recess.
He took a step forward inside the wood-railed dock. The buzz-cut
bailiffs tensed.

"Good afternoon, Your Honor." His voice was steady. It was the
first time anyone heard him speak more than two words; his Southern accent was pronounced, the consonants slurred. He spoke softly.
"For the last six weeks, I sat here in this courtroom and listened to
everything that everybody has to say about me. . . . This case here is a
very horrendous case. I feel sorry for the victim's family, her daughter, and her. And I never meant for this to ever take place, you know.

All through this whole trial, I sat here; and I was thinking to myself, you know, why me? Your Honor, I know there's nothing I can say to change your mind or anything. . . . But, Your Honor, all I can say is that I'm an innocent man in this case. And that's all I got to say, you know? Because"—he paused—"you know, all this time I've been innocent. And that's how I'm going to go out. Thank you, Your Honor."

Nickerson, jaw clenched, nodded. "Let the record reflect that the court indulged the defendant in his right of allocution and nothing more. Mr. Clerk?"

The word *indulged* stuck like a nettle in the throat. Nickerson's new tone announced that McCowen the human being had ceased to exist. The clerk announced the sentence: life without parole, to be served at the Massachusetts Correctional Institution at Cedar Junction, a.k.a. Walpole, the toughest prison in the state.

"Thank you, Your Honor," Welsh said.

"Thank you," Nickerson replied.

"Thank you, Judge," George said stiffly.

McCowen was led from the courtroom. Nickerson tidied his papers, then announced that he was denying the media's requests for jurors' names, that he was impounding the list "for good and just cause."

Within the hour, the unspecified "just cause" was clear: a threat made against jurors. Was it credible? Someone claimed that it was a woman who'd phoned the court clerk's office. Another said it was definitely an African-American bent on vengeance. But few in the press corps needed the judge's list anyway; one industrious newsman had already run the plate numbers of jurors' parked cars.

Outside, in front of the maze of TV cameras, cables, microphones, and floodlights, Welsh did his victory dance.

"I just thank God that it's over and that justice was done," he said, then stepped away from the makeshift podium and into his new judgeship. Once more, Rush would have been proud; the prosecutor managed to cram both "God" and "justice" into his pithy dozen-word statement.

Patenaude, who did not identify himself, was next. Jacketless and surrounded by other jurors, he read an equally uninformative statement: "Having completed our civic duty to the commonwealth, we wish to return to our private lives. We ask that you, the press and public, respect our privacy." He took no questions. Nickerson, out of his robes and wearing a beat-up country tweed jacket, stood nearby, listening.

George spoke to the press later, after seeing his client off in the sheriff's van. He was angry.

"It's obvious that over the past few days, there has been a tremendous amount of movement in the jury room," he said, stopping just short of accusing Welsh and others of improprieties. Asked if he thought authorities had set up the Hicks-Huffman calls, he scanned the sea of faces and replied, "If it walks like a duck and talks like a duck and smells like a duck, then to me, it's a duck."

Struggling to control himself, he had forgotten that ducks don't talk; they quack. He went on to say, "I'm going to do something about it."

He got angrier over the next few days, spoke more openly about the "very powerful appellate arguments for reversal": the Hicks cellphone calls, Huffman's expulsion, the twenty-seven-page unrecorded statement, Nickerson's restrictions on Brown and Ofshe.

Other potent arguments would emerge later.

He didn't talk about his mail. Within hours of the verdict, it had started to pour in, vile, stomach-turning, hate-filled messages worthy of the Klan. One e-mail read, "Have fun behind bars for the rest of your life, fucking rapist/murderer nigger garbage man!!!!" and then slashed at George, "You should have been aborted, too, Robert George, depraved defense atty." Another, replete with misspellings, instructed the attorney to contact Massachusetts Governor Deval Patrick, a black man: "Hay George, call Deval! Hep nigger will pardon him." Still another annotated a copy of the day's *Boston Herald* story, "Cape Killer Gets Life," putting racism to rhyme alongside a photo of McCowen in the dock, weeping: "Boo Who Who!! Crying won't d'oo wen It waz yoo!! YOU BLACK COWARD SCUM NIGGER." Still another well-wisher wrote on the outside of an envelope addressed to George's Newbury Street office, "Robert George Sucks Italian Cock" and "Hay Porky! Go Fuck Your BLACK Mother!"

Uplifting it wasn't. But who could claim surprise? The messages evoked all of the sins of Southie as captured in Stanley Forman's famous Pulitzer Prize–winning photo, "The Soiling of Old Glory," in which a black attorney, at the peak of Boston's school-desegregation crisis, is attacked by antibusing youths using an American-flag flag-pole as a lance. African-Americans had talked about Boston racism for generations, as had Southerners, tired of Northern finger point-ing. Boston was but an hour's drive from the Barnstable Superior Courthouse, where prosecutor and now District Judge Robert Welsh III stated with certainty that the trial had nothing to do with race and the learned Judge Gary Nickerson delivered his unforgettable *pronunciamento*, "Race is somewhat ambiguous in concept."

Ambiguous? Given the hatred behind George's mash notes, am-biguous for *whom*?

Some say that every cloud has a silver lining. The day after the verdict, George rushed downstairs from his Boston office to face two meter maids about to "boot" his Lexus. One recognized him. "Hey, you're Robert George! We love you! Put a quarter in the meter, will you?" she yelled as the two drove off, waving. Later that afternoon, as he wandered into his bank to deal with the bills he'd accumulated during the five-week trial, a young black bank officer intercepted him. "Mr. George, it's a pleasure to see you. Please come this way." He ushered the lawyer to a nearby cubicle; when he got the drift of George's mission, he said gently, "We know you've been very busy, Mr. George. How 'bout we give you a thirty-five-thousand-dollar line of credit?"

Ambiguous? The facts that were to surface during the next two weeks would show that, for many, race was the very armature of the McCowen verdict.

THE AFTERMATH

The verdict came as a shock. "We're just trying to hold on," Roy Mc-Cowen told the *Boston Globe*. "They got rid of the one juror who might have been holding up the rest . . . and then all of a sudden, twelve of them show up with the same answer. Something just ain't right."

Robert George agreed. But despite his anger and confusion, he recalled that the verdict had made him think about Chris McCowen's clothes. "He's about to get into a cold van to be taken the hour-and-a-half drive to prison. I knew he wasn't going back to the jail, so I went to Marshall's. Driving over there, my head was starting to clear. I just *knew* that the general public, intelligent people, believed he was innocent—no, not innocent, that's the wrong word. Most people had a reasonable doubt and wouldn't have convicted him, and I'm talking about people from all over the country. . . .

"So I brought McCowen back his sweatsuit. He had calmed down a bit. He was still crying, but he was calmer and happy that I had gotten him the clothes. . . . I said good-bye to him, which I don't want to talk about. That's between him and me. It was an emotional good-bye."

George had difficulty getting through to his client. McCowen couldn't concentrate. Previously, when they tried to parse his statement, he'd gotten exhausted after an hour and a half to two hours, "almost ready to go to sleep on the table," George recalled. "His speech pattern changes. He doesn't slur, but I notice a change in his demeanor that shows he's totally wasted. He simply can't focus, and the most logical explanation is that Chris McCowen is diagnosably ADD."

Two weeks after the verdict came the whopper: eight jurors were videotaped having a dinner party with Assistant DA Welsh at Wimpy's Seafood Cafe, an upscale eatery in Osterville. Shot by a paparazzo through the restaurant's window, the tape showed Welsh talking in the middle of a circle of eager jurors, then seated at one of the party's two tables, with foreman Dan Patenaude, two other jurors, and the alternate. Two court officers were relaxing in crew-neck sweaters and chinos.

"What is this, *My Cousin Vinny?*" shrieked one prosecutor, quoted in the *Boston Herald.* Said another in *Massachusetts Lawyers Weekly,* "It leaves a bad taste in your mouth and engenders mistrust in the jury system." Mary-Ellen Manning, a member of the Governor's Council that appointed young Rob Welsh to his pending judgeship, also weighed in: "Prosecutors are all about asking jurors to send messages. So what message did this jury send? If you come in with a guilty verdict, you get to hang out and party with the prosecutor. That taints a jury pool."

Conspicuously absent from the dinner: Huffman, Audet, and Bohanna.

If anyone else, at any time or place, had attended such a party, the system's disciplinary process would have come down "like an avalanche," George said. "What was going on at Wimpy's, and what were they talking about—Christmas plans, vacation arrangements, or other subjects?"

Among those present was Gomes, the first juror to seek publicity. Four days after the verdict, he told Boston's Channel 4 that "90 percent of the arguments were about that police report. We just didn't think he would incriminate himself that much. Had the police taped that I think we would have come to a decision much faster." Deliberations, he said, were contentious: "Talking it out? It was more like boxing it out." Race had been "a big weight on my shoulders" but hadn't mattered because the DNA match was conclusive. Gomes also appeared on *Dateline* and *48 Hours.* Not long afterward, e-mails between Worthington family members and various jurors were leaked, the family lauding the jury's decision, the jurors praising the Worthingtons' dignity under duress, using obsequious phrases that called into question the authors' impartiality.

Gomes's was the worst. In his e-mail to Susan Worthington Brennan, his misguided class envy of Worthington WASP-itude, his need to bond, was blatant.

Subj: MY HEART

Dear Susan,
Are you serious? There is no reason you would or should ever have to say thank you. . . . I just tried to do the right thing.
I love my family and would hope if anything ever happened to them others would want justice and make sure the right thing was done.
I could definitely feel the emotions coming from all of you, and I thought you could probably read it off me. . . .
And *Thank YOU* . . . for calling us brave. But all of you are the brave ones. So many STRONG, SUPPORTIVE, CARING, FAMILY, FRIENDS. (WOMEN) . . .
I'm sure Christa would be proud of you all. I am.

(Billy)
Eric Gomes

While news reports of the Wimpy's party titillated the Cape's reading public, the U.S. Justice Department uncovered twenty-three matches in sexual-assault cases where a DNA database administrator at the state crime lab had dropped the ball, then failed to inform law enforcement. The administrator was suspended, and Governor Patrick was forced to hire an outside consultant to review the lab's operations, top to bottom.

Jeremy Frazier remained a hot topic, as well. In February, Eric Williams, *Cape Cod Times* reporter turned radio personality, Web meister, and homespun pundit, received a rap song in the mail titled "Life without Parole." It set sections of George's cross-exam of Frazier to music. Williams played it repeatedly on WOMR, where he'd previously interviewed Jan Worthington. The rap-music background was interesting, suggesting that one of Frazier's cronies might be trying to say something. Police did not investigate, which was no surprise. Days after the verdict, at *his* press conference, O'Keefe unambiguously declared the case closed and Frazier in the clear.

At the end of summer 2008, McCowen was stabbed four times by a white inmate at Walpole, then transferred to the Souza-Baranowski Correctional Center, another state prison in western Massachusetts, where his girlfriend Catherine continued to visit, commuting from Hyannis, where she was a psychiatric social worker.

Several months later, DA O'Keefe would fail to keep his pledge to return or destroy the roughly 120 DNA samples gathered during the investigation. At the request of Keith Amato, the ACLU filed and won a class-action suit against the DA for clinging to specimens. O'Keefe waffled, initially claiming that the samples had been destroyed, then acknowledging that some had been kept. He claimed that his office was not responsible for people like Amato, who neither retrieved his sample nor requested its destruction.

In legal circles, postverdict skepticism had initially revolved around McCowen's unrecorded six-hour interrogation condensed into twenty-seven pages. Arguments about the Mason report became irrelevant when Roshena Bohanna, the lone female black juror, called Robert George's Boston office the day after the verdict, then again the next day, leaving messages. She was uneasy with her vote to convict, had "caved in" under pressure from fellow jurors. These jurors, she explained, made racist comments both before and during deliberations. She had wanted to tell Nickerson when he came to the jury room right after the verdict but was afraid to speak up in front of the others.

A disturbingly similar call came from the wife of juror Norman Audet. Race had played a role in deliberations, and Audet, too, was tormented by having voted with the majority. Unlike Bohanna, he'd told Nickerson that he shouldn't have voted to convict; he believed McCowen innocent. The judge, he said, had reassured him that an automatic appeal follows all murder one convictions in the commonwealth. The day after the verdict, Audet asked his wife to call Nickerson, to repeat his misgivings. When Nickerson didn't call back, Audet contacted the defense attorney.

Bohanna's and Audet's claims were backed up by the dismissed Rachel Huffman, who had already switched to her second lawyer in trying to deal with O'Keefe. By mid-December, all three met with George to sign affidavits testifying to racial bias, noting names, dates, and specific comments. Bohanna was African-American, a single mom in her thirties;

Audet was a soft-spoken sixty-three-year-old white man; and twenty-two-year-old Huffman, white, had a child with her black boyfriend.

The affidavits painted a singular picture: cliques had formed early, during testimony, and particular jurors had engaged in racially charged cat-and-mouse games before deliberations began. At lunch during the second week, juror Carol Cahill reportedly looked up from her plate and said, "Guys, the defendant looked at me. He scares me." Huffman asked why. Cahill replied, "I don't know, he's this big black guy, you know. He frightens me." After lunch, Huffman told Bohanna, who later said, "I already felt these people had some type of bias, and I told [Huffman] that." In her affidavit, Huffman testified, "It was obvious to me that several of my fellow jurors were biased against blacks and against the defendant because he was black."

The day after the lunch incident, Huffman showed Cahill and two other jurors photos of her child and her black boyfriend, the baby's father. According to Huffman, Cahill said, "Oh, my God, Rachel, he's *big*." Huffman realized that for Cahill, all black males were "big."

Dark-skinned Eric Gomes, portrayed as leading the charge for conviction, was also accused of making racist statements. Days before deliberations began, Gomes told Bohanna, "I think he's guilty." Bohanna didn't agree. "He may have done it, but the state hasn't proved it." En route to the Piccadilly Deli, she asked about his race. Gomes identified himself as Cape Verdean, not black, and took pains to differentiate himself from the defendant. "I was brought up mainly by white people," he said, adding that his brother's wife was "white." Huffman backed up Bohanna's testimony, and Audet testified to hearing Gomes make a similar statement later, during deliberations: "Hey, I'm not like him. I was raised by white people."

Bohanna said that dealing with these jurors was an uphill battle even before the jury was charged. She'd made a mental note: "There was no way that man was going to get a fair trial on the Cape. No way. Impossible."

To begin deliberations, the jurors conducted a poll. Five or six believed McCowen guilty; two or three did not; the rest were undecided. The group for conviction included Gomes, Cahill, Marlo George, Daniel Patenaude, and Matthew Maltby. Audet believed the group had based its conclusion on gut reaction rather than on the evidence. "All they had was the DNA, and that meant nothing until we discussed it," he said.

Undecided were Laura Stacy, Sally Ann Powers, Charles Ivers, and Taryn O'Connell, the jury's "organizer," who set up daily checklists and other routines to facilitate deliberations.

For the next eight days, jurors were to sit at a long table in the jury room, facing one photo: Christa Worthington, half-naked, lying in a pool of blood with her legs splayed. Two smaller conference tables stood off to the side, one piled with exhibits, the other used for lunches delivered by court officers. An easel with a marker and an artist's pad in one corner was used for O'Connell's checklists. The room's lone window looked out over the parking lot, just above the entrance to the courthouse. They had to close it at times, so the screaming and the "Fuck yous" couldn't be heard below.

Marlo George didn't help. A vociferous "hang 'em high" advocate, she waxed near giddy about her attraction to the chiseled Chris Mason and about fixing up a friend with the youngest of the muscular bailiffs.

On day two of deliberations, tensions exploded. Bohanna was at the easel, using a rubber-tipped pointer, arguing for reasonable doubt. As she sat down, Marlo George rose and turned the group's attention back to the photo, to Worthington's wounds, saying, "When a two-hundred-pound black guy beats on a small woman, he will leave these kind of bruises."

That was Audet's recollection. Bohanna remembered the remark slightly differently: "When a two-hundred-pound black guy beats up on a woman, bruises of that type happen." Bohanna yelled at Marlo George, "What the hell does black got to do with it?" She whacked the table with the pointer, causing everyone to duck, and proceeded back to the easel, where she continued yelling, punctuating each point with another whack. "I don't appreciate this shit! First I hear a comment that you're afraid of the defendant because he's this 'big black guy.' Now I hear out of your mouth that 'if some big black guy'—*what the hell's going on here?*"

Huffman, sitting between Marlo George and Bohanna, put her leg out to separate the two. Bohanna recalled one juror yelling, "Don't play the race card." Cahill followed up: "You're acting like Bob George!"

Foreman Patenaude called for a break. Outside, Huffman testified, Gomes referred to Bohanna: "That's why I don't like black people. You see what they're capable of?"

Bohanna didn't hear that comment. When the group filed back upstairs, she overheard Marlo George echo Cahill's remark, made at lunch weeks before, about being afraid of the black defendant "looking at her." Bohanna blew up. "That means you're a racist," she yelled at George, then pointed at Cahill. "You're a racist, too! You're sitting in the jury box with your proud-ass rich self, taking a vacation, saying, 'I'm afraid of this guy.' You're a *racist*!"

Thereafter, no one in the guilty group wanted to talk about race, Audet said. For the rest of that afternoon, Bohanna sat in stony silence. The next day, she continued arguing for reasonable doubt, trying to convince the others that the sex between Worthington and the defendant might have been consensual. After all, not even the medical examiner had provided any evidence of rape.

"What I thought was reasonable doubt nobody agreed with," she said later. "All they wanted to say was, 'Well, we got this picture,'" the photo of Worthington's battered corpse. " 'He's guilty of it.'"

One female juror routinely looked at the crime-scene picture and murmured, "This could be my daughter." Another allegedly commented, "Who else would do such a thing as this?" Audet said they "wanted to blame somebody for it, especially the women. They didn't care. Someone had to pay because that child was now motherless."

Some would say that vengeance is in Cape Cod's DNA. In *History of Plymouth Plantation*, written between 1620 and 1647, the commonwealth's first governor, William Bradford, detailed the fate of a teenage boy convicted of buggery with "a cow, two goats, five sheep, two calves, and a turkey." The boy was forced to watch as every one of the beasts was slaughtered and thrown into a pit. And the boy was next.

The restraining orders against McCowen were used to argue for conviction, according to the affidavits, although Nickerson had strictly limited their use to evaluating Mason's justification for seeking an arrest warrant, "nothing more."

No matter. The restraining orders, along with the photo of Christa, had become touchstones of certainty for the hang-'em-high group.

Attempts to break the holdouts were insidious. Audet had been sitting at the foot of the table opposite the foreman, but after a few days, Gomes claimed that seat, effectively squeezing the not-guilty jurors between those clamoring for conviction. At another point, foreman Patenaude proposed ending deliberations by allowing a majority vote to win. An outraged Bohanna refused to be railroaded. "You just want to disregard my vote? That's baloney."

But as tough as she appeared to be, Roshena was feeling alone. "They weren't pressuring [Audet] like they were pressuring me. If I disagreed with something, it was, 'Why do you disagree?' 'You need to explain this, explain that.' I'm, like, 'Why the hell do I have to explain everything? I'm not on trial here—and I'm damn glad I'm not, because I'd be sent straight to prison dealing with you people.'"

Bohanna testified that Marlo George questioned her educational background, as well as her cornrows, trying to put her on the defensive. Even the timing of Marlo George's queries was inappropriate, fired when Roshena was trying to make a point. Every day, "something different would unfold like in a movie you never thought you'd be involved in," she recalled. "I'm going, like, 'This is some crazy shit,' and I'd have to tell them, 'We're not paying attention to what we're here for.'"

By now, Audet said, they were "not even using facts anymore." With the sequestration order, pressure rose to reach a verdict. Early in the day, they had announced their deadlock. Nickerson bent over backward to tell them that the order was not to be construed as a demand for a decision, but it clearly had that effect, especially on Bohanna when Huffman was bumped the next day. The twenty-two-year-old had served as a buffer between the two sides, intervening constantly so Bohanna would be heard. With Huffman gone, Bohanna was alone. Audet, still holding out for not guilty, was a quiet man, no substitute for Huffman.

Jurors spent Monday through Wednesday on a sealed floor of

the Hyannis Radisson, with phone use, meals, smoke breaks, and TV hours controlled by the ever-present court officers. Courthouse grounds were taken over by a bivouac of intimidating Massachusetts State Police troopers, at least fifty, many in black SWAT outfits, some straddling imposing motorcycles, others leaning against unmarked squad cars bristling with broccoli like bouquets of high-tech antennas. O'Keefe had posted this military presence, ostensibly in response to the vague telephone threat invoked by Judge Nickerson, but it also reminded jurors, who were driven past the brigade morning and night, of what they'd learned as children: the policeman is your friend; he protects you from harm.

Rachel Huffman reported that she walked in on the group playing charades during the first night at the Radisson and heard Marlo George mimicking Bohanna, "I'm a racist! I'm a racist!" "They were all laughing. They thought it was funny," Rachel said. The game stopped abruptly when she entered. The court later refused to acknowledge the incident because neither Audet nor Bohanna was present; neither could corroborate Huffman's account.

Bohanna's estrangement deepened. She knew that Hicks had been arrested over the weekend, but, like other jurors, she didn't know why. Later she said she was afraid of "what was going on," that there was something "weird" about it.

Huffman said she was uncertain about McCowen's innocence but not impressed with the arguments for guilt, either. Her replacement was less ambivalent. By all accounts, Mary O'Prey was pushy. The court ordered the panel to go back and start from scratch, but O'Prey insisted otherwise. She knew the case intimately, no need to backtrack. During her first day, she took Bohanna to task for writing notes to herself and "not sharing" with the others.

Audet saw that O'Prey's mind "was already made up."

After the seventh day of deliberations, the second of sequestration, Bohanna was exhausted. "I couldn't process. I was having a mental breakdown, I think," she said. Alone in her motel room that night, she sat for hours, staring at the snow-filled screen of the disconnected TV, and finally fell asleep at three A.M. The next morning, she said, "I tried to fix my eyes. I'd been crying all night."

At the courthouse, she vomited. In the jury room, the others noticed that she was quiet and asked why. "Whatever you say, I agree with," she mumbled, now throwing in the towel. Audet, unable to hang in as the lone holdout, agreed to vote with the majority, too. Both later testified that they didn't realize they could have returned to the courtroom and declared a deadlock, triggering a hung jury, ending their agony as decisively as voting with the majority did.

Nickerson claimed that he satisfied the commonwealth's requirements in charging the jury, then following up with sequestration. Bob George admitted that he never anticipated this consequence of sequestration. "I've had deadlocked juries many times, but I've never had a jury say anything like this before," he explained. "The jury was intimidated into believing that they were going to be locked up forever if they didn't come up with a verdict."

Audet recalled one female juror making "cha-ching, cha-ching" sounds, like a cash register, as jurors waited to be called to deliver their verdict. They believed they were going to cash in, like the O.J. jurors. While another rejected the idea of peddling interviews, Gomes allegedly commented, "It all depends on how much money is involved." Within days, four jurors accepted an invitation from *Dateline.*

With all of this information in hand, on December 11, three weeks after the verdict, George filed a motion seeking a new trial based on the affidavits of Bohanna, Audet, and Huffman. The motion cited the racism allegations but also charged that jurors had discussed deliberations with alternates and had inappropriately discussed the restraining orders and that Audet and Bohanna never knew that they had the right to hold out for a hung jury.

District Attorney O'Keefe trivialized it as "a routine postconviction relief motion," adding, "As a general proposition, lawyers exploit what they think they can exploit in order to further their interests." The response he filed a month later argued that the term *big black man* was an accurate, if insensitive, descriptor, not an expression of racism.

"Perhaps another juror would have used the term 'African-American' or not used any descriptor at all," he wrote. "There may be a more sensitive method of articulating one's views. However, there is no indication of racial prejudice or bias."

In February, in response to this author's *Boston Magazine* article presenting the racism allegations more fully than George was able to squeeze into the motion, a *Cape Cod Times* poll found that 36.7 percent of respondents thought that racial bias had tainted the verdict. Hilary Russ jumped in with her coverage of another murder trial, in progress on Nantucket. Defendant Thomas Toolan, "a tall, pretty, white former bank executive" from Manhattan, she observed, walked into court unaccompanied by court officers, "in contrast" to McCowen, who'd been shackled hand and foot. Why, Russ wondered, such disparity?

Five months passed before Nickerson acted. By late May, with time running out on the SJC appeal, George submitted a motion to compel the judge's ruling. Never one for half-measures, he used the occasion to lambaste Nickerson: "I don't know whether there's any design behind the delay, but the entire case is a hot potato," he charged, "and the juror issue is a very explosive, dangerous, and unique situation to deal with. The fact is, [Nickerson] hasn't done anything."

Along with this critique, he moved to discover the jailhouse records pertaining to Huffman's removal, further driving his point home.

Five weeks later, on June 8, Nickerson finally ruled: the racial-bias claims deserved investigation, but the other five issues were dismissed; they had no influence on the jury. These included the predeliberation comments by jurors and Audet's and Bohanna's ignorance about the consequences of reporting a second deadlock.

Nickerson's call for a postverdict hearing to question individual jurors was highly unusual. Jonathan Turley, a law professor at George Washington University quoted by the Associated Press, called the move "extraordinary. . . . The jury system depends on jurors being open and frank in their views. We protect the sanctity of the jury room for that reason."

The few historical exceptions have been triggered by racist comments. Racial bias in the jury room is considered grounds for reversal. In 1996, a federal court of appeals overturned a conviction after a juror allegedly used the word *nigger*. In 1991, the Massachusetts Supreme Judicial Court ordered hearings into the controversial Benjamin Laguer case, in which one juror said, "The goddamn spic is guilty." In response to his fellow jurors' speculating about how anyone could rape all night long, he replied, "Spics screw all day and night."

Considering these and other precedents, as well as the Bohanna-Audet-Huffman affidavits, many Cape and Boston-area lawyers opined that Nickerson had no choice but to grant the hearing. The format of the inquiry was another matter. During the next seven months, the principals met for six closed-door protocol conferences: George wanted the hearing held in open court; O'Keefe wanted it behind closed doors. Nickerson finally ruled that he, not the lawyers, would interrogate jurors in open court. The review would be fact-based only; in a proposed second "stage," jurors might be queried about how those facts affected their final vote. The hearing was scheduled for January 10–11, 2008.

At the end of November, George filed yet another motion, potentially as damaging to the prosecution as the racism motion. This time, he asked for a new trial based on the commonwealth's failure to turn over arrest records for a number of its witnesses, including a knife-wielding Jeremy Frazier.

News reports, as well as the motion, mentioned that this author had unearthed Frazier's records, as well as the records of Frazier's "crew," in the course of researching this book. Coincidence or not, while I was in California not long after the filing, a squad of Truro police, some reportedly dressed in body armor and carrying riot guns, entered my isolated Truro home, armed with a warrant signed by Orleans District Court Judge Robert Welsh, the father of prosecutor Rob Welsh.

"Truro biographer Peter Manso (Norman Mailer, Marlon Brando) is in hot water after a burglar alarm went off at his unoccupied Cape home and police found three unregistered guns inside," the *Boston Herald* wrote.

In fact, the firearms were not "unregistered." Years before, the Commonwealth of Massachusetts had changed "lifetime" licenses to revenue-generating five-year renewals without notifying license holders—724,028 of them, according to official sources. I was but one of many. My crime was failure to renew a permit, no more, no less, and soon the district court dismissed my case. But in one of his more outsized gestures as DA, O'Keefe had me hauled in front of the Barnstable County grand jury, which indicted on five felonies, each carrying a two-and-a-half-to-ten-year prison sentence, plus seven misdemeanors. The twelve charges, twice as many as originally filed, were unprecedented. Not satisfied, the Cape's number one lawman telephoned Truro police chief John Thomas, demanding that I be brought back from the San Francisco Bay area in handcuffs, "like a common drug dealer."

The fat, as they say, was in the fire. O'Keefe would retaliate against everyone who opposed him. He'd had his shot at Huffman and later went after Audet. Fortunately for Bohanna, she'd moved out of state, repelled by Cape Cod.

Fourteen days after my home invasion, eleven jurors, including the excommunicated Huffman, were brought before the judge. Powers and O'Prey had been excused for hardships. Bohanna had flown up from the Deep South; she needed to testify first, so as not to miss too many workdays. The two other dissident jurors followed. The testimony from all three proved consistent with that offered in their affidavits. All semblance of agreement ended there.

Marlo George, the first of the naysayers, flatly denied referring to McCowen's race in discussing Worthington's bruises, although she did admit describing the defendant as a 200-pound black man who had come to Worthington's house looking for sex. Other jurors insisted that her comments were not made in a racist manner.

"It was always used descriptively," O'Connell said. Maltby said that Marlo George had told Bohanna, "It doesn't have anything to do with race. The defendant *is* big and black."

Cahill denied ever using the word *black* in expressing her fear of the defendant and admitted saying that she was afraid of McCowen only once. Gomes rejected ever saying that he preferred whites to blacks and denied mentioning his brother's wife.

During morning break on the second day, an elderly dark-skinned woman named Delainda Julia Miranda introduced herself as Eric Gomes's great-aunt. Miranda, of Cape Verdean descent, had read an op-ed piece I'd penned for the *Cape Cod Times*, excoriating jurors for the Wimpy's do, and she needed an outlet. I met with her and two of her sons two days later, when she explained that her nephew, whom she called "Billy," had made antiblack statements similar to those alleged by Huffman ever since he was fifteen or sixteen years old. Among his reported comments:

"I don't like what black people have done to the Cape."

"These niggers come down here and they think they can do what they want. They're making us look bad."

"I don't hang with blacks because all they do is get in trouble."

"All niggers do is rob people, kill people, and sell drugs."

Two days later, I reinterviewed her, then wrote Nickerson, George, and O'Keefe to inform them of Miranda's statements. George then submitted Miranda's affidavit. On January 19, just before the defense put its expert on juror racial stereotyping on the stand, Nickerson asked if I had already copied the press on my hand-delivered letter to the court. I had. Both *Massachusetts Lawyers Weekly* and the *Globe* were to run front-page stories later that day. Nickerson, his hand forced, set a date for Miranda's testimony.

With the jurors' testimony and now Miranda's, the evidence was nearly overwhelming. Common sense dictated that the hang-'em-high jurors had been playing mind games.

Miranda took the stand on February 1. O'Keefe, making his first official appearance in the case as a participant, could barely contain his anger. During cross-examination, he demanded to know why the witness hadn't taken her concerns to a court officer, as opposed to "Mr. Manson or whatever he calls himself." Dubbing me Manson, as in Charlie, the sociopathic mass murderer, was but a small token of the DA's esteem, given what was to come. Several reporters laughed aloud at O'Keefe's childishness; Nickerson did not.

Courtrooms tend to intimidate (a key to their architecture), but Miranda stood up to the DA with great aplomb, eliciting chuckles from the audience when she told O'Keefe, "I could have gone to you, but sometimes I see you [and] say hello and you turn your face."

Here, Nickerson smiled. His amusement faded, however, when the seventy-four-year-old domestic reiterated her affidavit testimony. When O'Keefe couldn't get her to budge, Nickerson tried. He asked whether she knew, or had ever spoken to, any other jurors, whether she knew me prior to approaching me in the courthouse hallway, even if I had nodded to her covertly during juror testimony. Miranda did not back down: Gomes was a self-hating black man with a deep-seated problem, a liar, a racist.

After court, while she sat next to a former president of the Cape Cod chapter of the NAACP, a reporter asked if her testimony wouldn't negatively affect her family life. "Billy's sad," she said. "But it's something that had to be done."

Another four months would pass before the judge rendered his decision. In the meantime, a bizarre photo of the jurors came to light, not partying at Wimpy's but this time actually inside the jury room. It captured the group in two rows, one sitting, one standing, with a horizontal Dan Patenaude sprawled across the laps, it seemed, of Carol Cahill, Taryn O'Connell, and Marlo George. All three women beam at the camera, as does foreman Patenaude, giving off an air of the risqué. Bohanna, Huffman, and Audet are off to one side with Laura Stacy, none of them smiling.

The souvenir snapshot had been e-mailed to jury members by computer-savvy Matthew Maltby. Apart from its iconography, it raised an interesting question: twelve jurors and two alternates filled the frame, so who snapped the photo? Who else had entry to the jury room?

The answer: a court officer. Had jurors and bailiffs, including those who dinner-partied at Wimpy's, gotten too close? Court officers are to stand guard over the jury room, deliver lunches and requested exhibits, and at the end of each day collect jurors' notes. Had one or more bailiffs listened at the door? Noted the charts on O'Connell's easel? Had jurors and their handlers discussed McCowen's case, his guilt or innocence, during the two and a half days of sequestration at the Radisson?

Most important, unlikely as it may sound, had a bailiff tipped off the prosecution as to which way the wind was blowing during the critical time surrounding Huffman's expulsion?

Courthouse regulars, on-Cape and off, say the idea is not remotely far-fetched or historically unheard of. Traditionally, the iconography of the Massachusetts Superior Court system has court officers carrying a shepherd's crook bearing the Commonwealth's seal; they herd the jury, one officer in front, another in back, and escorted judges, too. As "shepherds of the court," they have always been integral to the judicial environment; some are conscientious, some not. Here, a dim view was warranted. "You can never tell me that those court officers didn't sit outside that jury room, listening, especially if there were voices raised," said one ex-prosecutor when shown the photo. "Look, if you've got a jury that's locked up, what does the government not want in a deliberation like this? They don't want a lot of discourse or dissidence . . . that favors the defense because of the burden-of-proof requirement.

"So, there is no way that that information stayed sealed up there on the second floor," the ex-prosecutor claims. "Who do court officers deal with day in and day out? They don't deal with defense lawyers, who come and go; they deal with the prosecutors, the people who work there, and with the judges. So I have every reason to believe that what was going on in that jury room got back to the district attorney. And I will tell you candidly, it would not surprise me in the least if it [got] back to the judge, too."

Off the record, George expressed similar concerns. The bailiff-as-spy scenario explained the targeting of Rachel Huffman as nothing else did. On the premise that the simplest explanation is the best explanation, this one seemed all but unimpeachable.

On April 4, almost fifteen months after the filing of the original motion, Nickerson rendered his decision: the racism allegations did not warrant retrial.

Reporters and members of the legal community alike questioned whether it had ever been realistic to expect a judge, even one as persevering as Gary Nickerson, to nullify his own trial. Such a decision would have overturned a career victory for Welsh and O'Keefe and branded tourist-dependent Cape Cod a racist backwater.

There was more to the ruling than the written word revealed, though. Nickerson is known as a courteous judge, respectful of lawyers, and he has a reputation for making thoughtful, common-sense decisions. But he is no Louis Brandeis. "He *loves* being a superior court judge," said one local practitioner, pointing out that while honor and evenhandedness are very much part of his persona, Nickerson is fundamentally a conservative whose scholarly immersion in the law serves to mask his ambition.

What he has always wanted most is a seat on the SJC. Reportedly, he has even shied away from an appeals court judgeship. The Worthington trial, in other words, was made to order, and the neater it emerged on the record, the better.

Continued the practitioner, "He's a complicated man. Here he got himself a big trial and was determined to be perceived as an extraordinarily fair man and a good judge. Flip side is, he probably believed one hundred percent that McCowen did it, and once the jury came down with their verdict, he'd be damned if he was going to participate in any undoing of that."

The key was his strategy, the way he tidied things up. Nickerson knew, as does any first-year law student, that appellate courts base reversals on misapplication of legal and constitutional principles, not factual findings or witness credibility. Those considerations are the exclusive province of the trial judge. Nickerson's response to George's motion was carefully tailored with that in mind. Anyone in doubt of this needs to be reminded that after Nickerson left the DA's office, Phil Rollins had him as the DA's appellate counsel for several years.

The forty-page ruling dismissed Huffman's testimony outright. She had "misled the court," largely because her discharge cast her in a "bad light in her community," giving her "a motive to wreak havoc on the judicial process at hand." During deliberations, she had been "meddlesome," causing Bohanna to mistrust fellow jurors. The charades incident, he ruled, had no weight, since neither Audet nor Bohanna could verify it. By comparison, the remaining jurors, among them Marlo George and Carol Cahill, he called "disinterested." They claimed that the racist taunting never happened, although all agreed that the charades game had taken place.

"This jurist," Nickerson concluded, "does not find [Huffman] credible."

Nickerson noted that Audet's affidavit closely tracked Bohanna's, but his testimony, "while sincere, [was] faulty." He was uncertain whether it was Cahill or George who said she feared the defendant; he was fuzzy about the chronology of incidents, although his testimony dovetailed with Huffman's and Bohanna's.

Nullification of Audet and Huffman left the racism charges squarely on Bohanna's shoulders. "The court accepts juror Bohanna's ire as a warning flag that careful scrutiny must be given to juror George's words. . . . Juror Bohanna was appropriately vigilant in keeping racial bias from infecting the deliberations. Her calling was honorable."

But honorable was not enough. Large parts of her testimony were ignored, and what wasn't failed to make the grade because her affidavit had been "filtered through defense counsel's draftsmanship."

The dissident jurors had been unanimous in reporting Gomes's racist statements, but here the judge relied on a discrepancy about *where* Gomes made those comments to conclude that Huffman fabricated them and Bohanna had not been present at all.

He similarly dismissed Miranda. "She is a pleasant woman known to this jurist from her frequenting the local courts . . . often enough that she leaves baked goods for the security staff," he wrote. But Miranda's decision to approach an author, rather than a court official, rendered her unreliable, someone "seeking her fifteen minutes of fame."

Two of Miranda's sons had criminal records, so it was likely that the volunteer witness, in addition to being a showoff, harbored "resentment towards law enforcement." Her refusal to be cowed by O'Keefe stemmed from that resentment putatively.

Even with these suppressions and misrepresentations, Nickerson also relied on a lopsided selection of case law: *Wright v. U.S.*, in which a juror who used the term *black bastard* was deemed unbiased; *Commonwealth v. Tavares*, in which a juror, who called a female African-American witness "Sapphire" was said to be "jocular"; and the previously mentioned Laguer case, in which the verdict against a Latino defendant was not overturned even though a juror remarked, "Spics screw all day and night."

More than anything else, these citations unveiled the agenda. The judge could have invoked a broader armada of decisions; he chose not to. Among the alternatives was the case in which a Washington State trial judge granted retrial based on bias toward the defendant's

Japanese-American lawyer, Kamitomo by name, whom jurors referred to as "Mr. Kamikaze," "Mr. Miyashi," or "Mr. Miyagi"; one juror said the verdict was "almost appropriate" because it was returned on Pearl Harbor day. The court ruled without a hearing, because "people are never forthcoming with their prejudice." In another case, the New Jersey Supreme Court ordered a new trial for an African-American after a juror announced that he intended to "get me a good rope so when we hang him, it won't break." The court concluded that the juror was "unfit to sit," and his presence was ruled presumptively prejudicial.

In *U.S. v. Henley*, 2001, the Ninth Circuit Court of Appeals held that racial prejudice is a mental bias unrelated to the true issues of a case and overturned on the basis of a lower court's failure to take action after a juror used the word *nigger*. Likewise, in *Tobias v. Smith*, habeas corpus was granted when a juror allegedly said, "You can't tell one black from another." Even more persuasively, in *U.S. v. Heller*, the court reversed when a juror, referring to a black defendant, said, "The fellow we are trying, I say, let's hang him."

At bottom, it's not necessary to demonstrate that "prejudice pervaded the jury room." The Sixth Amendment guarantees a verdict rendered by impartial, "indifferent" jurors. It's violated by "the bias or prejudice *of even a single juror*." As stated in *Tobias*, "the race of a defendant is an improper consideration for a jury, just as ethnic origin and religion are. There should be *no injection of race into jury deliberations*. . . . Certainly, where a probability of such prejudice can be demonstrated, it would constitute sufficient grounds for ordering a new trial" (emphasis added).

The doctrine is plain: like a biased judge, a biased juror introduces a structural defect not subject to "harmless error" analysis, notwithstanding O'Keefe's nonsensical response to Bohanna's objection, "What the hell's *black* got to do with it?"

Nickerson chose to structure his decision around precedents narrowly selected to preserve the status quo. In addition to shortchanging the defendant, the decision skewed the very purpose of the inquiry he'd so bravely granted in the first place. He didn't forget that the application of law involves choices, that the Constitution, including the Bill of Rights, is a living document, subject to evolving interpretations. Rather, he decided to eschew *balance*, the key even for today's most conservative jurists, such as Antonin Scalia and John Roberts.

Nickerson was nothing if not a canny lawyer. Early on, he'd deep-sixed most of the questions submitted by the defense, preferring to soft-pedal the probe. Having nullified the racism allegations, he omitted the hearing's second phase, on the effects that racist comments had on jurors' votes.

It was tidy, even elegant, and, again, all based on the man's knowledge that appellate courts don't tamper with lower courts' determinations of fact and credibility.

George, disheartened, called the decision a "wholesale endorsement of . . . wrongdoing." He was upset with himself, too, for expecting so much from this judge, whose blanket dismissal of Bohanna, Audet, Huffman, and Miranda was "stunning in its ignorance." Even so, he pinned his hopes on the exculpatory-evidence motion. At issue here was material less subject to judicial interpretation as long as he could prove that the prosecution had withheld arrest records of at least five of its witnesses, most important Frazier's Wellfleet pier knife incident of July 2, 2003. In addition, the prosecution had possibly allowed Frazier to lie before the grand jury, then again during cross-examination, when Frazier was asked, "What did you get arrested for?" Unaware of the knife incident at the time, he had let the matter drop, less interested in the details of Frazier's arrests than in the pattern of special treatment extended to him by police.

The motion cited other examples of the commonwealth's duplicity, such as when George asked Nickerson to order Shawn Mulvey's probation records and Welsh shook his head, stammering, "It's not in my—it's not readily accessible."

The prosecution also knew that Christopher Bearse, who'd backed up Frazier's alibi, had a lengthy rap sheet: assaults and batteries, forgery, larceny, intimidating witnesses, and stolen credit cards.

Three who were not called to testify—Arthur DuBois, Ryan Buckles, and Kevin Lord—had contact with Frazier only hours before the time the commonwealth posited for the murder; all had histories more violent, suggesting that even Welsh had limits regarding prosecutorial underhandedness.

DuBois, who'd been jumped at the party by Bearse and then Frazier, had convictions for assault with a knife, breaking and entering, striking a blood-covered victim in the head with a beer bottle, shouting "I should just kill you," and assault on a nurse at Cape Cod Hospital.

Buckles, who hid in a closet at the Bilbo party, had been arrested for assaults and batteries on his girlfriend and stepmother, for drunk driving after crashing through the town of Brewster during a police chase, and for home invasion and assault on a man who, shot three times, managed to survive.

Lord, who accompanied DuBois and Buckles to the party only hours before the time assigned to Christa's death, had been arrested five times; his rap sheet included a knife attack on a woman and kicking a male contemporary in the head.

The motion was based on case law and on the Massachusetts Rules of Criminal Procedure: upon arraignment, the court must order the probation department to turn over "the record of prior complaints, indictments, and dispositions of all defendants and of all witnesses."

This court had failed to do so. George needed to prove that the criminal files would have been admissible and that the records were either "sufficiently subject to the prosecutors' control" or in the possession of police who participated in the investigation.

It seemed he had a slam dunk. The district attorney's office that prosecuted McCowen had handled the very cases not disclosed; the paperwork was in their own files. Detective Michael Mazzone, McCowen's handler, was the investigating officer in the Frazier knife incident; Detective Lloyd Oja, who testified at trial, had assisted. Mazzone was the arresting officer in some of the Bearse cases as well. Even the most pro-prosecution observers would have to take notice that the Buckles home invasion was investigated by four MSP troopers who testified at McCowen's trial: Mason, Squier, McCabe, and Gilardi. All of the cases were overseen by Michael O'Keefe.

George's motion charged that the discovery violations had been systematic and deliberate, presenting "what appears to be an unsettling pattern of uncanny commonality . . . the same investigators, arresting officers, defendants/witnesses, and prosecutors thread through all of the withheld evidence." It also charged that the pretrial demand for information regarding problems at the state crime lab had not been met. Was George a nut case or, as O'Keefe told the *Cape Cod Times*, a run-of-the-mill sore loser?

By February 2009, another problem loomed: the deadline for McCowen's appeal to the SJC was fast approaching, and the DA's office had opposed his request for an extension. On March 31, the SJC stepped in: George would have sixty days from Nickerson's ruling to file the brief for McCowen's final appeal.

Five months later, on June 9, Nickerson ruled on the "Manso motion," so called because I unearthed the material on Frazier and his crew; it was another denial, even more surprising than the first, since here the facts seemed to speak for themselves. Nickerson's rationale was that the commonwealth had complied with discovery requirements by turning over 388 reports, and George had just been trolling during early discovery motions, casting about trying to find anything useful. The arrest report regarding the Frazier knife incident, for example, had never been "specifically" requested.

"A prosecutor cannot always know that a particular piece of evidence is or might be exculpatory," the judge wrote, adding that he would not have admitted any of the withheld priors. "Opening a pocket knife in defiance of two men in an innocuous argument is hardly congruent with the brutal stabbing of Christa Worthington."

The canny ex-defense lawyer should have been more careful in referencing traceable specifics. Nickerson claimed that Frazier's knife was just "two inches long," in no way comparable to the Worthington murder weapon. But the only source for that information was the Wellfleet police report, case #20033677 (Mazzone), quoting Frazier's brother, Jason, who had his own criminal history and, evidently, sought to minimize his brother's liability.

Departure from fact continued. If Nickerson had checked, officially or otherwise, with local residents or police, he would have learned that Frazier's weapon of choice was a four-inch "flick knife," not the gentleman's fingernail parer he referred to. The judge noted that the two British victims failed "to appear and testify after two trial dates." This, too, was a mistake. Records from the victim/witness assistance unit of the DA's office show that Keir Kennedy-Mitchell and Blake Fisher were never contacted by the court or the O'Keefe office. *Never.* Not about the trial date or even that Frazier had been arrested and indicted. The omission was colossal.

"To date [Keir] has never received any correspondence from the U.S. courts or indeed any U.S. lawyers about this matter," Kennedy-Mitchell's family retainer wrote to me in a May 2009 e-mail. Kennedy-Mitchell had "received no request formal or informal to attend as a witness in any hearing. . . . He will be very happy to respond to any official request from the courts."

Truth-seeking judges aren't obligated to explore collateral issues, granted. But had he been more alert, Nickerson could easily have discovered that Keir Kennedy-Mitchell would have made a highly reliable witness since his mother, Helena Kennedy, is regarded as the most influential Liberal member of the House of Lords, as one of Britain's leading lawyers, an author and TV commentator known for promoting human rights. As compared with Huffman and Miranda, who'd been seeking only "fifteen minutes of fame," the credibility of the well-off, college-educated Kennedy-Mitchell would have been much harder to impugn.

But more suggested a cover-up. Police reports and the court file claimed that the Kennedy-Mitchells were tourists. But in fact the family owned a home not three minutes' walk from the Wellfleet pier where the Frazier incident took place. The assault-with-a-dangerous-weapon case (penalty: "state prison not more than five years") against Jeremy Frazier was dismissed on March 9, 2004, three months before the Kennedy-Mitchells' regular summer return. Had he been notified of a trial date, Keir would have been available to testify without any complications or cost to the commonwealth.

Another consideration was that Judge Robert Welsh Jr., father of McCowen prosecutor Rob "Hide the Exculpatory Evidence" Welsh, was one of several judges involved in Frazier's nonpros. Had Welsh III been assigned to prosecute McCowen at that time? No. But the suggestion that he did not know about Frazier's knife play can only be regarded as persiflage; Cape Cod judges and prosecutors (particularly son-prosecutors) talk to each other all the time.

As for George's allegation of deficiencies at the state crime lab, Nickerson's ruling was even less forthcoming; he claimed that no evidence suggested that the DA's office was aware of the problems here. Yet both Boston dailies and the *Cape Cod Times* headlined the suspension of the lab's director, the FBI found problems beyond those that prompted the suspension, and most criminal lawyers in the state were on guard, many filing appeals based on the lab's inadequacies. There were also published reports that the governor, under pressure from legislators, had hired consultants to review all operations at the commonwealth's chief forensics unit.

Responding to Nickerson's ruling, George told the *Cape Cod Times*, "I wish I could tell you I am surprised, but this decision was expected. If the court did not feel that the juror misconduct was serious enough to warrant a new trial, I was certainly not expecting an epiphany as far as the second motion goes."

He was faking. He was deeply troubled by the judge's order. And he now had only sixty days to file the final appeal with the SJC. Attorney and client could only hope for a panel of fresh eyes and ears.

"I may have publicly acted as if this record rejection was expected," he said later, "but I had wanted and expected much, much more. The *Brady* case requires the prosecution to show all their evidence, and it stands for the proposition that society wins not only when the guilty are convicted but when criminal trials are fair. For the judge to ignore the Wellfleet pier incident was the same as the court's justification and defense of the behavior and comments of jurors like Eric Gomes."

WYDNK (WHAT YOU DID NOT KNOW)

Even now, sympathetic Cape Codders express dissatisfaction with the verdict, wondering what really happened, what outcome *might* have been reached if all of the facts had been in play. Some theories are delusional: Christa's murder was a "mob hit," or she was a majordomo in the Cape's ever-expanding drug underworld. Others are based on discrepancies apparent in the trial. But even the most adamant critics of the verdict weren't aware of all that was withheld or buried during the five-week trial. Facts that the jurors were never told. Facts that might have altered the verdict.

DNA was the deciding factor, but did it connect McCowen to the murder?

Experts testified that McCowen's sperm had likely been deposited before the time prosecutors said the crime occurred. McCowen himself didn't testify and the court refused to allow defense witness Dr. Eric Brown to address McCowen's Thursday afternoon sexual encounter with Worthington. The defendant's account is offered here for the first time, from Brown's notes of October 10, 16, and 27, 2006: "Mr. McCowen said that he happened to notice some extra trash on the back porch and went over to pick it up. As he was gathering up this trash, Ms. Worthington reportedly opened the door and asked, 'Can you take a Christmas tree?' Mr. McCowen answered, 'It depends on how big it is.' At this point, Ms. Worthington reportedly said, 'Come in and take a look.' Mr. McCowen then reported that 'I walked into the back door and followed her through the kitchen to the living room. I looked at the tree. It wasn't too big. I said I'll call my boss and then went back out to the truck. I told them it was a medium tree, and they said it was OK. I walked back in to take a closer look at the trunk. Then I stood back up and asked her when she was going to take off the lights and ornaments, and she said in a couple of days to a week. I told her just let me know when I can get it.'

"Allegedly, Ms. Worthington touched him and rubbed lightly against his arm with her arm while he was looking at the tree. As Mr. McCowen turned toward Ms. Worthington and looked down at her, she looked up at him, and they both allegedly kissed. It was immediately apparent to Mr. McCowen that both he and Ms. Worthington were sexually aroused, and after kissing, they each quickly undressed and became sexually engaged with one another in vaginal intercourse. According to Mr. McCowen, neither of them engaged in oral sex.

" 'When we kissed, our hands were roaming. I was touching her breasts. She didn't have anything on under her sweater or shirt. While I was standing and getting undressed, she was sitting down on the couch while I was still getting undressed because I had to get my shoes off. I didn't take my socks off. We started having sex on the couch and then ended on the floor.' "

McCowen told Brown the sexual encounter lasted for "approximately forty-five minutes, and he paced himself . . . before ejaculating. Mr. McCowen explained that 'she didn't want me to come inside her, so I came in her pubic hair and on her stomach.' . . . He added that he asked Worthington if she would be willing to have sex with him again, and he said she assented."

McCowen told Brown that he mentioned the Christmas tree discussion when first interviewed by police in 2002. For that reason, he assumed they knew he'd been inside the Worthington home. He left out the sex part, he explained, because Christa had asked him not to tell anyone.

The turning point in McCowen's interview came when police pushed the DNA report across the table. McCowen allegedly said,

"No way I can deny it." But admitting sexual congress was not an admission of murder. The distinction was lost in Mason's report.

Brown explained: "Although Mr. McCowen told me that he was attempting to provide an honest account of his sexual encounter with Ms. Worthington on Thursday, he stated that the police conducted an interrogation that tried to interweave his truthful narrative of how he had sex with Ms. Worthington on Thursday with their own theory of how Ms. Worthington had been murdered.

"Mr. McCowen insisted that the police would not accept his account of having consensual sex on Thursday with Ms. Worthington but repeatedly told him that they did not believe his story, and little by little, he gave in and modified his statements in order to appease the police, who he thought were treating him as a witness and not as a murderer. . . . Here and elsewhere during his long interrogation, the police cajoled and induced Mr. McCowen to make hypothetical statements that they later manipulated him into acknowledging as behavior that he actually exhibited."

The prosecutors expressed disbelief of the consensual sex scenario, but they had Christa's diary. Why didn't they use it? If they had, they would have realized that Christa might well have enjoyed secret sex with a black man, even a black garbage collector.

Cathy Nolan, a *People* magazine editor in Paris during Christa's high-flying *Women's Wear Daily* days, says that Christa appeared at art openings and dinner parties arm-in-arm with any number of men of differing backgrounds, including the award-winning war photographer Stanley Greene, a former Black Panther from the streets of Brooklyn. Greene, a star of today's photojournalism in France, refuses to confirm an affair but acknowledges that there was much *drague, drague,* courtship and attraction. Nolan, a close female friend, observed, "Race would never be an issue, never. Given the fact that Christa could quite often be snobbish, class was her thing, not race. How she could have dated a garbage man was a puzzler."

Or not, depending on Christa's circumstances. Vassar chums recall her attraction to "the illicit," her secret life that included a dalliance with at least one Vassar faculty member. Her attraction to the edgy and exotic led to her affair with Jackett, the Portuguese dope smuggler who was not only married but whose mahogany skin was in fact dark enough to have barred him from most '50s-era "white" restaurants in the Deep South. Tony was no high roller, either. Like McCowen, Jackett was even employed as—yes, you guessed it—a garbageman or "skilled laborer—sanitation," according to the Town of Provincetown's 1996–97 payroll records.

Others close to Christa made the same point. Cousin Pam, interviewed by detectives the evening the body was found, had indeed spoken of Christa's "dark side," how she was "looking for love through sex," and "did not want to be alone." Author Melik Kaylan, Christa's friend for some twenty years, insisted that she felt "isolated" and "lonely," and "if a male paid attention to her, she would like that." Christa "would not go out with a lowlife," he said, "but would [characteristically] look for someone below her status."

If the Jackett tryst didn't establish her predilection for the unconventional, enter alcoholic English boyfriend "Peter," then Thomas "Tarquin the Magician" Churchwell, the penniless vagabond who hit on her in the bar opposite her New York apartment. The McCowen jurors never knew about Tarquin, nor about Christa's diary entry on race after Churchwell's motor mouth one day upset her: he "said something racist apropos of nothing. I told him I wouldn't listen to that kind of talk, that I wasn't interested in hearing [it], and in words I don't recall, that he disgusted me when he spoke like that, that I was not at all entertained."

Neither the prosecutor nor the defense introduced the diary; it is doubtful that either lawyer took the time to look at it. But the diary was a more grave omission than Brown's disallowed report, even. It mirrored Christa's outlook more clearly than anything in the thousands of pages making up the trial record, referring, as it did, to Che Guevara, farm union organizer Cesar Chávez, muckraking journalist Jack Anderson, even the FBI's covert '60s COINTELPRO program, in addition to Molière, Shakespeare, and Pirandello. All evidenced a progressive intellect. But cops did not have the background to pick up on any of this, any more than Bill Burke, during cross, was able to ID *Catch-22,* misattributing the phrase to the TV show *M*A*S*H* rather than to Joseph Heller's best-selling novel.

It cannot be assumed that the jury was any better educated, any more receptive to a portrait of the victim as anything other than Miss Proper Main Line.

The long and short of it was that Christa Worthington was, actually, a free thinker, smart, educated, and a product of the '70s, whose sexual "looseness" didn't separate her from contemporaries or her relatives, either, for that matter. Her iconic grandmother Tiny reportedly had her extramarital affairs with fishermen. Cousins Patricia and Jan had liaisons known to more than a few Truroites, in Patricia's case, with *another* Ptown dope smuggler, in fact. And Jan's exploits weren't limited to getting locked in the back of the cruiser with Sergeant David Costa. Their parents dallied, too, between marrying and unmarrying each other three times. Another reported philanderer was Aunt Diana's late husband, Bob Loft. And Christa's father, Toppy, years before his bizarre, headline relationship with Elizabeth Porter, reportedly kept a love nest in Provincetown to service his girlfriends.

The Outer Cape's bohemian values played a role in Christa's life, but by family standards, she was normal. Promiscuity was in her DNA. She wasn't a bad or reckless person. She was a Worthington.

Like her daughter, Ava, Christa was also conceived out of wedlock, making her an outsider. And like a lot of outsiders, she gravitated to the fringe. But as grateful as she was for the gift of Ava, her midlife miracle child, she saw Jackett as a coward, herself as a fool. "He embroils me in the disgusting details of his deception," she wrote in the midst of their affair. "I serve to comfort him in the discomfort of his marriage. . . . I don't want this, really. . . . I don't like being immobilized by an animal."

There was no romanticizing the relationship, hard as jurors might try. Jackett abandoned her and the baby for the first two years of Ava's life. Even with the "family-ization" six months before the murder, prompted by Susan Jackett, not Tony, Christa wanted out. Paris, London, New York, it didn't matter.

Stuck in the wilderness of wintertime Cape Cod, spurned by relatives who wanted nothing to do with her, whom might the free-wheeling, formerly unrestrained Christa have turned to for a quickie, if only to sustain her while she plotted her escape?

Why wasn't the indictment questioned after a grand juror confessed to a conflict of interest?

A week after the grand jury handed down its indictment, one grand juror sought out Barnstable Superior Court Judge Richard Connon. The middle-aged woman was in tears. She confessed to a conflict, even thought of recusing herself.

"I was very, very upset at the end of the day because the case is close to me. I have been having nightmares," she explained, adding that she'd gone to a shrink. "There was stuff I didn't want to see . . . I shouldn't have been there. I'm too close to it."

The police crime-scene video in particular freaked her out.

"*I knew her*," she said, meaning Christa. "I knew her daughter. I knew the gal's daddy . . . *and to see her . . .*"

Connon, an old-school gentleman, sought to comfort her. He explained that he'd create a record of her visit, so if anyone were to question the "integrity of the process," she'd be in the clear. He wished the woman a good summer.

At the start of the trial, George moved for dismissal on the grounds that the grand juror's admission should have been taken more seriously; the woman had also spoken about the proceedings with a *Cape Cod Times* reporter. Nickerson denied the motion. Why? And why did the *Cape Cod Times* reporter not question, in print, the propriety of the grand juror's public disclosures?

Why was a key witness never called?

Wellfleet Detective Michael Mazzone was on the commonwealth's witness list but was never called to the stand. Mazzone had interacted with both McCowen and Jeremy Frazier for years. He quit the Wellfleet police force in September 2004, to work for the Barnstable Sheriff's Department, then departed for Florida. From there, he wrote a series of postverdict blogs, as if purging, or celebrating his escape from hell. Had Mazzone contributed these same words from the witness stand instead of online, he might have altered the trial's outcome.

On March 17, 2007, at 6:24 A.M., he wrote: "Ahhh . . . you folks ask
a lot of good questions about Frasier [*sic*]. I wondered for a long time
after McCowen was arrested and implicated JF, why wasn't there a
more extensive look taken at him. [W]hen JF was a teenager, he was
caught breaking into a house in Eastham. . . . The police surrounded
the house and one of the officers caught JF attempting to crawl from
a window. . . . He had socks on his hands! Even back then he knew
about leaving evidence behind at a crime scene. . . .

"JF told everyone he was in some gang [with] off-Cape connections. JF was the focus of a local long-term narcotics investigation. He
once bragged about being pulled over and laughed because he had 4
pounds of marijuana under his seat that was not detected. JF and his
friends' favorite sport was going to parties and finding someone who
they could all beat up on, and then leave before the police would arrive. . . . I could go on and on. The bottom line is, JF is a thug! I think
the only reason he isn't sharing a cell with McCowen is the lack of
physical evidence connecting him to the crime scene. . . .

"Mulvey is a liar. . . . Being a former drug dealer himself, his alle-
giances lay with nobody. I do not believe JF stayed with him the night
of the murder. My opinion . . . McC and JF both did this. I'd bet the
farm on it!"

Three days later, Mazzone posted again: "I wish I could tell you
why they killed CW . . . But one thing I learned about the Cape in the
12 years I lived there . . . really anything is possible. . . .

"The crime scene portion of the case appears to have been
botched from the beginning. . . . How many murders have the Truro
Police investigated in say the last 20 years? . . . I'm sure the state never
even shared some of the more sensitive information with them. . . .
I remember the rumor [that] one of the Truro PD people was being
'picked up' in connection with the case. Turned out to be false, I
think, but then again you have to remember, this is the Cape. . . .
Anything is possible.

"Something else . . . Chris Mason is a good officer . . . and I believe
an honorable man. I had enough dealings with him in the past to
know he is competent and would do his best to bring to justice those
who break the law. [But] if someone hands you a plate full of crap . . .

all you have to work with is a plate full of crap! Who knows the extent of the damage done to the crime scene . . . ? All it would take is one false step, wiping away one fingerprint or cross-contaminating some kind of biological evidence, and the case could be lost. . . .

"Since I began to deal with JF and several others . . . I had the opportunity over the years to watch them progress from teenagers to adults. I watched all the hype around town with the gang talk . . . and I stood by helplessly and watched as they sold drugs and basically had a free reign of the town . . . There was [*sic*] incidents like home invasion style burglaries, vehicles and houses being broken into, and all kinds of other crimes and situations directly related to the local drug trade. . . . People just didn't want to hear this was a problem. So nothing was ever really substantially done about it. . . .

"I watched as they became more and more violent. I watched it go from marijuana to cocaine. [T]hese guys, [who] belonged to some 'bush league' chapter of some ridiculous gang, always felt they needed to step up their game. What better way to make the big time then [*sic*] killing someone. . . . So McCowen knows this woman, who lives alone way out in the woods in Truro. Perfect target, right? We know they were together the night of the murder. . . . Maybe it wasn't even supposed to be a murder. Maybe just a rape. . . . But they go there . . . and CW is dead.

"DNA and the state lab? Ahhh yeah, speaks for itself at this point."

Later that day, he added: "[M]y take is small towns like that [Truro, Wellfleet, Eastham] want people to look like the police, but they certainly don't want them to act like it. . . . The locals want their little private army's [*sic*]. Inefficient . . . but on a leash and controllable by the board of selectmen in each town."

The next morning, Mazzone continued: "Couple of months before I left . . . I had two cases that really convinced me the place was changing, and not for the better. . . . One was a home invasion. . . . The victim, who's [*sic*] father owns half the town, was sleeping when some people knocked on the door and held a knife to his throat. Drug related. The second, and far more serious, same kind of incident, except the guy who broke in beat up the boyfriend and terrorized the girlfriend saying he was going to duck [*sic*] tape them up and kill them. . . . Yeah, also drug related. So JF pulling a knife on some tourist at the pier for really no reason, other [*sic*] to make a name for himself probably, is this not serious? We just don't talk about it there [on Cape Code]. . . .

"The other thing . . . Mason handled one part of this investigation. If you think for a moment he had anything to do with strategy, planning or any other aspect of the trial . . . you're sadly mistaken. The image, course and overall presentation of this would be handled completely by the DA's Office and in this case, O'Keefe himself. . . . Welsh was the prosecutor, but the man behind every segment of this would be MO."

Early the next morning, Mazzone posted again: "If you haven't already figured it out yet, the DA's office is run like any efficient business. If the DA loses cases . . . he loses customers (voters)."

And finally, late that afternoon, Mazzone commented on his history with McCowen, Frazier's phone calls the night of the murder, and, again, Shawn Mulvey's role, as whitewashed by the prosecution: "It is called empathy. . . . I went to a loud party call with another officer one night . . . McC . . . ends up getting caught with the bong and a small baggie of marijuana. We talked about it. He has several children, with different mothers. [He] seems to work pretty hard. He runs the trash truck, most days all day. I . . . remember some of his so-called restraining order cases. He had a way of really making women he was with mad at him. But for the most part, he was pretty easy going. Never seemed to be doing what some of his friends did, which was beat the hell out of someone every chance they had. . . . He wasn't disrespectful when you spoke to him. So I gave him a break, with the condition that we would have a conversation down the road about where he obtained the illegal substance. He agreed and was never charged.

"Phone calls: I don't know why all the calls came from the barracks. The only thing I might think of is that when a drug cop is working with an informant . . . and they slack off, as they tend to do . . . call them till they pick up. . . .

"JF: I had a good case against him. But the victim lived overseas. He was arrested at least twice to my knowledge. . . . Mulvey, on the other hand, was the key to JF's story. Without him it was just JF vs. McC."

Why wasn't Mazzone called to the stand? Possibly for the same reason investigators failed to follow up on rumors that Mulvey was paid $500 to back Frazier's alibi. More likely, because Mazzone was the officer who busted commonwealth witness Jeremy Frazier for the Wellfleet pier knife attack, an incident the O'Keefe office took great pains to bury. Putting the retired detective on the stand would have left Welsh wide open. It appears that even Mazzone didn't know that prosecutors never contacted the Brit victims or that Frazier had been charged.

Why was Kyle Hicks allowed to make the call that knocked Rachel Huffman off the jury?
Per prison regulations, throughout the twenty-one months he was incarcerated in the Barnstable County jail, McCowen had not been allowed to call attorney George's cell phone from the facility, yet Hicks was allowed to call Huffman. How come? And what was the possible relevance of the Barnstable County lockup being run by the Barnstable County sheriff's office, which was run by Sheriff James Cummings, retired CPAC detective, O'Keefe buddy, and head fund-raiser for the DA's 2006 reelection campaign?

Why did Judge Nickerson attempt to broker a plea bargain halfway through trial?
It was never disclosed to the jurors or the public, as it never is, but during the afternoon break on October 26, right after George's cross-examination of Frazier, the judge called the attorneys into his office to propose a second-degree-murder plea. Present, in addition to the lawyers, was the judge's lobby officer and the clerk of courts, Scott W. Nickerson (no relation). George said that if the rape and aggravated-assault charges were dropped, he'd take the proposal to McCowen. Welsh, for his part, refused outright, leading Nickerson to admonish him, "Counselor, I urge you to reconsider, because you *could* lose this case."

What was going on? One possibility is that the judge believed that McCowen was at Worthington's the night of the murder, but having heard Frazier testify, he doubted that the defendant was there alone. Another reading: Frazier's testimony fueled Nickerson's long-standing contempt for O'Keefe and his shortcuts; in the interests of justice, the judge wanted the charade to end. Still another: he believed Mc-Cowen guilty and was worried that Frazier's bumbling, contradictory testimony might enable the defendant to walk.

Why was Christa Worthington's house sold before any arrest was made?
By allowing the 50 Depot Road property to be sold before an arrest was made, the prosecutor ensured that no future defense team could examine it. This is a small point but a glaring procedural maneuver, indicative of the DA's determination to win. "I can't count the number of cases where I went to the crime scene. This was one of the rare times where the murder scene was lost to me," says George.

Why was there such disparity between the prosecution's reconstruction of the crime and the physical evidence? What did the autopsy **actually reveal?**
If the victim was dragged into the house from outside, across frozen ground encrusted with crushed clamshell, why were her hands and feet clean? Why were her bare feet uncut? Grass was in Christa's hair and on the back of her sweater. Her socks were found outside. Something happened there, but what?

According to a longtime Boston-area emergency-room doctor independently retained to analyze the autopsy report, the victim's body abrasions were consistent with being dragged by the right arm; three were on her left forearm, hip, and knee. But if someone knocked her down outside, grabbed her arm, and dragged her inside, then the parallel marks in the driveway remain unexplained. The doctor is adamant that the most serious blow to Worthington's head would not have knocked her out long enough to be dragged any distance, nor is the drag scenario consistent with the prosecution's suggestion that she ran from her attackers, locked herself in the house, and attempted to call 911.

The kind of blow the autopsy showed would have stunned her, knocked her to the ground, but she would likely have been awake, according to the doctor. If the blow had been strong enough to knock her out, he opines, "she would have had some cerebral edema . . . a concussion."

But the stabbing occurred where Christa was found, in the narrow hallway between kitchen and living room, a certainty, given the nick to the floor beneath her body. The angle of the knife as it passed through her chest further suggests that she was lying down.

The wound says more. According to the official autopsy, the knife entered Christa's chest fourteen and a half inches from the top of her head, one and a half inches left of the front midline, missing the hard-to-penetrate sternum and ribs. It perforated the left lung's upper lobe and the upper portion of its lower lobe. To do that, the blade had to be at least one and a half inches wide, consistent with the entry wound. How it missed the ribs is unclear. Most people's ribs are about one inch apart; a knife one and a half inches wide should have hit bone, given the angle, but no such injury was discovered. Rather, the report says that the knife entered near the second rib, hit softer cartilage, and exited the victim's back near the fifth. The seeming discrepancy in the angle is consistent with a straight, slightly downward thrust as the rib cage curves. The knife did not go in horizontally but made a two-to-eight-o'clock wound.

The angle suggests that the killer was left-handed. A right-handed person kneeling over the prone body would have had to twist his wrist dramatically to inflict the two-to-eight-o'clock wound. The autopsy also showed that the stabbing went from right to left. If the killer knelt to her left, the angle is achievable for a right-hander. But Worthington's body was found lying sideways in the small hallway: to create the two-to-eight-o'clock wound, with the knife meeting her body at an eighty-to-ninety-degree angle, the killer would have had to negotiate her right leg, elevated in the bookshelf. It's possible that the killer was turned in the other direction and stabbed from behind Worthington's head, but he would have had to stand inside the next room, Christa's study. More important, because the dull side of the knife was at the top of the wound, he would have had to hold the knife upside-down.

Three blows to her right side, including her chest, and the worst of the contusions—three inches between the right eyebrow and ear—suggest a left hook, further supporting the lefty scenario. The doctor who reviewed the report believed that it was a punch, not a kick: "If he had kicked her in the head, he probably would have broken her skull."

Attorney George, Cisneros, and Roy McCowen insist that Chris McCowen is right-handed, as does McCowen. Left-handedness never came up at trial. The overworked defense attorney focused on other aspects of the case, but what about investigators and forensics specialists? Did police never consider the problem? If they had, wouldn't they have watched McCowen sign his waivers? And if they had, wouldn't they have introduced his hand preference at trial? No more than 15 percent of the population is left-handed; some studies suggest 5 percent.

Where did the rape charge come from? For three and a half years, the crime was murder.

The autopsy tells us that Christa munched on carrots before her death, was drug-free, and had no diseases. It does not suggest rape. Only six words in the entire report are pertinent: "The neck and genitalia are unremarkable."

The emergency-room doctor who read the report has dealt with hundreds of sexual assaults. "Women are not happy when they get raped," he explained clinically. "Women who are raped, with rare exceptions, are not wet. Sex is a parasympathetic phenomenon, and if they are being attacked, they're in sympathetic fight or flight. They're dry." Trauma or bruises to the labia are normally evident after rape; at the very least, redness and mucus membrane bleeding are common. Bruising is a given with no lubrication.

"There's no traumatic rape, and it's pretty hard to have a rape without some tears. I suspect it was consensual sex," the doctor said. "You know, it's one of those things they try to sneak in, because if they can get it to the jury that the guy's black—if there's any flavor of rape, it just makes the conviction so much easier."

Welsh would say that's his opinion. But the medical literature on vaginal injury in sexual-assault cases, a substantial body of work that the prosecutor claimed he knew nothing about, supports the doctor's con-clusion and then some. One study published in the *American Journal of Obstetrics and Gynecology* maintains that advances in clinical forensic medicine enable examiners using colposcopy to obtain "evidence of genital trauma in 87% to 92% of rape victims seen within 48 hours." Trauma from consensual sex was found in only 11 percent of the women examined. Rape trauma is usually identifiable "in one or more of four locations, with tears appearing most often on the posterior fourchette and fossa, abrasions on the labia, and ecchymosis on the hymen."

Even more persuasive is the testimony of McCowen's girlfriend, Catherine Cisneros. "In the year and a half I was sleeping with Chris before he was arrested," Cisneros says, "I would bleed after the two of us had sex. I would bleed at least half the time. There was nothing I could do about it. He's *big*."

Dr. James Weiner's autopsy report indicates that Christa's genita-lia were "unremarkable." Dr. Henry Neilds concurred. Was the jury not listening?

Was Maria Flook quoting DA O'Keefe accurately?

On page 36 of *Invisible Eden: A Story of Love and Murder on Cape Cod*, O'Keefe is quoted, telling the author in late 2002 about the evidence lifted from the victim's body.

"We haven't got all the samples back. There were some stains, a dried smear on the inner thigh. If it comes back as semen on her leg, then it's fresh, or she would have already showered. But she did have semen inside her . . . The semen was old . . . The semen was degraded. Its age could be anywhere between four to eighteen days old. It didn't have tails."

If this is indeed accurate information, then the prosecution should have had a major problem in arguing rape and murder dur-ing the wee hours of Saturday, January 5. Given the state of McCow-en's sperm, more than anything the statement points to the Thursday consensual sex scenario alleged by the defense; i.e., to McCowen's innocence, not guilt.

Question is, why did the DA provide this information to the flaxen-haired Flook but not to the jury during the trial?

What was the significance of the restraining orders?

According to his pal Dave Nichols, the not-too-bright Chris McCowen never reckoned with the complications of sleeping around, and that's what got him saddled with the majority of his restraining orders, five in all. "He was still sleeping with Pam [Maguire] while sleeping with Kelly [Tabor] while sleeping with Jessica while sleeping with Rhonda while sleeping with Lisa while sleeping with Sandy while sleeping with a handful that I can't even think of. That's six people, and I know for a fact that some of them didn't appreciate it," Nichols said.

"The other thing that was never made clear was that several of the restraining orders were put-up jobs," he said. One of the girlfriends "filed in order to get section eight housing assistance. . . . She had Chris either admit to, or go along with, her saying he was violent. It was all about getting housing, so that she wouldn't be denied. I remember saying to him, 'Dude, I wouldn't do this. It might come back and bite you in the ass.' But Chris and her were in cahoots. It got him out of having to pay child support. . . . Afterward, they lived together . . . and while she was working, he was watching the kid."

Was Christa wearing a green bathrobe? If so, where is it?

"I have Tim Arnold clearly testifying that he saw Christa on the floor in a green bathrobe," Robert George says. "His father says that he saw her in a nightie, whatever that means. Jan Worthington in all her statements says she's on the floor in the sea-green bathrobe. Two of the EMTs see her on the floor in a bathrobe. Now, where is the fucking bathrobe? There was only one person other than Tim Arnold in that house alone with Christa Worthington's body for any period of time: Truro Sergeant Dave Costa. The importance of the green bathrobe is that if Christa had herself wrapped in the bathrobe, it might have the killer's blood on it. There *was* a green bathrobe there. The bathrobe has disappeared."

Why was so much evidence not tested?

Forensic scientist Dr. Richard Saferstein pointed out the most damaging omission: semen swabbed from Christa's outer genital area was never analyzed for DNA. Investigators also overlooked the eleven-and-three-quarter-inch hair found on the dead woman's breast; no microscopic testing was done on it. Not a single hair found at the crime scene was tested.

Also ignored were bloodstains that authorities assumed resulted from Ava trying to clean her mother, stains on the broom handle, the hand mitt, the bathroom rug, and the sink. Wash towels should have been tested to determine if anyone tried to clean blood from his hands, but they were not. Blood found on Christa Worthington's clog matched one male; the blood on her body matched another.

Police took a cast of a foot imprint found outside, near Christa's car, but never even attempted to determine the shoe size.

DNA under Christa's fingernails came from at least three unknown males. Investigators waited twenty-four months to swab the doorknobs. Incomprehensible.

Were police playing Liar's Poker?

Police eliminated Frazier as a suspect after he passed the polygraph. McCowen, whose fingerprints were not found at Worthington's house, either, was never asked to take a polygraph. Why? If passing the polygraph meant innocence, why didn't police arrest Toppy Worthington, Toppy's girlfriend Beth Porter, and the girlfriend's live-in partner, Ed Hall? All three, according to MSP reports, failed the lie-detector test.

DNA might be foolproof, but what about the lab that tested it?

At the time of the murder, the state crime lab limited county DAs to four DNA submissions per month. O'Keefe, sweeping the Cape for DNA, swamped the lab with samples from men under no suspicion whatsoever but failed to submit McCowen's sample until July 7, 2004, more than five months after it was collected. Nine months later, it was a match. A month before the match, the lab director was forced to resign after the U.S. Department of Justice discovered that the lab mishandled twenty-seven samples from sexual-assault cases statewide. Twenty-three of the cases couldn't be tried.

DNA had become the darling of crime detection. But in August 2009, the *Journal of Forensic Science International* reported that "standard molecular biology techniques" can "enable anyone with basic equipment and know-how to produce practically unlimited amounts of *in vitro* synthesized (artificial) DNA with any desired genetic profile."

DNA can be manufactured, faked.

"DNA is a lot easier to plant at a crime scene than fingerprints," said Tania Simoncelli, science advisor to the ACLU. And yet, she noted, "We're creating a justice system that is increasingly relying on this technology."

And yet, O'Keefe and his Republican colleague Timothy Cruise, DA of neighboring Plymouth County and president of the Massachusetts District Attorneys' Association, spearheaded a drive in the state legislature for funding to expand DNA services.

At the close of trial, Judge Nickerson spent two hours instructing jurors on the presumption of innocence and the meaning of "beyond a reasonable doubt." He cannot be faulted; he labored at it diligently. He wanted jurors to understand fully that the burden of proof rested with the commonwealth, that the defendant need not prove innocence.

"Reasonable doubt" is the highest standard of proof in our adversarial system, always coupled with "beyond." The state must debunk all reasonable scenarios other than the defendant's guilt. Beyond means *further than* or *more than*, according to legal theorist, ex-Manson prosecutor, and best-selling author Vincent Bugliosi. If a juror has any reasonable doubt, he must return a not-guilty verdict.

Reasonable doubt plays a vital role in American criminal procedure. "It is a prime instrument for reducing the risk of convictions resting on factual error," the U.S. Supreme Court declared as long ago as 1895. But because of the commonwealth's ineptitude or trickery, or because of inevitable mistakes made by overworked defense counsel, a host of evidence was withheld from the McCowen jury. The statement was unsigned; the defendant never confessed to the murder; a DNA match from a laboratory in disarray was the sole evidence linking him to the crime scene; key prosecution witnesses were permitted to lie. Given these facts, wouldn't reasonable arbiters remember the word *beyond* and conclude that the government's case was riddled with reasonable doubt?

THE MAN WHO PULLED THE STRINGS

Michael O'Keefe was handpicked for the top job in Cape and Islands law enforcement by his predecessor, Philip Rollins, a pragmatic politician who held the position for thirty-two years. O'Keefe won the election by a comfortable margin, the crowning moment of his career. And it was at that moment that his career, begun as a Dennis cop three decades earlier, began to unravel.

Rollins was a large, florid man known to hold his liquor, a master of "working the room" at rallies and political fund-raisers. Often, he'd take a roundabout route to work, zigzagging along the mid-Cape's sandy byways, stopping at coffee shops in Falmouth, Osterville, and Yarmouthport to stay in touch with voters. He showed up for Boy Scout jamborees and the annual Barnstable County Fair. Over the years, this carefully constructed power base enabled him to expand the DA's office from a half-dozen part-time prosecutors to a full-time staff of more than twenty by the time O'Keefe took over.

Equally, if not more, important, increased funding from cohorts in the legislature and the State Attorney General's Office had let him separate his office from the larger "southern district," including the off-Cape cities of New Bedford and Fall River, working-class towns that would have challenged Rollins and other Republicans. The move, made in 1975, was brilliant, indeed key: by putting New Bedford and Fall River under the control of another DA, he created a fiefdom on the Cape, one that voted for Nixon over JFK, even though Massachusetts was the only state in the nation later to back McGovern.

The TV show *Law & Order* has taught most Americans that police investigate crime and district attorneys prosecute. Not so on Rollins' Cape Cod. Two years into his first term, O'Keefe's mentor took the unusual step of assigning a State Police officer to the DA's office; in time, he assigned a dozen. The Crime Prevention and Control Unit—CPAC—vastly increased the DA's power by gutting traditional checks and balances. On the Cape, CPAC was under the DA's thumb. State Police had become the king's palace guards.

Concerns about the "neutrality" of police investigations were ignored under the affable Rollins; that changed when O'Keefe took over. Unlike his predecessor, O'Keefe never tired of boasting about convictions.

The case of Barnstable County Sheriff James Cummings demonstrates how the compact between the police and the DA can subvert justice. Cummings, a state trooper assigned to CPAC for twenty-one years under Rollins, resigned and got himself elected sheriff in 1998; in 2006, he became O'Keefe's campaign manager. But the Massachusetts State Ethics Commission was investigating the Cummings office for corruption and conflict of interest. Charges against the sheriff's deputies included assault and battery, shoplifting, drunk driving, weapons violations, and domestic abuse.

No charges were filed against Cummings, but five of his deputy sheriffs were arrested during the 2006 election year. The arrests raised questions not only about Cummings but also about O'Keefe when two of the deputies were cleared of all charges and a third reached a plea bargain. People said O'Keefe had no business investigating his campaign manager or the campaign manager's staff.

It did not matter that PR-conscious Cummings served on the boards of the YMCA and Big Brothers and Big Sisters and ran the Sheriff's Youth Ranch, a program aiding at-risk teenagers, or that O'Keefe was a founding member of Massachusetts Employees Against Domestic Violence and a Cape figurehead in the Republican Leadership Team for Romney for President. Throughout his career, O'Keefe had been perceived as a cop, and there were times, it seemed, he filed charges automatically, legitimate and frivolous, alike. Sometimes his decisions seemed based on personal grudges. The most common explanation of his style as DA was that he lacked experience working the "other side of the aisle." He'd spent less than a year in private practice before becoming a prosecutor; he was a cop before he earned his night-school law degree, and he'd remained a cop ever since.

The Commonwealth is an anomaly because of CPAC but the DA's power was further enhanced by Mass. G.L. ch. 38 secs. 3–4, which made the investigation of homicides the province of county district attorneys, not local police. Everywhere except Boston and Spring-field, the DA decides who gets investigated and who investigates. "In Massachusetts, murder is political because the cops are powerless," says journalist Jeff Blanchard. "If you call the State Police or the lo-cals, anywhere, anytime, they'll refer you to the district attorney."

Who investigates is paramount. State Police overtime pay isn't chump change, as commonwealth taxpayers are painfully aware. For each of the three and a half years of the Worthington investigation, O'Keefe's lead detectives took in an estimated $200,000 apiece, more than Gov-ernor Deval Patrick. To put this into perspective, in 2007 the O'Keefe office paid more than *twice* as much overtime as comparable-sized offices—Berkshire County, for example, with an operating budget of $3.4 million, paid 4.2 percent in overtime; the Cape and Islands office, with a budget of $3.5 million, paid 8.9 percent.

That kind of money buys loyalty.

One former prosecutor guessed it was this, plus the usual "men in blue" bonding, that made O'Keefe's investigators turn a blind eye to inconsistencies in the Worthington case. Another factor is that town police departments on the Cape are autonomous, run by chiefs who answer to local selectmen, and then only selectively. Officers are often related by marriage or went to high school together. And not one town of the Cape's fifteen has a civilian review board. Not one.

One former assistant DA, an admitted O'Keefe foe, said, "I'm going to suggest that it's routine for certain police officers to flat-out lie." Good cops don't, but a disturbing number of local defense at-torneys point out that planting evidence and falsifying statements is more common on the Cape than in many other places, especially on the lower Cape, farthest from Boston. "Before most juries, the cop usually wins. But from Yarmouth to Provincetown, the police can do anything they want. . . . They're all given the utmost courtesy and never criticized."

The peculiar structure of Massachusetts law made O'Keefe the most powerful elected official on Cape Cod, but incestuousness was partly to blame. Pro-police bias was tradition. Look no farther than the Welsh dynasty. The family has meted out justice on the Outer Cape for almost a century. When Rob Welsh's judgeship was announced during the McCowen trial, he became the *fourth* Welsh to be so appointed, leading one fearless local attorney to complain, "I thought we were a republic, not a monarchy."

In the context of such a small world, is it any wonder so few saw it as odd or improper that Welsh's father should issue the arrest warrant requiring Shawn Mulvey to return from Florida with Frazier's alibi? Drug charges had made Mulvey disappear; after he testified, the charges disappeared. The senior Welsh presided over pretrial hearings against Frazier for his 2003 Wellfleet knife attack on the British tourists; he co-signed the search warrant allowing Truro officers to sweep this author's home and file-filled office. In none of these instances was there an outcry or press scrutiny.

By 2006, O'Keefe's arrogance was causing problems among those he needed as allies. The Yarmouth Patrol Officers Association issued a letter to the press stating, "One of the flaws attributed to O'Keefe was his inability to communicate or his lack of social skills. . . . In fairness, O'Keefe has put together an excellent staff with which local law enforcement works very well. It is O'Keefe's personal attitude and lack of support for local law enforcement that is both disheartening and disrespectful."

Police chiefs up and down the peninsula created a campaign fund to encourage the DA to run for state attorney general, a Boston job. Anything to get him off the Cape. O'Keefe had won twenty murder convictions and been named prosecutor of the year, but not many officers on the front line wanted to work with him.

In 2004, he had sold the Palomino Road house he'd shared with his ex-wife, Judge Joan Lynch, and moved into one of the Cape's most exclusive condo communities, Sandwich's tony Ridge Club, where homes sell for $700,000 to more than $1 million. He lived alone in his 4,200-square foot, four-bedroom contemporary that overlooked the eighteenth hole of a private, par seventy-one golf course. Ridge Club management, according to an insider, "comped" him with home improvements and landscaping. Among his neighbors were hockey stars Derek Sanderson and Bobby Orr; Kathleen O'Toole, Boston's first woman police commissioner; and reportedly several Boston mob heavies, not an implausible claim. Over the years, the Cape has been the vacation destination for all kinds of hoodlums, including master mobster James "Whitey" Bulger, the head of Boston's Irish Mafia.

Despite the gated community's twenty-four-hour security, the Ridge Club experienced a rash of burglaries not long after O'Keefe's arrival, the most publicized being those at the home of the Cape's number one lawman. The first took place on December 27, 2006, the second nine months later. Among the items taken was the DA's snub-nosed .38 revolver.

Although the weapon was stolen in December, six weeks after the McGowen verdict, the theft was not reported until after the second break-in, and then only because an offhand remark led this author to look into it, then tip off several of his colleagues. According to the *Cape Cod Times*, Sandwich police chief Michael Miller would not release any details. O'Keefe offered only a terse, grandiose comment: "It's unfortunate that people suffer break-ins into their homes."

The DA refused comment when asked whether more than one gun had been stolen, whether the gun(s) was trigger-locked as required by law, or if the firearm(s) was loaded. When the *Boston Globe* called for comment, he repeated his bromide: *his* break-ins were no more important than other Ridge Club burglaries.

A week later, O'Keefe called in the State Police, raising the question, should the district attorney investigate a crime at his own home, one that might entail illegally stored firearms?

On August 27, 2008, with both burglaries still unsolved after almost a year, the Robbins Report, a popular webzine on the Cape's alternative news source Capecodtoday.com, asked Sandwich's Chief Miller if O'Keefe had a valid pistol permit at the time of the theft. "I don't know," Miller was reported saying. "But I know he has one now." One blogger wrote, "I'm sure if the gun were registered prior to the break-in, the answer from the chief would have been the affirmative, not 'I don't know.' So there we have it."

Reporters were unable to determine whether O'Keefe's weapon's serial number had been entered into the computerized National Crime Information Center or even if the DA had requested a federal Alcohol, Tobacco, and Firearms trace for the stolen gun. On September 12, with the story mushrooming, Capecodtoday.com demanded an explanation: "A question has arisen about whether O'Keefe, who told police he owned the gun, legally owned the weapon." The DA had again refused to answer questions, and the State Attorney General's Office said, "No comment," when asked how an investigation of a Massachusetts district attorney might proceed. The article concluded with a question: "Who polices the police?"

The same unhealthy behind-the-scenes absence of accountability cropped up in connection with an incident next door to the DA's former home in Barnstable Village. On Easter Sunday, 2007, one of his ex-neighbors, Dr. Ann Gryboski, shot her husband twice, killing him instantly. Gryboski claimed self-defense. Under O'Keefe's supervision, the grand jury voted not to indict.

Insiders say that a DA can "indict a ham sandwich." He can structure testimony as he sees fit; submit or withhold evidence; use snitches, rapists, and serial killers as witnesses. The Gryboski case raised eyebrows because the notoriously lecherous O'Keefe wouldn't say how well he knew the middle-aged white physician. When reporters raised the potential conflict of interest, O'Keefe again stonewalled, saying there was "more to the shooting than meets the public eye."

He then tried to pull the same stunt in July 2008, when Yarmouth police fatally shot a twenty-five-year-old Brazilian house painter stopped for speeding, refusing to name the victim or the officer who shot him. When the official silence went on for more than a day and a half, longtime locals as well as the 14,000-member Brazilian community in the Hyannis area focused angrily on O'Keefe.

"It's now 30 hours since the killing, and the public has the right to assume the DA and YPD are stalling until they get their stories straight," Capecodtoday.com editorialized. "We *may* learn the truth when the DA has a scheduled news conference today. . . . He might muddy the waters as he has done often in the past, Gryboski, Worthington, et al. DA O'Keefe's habit of sitting on vital information has got to stop, and it will, either while he's still in office or after he's been cashiered by an angry electorate."

But it wasn't until the next day O'Keefe faced the press, along with grim-visaged, jut-jawed Yarmouth PD chief Michael Almonte at his side. The victim was Andre Martins of Hyannis; the police officer, Christopher Van Ness, a three-year veteran of the force. Martins drew the policeman's attention when his Lincoln Continental sped out of a parking lot in downtown Yarmouth early Sunday morning. A chase ensued. Martins drove up on a lawn, then struck Van Ness's cruiser while attempting a U-turn. An "unknown number" of shots were fired. A female passenger, Martins's girlfriend, was not injured.

The deceased, O'Keefe added, had a marijuana cigarette in his mouth when paramedics reached him.

The pot-in-mouth allegation was patently ludicrous; the Brazilian had taken at least one close-range gunshot to the chest. No further explanation was available until the *Boston Globe* reported that the Yarmouth police officer had fired not "an unknown number" of shots, as O'Keefe alleged, but three or four rounds from his regulation-issue .9mm Beretta, killing the unarmed house painter instantly.

Another version came from Camilla Campos, Martins's girlfriend and the mother of their five-year-old son and two-year-old daughter. O'Keefe had said the woman was "cooperating" with investigators, but Campos was not. Nor was she silent. She told the Brazilian *Folha Online* that Van Ness got out of his cruiser, appeared at Martins's open window, and fired. Three times. Friend Alex Kovelski said that Martins had been previously cited for driving offenses and was terrified of being deported because his work visa had expired.

The Martins incident stirred memories of another police shooting of a Cape minority member: David Hendricks, a Wampanoag

Indian teenager killed by a Mashpee police sergeant in May 1988. O'Keefe, then still an assistant DA, and Cummings smeared the victim as a heroin user but had to back down when the Hendricks family won a $375,000 wrongful-death suit against Barnstable County and its trigger-happy lawmen.

The Martins slaying spotlighted the Cape's lack of police oversight: with no local civilian police-review agency, police misconduct could only be reported in Boston, at local police stations, or at selectmen's meetings. But town officials on the Cape have been notoriously slow to act when it comes to the cops. For example, Truro residents, alarmed by the Martins incident, accused local cops of "acting like some sort of quasi-military operation." In response, the head of the Truro Police Employees Federation threatened a police work stoppage, then launched a personal attack against one complainant and his wife, a former assistant DA whom O'Keefe had fired. The officer's letter was nearly anti-Semitic, describing the woman's husband, a Jew, as "wealthy" and originally "from New York." After a motion to censor the cops, selectmen voted instead to hold the matter over for a week; not one board member called for the recusal of co-chairman Jan Worthington because of her Truro PD affiliation. Days before the second meeting, the complainant found a dead rat aboard his boat, a warning to "back off."

Even in the face of such gangsterism, selectmen were reluctant to act. In the end, they voted only to have town police de-tint their cruiser windshields "so people can see who's driving."

By 2008, the situation was reaching a critical mass. The *Cape Cod Voice*, an independent monthly under veteran O'Keefe watcher Seth Rolbein, devoted its July issue to the DA, who appeared on the cover bare-chested, golf putter in hand, clothed only in his infamous bath towel. The montage was pure Photoshop, but what readers found inside amounted to the most sustained critique of O'Keefe to date.

"To say that the Cape and Islands has both the most notorious and the worst district attorney in all Massachusetts used to be one of those inflammatory comments bound to spark debate," Rolbein wrote. "Now, unfortunately, it has to be accepted, as the lawyers say, as a matter of fact. . . . A person of less hubris—and more sense of

civic responsibility—would have resigned long ago. . . . His conduct
has undermined his personal reputation, as well as the reputation of
the office, and while some people might think that's a crime, it car-
ries no sentence. The court of public opinion is the only one that can
judge him now."

The longest piece in the issue detailed O'Keefe's campaign ex-
penditures with a fine-tooth comb, confirming what many concerned
Cape Codders suspected. The DA was having a damn good time. On
a 2005 vacation, he dropped $700 on golf and dinner with "support-
ers," although he was in Hawaii. In 2007, he spent $4,700 on meals
during the first half of the year alone, nearly $1,900 more than any
other Massachusetts district attorney, although he'd run for reelection unopposed. In 2008, he grew bolder still, spending $209 for two
lunches, then another $1,510 for dinner in the course of a single day
in Washington, D.C.

It went on. The O'Keefe campaign fund was a self-generating cash
register. Aside from lawyers, businessmen, and bankers, his supporters included South Dennis marina owner Joe Buscone and Adam
Hart, the latter a convicted bookmaker. Buscone was known to host
an annual O'Keefe fundraiser where, it is said, sponsors would "cup"
$100 bills into the DA's palm during a friendly handshake, nontrace-
able contributions running to $1,000 and more.

These scenes evoked the pointed description of Boston graft rendered by novelist Edwin O'Connor in *All in the Family*, his companion
work to *The Last Hurrah*: "Corruption here had a shoddy, penny ante
quality it did not have in other states. . . . Here everything was up for
grabs . . . there seemed to be a depthless cushion of street-corner cyn-
icism, a special kind of tainted, small-time fellowship which sent out a
complex of vines and shoots so interconnected that even the sleaziest
poolroom bookie managed . . . to be in touch with the mayor's office
or the governor's chair."

The Cape's "governor" was Mike O'Keefe. One look at the records of the State Office of Campaign and Political Finance showed
that his contributors included lawyers, businessmen, Democratic and
Republican pols alike, and even author Maria Flook, who'd tossed
fifty dollars into the DA's ever-swelling war chest.

Another article in the *Voice's* special issue surveyed local attorneys on O'Keefe the prosecutor. Most criticism focused on the McCowen case.

Attorney William Henchy called the DA's investigation "a case of shoot first, ask questions later" and noted "the number of drug informants who got a pass."

Drew Segadelli, one of the Cape's more high-profile barristers, was bothered by the impropriety of prosecutor Rob Welsh showing up at the jurors' postverdict party, by the expulsion of juror Rachel Huffman, and by the call from State Police to prosecution witness Jeremy Frazier on the night of the murder. The implications of that call, he said, were "jaw-dropping."

Attorney Bruce Bierhans, who represented McCowen's employer, Cape Cod Disposal, in the civil suit filed by the Christa Worthington estate, also talked about Welsh's partying with jurors, which he called a matter for the Board of Bar Overseers.

Even the normally circumspect Russell Redgate, Tim Arnold's lawyer, said that Jeremy Frazier's testimony cast doubt on whether McCowen acted alone.

Within a week of the magazine hitting newsstands, the mail poured in, almost all critical of the DA. But O'Keefe seemed impervious. In mid-July, flaunting his power with the same brio he displayed in rejecting charges of financial impropriety, or questions about the theft of his possibly unregistered handgun(s), he initiated several prosecutions that seemed to test the limits, even on Cape Cod. The first was directed at Dr. Rapin Osathanondh, a research associate at Harvard School of Public Health, who'd performed a clinical abortion that ended in the death of a twenty-two-year-old woman.

"The first chapters of torts casebooks are filled with fascinating cases about intentional torts in medicine, and the distinction between battery and lack of informed consent," the *Wall Street Journal* wrote. "But it's rare that even the most egregious instances of medical malpractice qualify as crimes. Michael O'Keefe, the DA for Cape Cod, is apparently pushing the envelope."

O'Keefe defended the indictment, claiming that the doctor had taken procedural shortcuts. But the issue seemed theological for him. Was the DA another primitive right-to-lifer, misusing his office?

Even those who championed O'Keefe and his wooden, by-the-book methods questioned his arrest of a Sandwich-area father who'd e-mailed his two young sons in defiance of a court-issued restraining order. The defendant refused to cut a deal, opting to take his chances with a jury trial. The case dragged on for months, but O'Keefe dropped the charges three weeks before the 2006 election, leery of bad publicity.

Perhaps the DA's nuttiest prosecution of all was that of seventy-six-year-old retired carpenter Francis Bello for rape and kidnapping, on the say-so of Bello's ex-girlfriend, age sixty-six. Bello and his inamorata had lived together for almost fifteen years; when Bello decided to leave the relationship, the woman ran to the cops, bent on revenge. The performance issue was obvious but meaningless to O'Keefe, who was determined to put Bello away for twenty years, a virtual death sentence. After two years' wrangling in court, Bello's fate was "administrative probation."

Michael O'Keefe had thrown the proverbial book at e-mails, medical malpractice, and love gone wrong. But what about murder? "The O'Keefe office has lost its way," said one of the many assistant DAs who have come and gone under his tenure, fleeing the vindictive, Machiavellian world of the Cape and Islands District Attorney's Office. "Michael is, in my opinion, a great lawyer, but the role of a prosecutor under Massachusetts law is not merely to obtain convictions. It's to do justice for all the citizens of the commonwealth, including the defendant. He's not the right man for the job."

By 2008, even little-old-lady Cape Codders, the stay-at-homes glued to *Dr. Phil*, acknowledged the gnarled personality at work here. The DA was smart, knew the law, and was as ambitious as anyone in local government. But he was a miserable man, childless and alone. His divorce had reinforced his innate misanthropy and his adolescent sexual longings. He'd been passed over for a judgeship while his ex-wife was appointed to the district court bench. His drinking had accelerated to the point where, even as he targeted seventy-six-year-old "rapists," he was weaving in and out of mid-Cape bars, often during the late afternoon, unable to drive himself home. Worse, his choirboy upbringing had fostered an inflexible, black-and-white worldview that metastasized into the belief that he had a God-given right to make moral judgments. The agent of righteousness felt duty-bound to characterize Christa Worthington as a slut who'd take on the butcher, the baker, and the husbands of her friends, even as the fifty-seven-year-old harassed frightened teenage salesgirls and took payoffs disguised as campaign contributions.

O'Keefe believed he was "out there working for the forces of good against the forces of bad," one ex-prosecutor said. "It's a very typical sort of Catholic thing, a very Irish way of looking at things, right?"

It was, indeed. And not unexpected in the son of Dorothy Mary O'Keefe, who'd been the deathbed nurse to His Eminence, Boston's Cardinal Cushing, in addition to seving as head nurse at the Cardinal O'Connell home before moving to the Cape in 1975 to be near her Number One son.

But Mother's wonder boy lied when it suited his purposes. In August 2008, the ACLU won a court victory that compelled the DA to return Keith Amato's DNA sample. For nearly two years after McCowen's conviction, O'Keefe claimed that the sample had been destroyed by the state crime lab; then he changed his story, saying that the lab had been instructed to return it, then that the sample was shipped to State Police barracks in South Yarmouth, where it sat on a shelf for months when Amato failed to claim it. All hooey, just like the claims he made about 100 samples collected from others, who were represented by the ACLU in a follow-up suit.

Particularly galling for those who remembered was the op-ed piece the DA penned in response to a *USA Today* editorial criticizing his methods during the 2005 Truro sweep.

O'Keefe wrote: "Prosecutors and police perform the balancing test every day between individual rights and the right of citizens to be free of crime in their homes and neighborhoods . . . this balancing of rights is not an academic exercise but a real test where the consequence for being wrong is that a killer may go free or even worse, an innocent man may be convicted.

"While many have attempted to draw parallels to other perceived invasions of privacy, this geographically limited request is an investigative tool involving a small population for a defined purpose.

"In this instance it has been made clear to those who voluntarily participate that their sample, if unrelated to the case at hand, will be destroyed and not entered into any database."

His comments ignored the facts. In the course of the Truro sweep, Mason and his team used intimidation, pure and simple. Their spiel, delivered most often in public, urged men to give up their DNA "for Ava's sake," and when that failed, they made it clear that the nondonor's license-plate number would be placed on a "special list," subject to "special scrutiny," both now and in the future.

O'Keefe's detectives also secured DNA samples through more covert methods, plucking Coke cans and water bottles from trash bins and cigarette butts from ashtrays. Trial testimony established that a dozen locals were treated in this fashion, including painter Robert Bailey, Keith Amato's pal Gino Monteiro, and this author. Collecting "abandoned" items doesn't violate the law, but to what lengths would the DA go? When do the ends *not* justify the means? Mason asked me to autograph a recently published book of mine at a July 2002 Borders book signing in Hyannis; then, as his report shows, he sent the volume to the state crime lab to have my DNA "lifted" from the signature page. My palm, presumably, had left traces of sweat.

In the final analysis, the district attorney bears responsibility for these tactics, and it isn't a big jump to the broader issue that he lacked the capacity to appreciate reasonable doubt, to think dispassionately. His need for power, and the moral certitudes that fed that need, deprived him of any real semblance of balance, just as his anger predisposed him to see humankind as evil, predatory, and weak. The vast majority of people dragged into court, he believed, deserved to be there as if there might not be any question as to their guilt.

Despite his 1994 prosecutor of the year award, his Medal of Bravery as a Dennis cop, and even Bill Burke's characterization of him as "brilliant," O'Keefe's investigation of the Worthington murder, the number one case of his career, was doomed from the start. He was too narrow to focus on who Christa Worthington was—an ambitious, bright, unresolved woman who had gone through Vassar during the activist '70s; a freelance fashion writer who longed to become Virginia Woolf; the only child of a distant, alcoholic father and a mother who'd been unable to decide whether she was a wife or a person first; a single parent at age forty-three who would buy her beloved daughter only organic milk.

Instead, tough guy O'Keefe placed her in the world he understood, a world of hard angles. He decided that she'd brought on her death by having sex with her killer, who could be Tony Jackett, Tim Arnold, any of a half-dozen acquaintances—or was it a half-hundred? One caveat: the candidate could not be black. The idea of the highborn heiress taking an African-American lover was beyond him.

This was the man who'd greeted writer Maria Flook in his infamous towel, and Flook had all but burned him to the ground. Her revelations nearly cost him his career. He had to wrap up the case. Fast.

Characterizing the DA's management of the investigation, one source said, "It was, 'Let's shake those fucking people up over there, let 'em know we're here. Somebody's got to say something. Stay in their faces, do whatever you got to do. We know somebody's had sex with this broad. Get that guy's DNA any way you can!' . . . That kind of stuff has Michael's fingerprints all over it."

Were O'Keefe's methods illegal? Telephone taps require a court order; phone-records collection requires a court-approved subpoena tied to a grand-jury investigation or a pending case. Instead of securing judicial writs for the phone data, the O'Keefe office relied on formatted "request" letters; Verizon and Cingular were not obligated to provide the records, but they did, as O'Keefe expected. His warrantless demand was an abuse of prosecutorial power. More than several hundred pages of records were assembled that listed toll calls even from public defender Nicholas Grefe, the attorney McCowen tried to call from the MSP barracks the night of the arrest.

Detectives staged surprise visits to private homes at dawn or late in the evening, prompting comparisons to the Gestapo. During one such visit to the Hyannis-area residence of Catherine Cisneros' parents, Mason and Burke informed them that their daughter was "well rid" of McCowen, whom they promised to put away "forever." Likewise, they dropped in on McCowen pal Dave Amerault and Amerault's wife at dinnertime, then returned forty minutes later to see if the couple had "any afterthoughts." As with Cisneros, they left no doubt that they expected the Ameraults' "cooperation."

Except for strategic considerations, O'Keefe didn't seem concerned about the state crime lab, whose director was forced to resign after the lab mishandled twenty-seven samples from sexual-assault cases, then wrongly entered twelve samples into the national database CODEX. He dismissed the idea that lab foul-ups might bear on the defendant's guilt or innocence. *Globe* columnist Eileen McNamara wrote on April 17, 2005, "Flooding the crime lab with useless DNA samples would seem to have been a counterproductive strategy for a man who spent much of his press conference . . . complaining that the same overburdened laboratory had slowed his investigation."

Some suspected that the police polygraph tests were less than kosher and had been used essentially to clear people like Frazier. The press never mentioned that the tests were conducted by Massachusetts State Police technicians, not FBI operators, exams most shrewd defense lawyers would never allow their clients to take. A biased polygraph operator can tailor results by establishing misleading baselines: the subject is asked a series of "test" questions to establish his neurobiological thresholds; then answers to the "real" questions are measured against these ersatz parameters.

The Center for Public Integrity, an independent, nonadvocacy group dedicated to producing responsible investigative journalism on issues of public concern, reports that prosecutors in the nation's 2,341 jurisdictions have stretched, bent, or broken the rules in order to convict defendants in at least 2,013 cases since 1970. A plethora of literature, from a wide variety of organizations, makes the same point: cops lie more than we would like to admit.

Such misconduct has grown since September 11, 2001, to a degree that seems contrived. As al-Qaeda exacted a terrible toll on New York City, Washington, and Flight 93 in Pennsylvania, the Bush White House fed funds to American law-enforcement agencies at every level. Coupled with the administration's bellicose saber rattling ("Bring it on!"), the funding has endorsed a "proactive" police posture never seen before; low-ranking officers barely three years out of high school in towns like Truro were suddenly earning annual salaries in excess of $80,000, nearly half again more than teachers, and many assumed swaggers to match. The Cape's number one law-man, in his effort to "clear" the case, employed tactics that eroded the notion of justice. The trial stirred ugly race and class issues, leaving an acrid aftertaste. Middle-class white parents, the majority people of good will, felt compelled to tell their youngsters that the courts and the cops cannot be trusted and to explain the nature of race prejudice in America.

Among teenagers at Barnstable High and at Nauset Regional in Eastham, two of the Cape's largest secondary schools, investigators' tactics were the number one topic of discussion before, during, and after the trial. Students got the message: the ends justified the means, even if the means entailed warping the laws of the commonwealth and inciting racial bigotry.

The kids were better than adults in this respect, bonding with the defendant in a way that suggested that many of them might have had problems of their own with the cops and the courts. On the overpass that spans Orleans's Rock Harbor Road just before the turnoff to 2nd District Court (where McCowen was arraigned), one high school graffitist posted the message in two-foot block letters the week of the verdict: "Wu Did It!"

Were O'Keefe and his detectives unaware of the implications of letting the white guy "walk" while trying the black man, especially if both were at Christa's that night in January 2002, as investigators may well have known? Were they unaware of the route the jurors would likely travel, given ordinary American racial biases? And had they not sought to capitalize on those biases from the get-go, using peremp-tory challenges to bounce potential jurors from outlying areas such as Provincetown, statistically more open-minded than your typical Republican from Sandwich, Mashpee, and Falmouth? Tactically, they had seated the blond, ultrawhite Worthingtons cheek-on-jowl with the jury box, where day after day, the parties exchanged *gemütlich* eye contact and, yes, even whispers.

The prosecution and its supporters slammed reporters for "playing the race card." But the contrasts couldn't be ignored. O'Keefe exploited them every which way he could.

It might even be said that the DA's mishandling of the case mirrored the misconduct of the Sacco and Vanzetti prosecutor eighty-five years earlier, at least as Harvard law professor and future U.S. Supreme Court Justice Felix Frankfurter saw it, arguing, as he did at the time, for a retrial on the basis of bigotry and prosecutorial misconduct that included withholding evidence: "The powers of a district attorney under our laws are very extensive," Frankfurter wrote, almost clairvoyantly. "They affect to a high degree the liberty of the individual, the good order of society, and the safety of the community. His natural influence with the grand jury, and the confidence commonly reposed in his recommendations by judges, afford to the unscrupulous, the weak or the wicked incumbent of the office vast opportunity to oppress the innocent and to shield the guilty, to trouble his enemies and to protect his friends, and to make the interest of the public subservient to his personal desires, his individual ambitions, and his private advantage. . . ."

In the end, O'Keefe's legacy was irreparably damaged by the Mc-Cowen case. He permitted both his investigators and prosecutor to manipulate sworn statements and trample on the rights of the accused. He ordered McCowen arrested solely on the basis of a DNA match, then publicly proclaimed the case "solved," when McCowen could easily have been taken in for questioning, then more properly held on a lesser charge pending further investigation. The arrest and murder charge were precipitous. Both set the stage for what one Cape attorney called "the railroading of Chris McCowen," a farce that played out in the very Barnstable courtroom where, four years earlier, O'Keefe vowed to seek justice, fairly and squarely, surrounded by his cops and politico buddies singing "The Star Spangled Banner."

Reporter Dan Hamilton, who interviewed the DA after the controversial DNA sweep, said, "The guy felt that there was no one going to call him on anything, and that therefore if he makes a decision, that decision is right."

To which I say, good work if you can get it. As this book goes to press, a U.S. federal grand jury has been in session in Worcester, Massachusetts, for some eighteen months, investigating political payoffs and gambling operations on Cape Cod. The investigation is said to focus on Boston-area bookmakers; East Dennis marina owner and O'Keefe fundraiser Joe Buscone; Buscone's Milford business partner Johnny Pizzulo; Harwichport's James Peterson, whose now-defunct 400 Club on Route 28 was long recognized as a gathering place for Cape pols (including the late speaker of the U.S. House of Representatives, Thomas "Tip" O'Neill); restaurateur and convicted bookmaker Adam Hart; and Cape and Islands District Attorney Michael O'Keefe.

According to the *Boston Globe*, the investigation was initiated by Attorney General Martha Coakley in fall 2008 and "focused on the activities of several alleged members of a Cape Cod gambling ring. . . . But the focus shifted to O'Keefe early last year after a relative of Hart's made a comment on the wiretap that triggered concerns for investigators that the district attorney may have protected illegal gamblers in the past. . . .

"The name of a prominent former public official has also come up in the investigation: former lieutenant governor Thomas P. O'Neill III. Now a lobbyist on Beacon Hill and a friend of O'Keefe's, O'Neill, the son of the late U.S. House Speaker Thomas P. 'Tip' O'Neill Jr., was heard on a wiretap allegedly placing bets, said the source.

"Barnstable District Court Judge W. James O'Neill, speaking through his lawyer, and Joseph S. Buscone . . . have acknowledged testifying before the grand jury. . . . Buscone said he has known Hart, the Cape Cod restaurateur, for about 20 years and is 'very friendly with Mike O'Keefe.' Buscone and his wife have contributed $3,000 to O'Keefe's campaign war chest since 2005, according to records at the State Office of Campaign and Political Finance."

Initially, O'Keefe had "no comment" when called by a representative of the *Globe* who'd been tipped to the investigation. Like so much else on Cape Cod, it had become an open secret, turning on the allegation that the Cape Cod and Islands DA had received a call from Hart to discuss a pending case against the man's teenage grandson. With the publication of the *Globe* story, O'Keefe changed his tune, telling both the *Globe* and the *Cape Cod Times* that when he talked to the restaurateur-bookmaker in July 2008, he had no knowledge that Hart was under investigation, despite the fact that Hart pleaded guilty to a state gambling charge in 2001 and received one year of probation. "Any assertion of wrongdoing by me or my office is completely false," the DA said.

A week later, the *Globe* came back with more, reporting that O'Keefe "covered a bill of nearly $2,500" for District Court Judges Joseph J. Reardon and John M. Julian to attend a 2006 judicial training program in Las Vegas. Subsequently, Julian was moved off-Cape for ten months; Reardon was barred from sitting on criminal cases on the Cape for five months until he retired. "Although there is no indication that federal authorities are looking into O'Keefe's $2,459 payment . . . the arrangement raises fresh questions about the relationships between the district attorney and judges on the Cape."

Another testimonial to the DA's fine character, on June 26, 2009, only months before the start of the Worcester grand-jury investigation, Judge Richard Connon of Barnstable Superior Court ordered a continuance without a finding for docket 2008-112, effectively dropping all charges against this author after eighteen months of what many private Cape citizens, the New England ACLU, the Authors Guild, the Media Law Resource Center, and other national groups saw as O'Keefe's efforts to silence this book.

In the larger scheme of things, it was as if the McCowen trial cast a pall on almost all those involved. McCowen remained in prison, awaiting the SJC appeal. The younger generation of Worthingtons was in disarray, with Pam, Patricia, and Mary in the throes of separations and divorces, and even Amyra Chase, Ava's adoptive mother, was looking at the end of her marriage. Jan Worthington, still single after the cancer death of her fisherman husband in April 2006, continued to work the switchboard at the Truro police station, her film project dead and buried. Tim Arnold was a diminished man, closer to the grave than to any new romance. As for Tony Jackett, locals weren't so sure about Tony, even though his newly dominant wife was keeping him on a very short leash, as evidenced by his absence from Ptown's waterfront bars.

Ava, reportedly, was thriving. "She's a perfectly happy, well-adjusted nine-year-old. You'd never know . . ." said a Cohasset neighbor of Amyra's. But how could any youngster cope with the nightmare of January 4–6, 2002? Blood and violence were Ava's legacy—the shrieks, then the empty silence that stretched out for two days and nights while she was alone with her mother's incarnadine corpse. How could anyone say she was OK? Might she someday return to Truro and sit on the banks of the Pamet to bask in the roseate warmth of a May sunrise? Listen to the whip-poor-wills, or smell the sweet- ness of a gentle incoming tide? Frolic in the surf at Balston beach on an August afternoon with Truro's new summer elite that had never heard of Tiny Worthington until Christa's murder? Not likely. Only time, and time alone, would tell, but even then there might be no sure answer.

EPILOGUE

On May 7, 2010, the Christopher McCowen appeal was argued in the Supreme Judicial Court at the historic John Adams Courthouse in downtown Boston. Trial attorney Robert George, who had remained on board to handle the appellate proceedings despite the disappointments of the Barnstable verdict and post-trial motions, had filed a brief far in excess of the fifty-page maximum allowed by Court rules. He had many issues: the removal of Rachel Huffman from the deadlocked jury; the police failure to tape-record McCowen's interrogation as purportedly reflected in the twenty-seven-page statement; the exculpatory evidence withholding claims; the restraining order admissions; and of course the central issue of racial bias. Put together, there was more than enough here, George felt, for the high court to reverse, but the odds were extraordinarily against him; only five percent of homicide appeals get reversed in Massachusetts.

He also was not ignorant of the politics of such a reversal; how, within the tight, hermetic world of judges high and low, it would be seen as a betrayal of one of the Court's robed colleagues, not to say how such a ruling might shake the public's confidence in the courts.

The justices' tough and right-out-of-the-box questioning of George, who argued first, was at times intense, but so were the pointed inquiries directed to Julia K. Holler, the Assistant District Attorney arguing for the Barnstable County District Attorney's Office.

Margaret H. Marshall, the retiring Chief Justice, sat at the center of the five-member appellate panel, which included Judith A. Cowin, a former Assistant District Attorney, Harvard Law graduate and former Superior Court judge; Ralph D. Gants, also Harvard Law School and Law Review, as well as a former Superior Court compadre of trial judge Nickerson; Robert J. Cordy, another Harvard Law graduate and former head of the criminal division at the United States Attorney's Office; and Margot Botsford, another former Superior Court associate of Nickerson. Ominously perhaps, Associate Justice Roderick L. Ireland, the Court's only black judge, came up with a conflict on the case despite being scheduled to hear the arguments. Ireland would later be named as Marshall's replacement for Chief Justice by Governor Patrick in November 2010, while the case decision was still pending.

The hearing was over in a half hour. Then came the waiting for attorney George and his client.

The Massachusetts Supreme Court has a time standard of 130 days for decisions, but with the deadline looming on September 17, 2010, the justices extended the time indefinitely for McCowen in what could be seen as a good sign. Equally encouraging, there had recently been two murder case reversals, one resting on the Massachusetts crime lab reporting issue; the other, centering on police failure to tape-record. To make matters more intriguing, the appeals on both cases had been heard before the McCowen brief, meaning that there might be a likelihood of case-law carryover, not to say a sensitizing of the justices to the common issues. The clock was ticking down.

In the meantime, Ireland was appointed Chief Justice on December 8, 2010, with still no decision. Then, like a thunderbolt, the Court issued its opinion two days later on December 10, 2010. The decision brushed aside all the defense arguments in affirming not only the trial jury's verdict but also the denial of the post-trial motions.

The Court was unanimous, but Ireland wrote an oddly concurring opinion, acknowledging he was bothered by the superficiality of Nickerson's questioning of jurors on their alleged racial bias during deliberations, especially Marlo George's mockery of Roshena Bohanna's hairstyle, education, and behavior. Juror George's comments in the jury room had raised "the specter of racism, warranting closer examination," the Chief Justice wrote, adding that further examination by Nickerson might have demonstrated whether these comments were "simply small talk or indicative of implicit bias."

But no matter, in the end he went along with the majority in failing to undermine the verdict or Nickerson's judgment.

It was bad sociology, to be sure, not to say out-and-out PC bullshit, and one Boston-area attorney wrote me the next day, "the Justices aren't the best. Most of the very best don't want the job . . . As far as fawning to hizzoner, entirely predictable. I haven't read [the decision] yet but I'll bet there's dicta about his extraordinary effort to preserve the impartiality of the jury, etc."

Another, "I could not believe the SJC opinion . . . it appears that they put it on Bob George—i.e., he played the race card and it blew up? Great praise for that wise Judge Nickerson . . . blaaaah! Another ball-less decision from the once liberal ballsy bastion of appellate decisions that stood out nationwide!"

The praise for Nickerson was so voluminous as to suggest he was being canonized, and it showed just how masterfully he had played his hand, relying on the SJC's protocol of focusing on points of law while taking the lower court determination of fact as a given. A master questioner, Nickerson had gotten exactly the testimony on racial bias he'd wanted; likewise, thanks to his post-trial ruling that Jeremy Frazier's pocketknife wasn't comparable to the knife that killed Christa, George's exculpatory evidence appeal was tossed, also. Why had he set things up so? Judging from the way Nickerson had addressed McCowen after the verdict, the huge disparity in his tone before and after, probably because he personally believed the defendant was guilty, and also because he wasn't going to throw two good, career-minded cops like Mason and Burke under the bus.

O'Keefe he didn't seem to care about. But Mason and Burke, especially Mason, well, in the future there were going to be other cases on the Cape where genuinely bad, dangerous people were going to have to be brought in and tried before they did bad upon bad, disfiguring the community even more than they'd done already.

It was his Cape and he was going to take care of it, pure and simple.

George had been in California, watching his eldest daughter join the bar, when the court announced its decision. The *Boston Globe* quoted him, saying, "I can tell you, it's not over," as he promised to file in federal court by the end of the next week for a new trial based on the racial allegations. Three days later, back in Boston, he made the hour's drive west to the Baranowski-Souza prison to explain to his client what was to come next, the long haul that yet awaited them.

NOTES

3   "The normally staid *New York Times*": Charlie Savage, "F.B.I. Violated Rules in Obtaining Phoned Records, Report Says," *New York Times*, 01/21/10, p. A23. Cf. "Judge Rules Bush-Era Wiretapping Effort Was Illegal," AP, 04/01/10. Also, "The Eavesdropping Continues," *New York Times* editorial, 06/17/09; James Risen and Eric Lichtblau, "E-Mail Surveillance Renews Concerns in Congress," *New York Times*, 06/17/09; Leslie Cauley, "NSA Has Massive Database of Americans' Phone Calls," *USA Today*, 05/11/06; Electronic Frontier Foundation, www.eff.org, "The wellspring of recent domestic police misconduct is, undoubtedly, due to the Bush administration's belief that the Constitution's protection against unreasonable search and seizure did not apply to its efforts to protect against terrorism, i.e., the infamous Yoo memo of October 2001." Cf. Pamela Hess and Lara Jakes Jordan, "Memo Justified Warrantless Surveillance," AP, 04/02/08; Larry Neumeister, "ACLU: Military Skirting Law to Spy," AP, 04/02/08; *New York Times* editorial, "There Were Orders to Follow," 04/04/08.

3   "the ACLU, the Innocence Project in New York City": cf. Jon B. Gould, *The Innocence Commission: Preventing Wrongful Convictions and Restoring the Criminal Justice System* (New York: New York University Press, 2008). ACLU, *Fighting Police Abuse: A Community Action Manual*, Ira Glasser, ed., 12/01/97. Ryan Gallagher, "Study: Police Abuse Goes Unpunished," Chicago: Medill Reports, Northwestern University, 04/04/07. Kevin Johnson, "Police Brutality Cases on Rise since 9/11," *USA Today*, 12/17/07. "In the Shadows of the War on Terror: Persistent Police Brutality and Abuse of People of Color in the United States," United Nations Committee on the Elimination of Racial Discrimination, December 2007 ("Systematic abuse of people of color by law enforcement officers has not only

continued since 2001 but has worsened in both practice and severity. According to a representative of the NAACP, the degree to which police brutality occurs . . . 'is the worst I've seen in 50 years' ").

4 "The file showed . . . my own phone records had been grabbed without a subpoena": Office of District Attorney/Cape and Islands District, Verizon New England letter of 01/07/02, requesting 12/31/01–01/06/02 toll call records for nos. 508-487-37--, 508-349-39--, 781-335-10--, 508-487-7707, 508-349-51--, 508-349-26--, 508-487-1402, signed "Michael O'Keefe." Cf. additional request letters, discovery items 293, 295, 298, 305, 307, 320, 372.

4 "My DNA was snatched": MSP (Tpr. Christopher S. Mason), conversation with Peter Manso in Hyannis on 07/25/02 re Worthington Homicide ("This officer selected a copy of Manso's book, pulling the book from the middle of a stack of books available for purchase. This officer then asked Manso for a lengthy inscription on the title page. . . . This officer then secured the book in paper packaging for possible future examination by the Massachusetts State Police crime lab").

5 "The ACLU and the *Boston Globe* called": Emily C. Dooley and Eric Williams, "DNA Sweep Bogus in Truro," *Cape Cod Times*, 01/06/05 ("Police say it's a voluntary thing, but they will take note of the dissenters. 'We have an awareness of the people who fail to consent,' Mason said"). Eric Williams, "ACLU Wants End to Truro Testing," *Cape Cod Times*, 01/11/05 (" 'This is a particularly insidious form of coercion . . .' Carole Rose, executive director of the Massachusetts chapter, said.") "ACLU of Massachusetts Calls for End to DNA Dragnet," ACLU news release, 01/10/05 (www.aclu.org/privacy/medical/1576/prs 20050110 html); also, ACLU of Massachusetts letter to police, www.aclu-Mass.org/Truro%20DNA%20 Letter%201-10-05.pdf. Eileen McNamara, "Flunking the Swab Test," *Boston Globe*, 01/09/05 ("Most problematic is O'Keefe's assertion that investigators will be compelled to look at why 'a man would choose not to cooperate with the police' "). Cf. Pam Belluck, "To Try to Net a Killer, Police Ask a Small Town's Men for DNA," *New York Times*, 01/10/05. Mac Daniel, "DNA Testing Troubles Some in Truro," *Boston Globe*, 01/11/05. *Boston Globe* editorial, "Suspicious Minds," 01/11/05 ("Civil Libertarians from the American Civil Liberties Union are right to call for an end to the practice. The DNA dragnet is both an abuse of power and an affront to the spirit of the Cape Cod community"). Mike Barnacle, "Truro Men Have Right to Keep Mouths Shut," *Boston Herald*, 01/11/05. Amanda Ripley et al., "The DNA Dragnet: To Find a Killer, a Town Asks All Its Men to Give a Sample. Savvy Policing or Invasion of Privacy?" *Time*, 01/16/05.

5 "the director of the Massachusetts State Police crime lab was discharged": Jonathan Salzman, "US Audit Found More Problems at Crime Lab," *Boston Globe*, 02/01/07. Jonathan Salzman, "Crime Lab Botched 27 DNA

Results," *Boston Globe*, 02/14/07. "More DNA Cases Mishandled by Lab," AP, 02/21/07. David E. Frank, "Lawyer Challenges DNA Evidence in Wake of Crime Lab Mistakes," *Massachusetts Lawyers Weekly*, 02/23/07. "Administrator Given Most of the Blame," www.thebostonchannel.com, 03/18/07.

5   "nadir of police misconduct": MSP (Mason) Report of Investigation, 12/10/02. This blood collection, conducted with neither permission from next of kin nor judicial oversight of any kind, is another example of police overreaching, brought about, presumably, by Girard Smith's refusal to adopt investigators' version of who killed Christa, and when. This was not only a Fifth Amendment violation, however. The United States Supreme Court has held that drawing blood, even from a dead person, to obtain a DNA sample clearly constitutes a search that triggers the protections of the Fourth Amendment. Cf. *Skinner v. Railway Labor Executives' Assn.*, 489 U.S. 602 (1989); *California v. Greenwood*, 486 U.S. 35 (1988).

6   "OxyContin-fueled lifestyles": Doug Fraser, "Quest for OxyContin Fuels Cape Crime," *Cape Cod Times*, 03/07/10. K. C. Myers, "Yarmouth Police Secure 29,100 Pills," *Cape Cod Times*, 12/13/09. Stephanie Vosk, "Dead at 16: Cape Cod Juvenile Crime," *Cape Cod Times*, 12/13/09. Stephanie Vosk, "Younger and Twice as Violent," *Cape Cod Times*, 12/14/09. Cf. "State Estimates of Substance Abuse from 2005–2006, National Surveys on Drug Use and Health," Dept. of Health and Human Services, Substance Abuse and Mental Health Services Administration (http://samusa.gov).

13   "As Henry David Thoreau once observed": Thoreau, *Cape Cod* (New York: Penguin Books, 1987), p. 318.

13   "Just outside the kitchen of the bungalow": Details of 50 Depot Road crime scene drawn from MSP Crime Scene Services Section sketch, case 02-102-0007/07-06-02; MSP Report of Investigation (Tpr. James M. Massari), 02/20/02; MSP Crime Scene Reports, 02/05/02, 02/07/02, 07/09/02; MSP Criminalistics Reports, 01/06/02, 02/04/02; Postmortem Examination Report, Office of Chief Medical Examiner (Pathologist James Weiner, M.D.), 02/07/02. Also, MSP (Sgt. Robert J. Knott, Jr.) ints. of Tim Arnold, 01/06/02, 01/07/02, 01/09/02; Robert Arnold, 01/06/02; MSP (Tpr. Kimberly A. Squier) ints. of fire rescue personnel, 01/10/02; Truro Fire Dept. Incident Report with narratives (Officer in Charge Captain Leo Childs), 01/07/02; MSP (Tpr. Carol Harding) ints. of rescue personnel regarding Worthington homicide, 01/09/02.

14   "The little girl who owned the toys": MSP (Sgt. Robert J. Knott, Jr.) Investigation Reports, 01/25/02, 02/05/02; Truro PD (Sgt. David J. Costa) Incident Report, 06/11/02. Also, Ellen Barry and John Ellement, "Friends Say Truro Victim Lived No Ordinary Life," *Boston Globe*, 01/09/02; Todd

Venezia, "Slay-Tot Tug-of-Love," *New York Post*, 09/11/02; Susan Schindehette, "Death on the Cape," *People*, 01/28/02; Ellen Barry, "Murder on the Cape," *Boston Globe*, 01/20/02; Vanessa Grigoriadis, "The Single-Mom Murder," *New York*, 01/28/02; Alex Kuczynski, "A Murder in Cape Jolts the Fashion World," *New York Times*, 01/13/02.

15 "she gave up on the juice for the familiarity of her mother's nipple": Tim Arnold testimony, trial trans.; MSP (Knott) int. of Tim Arnold, 01/06/02. Cf. Franci Richardson and Jessica Heslem, "Cape Fear; Cops Hunt Killer in Brutal Slaying of Truro Mom," *Boston Herald*, 01/08/02.

15 "Since his brain surgery seven months earlier": MSP (Knott) int. of Tim Arnold, 01/06/02; background info on Tim Arnold, 02/05/02; MSP (Tpr. Christopher Mason) int. of Tim Arnold, 06/13/02.

16 "'There is such an ache where she and Ava used to be . . . so caustic, on the attack'": Tim Arnold journal; also, trial trans.

16 "As they slowed": MSP (Knott) ints. of Tim Arnold, 01/06/02, 02/05/02; MSP (Mason) ints. of Tim Arnold 06/13/02, 04/18/03; MSP (Knott) int. of Bob Arnold, 01/06/02. Region V, Standard Ambulance Report (Lisa Silva, Jeff Francis), 01/06/02.

18 "The right side of the young woman's face": injury description drawn from Postmortem Examination Report (Office of the Chief Medical Examiner, Pathologist Weiner), 01/07/02.

18 "Meanwhile, Christa's cousin Jan Worthington": MSP (Mason) ints. of Jan Worthington, 01/06/02, 01/09/02.

19 "Francis was the first official responder to step inside": Truro Fire Dept. Incident Report with notations (Childs), 01/07/02; Region V, Standard Ambulance Report (Silva, Francis), 01/06/02; MSP (Tpr. Julie A. Sabota) int. of Leo Childs, 01/10/02; MSP (Squier) ints. of fire rescue personnel, 02/15/02.

20 "'Anybody who says she didn't'": Author int. of George Malloy, 11/07/07.

22 "People who knew Christa": Author ints. of Victoria Balfour, 06/04/09; Leila Levinson, 06/23/09; Warren Roderick, 10/28/06; E. J. Kahn III, 07/09/06; Anthony Jackett (15 ints.), 03/07/00–03/23/01. MSP (Mason) ints. of Jan Worthington, 01/06/02, 01/09/02; John Worthington, 01/06/02, 01/09/02, Lucinda Worthington, 01/06/03, 01/09/02; Francine Randolph, 01/06/02; Pam and Ted Franklin, 04/08/02; Ethan and Natalie Cohn, 01/08/02; Melik Kaylan, 01/08/02; Christopher Worthington, 01/06/02, 01/07/02, 01/14/02; Diana Worthington, 01/23/02, 08/19/02; Martha Ingram, 01/19/02, et al. Also, Maria Flook, *Invisible Eden: A Story of Love and Murder on Cape Cod* (New York: Broadway, 2003); Leila Levinson, "Remembering Christa Worthington," *Vassar Alumnae Quarterly*, Winter 2003.

22 "The media would portray": Cf. K. C. Myers and Emily C. Dooley, "A Small-town Family," *Cape Cod Times*, 01/13/02; Barry and Ellement, "No

Ordinary Life"; Jessica Heslam and Franci Richardson, "Cape Victim Was Brilliant Writer, Doting Mom," *Boston Herald*, 01/09/02; Sally Jacobs, "An Open Case," *Boston Globe*, 12/10/02; Kuczynski, "Murder Jolts Fashion World"; Emily C. Dooley, "Unresolved: The Christa Worthington Case One Year Later," *Cape Cod Times*, 01/05/03.

22 "After a string of affairs": MSP (Sgt. William Burke) ints. of Kerry Radlaver, 08/05/02; Richard Blakeley, 04/07/02; Pam and Ted Franklin, 04/08/02; Pam Worthington Franklin, 01/06/02; Jan Worthington, 01/06/02, 01/09/02; Lucinda Worthington, 01/06/02, 01/09/02.

23 "Close friend Leila Levinson had seen": Author int. of Leila Levinson, 06/10/09. Cf. Levinson's "Remembering Christa Worthington," *Vassar Alumnae Quarterly*, Winter 2003, for what remains the most movingly forthright portrait of Christa in print.

23 "And Tiny's affairs were not always discreet": Author ints. of multiple locals insisting on anonymity, 09/28/06, 08/12/07, 06/11/06, as well as Lloyd Rose, 07/19/06; E. J. Kahn III, 07/19/06; George Bryant, 04/10/06; Flook, p. 19.

23 "Ben Brantley, nowadays the *New York Times* drama critic": MSP (Burke) int. of Ben Brantley, 08/05/02.

23 "While in Europe": Flook, pp. 24–25, 202, 208, 247–50, 253. MSP (Burke) int. of Ben Brantley, 08/05/02.

24 "The next man in her life was": Christa Worthington diary, n.p. Flook, pp. 96–97, 288–98. MSP (Burke) int. of Kerry Radlauer, 08/05/02. MSP (Mason) int. of Thomas C. Churchwell, 08/05/02.

26 "Christa had barely unpacked when": Author int. of Warren Roderick, 09/30/06.

26 "Married for twenty-seven years and the father of six, Tony was nonetheless": Not only was Jackett known as a philanderer, but Christa herself spoke of his wanderlust, expressing concern that he was "two-timing" her as well as his wife. Cf. MSP (Mason) int. of Sharon Ferrito, 02/07/02 ("Ferrito said that she recalled Christa telling her that Jackett had been involved in 'many' affairs and that Jackett had continued to have affairs after he left Christa. Ferrito said that Christa explained to her, 'This summer I'm his fling'"). Also, MSP (Burke) int. of Ben Brantley, 08/05/02 ("Brantley stated Christa was worried about Tony fooling around on her"). Jackett was, in fact, so bold that at the point he felt he needed to distance himself from Christa and their child, he instructed intermediary Warren Roderick to "fix Christa up with other men in town." Then, when no suitable candidates could be identified, Tony, according to the harbormaster, asked Roderick to "lay it on her about his philandering." Roderick stated that he "told Christa that she was but one of many women Tony had affairs with, and Roderick stated that Christa was devastated." MSP (Mason) int. of Warren Roderick, 04/30/02. In the

same interview, "Roderick stated that he had heard from Tony about a Provincetown girl named Wendy who Tony had slept with." Jackett, on the record, spoke of his peccadilloes for Peter Manso, *Ptown: Art, Sex and Money on the Outer Cape,* saying (pp. 227–28), "I always had that feeling of guilt and I never wanted to hurt my wife. But I wanted to have my cake and eat it, too. I got away with it for a long time. . . . My romances have always been something of a little game—you know that little game? You see somebody, who's that?"

26 "Another old Vassar friend": Author int. of Victoria Balfour, 06/04/09.

26 "Christa's affair with Jackett continued": Manso, pp. 226–32. Hurt by Tony's abandonment of her and their child, Christa was not beyond self-interest and games of her own, including drafting her letter to Jackett's wife, Susan, that was never sent. The letter, which the trial jury was not exposed to, shows a side of the case insufficiently explored.

27 "The Worthingtons, like other staunch Yankee families": Worthington family background drawn from author ints. of E. J. Kahn III, 07/09/06; Valerie Falk, 02/25/07; anon. Truro old-timer, 09/28/06; Warren Roderick, 09/30/06; Marilyn Miller, 10/15/06, 01/03/07; Gerry and Marietta Hermanson, 09/29/06; George Bryant, 01/29/08; Lloyd Rose, 07/16/06; Malcolm Preston, 06/11/06; Joel Grozier, 08/12/07, 10/07/07. Also, Richard F. Whalen, *Truro: The Story of a Cape Cod Town* (Charleston, S.C.: History Press, 2007); Susan W. Brennan and Diana Worthington, *Images of America* (Charleston S.C.: Arcadia, 2002); Flook, pp. 18–19, 158–67; Myers, "A Small-town Family"; E. J. Kahn, "Images, Tiny Worthington," *Provincetown Advocate,* 06/24/68; John C. Worthington obituary, *Provincetown Advocate,* 12/26/88; Tiny Worthington obituary, *Provincetown Advocate,* 04/20/89; Ada Elizabeth and John C. Worthington Papers, Arthur and Elizabeth Schlesinger Library, Radcliffe Institute for Advanced Studies, Harvard University, call MC507 ("Papers of Ada E. Worthington, founder of Cape Cod Fish Net Industries, and her husband, John C. Worthington, oil driller, pilot, and general manager of Pond Village Cold Storage Company"); "Conservation Use Found for Netting, Saving Paper," *Provincetown Advocate,* 02/26/42; Margaret Worthington obituary, "Honored Activist Was Longtime Truro Summer Resident," *Provincetown Banner,* 01/03/02. Town of Truro Assessor's Office, Tax Collector forms, Truro Town Hall; Trust Certificate, doc. 970489 (Christa Worthington Revocable Levy Trust Agreement dated Nov. 14, 2001), and various Worthington family members. Quitclaim Deeds, Barnstable Land Court Registry.

28 "she became the family spokesperson": Todd Venezia, "Fashion Writer Slay Mystery Fitting for TV," *New York Post,* 07/29/02. Jared Stearns, "Film Underway on Writer's Slaying," *Boston Globe,* 03/21/04. Franci Richardson, "HBO Takes Up Truro Murder," *Boston Herald,* 03/21/04.

29   "lost their second, more modest place to foreclosure in spring 2007": "Notice of Mortgagee's Sale of Real Estate," *Provincetown Banner*, 04/15/07.

29   "Patricia, the youngest": Author int. of E. J. Kahn III; also Michael Iacuessa, "Benefit Saturday as Popular Goat Recovers," *Provincetown Banner*, 10/20/05.

30   "Police knew Jackett had engaged in other affairs before and during the time": MSP (Burke) int. of Warren J. Roderick, 04/30/02. MSP (Squier) int. of Katherine Izzo, 02/13/02. Author ints. of Anthony Jackett; Warren J. Roderick, 10/28/06; Keith Amato, 09/04/06, 10/28/06, 11/21/06, 12/02/06, 02/25/07, 03/30/07; MSP Lt. Robert Melia, 01/27/01. MSP (Squier) int. of Ethan Cohen, 01/08/02 ("On January 10, 2002, this officer received a phone call from Ethan in regards to a television interview with the Jacketts. . . . Ethan stated Tony had been with many women. Ethan said, in his opinion, the reason the Jacketts embraced the child was to stop the lawsuit"). Also, MSP (Mason) int. of Jan Worthington, 01/06/02 (Jan stated that Jackett has a reputation for 'sleeping around'").

30   "he'd bungled a big Colombia-Ptown dope run": Manso, pp. 80, 159–77, 225, 231–32. Flook, 225–26. Author int. of MSP Lt. Melia, 01/27/01. Cf. Comm. of Mass. Criminal History Systems Board, Persons Chart Summary: Anthony Jackett, DOB 03/18/50.

30   "The examiner's four-page report concluded": Cf. "Report of the Polygraph Examination of Anthony Jackett," 01/11/02, Christopher J. Dolan, 0910, Polygraph Examiner, MSP; observer Tpr. J. Sabota.

30   "'Read this: The unexamined life'": Diary of Christa Worthington, n.p.

30   "Police knew Susan served": Cf. "Report of the Polygraph Examination of Susan Jackett," 01/22/02, Christopher J. Dolan, 0910, Polygraph Examiner, MSP; observer Tpr. J. Sabota.

31   "as Christa (and her lawyer) pressed him for support and health insurance": MSP (Mason) ints. of Tony Jackett, 01/06/02; Keith Amato, 02/06/02, 06/13/02. MSP (Squier) ints. of Ethan and Natalie Cohen, 01/08/02; Steve F. Minninger, 04/02/02, 10/03/02; Melik Kaylan, 01/08/02. MSP (Burke) int. of Pamela Worthington Franklin, 01/06/02. MSP (Sabota) int. of Ellen Webb, 01/08/02.

31   "At High Toss Pizza, where he frequently": MSP (Mason) int. of Ralph Pechukas, 03/29/02.

31   "In their profile of Arnold, police noted": MSP (Knott, Jr.) int. of Tim Arnold, 02/05/02 ("Mr. Arnold stated he was diagnosed ADD as an adult. He stated he is currently on medications as follows: Effexor 125 mg. for depression taken daily, Remeron 75 mg. taken at night. . . . Mr. Arnold stated that he sees Dr. Vance in Provincetown and has been treated for depression. . . . He stated he also sees a therapist at South Bay Mental Health in Yarmouth, MA").

31 "He had been married for twelve years": Comm. of Mass. Probate and Family Court Dept., Worcester Division, docket 98DR2279DU1, "Judgment of Divorce," 10/31/98; Comm. of Mass., Record of Marriage, Timothy Arnold and Elise Anne Paradis, Andover, MA, 06/23/85. Tim Arnold vita ("Education," "Employment," "Publications," "References," through 1998).

32 "'We drove each other crazy'": MSP (Mason) int. of Tim Arnold, 06/13/02; trial trans.

32 "Christa had complained to Vassar classmate Sharon Ferrito": MSP (Mason) int. of Ferrito, 02/07/02.

33 "on Friday morning, January 4, Tim": MSP (Knott) ints. of Tim Arnold, 01/06/02, 01/09/02.

33 "In June, Detective Mason": MSP (Mason) int. of Tim Arnold, 06/13/02.

33 "after Thanksgiving, he'd left seven consecutive, increasingly whiny messages": MSP (Mason) review of telephone (508-349-61--) answering-machine tape in study of 50 Depot Rd., Truro, Christa Worthington residence (side 2 counter 0080; side 1 counter 0000).

34 "'I asked Arnold what, if anything'": MSP (Mason) int. of Tim Arnold, 06/13/02.

34 "Arnold telephoned Detective Bill Burke": MSP (Mason) int. of Tim Arnold, 06/13/02.

34 "'I do want this to be solved'": Tim Arnold journal, n.p.

35 "his therapist came to believe he was suicidal": MSP (Knott) information on Tim Arnold (Report), 02/05/02. MSP (Mason) int. of Tim Arnold, 01/18/03.

35 "the next day, Mason and Burke": MSP (Mason) int. of Tim Arnold, 01/18/03.

35 "But Christa's father . . . would all fail the same exam": MSP Report of Polygraph Examinations: Elizabeth Porter, 01/14/02; Edward L. Hall, 01/11/02; Christopher H. Worthington, 01/15/02 (all exams administered by Christopher J. Dolan, 0910, Polygraph Examiner, MSP; Tpr. J. Sabota, observer).

35 "had married outside": Flook, 158–67. MSP (Mason) ints. of John Worthington, 01/09/02; Pam and Ted Franklin, 04/08/02. MSP (Burke) int. of Ted Franklin, 01/06/02. MSP (Mason) int. of Lucinda Worthington, 01/09/02 ("When asked to describe Christopher Worthington, Lucinda described him as 'weird.' Lucinda stated that Christopher had been an alcoholic for many years when Christa was younger. Lucinda stated that both Gloria Worthington and Christa had 'difficult' relationships with Christopher. Lucinda stated that Christopher had been a lawyer in the State Attorney General's Office and left after the Bellotti administration. Lucinda stated that Christoper receives a state pension. Lucinda stated that Christopher bought an insurance company and after

that worked as a bike courier in Boston. Lucinda stated that Christopher served in the service in Japan and married Gloria when she was three months pregnant with Christa. . . . Lucinda stated that Christa was always arguing with Christopher and even Gloria about money management. . . . When asked if she had anything to add with regards to Tony Jackett, Lucinda said that she had heard that Tony was still cheating on Susan").

36   "Toppy had a succession of girlfriends and at times drank heavily": Flook, p. 163. MSP (Mason) int. of Lucinda Worthington, 01/09/02. MSP (Squier) int. of Dr. John Livingston, 01/10/02. Letter received by *Cape Cod Times* reporter Karen Jeffrey and turned over to MSP (Mason), 08/13/02. MSP (Mason) int. of John Worthington, 01/09/02. Author ints. of Leila Levinson, 06/23/09, and Victor Balfour, 06/20/09.

36   "private practitioner to become a bicycle courier": Flook, p. 163. MSP (Mason) int. of Lucinda Worthington, 01/09/02. Author int. of E. J. Kahn III, 07/25/07.

36   "Christa told friends in New York and Truro that she was afraid her father was": Truro PD (Sgt. David Costa) ints. of Linda Miner, 05/15/02; Melik Kaylan and Angela Marianie, 06/11/02; Jean Louise Doublet, 6/11/02. MSP (Squier) ints. of Dr. John Livingston, 01/10/02; Steve F. Minninger (Christa Worthington's financial advisor), 04/02/02.

36   "the funds wire-transferred . . . had introduced him as her 'gay' black friend who was studying to be a nurse": MSP (Mason) int. of Elizabeth J. Porter, 01/16/02. Weymouth PD Incident Report, "911—15 Castle Road, East Weymouth, MA. Medical Assist," 02/01/02. Boston PD arrest booking form, "Porter, Elizabeth," incident 98607292, 01/15/02. MSP (Mason) ints. of Eddie Hall, 01/10/02; Elizabeth J. Porter, 01/09/02; Warren J. Roderick, 04/30/02; Janet Lamprey, 01/13/02. Comm. of Mass. Criminal History Systems Board re Joanne A. Lamprey a.k.a. Joanna A. Lamprey, CJCS 945302, 01/13/03, 0922. Christopher and Christa Worthington documents from Financial Perspectives, 164 Canal St., Boston. Also, MSP (Sabota) int. of Ellen Webb, 01/08/02; MSP (Mason) ints. of Susan Worthington Brennan and Jan Worthington, 01/07/02.

37   "Toppy replied no, he simply": MSP (Burke) int. of Christopher Worthington, 01/06/02.

37   "No one had told him": MSP (Burke) int. of Christopher Worthington, 01/06/02.

37   "What Toppy failed to mention": MSP (Burke) int. of Pamela Worthington Franklin, 01/06/02. MSP (Mason) int. of Lucinda Worthington, 01/06/02. MSP (Squier) int. of Francine Randolph, 01/06/02. MSP (Mason) int. of Pam and Ted Franklin, 04/08/02 ("both Pam and Ted Franklin stated that Christa was obsessed with personal financial matters and money. They indicated that although Christa was given properties in Truro by her father she was concerned about having enough money for

the future and for Ava"). MSP (Burke) int. of Melik Kaylan, 08/05/03. MSP (Massari) ints. of Susan Brennan and Jan Worthington, 01/07/02 ("Christa had first mentioned about hiring a private investigator three years ago"). Cf. Jessica Heslam, "Finances May Provide Clue in Worthington Murder Case," *Boston Herald*, 01/20/02.

37 "'It is the opinion of this examiner'": MSP Report of Polygraph of Elizabeth Porter, 01/14/02.

38 "when police found her and Hall": Boston PD Arrest Booking Form, Report Date 01/15/02, District 02, UCR Code 1842, Elizabeth Porter, Booking 02-00134-02, Incident 98607292, CR 9459-98. MSP (Mason) consent search of 3 Cottage Ave., #4, Quincy, MA on 01/15/02. Cf. Andrea Estes, "Woman Tied to Truro Case Back in Court," *Boston Globe*, 01/17/02. Jose Martinez, "Truro Slay Suspect in Court," *Boston Herald*, 01/16/02.

38 "provided Mason with a more accurate version": MSP (Mason) int. of Elizabeth J. Porter, 01/16/02.

39 "Porter was now hot news": Ellen Barry and Janelle Meut, "Greineder Ex-Escort Is Tied to Truro Case," *Boston Globe*, 01/15/02. Tom Farmer and Franci Richardson, "Wellesley Doc's Hooker Tied to Truro Slay Case," *Boston Herald*, 01/15/02. Todd Venezia, "Shock Twist in Fashion-Writer Murder Case," *New York Post*, 01/16/02. John Ellement and Ellen Barry, "Woman Tied to Truro Case under Arrest," *Boston Globe*, 01/16/02. Estes, "Woman Tied to Truro Case." MSP Detectives, Cape and Islands District, consent to search form (3 Cottage Ave., #4), signed Elizabeth Hall, witnessed Christopher Worthington. Dept. of State Police, South Yarmouth, MA, receipt of seized property (one Compaq computer, one set of keys, one telephone answering machine), witnessed Tpr. Mason, 02/05/02.

40 "Their morning meetings involved the exchange of oral sex for money": MSP (Mason) ints. of Eddie Hall, 01/10/02; Edward Hall, 01/24/02.

40 "Both the *Globe* and the *Herald*": Barry and Ellement, "Greineder Ex-Escort." Farmer and Richardson, "Wellesley Doc's Hooker." Ellement and Barry, "Woman Tied to Truro Case." Jose Martinez, Tom Farmer, and Jessica Heslam, "Ex-Hooker Eyed in Truro Killing," *Boston Herald*, 01/16/02. Jose Martinez and Jessica Heslam, "Link between Dad, Ex-Hooker Confirmed," *Boston Herald*, 01/17/02. Cf. MSP (Mason) int. of Eddie Hall, 01/10/02.

41 "The big news was": MSP Report of Polygraph Examination of Christopher H. Worthington, 01/15/02, Christopher J. Dolan, Polygraph Examiner, MSP, witnessed Tpr. Sabota.

41 "Their exchanges were": MSP (Massari) int. of Christopher Worthington, 01/14/02.

42 "On January 29, she defaulted": "Woman in Investigation Is Sought," *Bos-

ton Globe, 01/30/02. "Former Prostitute Turns Herself In," *Boston Globe*, 01/31/02.

42   "The next day, paramedics and police responded": Weymouth PD Incident Report I0202264, 02/01/02: "911—15 Castle Road, East Weymouth. Caller's info: Worthington, C.H.; Vic/off: Porter, Elizabeth J., DOB 05/01/1972. Reported as: Medical Assist; found as: Drug Violation."

42   "'He showed me three hypodermic needles'": Weymouth PD Incident Report I0202264, Francis J. Beatrice narr., 02/02/02, p. 1.

42   "Back on the Cape, Keith Amato": MSP (Burke) int. of Ted Franklin, 01/06/02. MSP (Mason) ints. of Pam and Ted Franklin, 04/08/02; Braunwyn Jackett, 03/28/02; Steve Parlaute, 02/26/04. MSP (Tpr. Carol Harding) ints. of Vanessa Vartabedian, 02/26/02; Eugene Monteiro, 02/26/02. MSP (Squier) int. of Jessica Kode-Wingate, 02/28/02. MSP (Tpr. Richard W. Cosgrove) int. of Frederick Simonin, 02/27/02. MSP (Massari) int. of Diana Worthington, 01/23/02.

42   "The Amato marriage was rocky": MSP (Mason) ints. of Susan Jackett, 03/05/02; Braunwyn Jackett, 03/28/02; Luke Jackett, 03/29/02; India Conklin, 03/29/02; Keith Amato, 06/13/02. MSP (Cosgrove) int. of Frederick Simonier, 02/27/02. Author ints. of Keith Amato, 10/22/06, 10/28/06, 12/02/06, 02/25/07.

42   "The idea was buttressed by": MSP (Massari) ints. of Diana Worthington, 01/23/02, 08/19/02. Author int. of Pam Worthington Franklin, 01/20/02.

43   "and was busted for felony cocaine possession. . . . Outside, he vomited in the bushes": Author ints. of Keith Amato. MSP (Sabota) int. of Keith J. Amato, 01/23/02. MSP (Mason) ints. of Keith Amato, 02/06/02, 06/13/02.

45   "the prescription painkiller OxyContin": Author ints. of anon., 05/05/06; anon. II, 08/11/09; anon. III, 12/04/07; anon. IV, 11/11/06.

45   "According to the U.S. Department of Health": Massachusetts ranked fourth": Cf. "State Estimates of Substance Use from 2005–2006, National Surveys on Drug Use and Health," Arthur Hughes et al., Dept. of Health and Human Services, Substance Abuse and Mental Health Services Administration, Office of Applied Studies, DHHS Publication SMA 08-4311, NSDUH series H-33, Rockville, Md., Feb. 2008, pp. 20–35, 41–45. Also, Patrick Cassidy, "Cape Drug Deaths Follow Grim Trend," *Cape Cod Times*, 11/20/07; SustainCapeCod.org, "Health Risks: Social ("Because much of the crime committed on Cape Cod is drug-related . . ."); "Crime in Massachusetts, 2004–2005," Commonwealth Fusin Center, Nov. 2006; "Crime by County, 45 Years of Massachusetts Crime Data (1960–2005)"; U.S. Census Bureau, Barnstable County, Mass. "Demographic Profiles, Highlights"; Vosk, "Younger and Twice as Violent." Cf. Keith O'Brien, "A

Short Life in the Cape's Underside," *Boston Globe*, 01/12/09 ("Cape Cod, with its pristine beaches and ocean views, is known as a summertime playground for the masses and a haven for the rich and famous. Yachts and second homes are commonplace here—and so are big names. Jordan Mendes grew up just 2 miles from the Kennedy compound in Hyannis Port. But Mendes's gruesome killing ['shot, stabbed, dumped into a shallow hole, and set afire']—which police say was carried out by his 13-year-old half-brother, Mykel Mendes, another 13-year-old, and 20-year-old Robert B. Vacher—pulled back the curtain on a dark corner of paradise, revealing a world of drugs, violence and crime handed down from father to son"). Cf. Brian Fraga, "OxyContin: 'A Rocket Ship to Heroin,'" *Cape Cod Times*, 11/07/09, which points out that since the millennium, the problem has only worsened: " 'Massachusetts has a silent public health crisis on our hands,' said state Sen. Steven A. Tolmon. . . . OxyContin has become so widely abused that the addiction rate for the drug in Massachusetts increased by 950 percent over the past 10 years."

45 "unemployment in Provincetown, for example": Provincetown Chamber of Commerce. Barnstable County Dept. of Human Services, "The Human Condition, A Decade of Community Assessment, 1995–2004, CD-ROM.

46 "emerged as a class bully": Author ints. of David Wood, 08/02/07, 08/06/07; Hannah Lum, 08/05/07; Savannah Bremmer, 06/16/07; Sarah Locke, 08/31/07; anon. sources, 08/09/07, 08/31/07 ("He's creepy. . . . His father alone used to scare the entire police department when he was younger. When Froggy was drinking, they wouldn't even try to calm him down. [Jeremy] was one of those kids who always got in trouble. . . . He was just a bully and a jerk. I'm sure some people were afraid of him").

47 " 'And everyone knew about the Wu-Tang Clan' ": Author int. of anon., 10/06/06. On Wu-Tang Clan rap group, see "History of Hip hop Music," http:/www.en-wikipedia.org/w/index.php?title=History_of_hip_hop_music&printable.

47 "A mother who'd watched Frazier grow up": E-mail to author from anon., 10/27/06.

47 " 'Jeremy was selling blow, too' ": Author ints. of anon., 11/11/06; anon. II, 08/11/09; anon. III, 02/21/06.

47 " 'I watched as they became more and more violent' ": Blog DT MAZ0054, 03/20/07.

47 "Dave Amerault, a close friend": Author int. of Dave Amerault, 05/05/06.

47 "had close ties to the off-Cape drug world:" Author ints. of anon. sources, 08/11/09. Cf. Wellfleet PD Incident Report, 07/05/03; "Jeremy P. Frazier, Assault by Means of a Dangerous Weapon (Knife)." Author ints. of anon. sources re Frazier's drug connections, 08/09/07, 08/11/09. Au-

thor ints. of Dave Amerault, 08/12/09; Kim Deane, 12/04/07. Cf. trial trans., testimony of Shawn Mulvey. Wellfleet PD Narcotics Intelligence Report, 01/08/02.

48   "The older, tougher, more experienced city dealers": Author ints. of anon, 08/11/09; anon II, 08/12/09.

48   "Yet when the grand jury eventually indicted": Cf. In the Matter of Christopher M. McCowen, Superior Court Grand Jury, Friday, June 14, 2005, Bernice R. Rose, court stenographer.

48   "recently released from a Florida state prison": Cf. database records supplied by State of Florida: Christopher M. McCowen, DOB 03/08/72, SSN 442-70-xxxx (Monroe County, case nos. 9300438, 9101828, 9130163). Cf. Eastham PD Incident Report (M. Kelly) 09/21/95; Criminal Complaint 9526 CR 2405, Orleans District Court (Judge Robert A. Welsh, Jr.), Fugitive from Justice C276 S20R, 09/21/95; Eastham PD Master Card M9802946, Christopher M. McCowen, 04/15/02.

48   "he was met by Pam Maguire": MSP (Squier) int. of Pam Maguire, 04/14/05. Cf. ACE Investigations Supplementary Report, int. of Pam Maguire, 05/02/05.

48   "But black men . . . have always been rare": U.S. Census Bureau reports (2005), Cape-wide "Black or African-American population of 1.7%, compared with 12.1% nationally." USAelectionpolls.com reports black population figures for Cape Cod towns: Provincetown (7.4%); Truro (0.7%); North Truro (0.1%); Wellfleet (0.9%); Eastham (1.5%); Orleans (0.6%). Statewide, African-Americans make up 6% of the population. Author ints. John Reed (NAACP), 10/12/06, 10/15/06, 12/26/06.

48   "but women liked Chris": MSP (Mason, Burke) int. of Aaron Walters, 05/23/05. MSP (Sabota) int. of Amy L. Giangregorio, 04/14/05 ("described Chris as having 'a young girls fan club.' She stated she thinks they liked him because there aren't many black guys down Cape. . . . She stated, 'if he thought he could get women into bed he would. He is not a shy guy and he's very flirtatious and polite'"). ACE Investigations int. of Kelly Tabor, 04/25/05 ("She said she and McCowen lived together from 1999 through 2004 . . . She described him as definitely being a lady's man but also a hardworking father. . . . She knew that he was cheating on her but thought she could change him. . . . His anger was more verbal than physical. He never punched her but he has slapped her a handful of times. . . . She . . . never called the police as a result of his actions"). Author ints. of Dave and Juanita Amerault, 08/01/06, 10/06/06; Dave Nichols 10/01/05, 11/25/05; Roy McCowen, 08/27/06, 09/23/06, 09/24/06, 09/26/06, 10/13/06, 10/14/06, 10/25/06. Cf. Jenna Russell and Beth Daley, "Friends, Kin Describe Defendant as Caring, Generous," *Boston Globe*, 04/17/05; Jennifer Fermino, "Exes Trash Cape Cod Murder Suspect," *New York Post*, 04/28/05.

49 "rejection didn't seem to bother him": Author ints. of Dave and Juanita Amerault, 08/01/06, 10/06/06; Dave Nichols, 10/01/05, 11/25/05.

49 "led to friction with whatever woman": MSP (Squier) int. of Pam Maguire, 04/14/05. MSP (Sabota) int. of Amy L. Giangregorio, 04/14/05. Author ints. of Dave Nichols, 10/01/05, 11/25/05.

49 "Few on the Outer Cape were aware that . . . diagnosed as epileptic": Christopher McCowen Medical File, USAF Hospital, Altos, Okla. Dept. of Institutions, Social and Rehab. Services, Dept. of Public Welfare, State of Oklahoma. Medical Records, Hospitals of the University of Oklahoma, Oklahoma City, Oklahoma Children's Memorial Hospital, Pediatrics Clinic, Records of Christopher McCowen. Diagnostic letter, University of Oklahoma Health Science Center, to Dr. Jack Honaker, Frederick, Okla., re Christopher Jackson [McCowen], C.N. 48-13-61, mother Kathleen Jackson Freeman, grandmother Mrs. McCowen, 08/10/72:

"This letter is being written to allow you to complete your files on this child, as we had a request from you on July 31, 1972, to see the above named child for a convulsive disorder. The child was seen in Pediatric Clinic on August 7, 1972, and the history was obtained from the paternal grandmother. The mother, as you know, is rather severely mentally retarded, and the amount of her retardation precludes her giving either an adequate history or caring for this child. Dr. Bill Jackson, the medical student, called you that morning and verified most of the history, we do appreciate your cooperation.

"Essentially the impression was that the child did indeed have a seizure disorder. . . . The seizure work-up included a CBC, urinalysis, EEG, Skull X-rays, Serum Chemistries, Sickle Cell Prep, and Skeletal Survey. We also had the medical social worker . . . speak at length with the paternal grandmother, Mrs. McCowen, to have her secure the proper papers to show that she has temporary legal custody of the child, because as you know a seizure disorder such as this child exhibits would need chronic medical care, and medication for follow-up, and the barbiturates that the child would need, would be needed in specific amounts and given or administered on a routine basis. We did not feel that the child's natural mother would be able to carry out such responsibilities and hopefully Mrs. McCowen will carry through on our suggestions. . . . I believe that the situation is such that this mother will be unable to, at any time in the future, be able to administer correctly Phenobarbital medication for this particular child."

50 "he also believed he could": Author ints. of Dave Amerault, Dave Nichols, Catherine Rios-Cisneros, 09/11/06, 10/12/06, 12/18/06, 12/22/06, et al.

50 "McCowen had met with police": Wellfleet PD Narcotics Intelligence Report, 01/08/02. Trial trans. cross-examinations of Jeremy Frazier and Shawn Mulvey.

50   "both were 'functioning drug addicts'": Author ints. of anon., 05/05/07, 04/08/07.

50   "Later, some people said it was incomprehensible": Cf. Comm. Mass., Barnstable Superior Court, Grand Jury, *In the Matter of Christopher M. McCowen*, 06/14/05, Bernice Rose, court reporter, trans. pp. 2, 70–84.

51   "to take O'Keefe off the case": Bill Hewitt and Anne Driscoll, "Murder, She Wrote," *People*, 06/30/03. Franci Richardson, "Slain Writer's Kin: Take Cape DA Off Case," *Boston Herald*, 06/21/03. Elizabeth Bloch, "New Investigator to Join Probe in Cape Slaying," *Boston Globe*, 06/22/03. "Guardian Wants DA Off Murder Case," *Boston Globe*, 06/26/03. Hilary Russ, "Asst. DA Quiet but Confident," *Cape Cod Times*, 10/15/06.

51   "'More Theories Than Answers'": Brian Gregory, "More Theories Than Answers," *Boston Globe*, 06/03/03. Eric Williams, "Community on Edge," *Cape Cod Times*, 01/05/03. Dooley, "Unresolved." Jessica Heslam, "Story of Slain Writer Still Missing Ending," *Boston Herald*, 01/05/03. Todd Venezia, "25G Reward Set for Clues to Cape Cod Writer Slay," *New York Post*, 01/10/03. Richardson, "Slain Writer's Kin." Bloch, "New Investigator."

51   "which the *New York Times* called": Pam Belluck, "To Try to Net a Killer, Police Ask a Small Town's Men for DNA," *New York Times*, 01/10/05. Also, Kathleen Burge and John Ellement, "Police Seek DNA Samples in 2002 Truro Slaying," *Boston Globe*, 01/08/05; McNamara, "Flunking the Swab Test"; Jennifer Fermino, "DNA Male Call—Slogtown: Test All," *New York Post*, 01/06/05; "ACLU of Massachusetts Calls for End to DNA Dragnet," 01/10/05, www.ACLU.org; Laura Crimaldi, "DNA Swab Sweep Clash; Cape Authorities Ignore ACLU Protest," *Boston Herald*, 01/11/05; Ripley et al., "The DNA Dragnet."

52   "given a lie-detector test the next morning": MSP Polygraph Examination, Jeremy P. Frazier, DOB 05/26/83, 24 Leeside Hollow, Wellfleet, case 2005-113-0174, 04/16/05, Christopher J. Dolan, 0910, Polygraph Examiner MSP, no observer indicated.

53   "Kinton's description of Frazier": Author ints. of anon., 05/05/07; anon. II, 12/04/07; anon. III, 04/08/07.

54   "The Trial": All quoted dialogue, including sidebar dialogue normally unheard by jurors and spectators, is taken from the nonredacted trial transcript, Comm. of Massachusetts, Barnstable Superior Court BACR 2005-00109, *Comm. v. McCowen, Christopher M.*, Oct. 16–Nov. 16, 2006, Daniel E. Horgan, court reporter. In using ellipses, the author has made every effort not to distort content.

55   "'I don't want to fall back'": Author int. of Robert George, 08/19/09.

56   "I took it because I thought": Author int. of Robert George, 08/02/09.

60   "But on September 27, 2006, weeks before trial began": Hilary Russ, "Injured Judge Leaves Courtroom Vacancy," *Cape Cod Times*, 09/26/06.

62 "often boasted that he'd seen the body of every Cape murder victim": Flook, p. 6.

62 "According to one oft-repeated story": Author int. of Seth Rolbein, 12/15/06.

62 "earning the nickname": Author int. of attorney Nancy Correa, 06/27/09.

62 "His most embarrassing moment": Flook, pp. 6–13, 149–54, 192–201.

63 "Declared the *Boston Herald*": Jessica Heslam, "Tell-All Sheds Light on Cape DA," *Boston Herald*, 06/02/03. Margery Egan, " 'Dramatized' Book on Cape Cod Murder Hits Its Target: Sales," *Boston Herald*, 06/26/03. Also, John Leland, "Murder She Wrote," *New York Times*, 06/22/03; Erica Noonan, "Author's Tactics Cloud a Compelling Look into Unsolved Murder," *Boston Globe*, 06/30/03; Hewitt and Driscoll, "Murder, She Wrote" K. C. Myers, "Family Outcry Shakes Worthington Probe," *Cape Cod Times*, 06/21/03; Joanna Weiss, "Truro Buzz Is about Author, Not Book," *Boston Globe*, 06/25/03; Ellen Barry, "Book on '02 Cape Slaying Uses Lurid Details from DA," *Boston Globe*, 05/22/03.

63 "Flook's 'sex-omatic' tell-all": Alex Beam, "Dirty Politics, Clear Power on the Cape," *Boston Globe*, 04/04/07.

63 "demanding that the priapic DA be yanked": "Guardian Wants DA Off Murder Case"; Elizabeth Boch, "New Investigator to Join Probe on Cape Slaying," *Boston Globe*, 06/22/03; Richardson, "Slain Writer's Kin."

63 "Visibly shaken, O'Keefe announced": Quoted in Hewitt and Driscoll, "Murder, She Wrote."

63 "One weepy neighbor came to the DA's defense, explaining": Author int. of anon., 10/10/06, 10/13/06.

63 "One assistant DA insisted": Author int. of anon., 12/07/07.

63 "Another spoke of his openly enjoying": Author int. of anon., 05/16/07, 05/20/07, 01/13/08.

63 "In another account, O'Keefe was spotted at the Hyannis Mall": Author int. of anon., 10/02/09.

64 "An ex-Barnstable County Sheriff's Department detective reported": Author int. of anon., 01/13/08. Months after this interview, at a Cape cocktail party, I ran into the defense lawyer who'd reportedly been frolicking in the hot tub with the DA, the dope dealer, and the bimbos. Queried about the story, the man smiled, replying, "Hot tub? If memory serves, not a hot tub, a *sauna*, Mr. Manso. Please, let's get it right." He then turned and walked away, giggling. I have chosen to leave the original version of the story intact, satisfied that in its broad outlines, the episode has been adequately confirmed.

64 " 'He's a skirt chaser' ": Author int. of Seth Rolbein, 12/15/06.

64 "And the big head didn't seem to control": Author int. of Michael O'Keefe, 05/10/06. What did the O.J. verdict have in common with Chris McCowen? Simpson, an internationally known screen personality

who'd parlayed a Heisman Trophy into tens of millions of dollars, akin to McCowen, a $120-a-week garbageman and petty crook with a 76 IQ, a drifter who'd worked as a bar bouncer and a supermarket bagger? The comparison was ludicrous—except for the fact that the DA, obviously, saw all blacks as one. The other consideration was, of course, the man's tendency to blab even after his Flook experience. Was the DA deranged? So self-absorbed and arrogant, so ego-driven as to completely misjudge his audience?

65 "a graduate of Georgetown University and": Robert Welsh III bio, courtesy Cape and Islands District Attorney's Office. Russ, "Quiet but Confident."
65 "what bearing the 1.7 percent statistic": Trial trans.
74 "But he was wrong": Author int. of George Malloy, 09/08/07.
78 "Robert George spent the night": Author int. of Robert George, 10/19/06.
80 "The allusion was, plainly, to": Manso, pp. 164, 173–77, 209–32. Also, Flook, pp. 44–48, 50–51, 258–62; Grigoriadis, "The Single-Mom Murder."
88 "one of Truro's more amusing incidents": Author int. of Phil Tarvers, 11/11/07.
88 "The Worthingtons owned multiple homes in Truro, including four on Depot Road": Barnstable County Registry of Deeds (Worthington), index dates 1939–2006. Also, Cape Cod and Islands Multiple Listing Service; Truro Town Hall, Assessor's Office, books 2006, 2000, 1995, 1983; Tax Collector's Office, book 1960.
91 "Jan had pinned her hopes on screenwriting": Cf. records check re bankruptcies and tax liens; GVB Security and Investigation Group, Westwood, Mass. (Subject Information: Name Janet W. Worthington, DOB 11/16/51, SSN 032-40-xxxx); author int. of Richard J. Cohen, Esq., 10/20/06.
91 "More recently, Worthington received $60,000": Kaimi Rose Laur, "Worthington Cousin to Write Screenplay," *Provincetown Banner*, 04/11/02; Todd Venezia, "Fashion Writer Slay Mystery Fitting for TV."
91 "Jan had opened the door to the exploitation issue": Despite Worthington's insistence on "doing the right thing," not all of the press was taken in. In May 2002, within weeks of the announcement of Jan's film deal, Ann Kalill Wood wrote: "And then there's Jan Worthington, Christa's cousin, who is reportedly at work on (or maybe done with) a screenplay or teleplay—I'm not sure which, or the difference really—about the murder. I haven't seen it so I can't say how cheesy or tasteful a thing it is. Maybe she won't portray her cousin as a slut but, damn, it's got sell-out written all over it. . . . I can't stop thinking about Worthington and how she epitomizes the victimization of the victim." Ann Kalill Wood, "Victimizing the Victim: What Really Happened to Christa Worthington," *Provincetown Banner*, 05/05/02.

92   "Given the witness's high-toned stance": If Worthington's confabula-
tions stemmed from a need to hide her exploitations of her cousin's
death, then there may have been another reason—feelings of guilt. On
Saturday and Sunday, January 5 and 6, 2002, Jan and her parents took
their usual morning constitutional around the neighborhood, passing
Christa's driveway. Both mornings, they noticed Christa's *New York Times*
in its blue plastic wrapper at the foot of her drive yet did nothing. John
Worthington added that he'd also seen his niece's lights on early Saturday morning before sunrise, then again when he got up to pee several
times during the next night. Again, neither he nor Cindy bothered to
telephone to see that the single mother and her infant in the bungalow
across the road were all right.

From Tpr. Mason's 01/06/02 interview of John Worthington: "[T]he
last contact he had with Christa was approximately seven to ten days
ago when he saw her . . . pickup [*sic*] a newspaper which was wrapped
in blue plastic. John explained that he frequently walks with his dog
on Depot Rd. and often sees the N.Y. Times or Globe at the base of the
driveway. . . . [H]e saw lights on at Christa's house at approximately
0530 hours on Saturday morning when he got up. John Worthington stated that he walked by Christa's driveway at approximately
0630 hours on Saturday morning and noticed a N.Y. Times paper in
Christa's driveway. . . . [H]e noticed on Saturday evening after returning from the movies, that the lights were still on at Christa's. John
Worthington stated that he can see Christa's house when he gets up
at night from his house and that Saturday night at around midnight
he saw that Christa's lights were on and that they were on when he
awoke at 0200 hours, Sunday morning. . . . [O]n this Sunday morning
he went for a walk and noticed two (2) papers at the head of Christa's
driveway. John Worthington said that Christa has been 'negligent' in
the past about picking up her papers and he was not concerned when
on his return trip by Christa's driveway he saw the papers still there."

In the end, how long it took for Christa to "bleed out" remains an
open question. Had her relatives bothered to make a phone call, while
it might not have saved her, Ava certainly would have been spared the
unspeakable horror of being locked in that house for two days alone
with her mother's corpse. Cf. MSP (Mason) ints. of John Worthington,
01/06/02; Jan Worthington, 01/06/02.

92   "Jan admitted that she had not": Rose Connors, "How Strategy—and
Flaws—Showcase in the Christa Worthington Murder Trial," *Cape Cod
Voice*, 11/02–11/15/06.

92   "A new VW and a sporty Audi convertible sat": Cf. GVB Security and
Investigative Corp. report, 10/02/06, listing two vehicles registered to
Janet W. Worthington: a blue 2007 Volkswagen Passat 2.0T luxury station

wagon, VIN WVKTK73C67E003357, Title BD0090306, lien holder VW Credit; and a green 2005 Audi II Roadster, VIN TRUTC28NX51007965, lien holder none. Per [Town of] Truro Assessor's Office, book 2006, Worthington's home at 51 Depot Road was assessed at $1,137,300. The Town of Truro Annual Town Report 2008 lists Worthington's annual wages as $14,100.

98 "Do you recall telling him again on the ninth": MSP (Mason) int. of Jan Worthington, 01/09/02: "Worthington indicated that Arnold told her that Christa was dead and inside the residence. Worthington said she then climbed the steps to the front door and looked inside. Worthington stated that she was not prepared for the sight of [*sic*] family member and 'lost all professional composure.' I asked Worthington what she meant and she indicated that she began to scream and ran from the doorway down the driveway towards her parents [*sic*] house on Depot Rd. . . . Worthington stated that it was obvious to her from her vantage point at the doorway that Christa was dead and stated that she did not enter into the house more than one or two steps, if at all."

99 "He directed the witness to her interview": Eric Williams, "Worthington Cousin Recounts Discovery of Body," *Cape Cod Times*, 05/13/04, for reprint of Jan's remarks. Here, Worthington claimed, "I was in action. . . . I felt for a pulse and knew she was not alive. And then I wanted a phone to call the police because I wanted the police to get there before the rescue squad. Because I knew it was a police matter at that point. . . . After that I wanted to be with my family . . . so I walked down the hill. . . . I feel a certain obligation to Christa and to Ava to keep this story alive and to tell this story the best way I can," she added.

102 "Tim Arnold had told police": MSP (Knott) int. of Tim Arnold, 01/06/02.

102 "she told him 'she kind of "freaked out"'": MSP (Massari) Report of Investigation, 01/06/02 ("Jan Worthington stated that she went up to the rear door and could see the body of Christa Worthington lying in the hallway . . . after seeing the body of her cousin she kind of 'freaked out.' Subsequently, Jan Worthington did not perform any rescue measures on the body").

102 "And after the January 9 interview": MSP (Mason) int. of Jan Worthington, 01/09/02. Cf. Mason int. of Jan Worthington, 01/06/02.

102 "'How could you let him do that to me?'": Exchange overheard in lobby, repeated to author, 10/20/02.

102 "He called in his Code 99": Region V, Standard Ambulance Report Form, 01/06/02, Lower Cape Amb., CMed No. 387, SARF No. 96211. Re Krista [*sic*] Worthington, 50 Depot Road, Truro, Mass. Priority 1. Clinical Impression: Code 99/Condition 13.

106 "and in his inimitable style, District Attorney O'Keefe": Author int. of Michael O'Keefe, 08/16/06.

110 "the proceedings had begun to evoke": "According to Tuskegee Institute records, in the period 1862–1968, 3,446 blacks were lynched in the
United States, more than seventy percent of whom were accused of rape
or attempted rape, assault upon, or the 'crime' of insulting Caucasian
women. Willie McGee, convicted and sentenced to death after being accused of rape by his white lover, spawned an international outcry in the
early '50s when Mississippi's highest court refused to consider the notion that consensual sexual relations were possible between a black man
and a white woman." Tuskegee Institute records: www.yale.edu/ynht;/
curriculum/units/1979/2/79.02.04.x,html#b; www.umkc.edu/faculty/
projects/ftrials/shipp/lynchingssate.html. Cf. Philip Dray, *At the Hands
of Persons Unknown: The Lynching of Black America* (New York: Modern Library, 2003); Robert Whitaker, *On the Laps of Gods: The Red Summer of
1919 and the Struggle for Justice That Remade a Nation* (New York: Crown,
2008). Arguably, the fullest realization of the lynching phenomenon in
an urban context is Richard Wright's *Native Son* (New York: Library of
America, 1991).

121 "Megan Tench of the *Boston Globe* wrote": Megan Tench, "Trooper Says
McCowen Changed His Story," *Boston Globe*, 10/25/06. Cf. Harriet Ryan,
"Knife Wound Killed Cape Cod Writer, but Rape Unconfirmed, Pathologist Says," *Court TV News*, 10/23/06; Michael Iacuessa, "McCowen Murder Trial: Day 5," *Provincetown Banner*, 10/26/06.

123 "used effectively by Peter Neufeld and Barry Scheck of the Innocence
Project": Cf. www.innocenceproject.org.

128 "at the barracks": Cf. MSP (Mason) int. of Christopher M. McCowen,
04/14/05.

128 "Under Massachusetts law, police must advise": In *Commonwealth v.
DiGiambattista*, decided in 2004. Ironically, after a similar warning eight
years earlier in *Commonwealth v. Diaz*, 422 Mass. 269 (1996), Massachusetts' highest court warned that it was ready to issue a bright-line rule
on the exclusion of nonrecorded interrogations. As in many legal situations, unfortunately, the SJC compromised by "splitting the baby" with a
required jury instruction on the issue but offered no prohibition despite
statistics and the many scholarly studies calling for exclusion. The failure
to do so, according to Robert George and other defense lawyers, has
"led to the morphing and perversion of the very safeguards" the court's
instructions were meant to protect. Alaska was the first state to require
electronic recording in felony cases, in 1985. Since then, six states and
the District of Columbia have required police to record in at least some
criminal cases. In Massachusetts, police know that the courts prefer
but do not require taping, a nonrule that provides incentive to suggest
that a suspect need not participate in taped interrogations. If nontaped
statements were inadmissible, borderline interrogation tactics would be

forced from the shadows. Cf. Edwin Colfax, "Electronic Recording of Cus-
todial Interrogations, Summary of HB 223/SB 15," Center on Wrongful
Convictions, Northwestern University School of Law, 07/17/03, www.law
.northwestern.edu/depts/clinic/wrongful/SB15Summary.htm; Thomas
P. Sullivan, *Police Experiences with Recording Custodial Interrogations*, Center
on Wrongful Convictions/Bluhm Legal Clinic, Northwestern University
School of Law, 2004, www.law.northwestern.edu/wrongfulconvictions/
Causes/Custodial Interrogations.htm; Steve Mills and Michael Higgins,
"Cops Urged to Tape Their Interrogations," *Chicago Tribune*, 01/06/02;
Gould, *The Innocence Commission*; Barry Scheck, Peter Neufeld, and Jim
Dwyer, *Actual Innocence: When Justice Goes Wrong and How to Make it Right*
(New York: New American Library, 2003).

164   "the business and personal phone records of this author": Cf. letter to
Verizon–New England from Office of the District Attorney, Cape and
Islands District, 01/07/02: "Pursuant to an official criminal investigation . . . it is *requested* [emphasis added] that your company supply
tolls for the completed billing period . . . from December 3, 2001 to
January 6, 2002 for the following numbers. . . . You are not to disclose
the existence of this request as any such disclosure could impede the
investigation being conducted and thereby interfere with the enforcement of the law." This letter, which should not be confused with a
court-issued subpoena, was signed by then-first-assistant-DA Michael
O'Keefe. Records were requested for Tony Jackett, Tim and Robert Arnold, Durand Echeverria (owner of the home Tim Arnold was house-
sitting), Christopher Worthington, myself, and my then-girlfriend, now
my wife, Anna Avellar. By the close of the investigation, the records
of some forty-five telephone numbers would be similarly "requested,"
according to trial documents. An abuse of prosecutorial powers or legitimate police protocol? The courts have ruled on this issue, deeming
relevant the factors of urgency, the status of an investigation, reasonable cause, and, as always, the principle of "overriding" interest. The
role of Verizon, the principal supplier of the "requested" records, is
another matter.

178   "He said he didn't have a copy of Frazier's full record": This is chutzpah
writ large. In addition to the July 2, 2003, Wellfleet pier incident, which
led to Frazier being charged with assault with a dangerous weapon
(knife), his record is readily available at the clerk's office of the Orleans
District Court and includes arrests for destruction of property, assault,
possession of liquor person under 21, OUI, disorderly behavior, and a variety of traffic violations. With the exception of the assault charge, these
are all "lightweights" that conspicuously skirt Frazier's reputation among
cops as a local drug dealer.

178   "The facts weren't negligible": Cf. Case 20033677, assault by means of a

dangerous weapon (knife), Jeremy Frazier, 07/05/03, Wellfleet PD Incident Report, Det. Michael Mazzone.

191 "He handed the witness": Cf. Criminal Complaint 0326CR000558, Orleans District Court. Defendant Shawn Mulvey; date of offense 05/08/2002; complainant David Hagstrom, Eastham PD Count-Offense, 94C/32 C/A Drug, Distribute Class D c.94C s. 32c(a). Also, Report of Deputy Sheriff Michael Mei to Orleans PD re Undercover Purchase of Exhibit 1 from Shawn Mulvey in Eastham, Mass., on 05/08/02 ("At approximately 8:00 PM, D/S Mei along with the CI arrived at Mulvey's residence, a basement apartment located in the rear of the house. . . . Mulvey asked D/S Mei how much ecstasy he was looking for. . . . Mulvey then told D/S Mei he could get ecstasy tomorrow afternoon").

192 "On May 13, Whitcomb called back": MSP (Mason) int. of Shawn Mulvey, 05/13/05.

203 "relished the memory of Costa's wife": Author ints. of Phil Tarvers, 11/11/06, and anon., 09/14/06.

205 "Costa and another man had been spotted": Truro PD Incident Report, 06/11/02, Staff Sgt. David J. Costa, Jerry Costa, Assist.

205 "Costa first injected himself into the investigation": Truro PD Incident Report, narr. 4, 06/11/02, Staff Sgt. David J. Costa, Internal Report ("After the briefing, I responded to John and Cindy Worthingtons [sic] residence to update the family on the situation at hand").

205 "He took the liberty of interviewing Truro harbormaster Warren Roderick": Truro PD Incident Report, 06/11/02, narr. 8, Staff Sgt. David J. Costa, Warren Roderick int.

208 "his 1999 conviction for lobster scrubbing": Felix Carroll, "Truro Officer Convicted in Lobster-Scrubbing Trial," *Cape Cod Times*, 12/09/99. Michael Iacuessa, "Truro Police Protest, Letter Objects to Sgt. Working While Charged," *Provincetown Banner*, 07/22/99 ("The Truro Police Employees Federation . . . presented a six-page letter to the Town Administrator's Office July 6 stating unanimous opposition to Costa remaining on active duty. . . . Costa returned to active duty June 13 and, as he is normally second in command, was officially in charge of the Department at the time the letter was drafted. . . . He was arrested by State Environmental Police while on his boat"). Michael Iacuessa, "Accused Lobsterman Scrubs Deal. Boat's Back but Costa Counsel Claims Prosecutorial Misconduct," *Provincetown Banner*, 11/11/99 ("Costa faces four counts related to scrubbing female egg-bearing lobsters and three counts of failing to obey commands from authorities during the arrest").

208 "unless he was 'the sole witness in an ax murder'": Michael Iacuessa, "Costa Credibility Remains an Issue," *Provincetown Banner*, 03/09/2000.

209 "Amato lived in New York City": Author ints. of Keith Amato, 09/04/06, 10/05/06, 10/22/06, 11/05/06, 01/07/07.

210 "pursuant to rumors that he'd had an affair": MSP (Mason) ints. of Luke Jackett, 03/29/02; India Conklin, 03/29/02; Braunwyn Jackett, 03/28/02; Tony Jackett, 05/02/02; Susan Jackett, 03/05/02; Pam and Ted Franklin, 04/08/02; Keith Amato, 01/23/02, 02/06/02, 06/13/02. MSP (Massari) int. of Diana Worthington, 01/23/02. MSP (Sabato) int. of Kyle Jackett, 01/17/02. MSP (Harding) ints. of Vanessa Vartabedian, 02/26/02; Eugene Monteiro, 02/26/02. MSP (Squier) int. of Jessica Kode-Wingate, 02/28/02.

211 "Etel, age four in 2000": MSP (Mason) int. of Susan Jackett, 03/05/02. Author ints. of Keith Amato.

212 "especially after Braunwyn confronted Christa": MSP (Mason) ints. of Susan Jackett, 03/05/02; Braunwyn Jackett, 03/28/02. MSP (Sabota) ints. of Braunwyn Jackett, 01/09/02, 01/17/02. Also, author int. of Braunwyn Jackett, 05/18/02.

212 "Amato explained that the idea was to": Author ints. of Keith Amato.

212 "'My son actually called me'": Author ints. of Keith Amato.

213 "He didn't know investigators had": Cf. Comm. Mass., Dept. of State Police, Crime Laboratory, DNA-STR Status Report, Lab 02-00157 Truro, Incident 2002-102-0900-0007, p. 3 of 19: "On September 20, 2002, Sergeant William O. Burke of the MSP Cape & Islands Detective Unit delivered the following items to the laboratory for DNA analysis: Item #26-6, Pen used by Ian Amato; Item #26-7, Pen used by Ian Amato; Item #26-8, Can for Alternate DNA Standard—Ian Amato."

226 "in January 2000, he was arrested in West Haven, charged with": John Leaning, "Eastham Chief Faces Charges of Stalking," *Cape Cod Times*, 01/22/00. Doug Fraser, "Eastham Fire Chief Had Been Warned," *Cape Cod Times*, 01/26/00. Doug Fraser, "Eastham Decides to Terminate Fire Chief," *Cape Cod Times*, 05/09/00. "Former Eastham Fire Chief Gets Probation for Stalking Woman," *Cape Cod Times*, 09/16/00. Doug Fraser, "Eastham Chief's Hockey Background Makes Him Eager to Stick Around," *Cape Cod Times*, 04/07/99.

233 "echoed Pam's statement": MSP (Burke) int. of Pamela Worthington Franklin, 01/06/02.

238 "McCowen's history of epilepsy": Christopher McCowen medical records, previously cited.

239 "according to *Cape Cod Times* reporter": Hilary Russ, "McCowen's Mental Status at Issue," *Cape Cod Times*, 11/04/06.

252 "the Central Park jogger case": The reference was to the 1989 New York City rape case that left the victim nearly dead and the nation outraged. Four of five teenagers charged with the crimes confessed; a fifth made incriminating verbal admissions. All five were convicted in 1990. Twelve years later, their convictions were vacated after DNA evidence confirmed another man's confession.

253 "Michael Iacuessa wrote": Michael Iacuessa, "McCowen Murder Trial, Day 14," *Provincetown Banner*, 11/02/06.

259 "prompted Beth Karas of Court TV": Court TV live coverage of the McCowen trial, 11/06/02.

259 "Again, members of the out-of-town press": According to the late Milton Helpern, retired chief medical examiner of New York City, widely regarded as the world's best-known forensic pathologist, the *habitude* of the New England courts has an identity all its own. Helpern writes in *Autopsy*, with Bernard Knight, M.D. (New York: New American Library, 1977), p. 92: "I have always had the feeling that New England still lives in the past as far as crime and punishment are concerned. The atmosphere of the old Salem witch trials still persists—they're out to get you and they're going to convict someone if it's the last thing they do!

"I got mixed up in one such affair some years ago, and I think it was one of the most horrible cases I remember—not because there was anything revolting or horrific about the pathology, but because Boston was out to get this poor guy, come hell or high water."

270 "The story is told in the celebrated study of": J. Anthony Lukas, *Common Ground: A Turbulent Decade in the Lives of Three American Families* (New York: Vintage, 1986), pp. 53–55. Also, Kerri Greenidge, *Boston's Abolitionists* (Beverly, Mass.; Commonwealth Editions, 2006), pp. 28, 39. In addition to "set[ting] the precedent for federally sanctioned racial segregation that would haunt the country for more than sixty years," Shaw used his bench to return runaway slaves to their irate owners, sometimes unsuccessfully. In one case, fugitive slave Shadrach Minkins had made the journey from Virginia to Boston, gotten a job at the Cornhill Coffeehouse downtown, a short distance from William Lloyd Garrison's *Liberator* office, when, in 1851, he was arrested by two Virginia slave catchers. Almost immediately, abolitionist lawyers pled Minkins's case, but their pleas, according to Greenidge, came to nothing, with Shaw ruling that Minkins be returned to slavery under the Fugitive Slave Law. Just as Shaw delivered his ruling, however, the courtroom erupted as more than fifty blacks stormed the proceedings and grabbed Minkins, still clad in his waiter's uniform, before any of the shocked attorneys and court officers could respond. Shadrach Minkins was spirited to freedom in Canada. The abolitionist community was as joyful as federal officials were flummoxed, leaving Minister Theodore Parker to praise the rescue as "the noblest deed done in Boston since the destruction of the tea." Shaw's performance hardly qualified him as an enlightened, forward thinking jurist.

270 "'Justice Shaw's ruling,' Lukas concluded": Lukas, p. 55.

275 "Like Jan Worthington, Jackett had snagged his own film deal": Connor Berry, "Reel Life: Truro Murder as Movie," *Cape Cod Times*, 12/30/03.

Also, Jennifer Longley, "Cape Man Sells Film Rights to Murder Saga," *Boston Globe*, 12/31/03 ("Independent filmmaker Arthur Egeli says his movie would be a fictionalized account, focusing on Worthington's life in Truro, the affair and birth of her child, and how the Jacketts put their lives back together after the murder. . . . Neither Jackett nor Egeli would say how much Jackett will earn for sharing his story, but Jackett said it would be a percentage of the movie's revenue").

275 "he briefed counsel": Megan Tench, "Deliberations Continue in Worthington after a Delay," *Boston Globe*, 11/13/06. Joe Dwinell, "Jury Deadlocked," *Cape Codder*, 11/13/06. Denise Lavoie, "Jurors Claim They're Deadlocked in Cape Cod Slaying Trial," AP, 11/31/06; "Juror Kicked Off Cape Cod Murder Case," AP, 11/14/06. Also, George Brennan, "Family Squabble Led to Weekend Shooting," *Cape Cod Times*, 11/15/06; Jack Coleman, "Christa Twist," *New York Post*, 11/15/06; author ints. of Robert George, Drew Segadelli; trial trans.

277 "With the jurors out of the courtroom": Megan Tench, "Juror in Worthington Case Dismissed, Deliberations Start Over," *Boston Globe*, 11/14/06. Megan Tench, "Judge Orders Jurors Secluded," *Boston Globe*, 11/14/06. Denise Lavoie, "Juror Booted from Cape Cod Murder Trial," AP, 11/15/06. "Massachusetts Juror Dismissed," *New York Times*, 11/15/06.

278 "But O'Keefe was not to be relied on. Huffman soon would be charged": George Brennan, "Police Investigate Juror Linked to Shooting," *Cape Cod Times*, 11/16/06. George Brennan, "Dismissed Juror Not a 'Holdout,'" *Cape Cod Times*, 11/17/06. Denise Lavoie, "Ex-Juror Arrested in Connection with Boyfriend's Case," AP, 11/29/06. George Brennan, "Former Juror Faces Charges in Shooting," *Cape Cod Times*, 11/30/06. "Former Worthington Juror on Other Side," Top-News, CBS4, Boston, www.cbs4boston.com, 11/30/06. George Brennan, "Dismissed Juror in Worthington Case Arraigned," *Cape Cod Times*, 12/01/06. Amanda Lehmart, "Key Charges Dropped against Ex-Juror," *Cape Cod Times*, 12/05/06. Denise Lavoie, "DA Drops Accessory Charge against Former Juror" AP, 12/05/06. Author ints. of Huffman attorneys Drew Segadelli, 12/14/06, and Kevin Reddington, 11/05/09.

281 "Nickerson had already heard the tape but agreed to play it": Hilary Russ, "Jury Back to Square One," *Cape Cod Times*, 11/15/06.

283 "Brought into the courtroom, Huffman stood": Joe Dwinell, "Juror Tossed over Bad Call: Defense in Cape Slay Fumes at Replacement," *Boston Herald*, 11/15/06. Michael Iacuessa, "Legal Questions Raised as Juror Removed," *Provincetown Banner*, 11/16/06.

285 "A number of Cape attorneys could not recall": Weinstein quoted in Iacuessa, "Legal Questions."

285 "another written question": Denise Lavoie, "Jurors in Cape Slaying Trial

Ask about Police Interrogation," AP, 11/15/06. Jack Coleman, "Among the unfortunate legacies of the Worthington case are the mixed signals being sent to police about audio and videotaping of interrogations," www.capecodtoday.com, 11/15/06.

286 "According to Megan Tench of the *Boston Globe*": Megan Tench, "Jury Query Focuses on Interrogation," *Boston Globe*, 11/16/06.

287 "the *Cape Cod Times* was preparing a motion": "Times Identifies Dismissed Juror," *Cape Cod Times*, 11/15/06. Denise Lavoie, "Judge Rules Media Can Use Dismissed Juror's Name," AP, 11/16/06.

289 "Nickerson announced": It is interesting that with the verdict, much of the press, including the refined, politically correct *New York Times*, felt justified in running headlines IDing McCowen as a garbageman. Cf. Pam Belluck, "Trash Collector Guilty in Cape Cod Slaying," *New York Times*, 11/17/06; Denise Lavoie, "Trash Man Convicted in Cape Slaying," AP, 11/16/06; and, most crudely, Jack Coleman and Rita Delfiner, "Piece of Trash Guilty of Murder," *New York Post*, 11/20/06.

291 "Within the hour": Denise Lavoie, "Worthington Judge Said Jurors Faced Death Threats," AP, 12/03/06.

291 "'I just thank God that it's over'": Quoted in K. C. Myers and Mary Ann Bragg, "Two Men, Two Lives Forever Altered," *Cape Cod Times*, 11/17/06. Michael Iacuessa, "McCowen Guilty on All Counts," *Provincetown Banner*, 11/16/06.

291 "'Having completed our civic duty'": Quoted in Iacuessa, "McCowen Guilty."

292 "'If it walks like a duck and talks like'": Author's notes re Robert George press conference, 11/16/06.

292 "'very powerful appellate arguments for reversal'": Megan Tench and John Ellement, "Lawyer in Cape Case Eyes Retrial, Alleged Threats to Jury Are Under Investigation," *Boston Globe*, 11/18/06.

292 "'Have fun behind bars' . . . 'Go Fuck Your BLACK Mother!'": Postverdict messages received by Robert George, provided to the author by George's office.

293 "The day after the verdict, George rushed downstairs . . . to face two meter maids": Author int. of Robert George, 12/03/06.

294 "Roy McCowen told the *Boston Globe*": Tench and Ellement, "Lawyer in Cape Case Eyes Retrial."

294 "Robert George agreed . . . 'diagnosably ADD'": Author int. of Robert George, 02/17/07.

295 "Two weeks after the verdict": Laurel J. Sweet, "Prosecutor Partied with Jurors: Conduct after Cape Trial Raises Judgment Questions," *Boston Herald*, 12/08/06. David E. Frank, "Videotape Shows McCowen Prosecutor Dining with Jurors," *Massachusetts Lawyers Weekly*, 12/08/06.

295 "'What is this, *My Cousin Vinny*?'" Quoted in Sweet, "Prosecutor Partied."

295 "Said another in *Massachusetts Lawyers Weekly*": Quoted in Frank, "Video-tape Shows."

295 "Mary-Ellen Manning": Quoted in Sweet, "Prosecutor Partied." Joe Dwinell, "Juror: Dinner with Prosecutor No Party," *Boston Herald*, 12/09/06 ("'This was not a party,' said [a] female juror, who requested anonymity, citing death threats reportedly made against the jury. 'This was not a celebration. . . . Mr. Welsh was contacted by one of us . . . because we had a lot of unanswered questions. . . . ' The juror said she and other members of the jury will be appearing soon on *Dateline NBC*. 'We kept telling each other you couldn't write this stuff if you tried,' she said. . . . The woman reportedly contacted the *Cape Cod Times* in addition to the *Boston Herald*. In the *Times*, she was quoted, 'If anything, we respect [Welsh] tremendously for going out on a limb and meeting with us, knowing that people would view it as inappropriate. But he felt he owed that to us. We are forever grateful to him. I know I can sleep better now'").

295 "Among those present": Hilary Russ, "Prosecutor Welsh Seen Socializing with Jurors," *Cape Cod Times*, 12/09/06 (queried about the dinner, DA O'Keefe is quoted: "There is nothing at all inappropriate in what this jury did and nothing inappropriate about [Welsh's] accepting the invitation").

295 "Gomes, the first juror to seek publicity": Denise Lavoie, "Juror in Worthington Trial Says Jury Struggled with Decision," AP, 11/21/06.

295 "'90 percent of the arguments were about'": Quoted in T. J. Winick, "Juror Sheds Light on Worthington Murder Trial," CBS4/Falmouth-Boston, www.cbs4boston.com, 11/20/06.

295 "'Talking it out? It was more like'": Quoted in Kevin Dennehy, "Juror Swayed by DNA, *Cape Cod Times*, 11/21/06.

296 "Gomes's was the worst": Copies of e-mails provided to author by anonymous source.

296 "the U.S. Justice Department uncovered twenty-three matches": Jonathan Saltzman, "FBI Begins Review of Crime Lab, Downloads DNA Data after Aide's Suspension," *Boston Globe*, 01/20/07. Editorial, "Our View: Crime Lab Incompetence," *Patriot Ledger*, 01/24/06. Eric Williams, "Crime Lab DNA Work under Microscope," *Cape Cod Times*, 01/25/07. Jonathan Saltzman, "Lawyers Question Lab's DNA Results," *Boston Globe*, 01/24/07. "US Audit Found More Problems at Crime Lab," *Boston Globe*, 02/01/07. "Crime Lab Botched 27 DNA Results, Nearly Twice as Many as State Found Earlier," *Boston Globe*, 02/14/07. Denise Lavoie, "More DNA Cases Mishandled by Lab," AP, 02/21/07.

296 "At the end of summer 2008": Jessica Van Sack, "Inmate Stabs Truro Killer," *Boston Herald*, 06/10/08. Hilary Russ, "Christopher McCowen Stabbed in Prison," *Cape Cod Times*, 06/11/08.

297 "Several months later, DA O'Keefe": Eric Williams, "O'Keefe to Return

120 DNA Samples," *Cape Cod Times*, 11/22/06. David Abel, "DNA Samples in Cape Slaying to Be Returned," *Boston Globe*, 11/22/06.

297 "At the request of Keith Amato": "Men Sue for Return of DNA in Cape Cod Slaying Case," AP, 06/19/08. Hilary Russ, "Contested DNA Samples Ignite Cape Legal Clash," *Cape Cod Times*, 06/20/08. Pru Sowers, "Lawyers Demand Proof DNA Samples Have Been Destroyed," *Cape Cod Times*, 06/25/08. Pam Belluck, "ACLU Seeks End to DNA Sweep," *New York Times*, 01/11/05.

297 "In legal circles, postverdict skepticism": Kevin Dennehy and Hilary Russ, "New Doubts Raised on Police Interviews," *Cape Cod Times*, 11/20/06.

297 "Arguments about the Mason report became": Jonathan Saltzman, "Jurors: Race Talk Tainted Panel," *Boston Globe*, 12/12/06. Saltzman, "Bid for Retrial in Slaying Alleges Racism by Jurors," *Boston Globe*, 12/13/06. Hilary Russ and Kevin Dennehy, "Defense: Jurors Claim Racial Bias," *Cape Cod Times*, 12/13/06. Denise Lavoie, "Jurors Were Racist, Defense Says," AP, 12/13/06. Cf. Motion (p. 211) *Comm. v. Christopher McCowen*, Barnstable Superior Court, No. 05-109-03, Motion for Post-Verdict Inquiry of Jurors Pursuant to *Commonwealth v. Fidler*, filed 12/12/06 pursuant to Rule 61A(c) of the Superior Court Rules. Also, Peter Manso, "An Unjust Conclusion," *Boston* magazine, February 2007.

297 "when Roshena Bohanna, the lone female black juror": All descriptions and testimony pertaining to the Bohanna, Audet, and Huffman affidavits and to all events and dialogue taking place inside the jury room are drawn from juror affidavits, Barnstable Superior Court. Also, author ints. of Bohanna, 12/22/06, 05/17/07; Audet, 12/16/06; Huffman; attorneys Segadelli and Reddington; Taryn O'Connell, 03/07/07; Laura Stacey, 03/05/07. Cf. Manso, "An Unjust Conclusion."

303 "District Attorney O'Keefe trivialized it as": Quoted in Denise Lavoie, "Prosecutors in Cape Cod Slaying Deny Racial Bias on Jury, AP, 01/10/07.

304 "In February, in response to this author's *Boston* magazine article": Eric Williams and Hilary Russ, "Writer Questions McCowen's Guilt," *Cape Cod Times*, 02/23/07 ("When fielding questions yesterday about his contention that the Cape was home to a quiet sort of racism, Manso was asked whether he felt a black man could get a fair trial on Cape Cod. In Barnstable County, 94 percent of the population is white, according to 2000 US Census data. 'While recognizing that nothing is an absolute, I would say no,' Manso replied. 'If I were a black person on trial charged with murder, I would far prefer to be tried off Cape Cod. . . . This jury seemed to have been made up of either terribly frivolous people, or people who were not going to look at the evidence because they were convinced that the "big black man" was the only person who did the killing.' One juror, who would speak only on the condition of anonymity for this report, called Manso's opinion 'insulting' and Manso himself 'antagonistic.'

Manso said yesterday he hoped his article would 'serve to goose [Barnstable Superior Court] Judge Gary Nickerson into seriously entertaining the motion that was filed in mid-December for an open and thorough hearing'").

304 "a *Cape Cod Times* poll found": Cf. Cape Cod On Line/*Cape Cod Times*, 02/27/07, "Times Quick Poll."

304 "Defendant Thomas Toolan, 'a tall, pretty, white former bank executive'": Hilary Russ, "Murder Defendant Toolan Given Room to Move," *Cape Cod Times*, 06/07/07.

304 "Five months passed before": Jonathan Saltzman, "Lawyer Criticized Judge in Slay Case," *Boston Globe*, 06/02/07.

304 "Nickerson finally ruled": Cf. Comm. of Massachusetts, Barnstable Superior Court Criminal Action No. 2005-00109(01-03), *Comm. v. Christopher McCowen*, "Order Regarding Defendant's Motion for Post-Verdict Inquiry of Jurors," Gary A. Nickerson, Justice of the Superior Court, 06/08/07. Also, Katie Zezima, "Jurors Ordered to Hearing on Bias Remarks," *New York Times*, 12/01/07.

304 "Jonathan Turley, a law professor at": Quoted in Denise Lavoie, "Massachusetts Jury's Racial Attitudes Questioned," AP, 01/03/08.

305 "During the next seven months": Hillary Russ, "Lawyers, Judge Confer in McCowen Challenge," *Cape Cod Times*, 09/08/07.

305 "George wanted the hearing held in open court": Cf. Comm. of Massachusetts, Barnstable Superior Court No. 05-109-01-03, *Comm. v. Christopher M. McCowen*, "Defendant's Proposed Questions for Post-Verdict Inquiry of Jurors" and "Defendant's Supplemental Proposed Questions for Post-Verdict Inquiry of Jurors." Also, author int. of Robert George, 07/10/07.

305 "George filed yet another motion": Cf. Comm. of Massachusetts, Barnstable Superior Court No. 2005-109-01-03, *Comm. v. Christopher M. McCowen*, "Motion for New Trial Pursuant to Rule 30(b) of the Rules of Criminal Procedure and Exhibits," filed 12/12/06, refiled 11/27/07. Also, "Man Convicted in Writer's Death Says Prosecutor Withheld Evidence," *International Herald Tribune* (AP), 11/29/07.

305 "News reports, as well as the motion": Cf. "Worthington Revisited," *Boston* magazine, www.bostonmagazine.com, 12/01/07.

305 "Coincidence or not, while I was in California . . . armed with a warrant signed by Orleans District Court Judge Robert Welsh, the father of prosecutor Rob Welsh": Search Warrant docket 82785, 18 Long Nook Road, Truro, Mass. Town of Truro Assessor's atlas 43-123-O-R . . . "You are also commanded to search any person who may be found to have such property in his or her possession. . . ." Date issued 12/27/07, witnessed Robert A. Welsh, Jr., signature of Justice Clerk-Magistrate Stephen I. Ross.

305 "'Truro biographer Peter Manso (Normal Mailer, Marlon Brando) is

in hot water'": Inside Track, "We Hear . . . ," 01/10/08. Cf. Jonathan Saltzman, "Writer on Cape Slaying Indicted on Gun Charges," *Boston Globe*, 08/23/08; Corey Kilgannon, "Cape Cod Murder Case Adds Another Chapter," *New York Times*, 08/28/08.

305 "the Commonwealth of Massachusetts had changed 'lifetime' licenses to revenue-generating five-year renewals without notifying license holders—724,028 of them": Cf. Gun Control Act of 1998; Comm. of Massachusetts, House of Representatives, House Post Audit and Oversight Bureau, "Preliminary Report: Firearms Identification Cards (FIDs) and Licenses to Carry (LTCs)—After the implementation of the 1998 Gun Control Act," July 2002. *Findings*: "Pre-1998 recordkeeping varied by locality. The CHSN made significant efforts to contact holders of pre-1998 (lifetime) FIDs to notify them of changes in the law. Civil penalties for being in possession of a weapon with an expired FID or LTC are currently unenforceable as written." *Recommendations*: "Civil penalties for being in possession of a weapon with an expired FID or LTC should be enforceable through noncriminal proceedings similar to motor-vehicle infractions. The legislature should consider statutory changes to this effect. Efforts to improve recordkeeping and communication between localities and the state should continue." *Mechanics*: "The Criminal History Systems Board is required to send notice of expiration at least ninety days prior to the expiration of the FID." *Conclusion*: "Now that the requirements have changed and technology is ubiquitous, records must be centralized and well maintained."

Response letter, Commonwealth of Massachusetts, CHSB, 08/19/08, Re: Request for Records: Dear Mr. Manso: The Criminal History Systems Board (CHSB) is in receipt of your July 26, 2008 request for 'research whether the CHSB has records or other evidence showing that it contacted, or attempted to contact . . . Mr. Peter Manso, with respect to the need for "lifetime" FID card holders to bring their gun permit(s) into conformity with MBCA 1998.' In response to your request for information, please be advised that the CHSB is not in possession of documents that are responsive to your request. Sincerely, Georgia K. Critsley, General Counsel."

306 "and soon the district court dismissed my case": Letter from Stephen I. Ross, clerk magistrate, to Peter Manso, 01/14/09.

306 "had me hauled in front of the Barnstable County grand jury . . . which indicted": Jonathan Saltzman, "Writer on Cape Slaying Indicted."

306 "'like a common drug dealer'": Anonymous to author.

306 "He'd had his shot at Huffman": Amanda Lehmert, "Key Charges Dropped against Ex-Juror," *Cape Cod Times*, 12/05/06. "DA Drops Accessory Charge against Former Juror," AP/*Boston Herald*, 12/05/06.

306 "later went after Audet": Cf. Falmouth District Court, 06/25/09, "Dis-

positions: AUDET, Norman, 65, 630 MacArthur Blvd., indecent assault and battery on child under age 14, June 1, 2008, in Bourne, not prosecuted, indicted and arraigned in Superior Court. Audet attorney David R. Zanetti, Boston.

306 "Fourteen days after my home invasion": Abby Goodnough, "Jurors in a Cape Cod Murder Case Testify about Racial Remarks," *New York Times*, 01/11/08. Laura Crimaldi, "Cape Jury Bias Probe Now in Judge's Hands," *Boston Herald*, 01/12/08. "Jury Called Back to Discuss Racial Bias in 2006 Murder," AP/www.CNN.com, 01/12/08. Jonathan Saltzman, "Worthington Jurors Confirm Quarrel," *Boston Globe*, 01/12/08. Sheri Qualters, "Lawyers Say Post-Verdict Inquiry Is Necessary Check on Juror Impartiality," www.law.com. Jeff Blanchard, " 'Extraordinary' Hearing Allows Glimpses into Jury Room, and It's Not a Pretty View," www.capecod today.com, 01/10/08. Cf. Comm. of Massachusetts, Barnstable Superior Court, No. 0572CR0109, *Comm. v. Christopher M. McCowen*, before Gary A. Nickerson, Superior Court Justice, 01/10–11/08, Hearing trans. (Daniel E. Horgan, court reporter).

306 "Marlo George, the first of": Hearing trans., proceedings 01/10–11/08, Barnstable Superior Court, *Comm. v. Christopher M. McCowen*, Appearances: Michael O'Keefe, Robert A. George.

306 "an op-ed piece I'd penned for the *Cape Cod Times*": Peter Manso, "Party to a Grave Injustice," *Cape Cod Times* (op-ed), 12/13/06. ("Some jurors, post-trial, are disturbed enough about the many questions they have that they initiate a private meeting with the prosecutor so as to get answers? These same jurors who've recently made arrangements with the television networks . . . to appear on prime-time programs to discuss the very deliberations that are supposedly secret and sacred? . . . Cape Cod, listen to me, please. None of this is right and none of it would be accepted anywhere on this planet where due process is the accepted form of justice. . . . No matter what your District Attorney or anyone else tells you, or what your personally choose as your method of jurisprudence— or what your feelings about the verdict in this case may happen to be— these types of activities are unacceptable.")

307 "George then submitted": Cf. "Affidavit of Delainda Julia Miranda," filed with Barnstable Superior Court, 01/18/08. Miranda's allegations about Gomes's anti-black statements appeared in her sworn affidavit and formed the basis of direct- and cross-examinations when she took the stand.

307 "Miranda took the stand": David Frank, "Further Allegations of Juror Bias Surface in McCowen Murder Case," *Massachusetts Lawyers Weekly*, 01/18/08. Jonathan Saltzman, "Juror's Kin Says He Lied about Bias," *Boston Globe*, 01/19/08. K. C. Myers, "New Racism Charges Surface in McCowen Case," *Cape Cod Times*, 01/20/08. Rose Connors, "The Next Phase: Jurors Tell Very Different Tales in Court," *Cape Cod Voice*,

01/24/09. Marilyn Miller, "Judge Takes McCowen Retrial Motion under Advisement," www.wickedlocal.com, 12/01/08. Hilary Russ, "McCowen Juror a Racist, Says Aunt," *Cape Cod Times,* 02/01/08. Jonathan Saltzman, "Great-Aunt Says Worthington Juror Is Racially Biased," *Boston Globe,* 02/02/08. Author ints. of Delainda Julia Miranda, 01/13/08, 01/15/08. Again, I found myself in the headlines, and after interviewing Miranda, I brought this potential witness to the court's attention via a letter addressed to Honorable Gary A. Nickerson, DA Michael O'Keefe, and Robert George. The letter read:

"Gentlemen,

"I am writing to advise the Court, the defense and the Commonwealth of the following developments that bear directly on the credibility of Eric Gomes, a trial juror in the case of *Commonwealth v. Christopher McCowen.* I was present in Barnstable Superior Court when Mr. Gomes testified before the Court on January 10, 2008, that he had not made racially biased statements attributed to him by trial juror Rachel Huffman. . . .

"During a recess in the proceedings on January 11, 2008, I engaged two women named Julia Miranda and Andrea Robinson in a conversation and they stated they wished to speak to me about Gomes' testimony at the hearing. As a result of this meeting, I met with Julia Miranda on January 13, 2008 at her home located at xxxx in Mashpee, Massachusetts 02649. At that time, she told me that Mr. Gomes is her great-nephew (Gomes' mother is Miranda's niece, and Gomes' grandfather is Miranda's oldest brother). Also present at the time I spoke to Ms. Miranda were her sons Rodney Miranda and Jeffrey Perry, who are Gomes' 'cousins.'

"At this meeting, I was told by Ms. Miranda that Mr. Gomes has been 'a racist' since he was 15–16 years of age and has been making anti-black statements similar to those alleged by Rachel Huffman in her presence for many years. She stated that he has made negative comments about blacks being criminals, just as he has also insisted that he is not black and prefers to be with whites. Ms. Miranda told me that she came forward after reading that Mr. Gomes had denied making such statements in his testimony under oath before the court at the hearing. . . .

"She also told me that when Mr. Gomes was selected as a juror in the McCowen case in 2006, she ran into him and congratulated him on what she thought was a great civic honor. She told me that Gomes told her that he did not want to serve as a juror in the case and that 'he did not like blacks anyway.' After hearing these allegations, I immediately contacted Attorney Robert George that day by telephone and suggested that he meet with Ms. Miranda to discuss these matters. Ms. Miranda later talked with Attorney George by telephone.

"It is my understanding that Ms. Miranda is prepared to execute an affidavit and testify to these matters. She has unequivocally told me that Gomes testified falsely to the Court at the hearing and in his voir dire selection proceedings (at which I was also present) when he swore that he was not racially biased against persons who are black. . . .

"I am certain I need not point out that Ms. Miranda's statements support the claims of Rachel Huffman.

"I did not solicit the comments of Ms. Miranda and her family nor had I met her before our discussion at the Courthouse. Therefore, I am advising the Court, the District Attorney and Mr. McCowen's lawyer of this evidence and leave it to the parties to deal with this development, which in my opinion clearly supports the fact that Mr. McCowen did not receive a fair trial free of racial bias.

"Very truly yours, Peter Manso."

Needless to say, O'Keefe saw my notifying the court as meddlesome, which prompted him to call me "Mr. Manson" during his cross-examination of Miranda. He could not have been made happy by my comments to the press, either—my reference to the Cape as "a suburb of racist Mississippi" and the quote attributed to me in the *Boston Globe*, calling the DA's conduct "criminal" (Jonathan Saltzman, "Author Takes Center Stage in the Worthington Trial," 02/10/08). There is little question that my contributions to the case were what prompted him to ramp up the number of charges against me from five to twelve, and, flying in the face of all recent Commonwealth legal precedent, see to it that I was indicted on multiple felonies in Superior Court for what was, finally, my innocent failure to renew a gun permit.

307 "as opposed to 'Mr. Manson or whatever he calls himself'": Cf. hearing trans. Comm. of Massachusetts, Barnstable Superior Court, Criminal Action No. 2005-00109, *Comm. v. Christopher M. McCowen.* Motion for New Trial, Friday, February 1, 2008 (Victoria Gordon, court reporter); Saltzman, "Author Takes Center Stage."

307 "Nickerson tried. He asked": Hearing trans. 02/01/08.

308 "'Billy's sad'": Hilary Russ, "Post-Trial Witness: McCowen Juror Racist," *Cape Cod Times,* 02/02/08.

308 "The souvenir snapshot had been e-mailed to jury members": Matt Maltby e-mail, "Hi guys, thought you might like to have these . . . you can get them printed at CVS if you want . . . your pal, Matt." Response from Pam Worthington to Maltby.Matthew@hal.sysco.com, 11/29/06: "Matthew, thank you so very much for your note and photo's [*sic*] they all came and gave me so much joy!!!! I forwarded them to my sisters May and Susan and Amyra (Ava's Mom #2!!!) Very Fondly, Pam Worthington."

309 "'You can never tell me'": Author ints. of anon., 05/10/06, 05/16/06.

309 "Off the record, George expressed": Author int. of Robert George, 11/23/06.

309 "Nickerson is known as": Megan Tench, "A Judge Willing to Make Hard Calls," *Boston Globe*, 11/15/06. Hilary Russ, "Judge Keeps Court under Strict Control in Christa Worthington Murder Trial," *Cape Cod Times*, 10/31/06.

309 "'He *loves* being a superior court judge'": Author ints. of anon., 10/18/09, 11/02/09.

310 "The forty-page ruling": Comm. of Massachusetts, Barnstable Superior Court, CR 05-109, *Comm. v. Christopher M. McCowen*, "Order Regarding Defendant's Motion for a New Trial Pursuant to Rule 30(b) of the Rules of Criminal Procedure," Gary A. Nickerson, Justice of the Superior Court, April 4, 2008. All subsequent quotes are from this Nickerson ruling.

311 "the case in which a Washington State trial judge": Cf. *Turner v. Stime*, No. 05-2-0537-1, 2008 WL 4375521 (Wash. Super. Ct., March 27, 2008).

312 "the New Jersey Supreme Court ordered a new trial": Cf. *State v. Loftin*, 922 A.2d 1210 (N.J. 2007).

312 "the Ninth Circuit Court of Appeals": Cf. *U.S. v. Henley*, 238 F.3d 1111 (9th Cir. 2001).

312 "in *Tobias v. Smith*, habeas corpus was granted": Cf. *Tobias v. Smith*, 468 F.Supp. 1287, 1289 (W.D.N.Y. 1979).

312 "At bottom": Cf. *Dyer v. Calderon*, 151 F.3d-20970, 973, 974 (9th Cir. 1998); *Smith v. Brewer*, 444 F.Supp. 482 (S.D. Iowa 1978); *U.S. ex rel. Haynes v. McKendrick*, 481 F.2d 152 (2d Cir. 1973); *U.S. ex rel. Owen v. McMann*, 435 F.2d 863 (2d Cir. 1970); *Parker v. Gladden*, 385 U.S. 363, 366 (1966).

312 "The doctrine is plain": *U.S. v. Allsup*, 566 F.2d 68, 71 (9th Cir. 1977); *Tumey v. Ohio*, 273 U.S. 510, 535 (1927); *Arizona v. Fulminante*, 499 U.S. 279, 307-10 (1991).

313 "Early on, he'd deep-sixed": Cf. Comm. of Massachusetts, Barnstable Superior Court, No. 05-109-01-03, *Comm. v. Christopher M. McCowen*, Defendant's Proposed Questions for Post-Verdict Inquiry of Jurors, filed under seal per Order of Court, 09/04/07.

313 "called the decision": Quoted in Denise Lavoie, "Judge Rejects New Trial for Man Convicted in Worthington Murder," AP, 04/04/08.

313 "most important Frazier's Wellfleet pier knife incident": Cf. Case No. 20033677, Assault by Means (Knife), Jeremy Frazier, 7/5/03, Wellfleet Police Dept. Incident Report. The Frazier knife-incident file, including arraignment and court proceedings, as well as the criminal histories of the other relevant prosecution witnesses, was found by this author; all material is on file at Orleans District Court, Court Clerk's Office. Cf. Comm. of Massachusetts, No. 05-109 (01-03), *Comm. v. Christopher M. McCowen*, Defendant's Motion for a New Trial Pursuant to Rule 30(b) of the Rules of Criminal Procedure.

313 "The prosecution also knew that Christopher Bearse": Cf. Criminal

docket 0226CR000545, SP Yarmouth PD, offense date 02/07/02, RMV document, forge/dvrs. lcse.; docket 9725CR000130, SP Yarmouth, offense date 01/11/97, A&B on police officer, resisting arrest; docket 9725CR002004, Yarmouth PD, offense date 05/27/97, A&B; docket 0325CR002578, Barnstable PD, offense date 08/07/03, A&B, destruction of property, intimidating witness; docket 02CR2303, Barnstable PD, offense date 05/17/02, op. MV with license suspended, credit card fraud; docket 0225CR003248, SP Yarmouth PD, offense date 09/12/02, larceny over $250, improper use of credit card, forgery of document, counterfeit note.

314 "DuBois, who'd been jumped": Cf. docket 0325CR003493, Yarmouth PD, offense date 10/23/03, B&E building daytime for felony, poss. burglarious tools; docket 0526CR001710, Orleans PD, offense date 08/19/05, assault w/ dangerous weapon (knife), destruction of property over $250; docket 0626CR000504, Orleans PD, offense date 03/18/06, A&B w/ dangerous weapon (bottle), resisting arrest, B&E building nighttime for felony, A&B on ambulance personnel, disorderly conduct.

314 "Buckles, who hid in a closet": Docket 0326CR 000586, Orleans PD, offense date 03/22/03, OUI/liquor, drug possession, Class C; docket 0326CR001298, Eastham PD, offense date 06/16/03, A&B; docket 0426CR002023, Eastham PD, offense date 07/05/04, burglary (unarmed), B&E building nighttime for felony, prob. violation; docket 0426CR2023, Orleans Court Prob. Dept., offense date 10/10/06, intimidating witness, failure to remain alcohol-free; docket BACR2005-00063, Orleans PD/MSP, offense date 11/20/04, home invasion, burglary (armed) A&B w/ a dangerous weapon.

314 "Lord, who accompanied": Docket 0426CR000057, Orleans PD, offense date 01/05/04, destruction of property over $250; docket 0426CR000324, Orleans PD, offense date 02/17/04, A&B w/ a dangerous weapon (shod foot); docket BACR2007-00061, Orleans PD, offense date 02/02/07, A&B w/ a dangerous weapon (knife).

314 "the Buckles home invasion was investigated by": Statement of facts re shooting at 23 Greenwood Lane, South Chatham, 11/20/04, Det. Sgt. Mark R. Goodspeed, Chatham PD. Cf. Comm. of Massachusetts, Barnstable Superior Court, docket 0572CR00063-02, 07/11/06. Also, nolle prosequi, in which defendant Buckles pleaded guilty and was released from the House of Corrections on condition of his entering a halfway house and SHOCK rehab program, by court order of Gary A. Nickerson(!).

314 "George's motion charged that the discovery violations had been systematic and deliberate": Comm. of Massachusetts, Barnstable Superior Court, No. 2005-109-01-03, *Comm. v. Christopher M. McCowen*, Defendant's Motion for a New Trial Pursuant to Rule 30(b) of the Rules of Criminal Procedure.

315 "Five months later, on June 9": Cf. Comm. of Massachusetts, Barnstable
     Superior Court, CR05-109, *Comm. v. Christopher M. McCowen*, Memoran-
     dum of Decision and Order on Defendant's Renewed Motion for New
     Trial, Gary A. Nickerson, Justice of the Superior Court, June 9, 2009.

315 "But the only source for that information was": Case 20033677, Wellfleet
     PD Incident Report.

315 "If Nickerson had checked, officially or otherwise, with local residents":
     Author ints. of anonymous sources, 10/06/05, 02/21/06, 04/08/07,
     05/05/07, 08/12/07, 08/13/08; Dave Nichols, 01/21/07.

316 "Records from the victim/witness assistance unit": Author's telephone
     queries to Barnstable County District Attorney's Office, 07/08/09, and
     Orleans District Court (court clerk's office).

316 "'To date, [Keir] has never'": E-mail to Peter Manso/Christophe Laf-
     faille, 05/08/09, from Hilary Hard, secretary/assistant to Helena Ken-
     nedy-Mitchell and Keir Kennedy-Mitchell.

316 "the family owned a home not three minutes' walk from": Cf. Quitclaim
     Deed, book 15326, p. 290, 5767007-01-2002, between Robert H. Wharf
     and Iain L. Hutchison and Helena A. Kennedy of 2 Eton Road, Lon-
     don, NW34SP, United Kingdom, property located at 161 Commercial St.,
     Wellfleet, Mass. 02667. Also, Town of Wellfleet, Fiscal Year 2010, Hutchi-
     son, Iain L., and Kennedy, Helena A., 161 Commercial St., parcel ID
     21-119-O-R, DOS 07/01/02.

317 "allegation of deficiencies": Saltzman, "Lawyers Question Lab's DNA Re-
     sults" and "U.S. Audit Found More Problems."

317 "Responding to Nickerson's ruling, George told the *Cape Cod Times*":
     Quoted in Stephanie Vosk, "Christopher McCowen Murder Retrial De-
     mand," *Cape Cod Times*, 06/10/08.

317 "'I may have publicly acted as if'": Author int. of Robert George, 04/08/09.

318 "Even now, sympathetic Cape Codders express": Cf. Comm. of Massa-
     chusetts, Supreme Judicial Court, No. SJC-09935, *Comm. v. Christopher M.
     McCowen*, Defendant-Appellant's Brief, Robert A. George, Attorney for
     Defendant-Appellant, filed 12/14/09.

318 "all that was withheld or buried": Clinical and evaluative reports of Dr. Eric
     L. Brown, PsyD, Clinical Synopsis, 10/10/06; Suppl. Report, 10/16/06;
     Second Supp. Report, 10/26/06; Notes of 09/15/06, 09/18/06,
     09/19/06, 09/28/06, 10/05/06, 10/07/06, 10/19/06; Wechsler Memory
     Scale, 10/07/06; Wechsler Adult Intelligence Scale, 09/15/06.

320 "Cathy Nolan, a *People* magazine editor in Paris": Author ints. (Chris Laf-
     faille) of Cathy Nolan, 08/10/02, 02/27/09.

320 "Greene, a star of today's photojournalism in France": Author int. (Chris
     Laffaille) of Stanley Greene, 11/21/09.

320 "'Race would never be an issue, never'": Author ints. (Chris Laffaille) of
     Cathy Nolan, 08/10/02, 02/27/09.

320 "Vassar chums recall her attraction to 'the illicit'": Author ints. of anon., 06/04/09; Leila Levinson, 06/10/09.

321 "Cousin Pam": MSP (Burke) ints. of Pamela Worthington Franklin, 01/06/02; Melik Kaylan, 08/05/03.

321 "enter alcoholic English boyfriend": Flook, pp. 249–51.

321 "'said something racist'": Cf. Christa Worthington diary entry, n.p.

322 "Cousins Patricia and Jan had liaisons": Author ints. of anon., 09/28/06; Warren Roderick, 09/30/06; Phil Tarvers, 11/11/06; anon. II, 08/12/07; E. J. Kahn III, 07/19/06.

322 "Their parents dallied, too, between marrying and unmarrying each other three times": MSP (Massari) int. of John Worthington, 01/14/02. Also, author int. of E. J. Kahn III, 07/09/06.

322 "Diana's late husband, Bob Loft . . . love nest in Provincetown": Cf. *Cape Cod Times* fax 08/13/02 to MSP; Discovery 185 ("My friend . . . was going out with [Toppy] for a while—totally in love with him—he told her he was broken up with his wife. She totally believed it because she use [*sic*] to go to his house with him all the time in P-town! . . . He actually rented the place in P'town JUST for his relationship with her! . . . Diana's husband, Bob, cheated on her constantly! He use [*sic*] to try it EVEN with her friends! He use [*sic*] to hit on me . . . any woman within any distance of him! I use [*sic*] to be afraid to go down cellar to do laundry because he'd follow me down there!"). Also, Flook, pp. 86, 161 ff.

322 "'He embroils me . . . I don't like being immobilized by an animal'": Christa Worthington diary entry, n.p.

322 "Jackett abandoned her": Cf. MSP (Squier) ints. of Nicholas Kahn, 02/07/02; Ethan and Natalie Cohen, 01/08/02; Debra Strain, 06/13/02 ("Strain said it seemed as though Christa got mad when she spoke of him and it bothered her that he didn't want to meet Ava"); MSP (Mason) int. of Gail Motlin, 01/18/03 ("Motlin stated that after Ava was born, Worthington began to become concerned that Ava would not have a family. . . . Motlin stated that Worthington told her that Jackett had stopped seeing her after she told him she was pregnant"); MSP (Sabota) int. of Ellen Webb, 01/08/02; MSP (Burke) int. of Pamela Worthington Franklin, 01/06/02; MSP (Knott) int. of Tim Arnold, 01/06/02; author int. of Warren Roderick, 09/30/06.

323 "one grand juror sought out": Proceedings trans., Judge Richard F. Connon lobby, Barnstable Superior Court, 06/14/05 (Daniel E. Horgan, court reporter).

323 "Had Mazzone contributed these same words from the witness stand": Mazzone blogs posted on www.capecodtoday.com, dates as indicated. Also, "Mazzone, the Cowboy Cop, Speaks Out on the Worthington

Case . . . An Exclusive Interview with a Former Wellfleet Policeman," by Crusader, www.capecodtoday.com, 04/12/08.

327 "which was run by Sheriff James Cummings": Cf. Cummings bio, Massachusetts Sheriff's Association, www.mass.gov. Also, Barnstable Sheriff's Office, www.bsheriff.net/sheriff-bio.htm. Cf. Editorial, "Call the Sheriff: The Most Outrageous Campaign Manager of All Is Michael O'Keefe's," *Cape Cod Voice*, 10/19/06.

327 "the judge called the attorneys into his office": Author int. of anon., 10/26/06.

328 "Nickerson's long-standing contempt": Author ints. of anon., 10/18/09, 11/02/09.

328 "'I can't count the number'": Author int. of Robert George, 07/09/09.

328 "What did the autopsy": Cf. Comm. of Massachusetts, Office of the Chief Medical Examiner, Postmortem Examination Report, Final, Case 200263, Christa Worthington, age 46, race white, gender FEMA. Date of death Sunday, January 6, 2002; date of autopsy Monday, January 7, 2002. Cause of death stab wound of chest, manner of death homicide. Signed, James Weiner, M.D., pathologist (5 pages). Autopsy reviewed by anon., int. by author, 09/16/06, 10/08/06.

330 "'The neck and genitalia are unremarkable'": Comm. of Mass., Office of the Chief Medical Examiner, Postmortem Examination Report, Case 200263, 01/07/02, p.3.

330 "'Women are not happy when they get'": Author ints. of anon., 09/16/06, 10/08/06. Note that not all autopsies are definitive. The review here cannot be regarded as final, either; it points to the obvious, however, in ways that only partly surfaced at trial.

330 "But the medical literature on vaginal injury": Laura Slaughter, Carol Brown, Sharon Crowley, and Roxy Peck, "Patterns of Genital Injury in Female Sexual Assault Victims," *Am. J. Obstet. Gynecol.* 1997, 176: 609–16. Also, J. R. Evrard and E. M. Gold, "Epidemiology and Management of Sexual Assault Victims," *Obstet. Gynecol.* 1979, 53: 381–87; L. Brown Slaughter, "Colposcopy to Establish Physical Findings in Victims of Sexual Assault," *Am. J. Obstet. Gynecol.* 1992, 166: 83–86; L. Bowyer and M. E. Dalton, "Female Victims of Rape and the Genital Injuries," *Br. J. Obstet. Gynecol.* May 1997, 104(5): 617–20.

331 "Even more persuasive": Author ints. of Catherine Cisneros, 04/05/09, 07/06/09.

332 "According to his pal Dave Nichols": Author ints. of Dave Nichols, 10/01/06, 11/25/06, 12/02/06.

332 "'I have Tim Arnold clearly testifying'": Author int. of Robert George, 07/09/09.

334 "But in August 2009, the *Journal of Forensic Science International* reported": Dan Franklin, Adam Wasserstrom, Ariane Davidson, and Aaron Grafit,

"Authentication of Forensic DNA Samples," www.fsigenetics.com. Andrew Pollack, "DNA Evidence Can Be Fabricated, Scientists Show," *New York Times*, 08/08/09.

334 "Beyond means": Vincent Bugliosi, *Till Death Us Do Part* (New York; Norton, 1979), p. 326.

336 "a master of 'working the room' at rallies": "Heartfelt Farewell," *Cape Cod Times*, 12/31/05.

336 "let him separate his office from": Author ints. of Jeff Blanchard, 05/16/07, 05/20/07.

337 "The Crime Prevention and Control Unit—CPAC—vastly increased": Cf. Code of Massachusetts Regulations, Title 515, Dept. of State Police, 515 CMR 5.01 ch. 5.00.

337 "The case of Barnstable County Sheriff James Cummings": Seth Rolbein, "The Pieces of a Puzzle Reveal an Outrageous District Attorney," *Cape Cod Voice*, June 2008. Author int. of Seth Rolbein and Dan Hamilton, 12/15/07. Patrick Cassidy, "Sheriff Cummings Vows to Punish Aides," *Cape Cod Times*, 08/06/09.

337 "Charges against the sheriff's deputies": Editorial, *Cape Cod Voice*, 10/18/06.

338 "The commonwealth is an anomaly because": Cf. Mass. G.L. ch. 3, sec. 8, "Special Responsibilities of a Prosecutor": "The prosecutor in a criminal case shall: (a) refrain from prosecuting a charge that the prosecutor knows is not supported by probable cause; (b) make reasonable efforts to assure that the accused has been advised of the right to, and the procedure for obtaining, counsel and has been given reasonable opportunity to obtain counsel; (c) not seek to obtain from an unrepresented accused a waiver of important pretrial rights . . . (d) make timely disclosure to the defense of all evidence or information known to the prosecutor that tends to negate the guilt of the accused or mitigates the offense, and, in connection with sentencing, disclose to the defense and to the tribunal all unprivileged mitigating information known to the prosecutor, except when the prosecutor is relieved of this responsibility by a protective order of the tribunal; (e) exercise reasonable care to prevent investigators, law enforcement personnel, employees, or other persons assisting or associated with the prosecutor in a criminal case from making an extrajudicial statement that the prosecutor would be prohibited from making under Rule 3.6; (f) not subpoena a lawyer in a grand jury or other criminal proceeding to present evidence about a past or present client unless: (1) the prosecutor reasonably believes: (i) the information sought is not protected from disclosure by any applicable privilege; (ii) the evidence sought is essential to the successful completion of an ongoing investigation or prosecution; and (iii) there is no other feasible alternative to obtain the information; and (2) the prosecutor obtains

prior judicial approval after an opportunity for an adversarial proceeding; (g) . . . refrain from making extrajudicial comments that have a substantial likelihood of heightening public condemnation of the accused; (h) not assert personal knowledge of the facts in issue, except when testifying as a witness; (i) not assert a personal opinion as to the justness of a cause, as to the credibility of a witness . . . or as to the guilt or innocence of an accused . . . (j) not intentionally avoid pursuit of evidence because the prosecutor believes it will damage the prosecution's case or aid the accused. Adopted June 9, 1997, effective January 1, 1998. Amended Dec. 9, 1998, effective Jan. 1, 1999. Comment: A prosecutor has the responsibility of a minister of justice and not simply that of an advocate. . . . Knowing disregard of those obligations or a systematic abuse of prosecutorial discretion could constitute a violation of Rule 8.4."

In the course of the Worthington investigation and trial, O'Keefe, it appears, failed to adhere to *eight* of these ten mandates.

338 "with an operating budget of $3.4 million": Editorial, *Cape Cod Voice*, 10/18/06. Dave Wedge, "Non-Campaigning Cape DA Eats Big Bucks from Election Account," *Boston Herald*, 07/30/07.

338 "'to flat-out lie'": Author int. of anon., 05/16/07.

339 "incestuousness was partly": Susan Milton, "End of the Line for Judge Robert Welsh Jr.," *Cape Cod Times*, 02/04/08.

339 "The senior Welsh presided": Cf. Arraignment Order: Pretrial Conference and Hearing, docket 03-26-CR1828, Orleans District Court, *Comm. v. Jeremy P. Frazier*, Setting of Trial Date, signed by Robert A. Welsh, Justice, 11/02/03. (If this wasn't enough, the Notice of Counsel Assignment, C3774229-4, docket 0326-CR-1828, "Assault w/ Dang. Weapon," dated 09/22/03, was signed by Charles Welsh, District Court Magistrate, who is Judge Robert Welsh's brother.)

339 "The Yarmouth Patrol Officers Association issued a letter": Rolbein, "The Pieces of a Puzzle."

339 "created a campaign fund": Author int. of anon., 08/01/06.

340 "Sandwich's tony Ridge Club": Cf. www.ridgeclubcapecod.com.

340 "'comped' him with home improvements": Author int. of anon., 09/26/07.

340 "the most publicized being those at the home": Hilary Russ, "Cape District Attorney's Home Burglarized Twice," *Cape Cod Times*, 10/19/07. Stephanie Ebbert, "Burglars Strike Cape DA's Home Twice in Past Year," *Boston Globe*, 10/26/07.

340 "the theft was not reported until": Russ, "Cape District Attorney's Home."

340 "When the *Boston Globe* called for comment": Ebbert, "Burglars Strike." Russ, "Cape District Attorney's Home."

340 "the Robbins Report": Peter Robbins, "A Cool Million Could Buy You the Cape & Islands' District Attorney's House," www.capecodtoday.com,

08/27/08. Also, James Kinsella, "Theft of Gun from DA Poses Continuing Questions," www.capecodtoday.com, 09/12/08 ("O'Keefe declined to answer questions from *Cape Cod Today* about the theft of the weapon. 'I wouldn't answer questions about an ongoing investigation,' he said. 'I would have nothing to say about it.' . . . A spokesman for the State Attorney General's Office said 'no comment' when asked how any investigation of an official such as a Massachusetts district attorney might be structured or proceed. The questions about O'Keefe and the stolen weapon come up at a time when one of the district attorney's critics, writer Peter Manso of Truro, has been indicted . . . on firearms charges").

341 "On September 12, with the story mushrooming": So frustrated was much of the Cape community that the Kinsella article elicited a flow of particularly outspoken e-mails. Three examples:

09/12/08, 6:45 P.M. "This is beyond words. . . . He's the chief law enforcement official. Hello! Anybody home in this State??????? . . . Well what do you expect from a justice system where saying 'I hate N's' is not considered racist in a trial where the defendant is black?? We're down the rabbit hole Alice."

09/12/08, 6:48 P.M. "So why is O'Keefe not indicted? All the evidence is here. He possessed a gun that has no serial numbers nor did he have a license to carry. Why doesn't the police department have the BALLS to arrest and indict this guy? . . . If it's ok for him, it's ok for Manso. O'Keefe is a hypocrite and should be shown the door as well as the police chief for not arresting this guy on something ANYONE else would have been arrested. . . . Flat out, this sucks."

09/12/08, 10:35 P.M. "The snub-nose .38! Excellent weapon for suicide. . . . Press the mouth of the barrel against the roof of the mouth and Blammo—Highway to Hell."

341 "there was 'more to the shooting'": Quoted in Jeffrey Blanchard, "When the Other Man Is District Attorney," www.capecodtoday.com, 08/06/07.

342 "the next day O'Keefe faced the press": Jake Berry, "DA Report: Gunfire Felled Brazilian Man," *Cape Cod Times*, 07/29/08. John Ellement and Michael Levenson, "Police Killing of Immigrant Challenged," *Boston Globe*, 07/29/08.

342 "Another version came from Camilla Campos": Quoted in Ellement and Levenson, "Police Killing."

342 "terrified of being deported": Cf. Editorial, "Officer's Perspective Still Doesn't Justify Execution," *Cape Cod Times*, 08/08/08. Also, Patrick Cassidy, "Yarmouth Police Officer, Town Sued in Fatal Shooting," *Cape Cod Times*, 11/05/09.

342 "The Martins incident stirred memories": Cf. "A Report on the Death of David C. Hendricks," David C. Hendricks Committee for Human Rights, December 1992. *Falmouth Enterprise*, n.a.; www.capecodtoday, 07/28/08.

Author ints. of John Reed, 10/12/06, 10/15/06; Ernest C. Hadley, 02/02/06; David and Peggy Lillienthal and Mary Ann Barboza ("Cape Codders Against Racism"), 05/20/07, 05/23/07.

343   "Truro residents, alarmed": Kevin Mullaney, "Leave It Alone, Counsel Advises on Perry Letter," *Provincetown Banner*, 07/09/08. Kevin Mullaney, "Reaction Grows over Perry Letter," *Provincetown Banner*, 07/02/08. Kevin Mullaney, "Police Reprisal Feared," *Provincetown Banner*, 07/24/08.

343   "Even in the face of such gangsterism": Mullaney, "Leave It Alone." Author int. of Robert Weinstein, 11/02/09.

343   "'To say that the Cape and Islands has both'": Rolbein, "The Pieces of a Puzzle."

344   "The longest piece in the issue": Jeffrey S. Davidson and Seth Rolbein, "Raising Money to 'Fight Crime,'" *Cape Cod Voice*, June 2008, pp. 60–62. Jeffrey S. Davidson and Seth Rolbein, "Some Tough Campaigning," *Cape Cod Voice*, June 2008, pp. 64–65. Also, Wedge, "Non-Campaigning Cape DA Eats."

344   "Aside from lawyers, businessmen, and bankers": Author ints. of anon., 10/15/09; anon. II, 10/30/09.

345   "Attorney William Henchy called the DA's investigation. . . . Even the normally circumspect Russell Redgate": All quoted in Doreen Leggett, "Following a Trail of Legal Smoke," *Cape Cod Voice*, June 2008, pp. 46–51.

345   "The first was directed": David Abel, "Doctor Indicted in '07 Death of Abortion Patient," *Boston Globe*, 07/17/08.

345   "'The first chapters of torts case books are filled'": "Making Malpractice a Criminal Matter," *Wall Street Journal*, 07/17/08. Abel, "Doctor Indicted."

346   "Even those who championed O'Keefe and his wooden, by-the-book methods": "Michael O'Keefe—What Does He Have against Fathers?" www.not mtwain.typepad.com/nader_for_president, 09/07/06.

346   "Perhaps O'Keefe's nuttiest prosecution of all": Author int. of Robert George. Barnstable Superior Court, docket 2000-45. Also, "District Attorney Michael O'Keefe: Not Exactly a Friend to Women, Infants and Children," www.welcometobarnstable.com, 08/07/09.

346   "'The O'Keefe office has lost its way,' said": Author ints. of anon., 05/10/07, 05/16/07, 10/18/09, 11/02/09.

347   "was 'out there working for the forces of good'": Author ints. of anon., 05/10/07; anon. II, 12/07/07.

347   "the son of Dorothy Mary O'Keefe": Cf. Dorothy M. O'Keefe obituary, *Cape Cod Times*, 10/12/06.

347   "But Mother's wonder boy lied": "Men Sue for Return of DNA." Russ, "Contested DNA Sample." Jonathan Saltzman, "ACLU Sues over DNA Sample, Alleges Cape DA May Have Kept It," *Boston Globe*, 06/20/08. Sowers, "Lawyers Demand Proof."

347   "compelled the DA to return": Hilary Russ, "DNA Sample Returned to Cape Man after Legal Fight," *Cape Cod Times*, 08/28/08.

347 "the op-ed piece the DA penned": Michael O'Keefe, "Sweep Can Solve Crime," *USA Today* (op-ed), 01/18/05.

348 "His comments ignored the facts": Saltzman, "ACLU Sues over DNA Sample." Cf. Burge and Ellement, "Police Seek DNA Samples" ("Cape and Islands District Attorney Michael O'Keefe has said that authorities would be compelled to look at those who refuse to give a sample. . . . John Reinstein, legal director for the American Civil Liberties Union of Massachusetts, said the legality of the DNA tests hinges on three factors: whether the DNA donor consents, whether he understands what he has consented to, and whether he is intimidated into consenting. Worthington's killer would almost certainly not agree to volunteer DNA, Reinstein argued. 'The only thing it reasonably does is narrow down the pool of people who they ask,' he said. 'That does suggest that the refusal to take the test is in fact what they're looking for'"); McNamara, "Flunking the Swab Test" Belluck, "To Try to Net a Killer"; ACLU, "ACLU of Massachusetts Calls for End to DNA Dragnet," 01/10/05 ("Officers seeking suspects in Truro . . . reportedly have been confronting people in public settings, asking them in front of other people if they are willing to do their part to help solve a heinous crime, and giving them little time to decide. Moreover, both police and the District Attorney have made public statements suggesting that anyone who refuses will, in effect, become a suspect in the case"); Barnacle, "Truro Men Have Right" ("And civil libertarians along with others were upset. . . . Call me naïve but I figure the refusal to submit a sample has more to do with rapidly disappearing individual privacies than it does with any desire to beat a murder rap or throw roadblocks in the path of detectives. . . . One of our most basic rights is the right to be left alone. And it's nearly gone. . . . Average folks are increasingly suspicious and rightfully raise questions about what happens to personal data and DNA. Who keeps it? Where? For how long? And why? . . . Sgt. David Perry of the Truro Police Department and other law enforcement authorities here say that the program is voluntary but that they will pay close attention to those who refuse to provide DNA. 'We're trying to find that person who has something to hide,' Sergeant Perry said").

348 "the nondonor's license-plate number": Amanda Ripley, Theonis Bates, Marc Hequet, and Ruth Caney, "The DNA Dragnet in Truro," *Boston Globe,* 01/16/05 ("Do DNA dragnets work? The answer so far is . . . rarely. . . . Of the 18 publicized U.S. sweeps, only one—a narrow sampling of 25 workers at a nursing home—has been successful, according to a 2004 study. . . . Given the history of Massachusetts' crime lab, it's hard to imagine Truro's DNA samples getting processed anytime soon. It took several months just to get the DNA from the initial suspects processed in the Worthington case. But DA O'Keefe insists, without elaborating, that the effort will have . . . 'ancillary benefits'").

348 "secured DNA samples through more covert methods": MSP (Massari) int. of Richard Emerson, 06/05/02 ("After Emerson left I took the can of Coca-Cola that Emerson was drinking out of while I interviewed him and preserved it in the event I would need it for a DNA sample"). Report of Investigation, "DNA Collection from Robert Lynn Bailey," MSP (Squier, Mason, Milos, Burke, Plath), 09/13/02: "On September 13, 2002 this officer, Tprs. Chris Mason, John Milos, Sgts. William Burke and James Plath set up a surveillance around the area of the DNA Gallery located on Bradford Street in Provincetown. This was done for the anticipation to obtain a DNA sample from Robert Bailey. . . . The Surveillance was set up for an Opening Night held at the DNA Gallery. The opening was scheduled to be held from 7:00 P.M. to 9:00 P.M. This officer, Tpr. Mason and Sgt. Burke were assigned to patrol the area. Sgt. Plath and Tpr. Milos were assigned to attend the Opening at the gallery. At approximately 1915 hours Sgt. Plath and Tpr. Milos entered the gallery. At approximately 1920 hours this officer and Tpr. Mason observed Robert Bailey, his wife, Breon, and son pull up in a dark green van . . . and park their vehicle on Bradford Street, diagonal from the DNA Gallery. At approximately 2015 hours, this officer and Tpr. Mason observe [*sic*] Robert Bailey, his wife and son leave the gallery. At approximately 2030 hours, Sgt. Plath and Tpr. Milos exit the gallery. Sgt. Plath advised that Bailey's son had asked for some water so Bailey bought a Dasani water bottle for him. Sgt. Plath and Tpr. Milos then observed Bailey and his son playing ping-pong, with the Dasani water bottle on the child's side of the table. Sgt. Plath and Tpr. Milos stated they did not observe the child drink from the bottle. Just before Bailey exited the gallery, Sgt. Plath and Tpr. Milos witnessed Bailey drink from the Dasani water bottle, finishing the water. Bailey then deposited the water bottle in a wastebasket located next to where Sgt. Plath was standing. Sgt. Plath then grabbed the plastic bag containing the Dasani water bottle. The bottle was then bagged as evidence. . . .

"On September 16, 2002, this officer, Tpr. Mason and Cosgrove again were assigned to obtain DNA from Robert Bailey. At approximately 1530 hours, this officer, Tpr. Mason and Cosgrove entered Willy's gym in Eastham, located on Route 6. At approximately 1600 hours Bailey enters the gym with his son. Bailey is observed to be carrying a Dasani water bottle. While in the gym, Bailey is witnessed to be using an elliptical exercise machine during the entire time. At the conclusion of his work-out, Bailey then went into the men's locker room. While in the locker room, Tprs. Mason and Cosgrove observe Bailey throw the Dasani water bottle away. Tpr. Cosgrove then recovers the Dasani water bottle, which is then bagged as evidence."

Re Peter Allner and Michael Denn, cf. Criminalistics Report, Comm.

Massachusetts, MSP Crime Laboratory (Sudbury), 02/11/04, Lab 02-00157 Truro; incident 2002-102-0900-0007: "Examination of Materials in Connection with a Fatal Stabbing in Truro on January 6, 2002. . . .

"On March 4, 2003, Trooper Christopher Mason of the Massachusetts State Police Cape and Island Detective Unit delivered the following item(s) to the laboratory in connection with the above subject . . . : 28-7, two cigarette butts, Peter Allner; 28-8, one envelope, Peter Allner; 28-9, one juice bottle, Peter Allner; 28-10, T-shirt, Michael Denn; 28-11, one water cup, Michael Denn; 28-12, one book with inscription page, Peter Manso. . . .

"Item 28-8, envelope—Peter Allner: This item consists of a white envelope addressed to 'GRISWOLD DRAZ, THE ZOE GALLERY, 207 NEWBURY STREET, BOSTON, MA USA.' . . . The adhesive flap of the envelope was sampled for DNA analysis.

"Item 28-10, T-shirt—Michael Denn: This item consists of a green 'Delta, Proweight' size 'XL' T-shirt with 'Boston Parks and Recreation, Thomas M. Manino, Myr' logo on the front and 'Staff' logo on the rear. The interior collar area of the T-shirt was sampled for DNA analysis.

"Comments: Specimens from the following item(s) were retained should comparative analysis be requested: item 28-8, envelope, Peter Allner, (2) swabs; item 28-10, T-shirt, Michael Denn, (2) swabs. . . .

"Robert J. Martin, Chemist III, Supervisor, Crime Scene Response Unit, Mass. State Police Crime Laboratory. Report to: ADA Sharon Thibeault, Cape and Islands District Attorney's Office. cc: Trooper Christopher Mason, MSP Cape and Islands County Detective Unit."

350 "The Center for Public Integrity": Steve Weinberg, "Breaking the Rules," 06/26/03, www.publicintegrity.org.

350 "grown since September 11, 2001, to a degree that seems contrived": Cf. Hess and Jordan, "Memo Justified" ("For at least 16 months after the Sept. 11 terror attacks in 2001, the Bush administration believed that the Constitution's protection against unreasonable searches and seizures on U.S. soil didn't apply to its efforts to protect against terrorism. . . . That program intercepted phone calls and e-mails on U.S. soil, bypassing the normal legal requirements that such eavesdropping be authorized"); editorial, "There Were Orders"; Jane Mayer, *The Dark Side: The Inside Story of How the War on Terror Turned into a War on American Ideals* (New York: Doubleday, 2008). Another mirror of this new lawlessness is the increased funding for law enforcement that starts with the Office of Homeland Security, then, in a true Reaganite vein, trickles down to local police departments in torrential volume. In 2008, the town of Truro, for example, employed fourteen full-time officers; five earned in excess of $100,000 a year; three others made $90,000-plus. Such remuneration not only bolsters the ego, especially among young officers, in places like

Cape Cod, it has turned law enforcement into a most desirable career path. For Truro calendar-year salaries, see *Town of Truro, Annual Town Report 2008*, pp. 136–39. Also, "Police Funding Awarded; Mass. Cities Can Hire Officers," *Worcester Telegram and Gazette*, 10/04/07 ("The Patrick administration yesterday made one of its first deliveries on a promise to put more police on the streets, distributing $4 million in grants to hire as many as 50 local police officers around the state. . . . Worcester will see $400,000. . . . Other grants will help police with hiring in 12 other cities and towns"). There can be no doubt that this "new" money has had its macho-izing effect, as suggested by, among others, Kevin Johnson, "Police Brutality Cases on Rise Since 9/11," *USA Today*, 12/17/07 ("Federal prosecutors are targeting a rising number of law enforcement officers for alleged brutality, Justice Department statistics show. The heightened prosecutions come as the nation's largest police union fears that agencies are dropping standards to fill thousands of vacancies and 'scrimping' on training. . . . Cases in which police, prison guards and other law enforcement authorities have used excessive force or other tactics to violate victims' civil rights have increased 25% . . . from fiscal 2001 to 2007 over the previous seven years. . . . For the past few years, dozens of police departments across the country have scrambled to fill vacancies. The recruiting effort, which often features cash bonuses, has intensified since 9/11, because many police recruits have been drawn to military service"). Also, United Nations Committee on the Elimination of Racial Discrimination, *In the Shadows of the War on Terror: Persistent Police Brutality and Abuse of People of Color in the United States*, December 2007 ("Since this Committee's 2001 review of the U.S. . . . there have been dramatic increases in law enforcement powers in the name of waging the 'war on terror' in the wake of September 11, 2001. . . . Systemic abuse of people of color by law enforcement officers has not only continued since 2001 but has *worsened in both practice and severity*. According to a representative of the NAACP, 'the degree to which police brutality occurs . . . *is the worst I've seen in 50 years*'" [emphasis added]).

351 "eroded the notion of justice": Cf. Michelle R. McPhee, *When Evil Rules: A True Story of Vengeance and Murder on Cape Cod* (New York: St. Martin's, 2009), pp. 78, 83, 87, 94, 96, 98–99, 102, 105, 145, 155, 162–63, 190, 193, 207. McPhee, an experienced crime reporter for the *Boston Herald*, CNN, MSNBC, and Fox News, comes to a similar conclusion about Michael O'Keefe, whom she characterizes as being at the beck and call of political allies, not focused on "finding justice."

351 "Among teenagers at Barnstable High and Nauset Regional": Author ints. of John Reed, 10/15/06, 10/29/06; Jamie Williams, 09/19/07; Diane Elder, 07/18/07.

351 "'Wu Did It'": Author ints. of anonymous sources and Diane Elder, 07/18/07.

352 "future U.S. Supreme Court Justice Felix Frankfurter": Felix Frankfurter, "The Case of Sacco and Vanzetti," *Atlantic Monthly*, May 1927.

352 "Both set the stage for what one Cape attorney called": Author ints. of anon., 05/10/07, 05/16/07.

352 "As this book goes to press, a U.S. federal grand jury": Author ints. of anon., 09/15/09; anon. II, 09/16/09. Subpoena records on file, Clerk-Magistrate's Office, Barnstable District Court.

353 "According to the *Boston Globe*": Jonathan Salzman and Shelly Murphy, "Grand Jury Scrutinizes Cape DA, O'Keefe Asserts Innocence, Says He Has No Tie to Illegal Betting," *Boston Globe*, 04/14/10. Jonathan Salzman and Shelly Murphy, "Judges Accepted Funds from O'Keefe, Two Barred from Criminal Cases on Cape Cod after DA Covered Bill for Training Program," *Boston Globe*, 04/18/10. Stephanie Vosk, "DA Michael O'Keefe Appears Safe, for Now," *Cape Cod Times*, 04/17/10. "Report: DA O'Keefe Target of Gambling Probe," www.masscops.com, 04/15/10. Stephanie Vosk, "O'Keefe Payment Got Judges Reassigned," *Cape Cod Times*, 04/23/10.

353 "Initially, O'Keefe had 'no comment'": Author ints. of anon., 09/16/09, 01/06/10.

354 "Ava, reportedly": Author int. of Rose Vella Kahn, 09/03/09.

BIBLIOGRAPHY

Books

Albright, Evan J. *Cape Cod Confidential: True Tales of Murder, Crime, and Scandal from the Pilgrims to the Present.* Harwich, Mass.: Mystery Lane, 2004.

Berger, Josef (Jeremiah Diggs). *Cape Cod Pilot.* Cambridge, Mass., and London: MIT Press, 1969.

Blackmon, Douglas A. *Slavery by Another Name: The Re-Enslavement of Black Americans from the Civil War to World War II.* New York: Doubleday, 2008.

Bradford, William. *History of the Plymouth Plantation.* Boston: Wright & Potter, 1899.

Brennan, Susan W., and Diana Worthington. *Images of America: Truro.* Charleston, S.C., Chicago, Portsmouth, N.H., San Francisco: Arcadia, 2002.

Bugliosi, Vincent. *Till Death Us Do Part.* New York: Norton, 1979.

Capote, Truman. *In Cold Blood: A True Account of a Multiple Murder and Its Consequences.* New York: Vintage/Random House, 1965.

Carr, Howie. *The Brothers Bulger: How They Terrorized and Corrupted Boston for a Quarter Century.* New York: Warner, 2006.

Carr, Robert K. *Federal Protection of Civil Rights: Quest for a Sword.* Ithaca, N.Y.: Cornell University Press, 1947.

Cohen, Stanley. *The Wrong Man: America's Epidemic of Wrongful Death Row Convictions.* New York: Carrol & Graf, 2003.

Damore, Leo. *In His Garden: The Anatomy of a Murderer.* New York: Dell, 1990.

De Tocqueville, Alexis. *Democracy in America.* New York: Bantam Classic, 2000.

Dray, Philip. *At the Hands of Persons Unknown: The Lynching of Black America.* New York: Modern Library, 2003.

DuBois, W. E. B. *The Autobiography of W. E. B. DuBois: A Soliloquy on Viewing My Life from the Last Decade of Its First Century.* New York: International, 1968.

Dunne, Dominick. *Justice: Crimes, Trials, and Punishments.* New York: Crown, 2001.

Egan, Leona Rust. *Provincetown as a Stage: Provincetown, the Provincetown Players, and the Discovery of Eugene O'Neil.* Orleans, Mass.: Parnassus, 1994.

Egan, Timothy. *The Worst Hard Time: The Untold Story of Those Who Survived the Great American Dust Bowl.* Boston and New York: Mariner/Houghton Mifflin, 2006.

Ellison, Ralph. *Invisible Man.* New York: Vintage/Random House, 1972.

Finch, Robert. *Outlands: Journeys to the Outer Edges of Cape Cod.* Boston: David R. Godine, 1986.

———, ed. *A Place Apart: A Cape Cod Reader.* New York: Norton, 1993.

Flook, Maria. *Invisible Eden: A Story of Love and Murder on Cape Cod.* New York: Broadway/Random House, 2003.

Gates, Henry Louis, Jr., and Cornell West. *The African American Century: How Black Americans Have Shaped Our Century.* New York: Free Press, 2000.

Ginger, Ann Fagan, ed. *Minimizing Racism in Jury Trials: The Voir Dire Conducted by Charles R. Garry in People of California v. Huey P. Newton.* Berkeley, Calif.: National Lawyers Guild, 1969.

Gould, Jon B. *The Innocence Commission: Preventing Wrongful Convictions and Restoring the Criminal Justice System.* New York: New York University Press, 2008.

Greenidge, Kerri. *Boston's Abolitionists.* Beverly, Mass.: Commonwealth Editions, 2006.

Hale, Grace Elizabeth. *Making Whiteness: The Culture of Segregation in the South, 1908–1940.* New York: Vintage, 1999.

Helpern, Milton, M.D., with Bernard Knight, M.D. *Autopsy: The Memoirs of Milton Helpern.* New York: New American Library, 1977.

Kadri, Sadakat. *The Trial: A History, from Socrates to O. J. Simpson.* New York: Random House, 2005.

Kelley, Shawnie M. *It Happened on Cape Cod.* Guilford, Conn, and Helena, Mont.: Globe Pequot, 2006.

Kittredge, Henry. *Cape Cod: Its People and Their History.* Hyannis, Mass.: Parnassus, 1987.

Lehr, Dick, and Gerard O'Neill. *Black Mass: The True Story of an Unholy Alliance between the FBI and the Irish Mob.* New York: Perennial/HarperCollins, 2001.

Litwack, Leon F. *How Free is FREE? The Long Death of Jim Crow.* Cambridge, Mass., and London: Harvard University Press, 2009.

———. *Trouble in Mind: Black Southerners in the Age of Jim Crow.* New York: Knopf, 1998.

Lukas, J. Anthony. *Common Ground: A Turbulent Decade in the Lives of Three American Families.* New York; Vintage, 1986.

Manso, Peter. *Ptown: Art, Sex, and Money on the Outer Cape.* New York: Lisa Drew/Scribner/Simon & Schuster, 2002.

Mayer, Jane. *The Dark Side: The Inside Story of How the War on Terror Turned into a War on American Ideals.* New York: Doubleday, 2008.

McGinniss, Joe. *Fatal Vision.* New York: New American Library, 1984.

McPhee, Michelle R. *When Evil Rules: A True Story of Vengeance and Murder on Cape Cod.* New York: St. Martin's Paperbacks, 2009.

O'Hara, Charles E. *Fundamentals of Criminal Investigation.* Springfield, Ill.: Charles C. Thomas, 1973.

Philbrick, Nathaniel. *Mayflower: A Story of Courage, Community, and War.* New York: Viking/Penguin, 2006.

Rosenbaum, Thane, ed. *Law Lit.: From Atticus Finch to* The Practice, *a Collection of Great Writing about the Law.* New York and London: New Press, 2007.

Scheck, Barry, Peter Neufeld, and Jim Dwyer. *Actual Innocence: When Justice Goes Wrong and How to Make It Right.* New York: New American Library, 2003.

Schneider, Paul. *The Enduring Shore: A History of Cape Cod, Martha's Vineyard, and Nantucket.* New York: Holt, 2000.

Sokol, Jason. *There Goes My Everything: White Southerners in the Age of Civil Rights, 1945–1975.* New York: Vintage/Random House, 2007.

Strahler, Arthur N. *A Geologist's View of Cape Cod.* Garden City N.Y.: Natural History Press/Doubleday, 1966.

Thompson, Thomas. *Blood and Money: A True Story of Murder, Passion, and Power.* Garden City, N.Y.: Doubleday, 1976.

Thoreau, Henry David. *Cape Cod.* New York: Penguin, 1987.

Vollen, Lola, and Dave Eggers, eds. *Surviving Justice: America's Wrongfully Convicted and Exonerated.* San Francisco: Voice of Witness/McSweeney's, 2008.

Vorse, Mary Heaton. *Time and the Town: A Provincetown Chronicle.* New Brunswick, N.J.: Rutgers University Press, 1991.

Weiland, Matt, and Sean Wilsey. *State by State: A Panoramic Portrait of America.* New York: HarperCollins, 2008.

Whalen, Richard F. *Truro: The Story of a Cape Cod Town.* Charleston, S.C.: History Press, 2007.

Whitaker, Robert. *On the Laps of Gods: The Red Summer of 1919 and the Struggle for Justice That Remade a Nation.* New York: Crown, 2008.

Wilson, William Julius. *More Than Just Race: Being Black and Poor in the Inner City.* New York and London: Norton, 2009.

Wolfson, Victor. *Cabral.* New York: Avon, 1972.

Woodward, Bob. *State of Denial: Bush at War, Part II.* New York: Simon & Schuster, 2006.

Woodward, Bob, and Scott Armstrong. *The Brethren.* New York: Simon & Schuster, 2005.

Woodward, C. Vann. *The Strange Career of Jim Crow.* New York: Oxford University Press, 1966.

Wright, Richard. *Native Son.* New York: Library of America, 1991.

ACKNOWLEDGMENTS

This book does its best to be fair and evenhanded. More than several hundred people were interviewed over a period of four years, some multiple times. Documents reviewed and re-reviewed amounted to some twenty running feet of files. Secondary materials, including news stories and editorials, magazine articles, books, and online blogs, were used for background on the law and legal procedure, as well as to ground the particulars of the McCowen case.

Plainly, a book of this kind cannot happen without sources, and for some Cape Codders talking to me was an alarming experience since my questions centered on a real-life murder that many felt (and still feel) has yet to be solved. Per their request, these individuals are not identified by name, but I want them to know that I thank them sincerely. In one case, I didn't want to take no for an answer and tried to get the source, an attorney who'd been especially helpful, to change his mind:

"No, you may not identify me," the lawyer responded. "That was the deal we made going in, and I must insist on it. The Cape is a small place, the Superior Court much smaller still, [and] if you publicly acknowledge me there is a very strong likelihood I'd be blackballed in that court, affecting my clients and my ability to provide for my family. . . . My contribution is to try to help right a wrong, and I need no accolades for doing it. The villain in this story is O'Keefe, and I believe his ending has not been written yet."

For editorial and research help my boundless gratitude to Susan Dooley Carey, Mike Iacuessa, and Rose Connors, who helped more than they know. Michelle Costantino once more came through with the transcribing. Lisa Baumgartel and Asya Passinsky kept things together in Berkeley. At Atria/Simon & Schuster my editors, Sarah Durand and Peter Borland, and Sarah's assistant, Sarah Cantin, more than held up their end, just as Jaime Wolf's vetting of the manuscript was as sensitive as it was prudent. Dan Strone at the Trident Media Group seemed to anticipate my every need, and I thank him, too.

No project of this kind can be completed without the assistance of town, county, and state libraries, historical societies, and various governmental agencies. Among those that contributed were the Truro Historical Society; Cape Cod Commission; Barnstable County Human Services Dept.; Barnstable County Human Rights Comm. (Ernest C. Hadley); Barnstable County Superior Court Clerk's Office; Barnstable County 2nd District (Orleans) Court Clerk's Office; Cape Cod NAACP; The Nickerson Research Center (North Chatham); Cape Cod Immigrants Center; Cape Cod Citizens Against Racism (David & Peggy Lillienthal, Mary Ann Barboza, Rev. Robert Murphy, "Scober" Frank Rhodes, Jacqueline Fields); Massachusetts Dept. of Public Health (Office of Substance Abuse); Center on Wrongful Convictions at the Northwestern University School of Law; the Innocence Project at New York City's Benjamin Cardozo Law School.

My colleagues in the media were also helpful. Here, I would single out Beth Karas, Harriet Ryan, and Carl Liebowitz of Court TV; editor-in-chief Paul Pronovost and photo editor Jim Preston at the *Cape Cod Times*; the *Cape Codder*'s Marilyn Miller; Sally Rose, editor of the *Provincetown Banner*, the AP's Denise Lavoie and Linda Deutsch in Los Angeles; Jonathan Saltzman of the *Boston Globe*; Walter Brooks of *Cape Cod Today* and PlymouthDailyNews.com; Seth Rolbein of *Cape Cod Voice*; David Frank, editor of *Massachusetts Lawyers Weekly*; Scott Button of Cape Media Networks, Jeff Blanchard, and Peter Robbins were also givers. Barry Levine, editor of the *National Enquirer* in New York, was kind enough to supply me with documents on Christopher McCowen's criminal history that neither attorney Robert George nor the Cape and Islands DA's office appeared to have. It is rumored that veteran Boston WCVB-TV correspondent Amalia Barreda has covered more than one hundred major trials; her willingness to share her insights, not to say put up with my pesky neophyte's questions about court procedure, were appreciated more than I can say.

Provincetown's George Bryant filled in a few cracks, much as he did for my last book, *Ptown: Art, Sex and Money on the Outer Cape*; whether it is sociology, economic history, or whaling, George is a treasure trove of information who should be decorated for his lifelong study of the Cape. On the west coast, thanks go to Dr. Risa Kegan for her valuable guidance on the gynecology of rape.

My gratitude also to John Reinstein and Laura Rotolo of the ACLU Foundation of Massachusetts; Christopher Conte and Vince Gay of the National Rifle Association; Jan Constantine of the Authors Guild, and Sandy Baron, Executive Director of the Media Law Resource Center in New York. All gave of their time and support.

To Mary Jo Avellar, John Lawler, and Susan Jacobson, my thanks, as well; Lawler was always there for me. Members of the security staff and the personnel in the Court Clerk's offices at both the 2nd District Court and Barnstable Superior were, almost without exception, more helpful than they had to be; I would be greatly remiss if I didn't acknowledge their assistance and good cheer.

Many friends listened to me while I was doing my research and writing, and were supportive when I found myself in that long surreal tunnel, looking at what felt like doomsday jail time: Jim and Denise Landis, Jeremy Larner, David Reid and Jayne L. Walker, Tom Goldstein, Nicholas Von Hoffman, Ishmael Reed, Charlotte Jerace, John Yingling, Dan Richter, Peter Bloch, David Fechheimer, Tom Luddy, Denne Abrams, John and Dagmar Searle, the late Charles Muscatine, and, especially, my dear friends Lizbeth Hasse and Joe Orrach. To all of them I owe an unforgettable debt of gratitude.

Thanks to Kyoungjoo Kim for help with case law, and to attorney David S. Hammer for his counsel and advice.

Joe Balliro and Kevin Reddington, gentlemen and master legal practitioners both, got me out of that particular mess, and I shall never forget them. In addition, during the trial I had numerous chats with Joe about the McCowen case that were so stimulating as to make me consider enrolling in law school.

Thanks also to Drs. John Shackelford, Alix Divigal, and Craig Bloom. Blessed be the healers; far too often do we take them for granted.

Chris Laffaille, one of Europe's best investigative reporters, did some amazing spadework in London and Paris, the fruits of which appear in these pages. *Merci, mon frère, camarade.*

Most of all, this book could not have been done without the trust and cooperation of Robert George, a.k.a. "Bobby." We worked together, became friends, fought the good fight side by side. Given our nonstop competitive banter, someone suggested that we should be doing a real-time TV show together, a latter-day "Mutt and Jeff." One thing is sure: it'd be great fun.

Finally, although words fail me, I must thank my dear wife, Anna Schenkelbach Avellar, who was unfailingly supportive throughout my year-and-a-half legal imbroglio that began with cops invading her home with shotguns. She never bargained for any of that, any more than she should have had to live with the nutsiness of my writer's moods as this book yo-yoed its way toward completion. She is an angel worthy of Fra Angelico (or, better, he of her.)

INDEX

For more detailed information about the case, the characters, and the research behind *Reasonable Doubt*, please consult the endnotes of this book.

Mason, Christopher *(cont.)*
222–23; style of, 126–27, 130,
145; surprise visits to homes by,
349–50; testimony of, 48, 124–40,
143–59, 160–73, 201, 202, 223,
235, 260; Worthington (Toppy)
as suspect and, 41
Mason, Christopher—interviews by:
Amato, 43–44, 212, 213, 214, 215,
216, 217, 218; Arnold (Tim), 33–
34, 35, 50, 77, 81, 83, 84, 85, 86,
151–52, 169–72, 206, 220; crime
scene responders, 50; Frazier, 52,
183; Jackett, 50; Kinton, 185, 228;
McCowen, 25, 52, 125–40, 143–
59, 160–73, 215, 238, 239, 243,
253, 255, 256, 259, 266, 267, 282,
297, 320; Mulvey, 193; "persons
of interest," 51; Porter, 38–39;
Roderick, 205; Worthington
family, 50; Worthington (Jan), 96–
99, 100, 101, 102; Worthington
(Pam), 229, 230, 232
Massachusetts crime lab, 5, 296, 315,
317, 325, 333–34, 335, 347, 348,
350, 358
Massachusetts Lawyers Weekly, 295, 307
Massachusetts State Ethics
Commission, 337
Massachusetts State Police: burglaries
in O'Keefe home and, 340;
corruption and, 338–39; DA
office relationship with, 337,
338; DNA sweep and, 347;
Frazier telephone records and,
169–72, 173, 175, 181, 185–86,
202, 203, 264, 326, 345; Huffman
situation and, 278, 282; jury and,
302; Manso decision to write
book and, 1; McCowen file of,
4; oversight of, 343; overtime
pay for, 338; politics and, 338;
polygraph tests and, 333, 350;

taping of interviews by, 11. *See also*
Crime Prevention and Control
Unit (CPAC); Massachusetts
crime lab; *specific person*
Massachusetts Supreme Judicial
Court (SJC), 7, 60, 66, 128, 248,
269, 270, 304–5, 310, 315, 317,
354, 357–60
Massari, James, 41, 102, 212, 233
Mawn, John, 34, 39, 44, 77, 85, 86,
213, 214, 215, 217, 222–23
Mazzone, Michael, 47, 168, 195, 196,
314, 323–27
McCabe, Scott, 199–201, 314
McCowen, Christopher: address to
court by, 290–91, 359; aliases
of, 118; alibi of, 130, 131, 132,
154, 207; appearance of, 48;
arrest and arraignment of, 2, 5,
52, 53, 56, 70, 127, 128, 148–49,
151, 164, 167, 172–73, 200–201,
206, 208, 269, 301, 349, 352;
childhood and youth of, 49;
comments about Christa by, 129;
"confession" of, 53, 210, 238–45,
261, 335; courtroom behavior
of, 93, 104, 108, 125, 197–98,
243, 265, 274, 276; criminal
background of, 48, 49, 50, 140,
269; DNA of, 5, 52, 53, 70, 107,
125, 126, 127, 130, 131, 133,
134, 138, 143–44, 151, 157, 163,
164, 196–97, 198–99, 206–7, 209,
244, 257–58, 263–64, 265, 266,
267, 295, 299, 318–23, 333, 335,
352; domestic violence history
of, 138, 140, 165, 167, 172–73,
189, 234, 237, 300–301, 303, 326,
332, 357; drugs and, 48, 49, 50,
155, 195, 220, 221, 236, 238, 240,
264, 326; George relationship
with, 173, 197, 284, 294–95;
image of, 47; indictment/